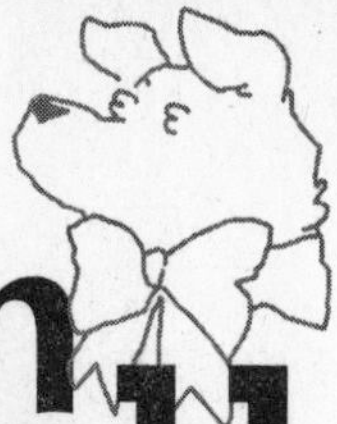

maison ikkoku 11

STORY AND ART BY RUMIKO TAKAHASHI

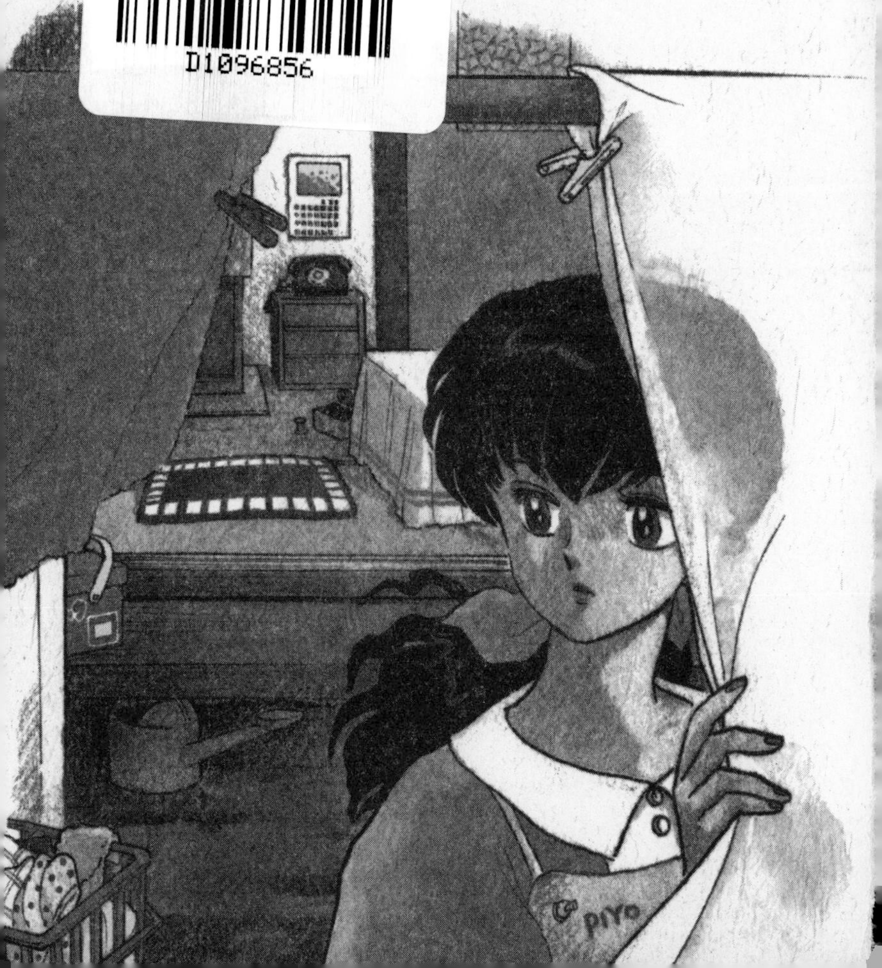
piyo

TABLE OF CONTENTS

PART ONE
THE DOOR SLAMS

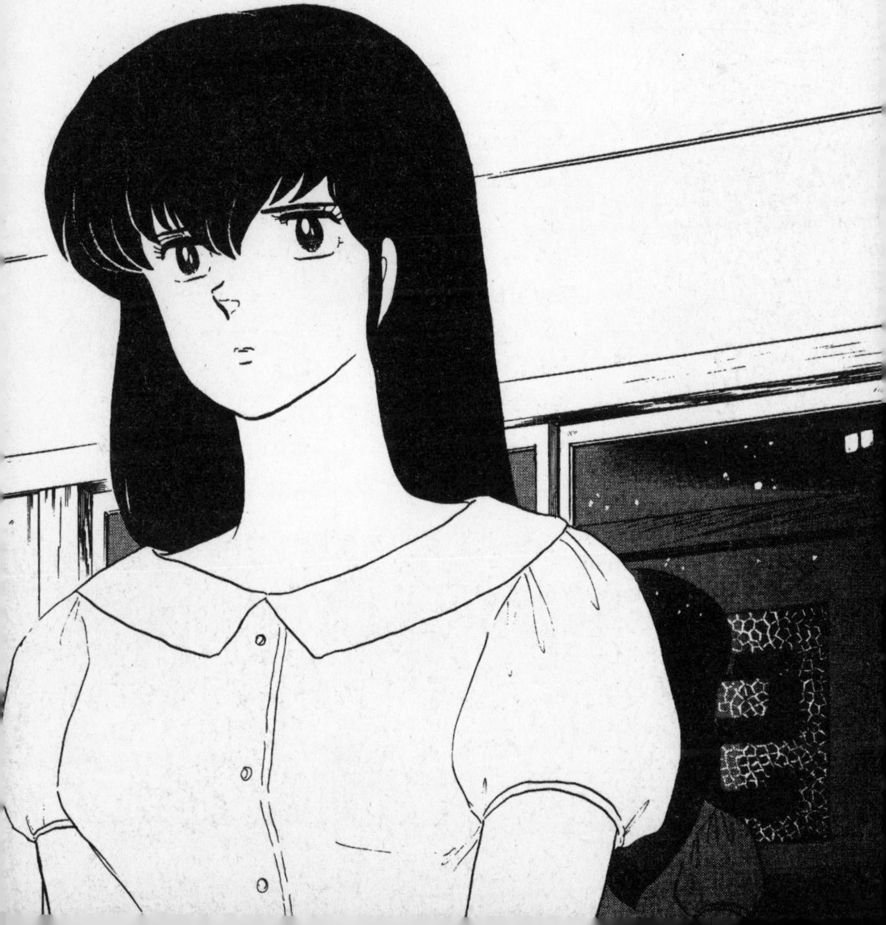

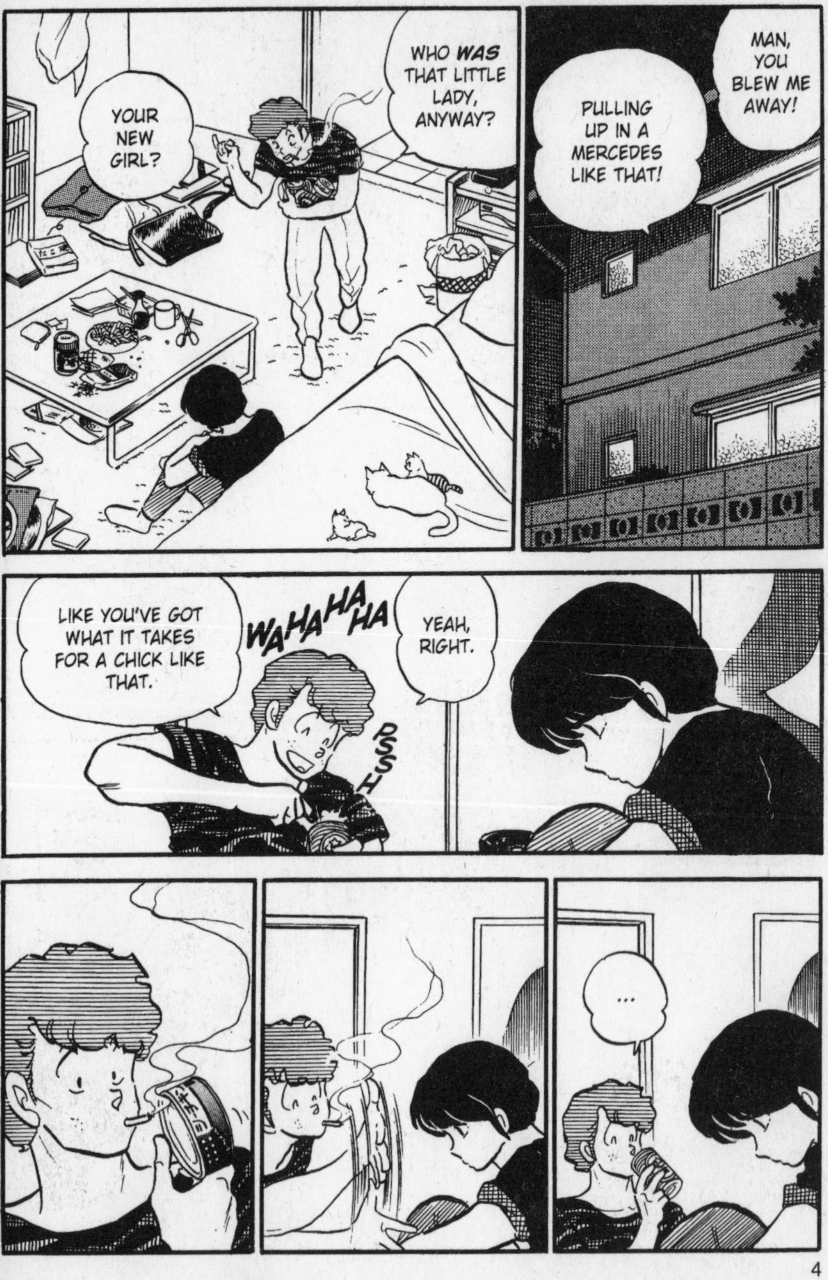
MAN, YOU BLEW ME AWAY!
PULLING UP IN A MERCEDES LIKE THAT!
WHO WAS THAT LITTLE LADY, ANYWAY?
YOUR NEW GIRL?
YEAH, RIGHT.
WAHAHAHA
PSSH
LIKE YOU'VE GOT WHAT IT TAKES FOR A CHICK LIKE THAT.
...

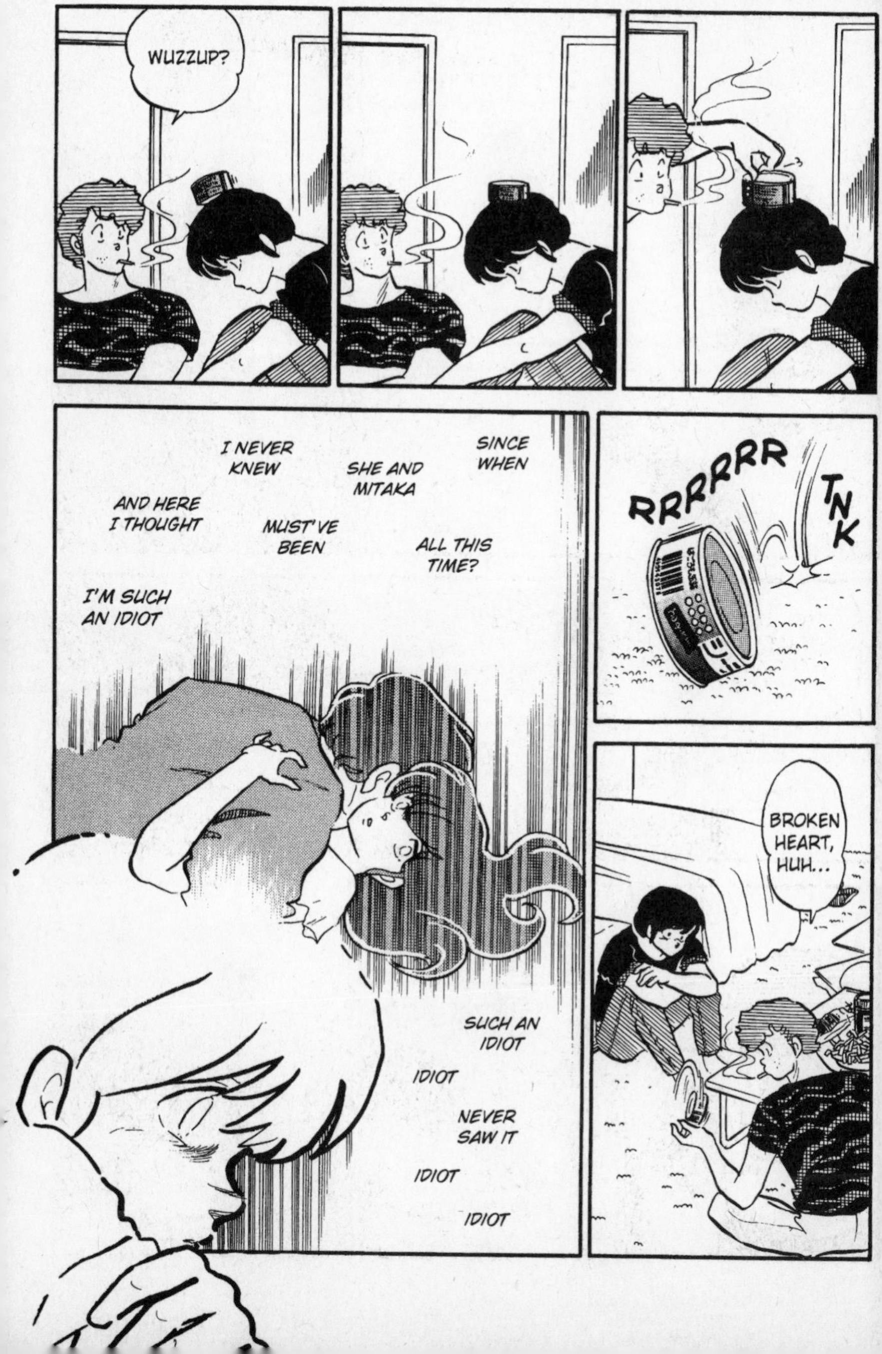
WUZZUP?
RRRRRR
TNK
BROKEN HEART, HUH...
SINCE WHEN
ALL THIS TIME?
SHE AND MITAKA
MUST'VE BEEN
I NEVER KNEW
AND HERE I THOUGHT
I'M SUCH AN IDIOT
SUCH AN IDIOT
IDIOT
NEVER SAW IT
IDIOT
IDIOT

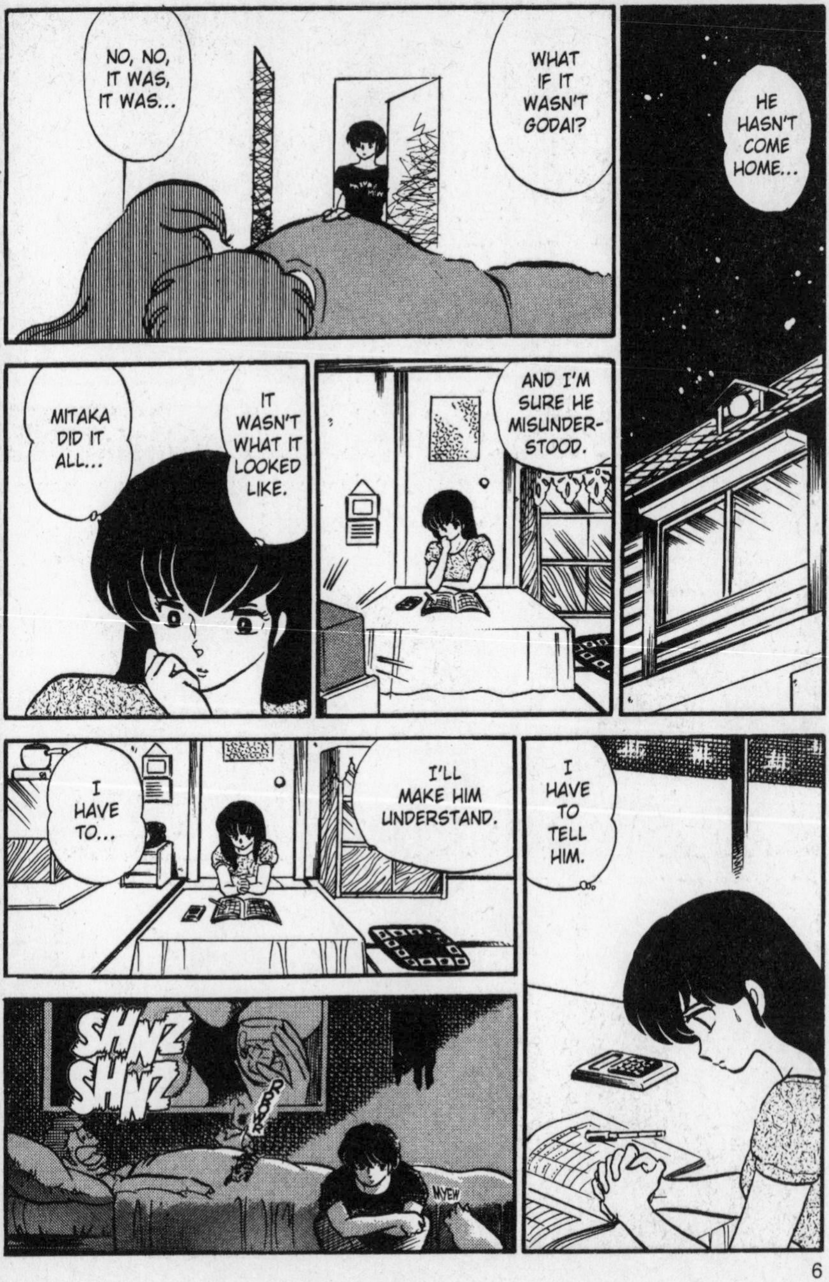
HE HASN'T COME HOME...
WHAT IF IT WASN'T GODAI?
NO, NO, IT WAS, IT WAS...
AND I'M SURE HE MISUNDERSTOOD.
IT WASN'T WHAT IT LOOKED LIKE.
MITAKA DID IT ALL...
I HAVE TO TELL HIM.
I'LL MAKE HIM UNDERSTAND.
I HAVE TO...
SHNZ SHNZ
MYEW

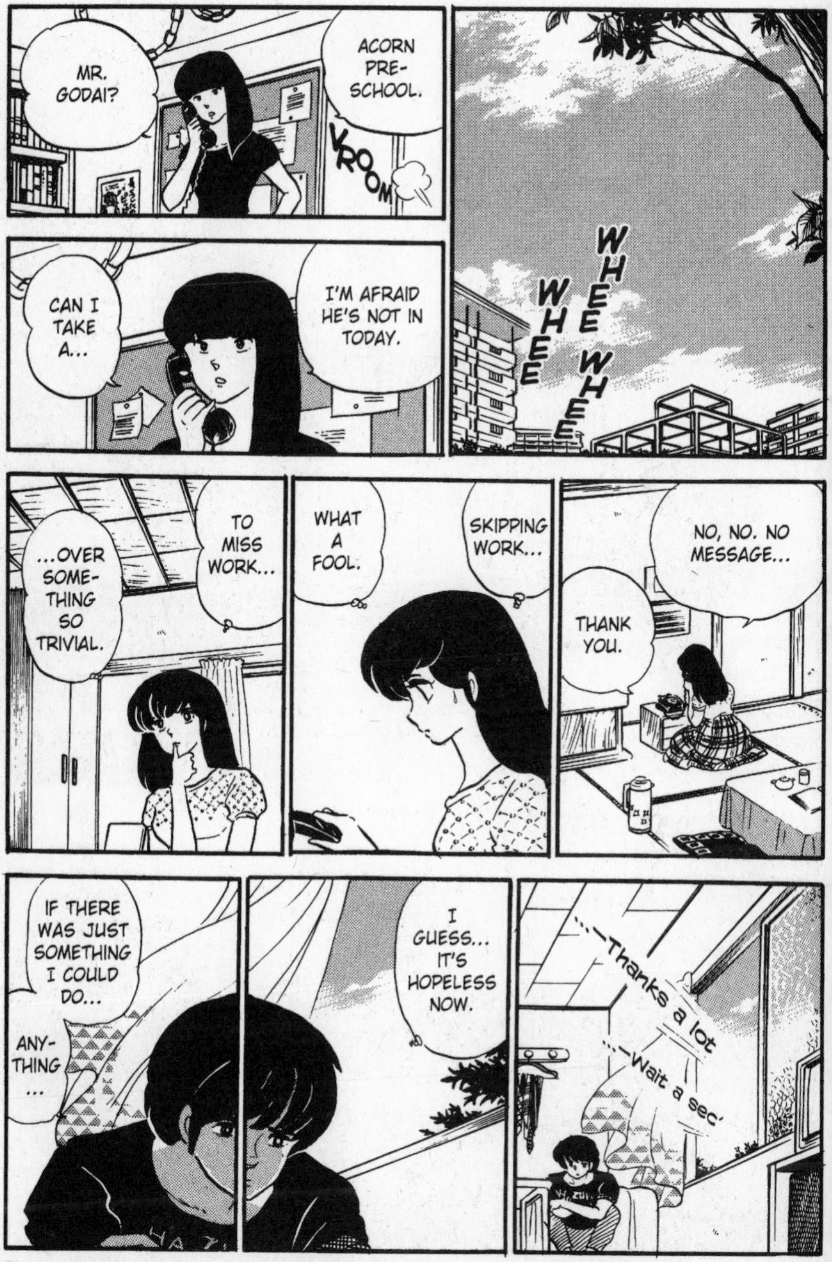

WHEE WHEE
WHEE
ACORN PRE-SCHOOL.
VROOM
MR. GODAI?
I'M AFRAID HE'S NOT IN TODAY.
CAN I TAKE A...
NO, NO. NO MESSAGE...
THANK YOU.
SKIPPING WORK...
WHAT A FOOL.
TO MISS WORK...
...OVER SOME-THING SO TRIVIAL.
...—Thanks a lot
...—Wait a sec'
I GUESS... IT'S HOPELESS NOW.
IF THERE WAS JUST SOMETHING I COULD DO...
ANY-THING...

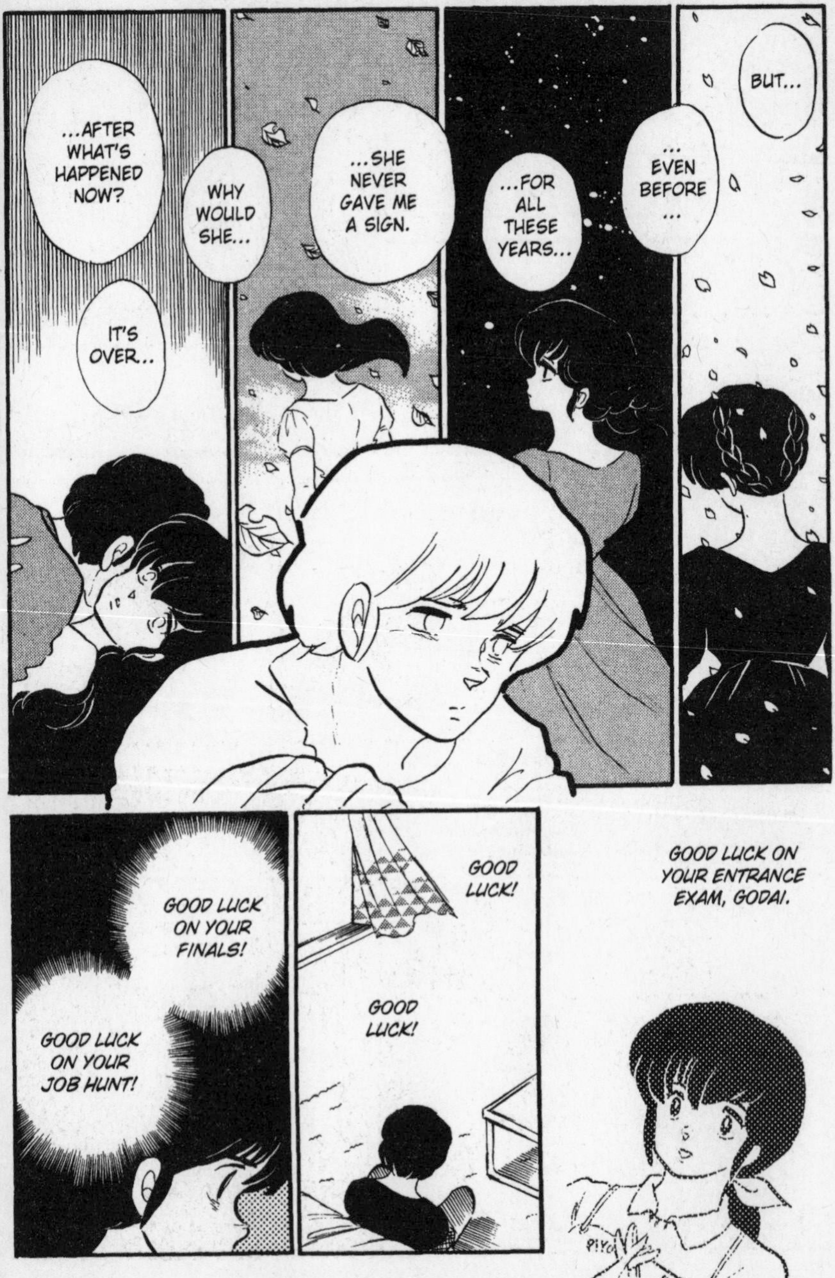
BUT...
...EVEN BEFORE...
...FOR ALL THESE YEARS...
...SHE NEVER GAVE ME A SIGN.
WHY WOULD SHE...
...AFTER WHAT'S HAPPENED NOW?
IT'S OVER...
GOOD LUCK ON YOUR ENTRANCE EXAM, GODAI.
PiYo
PiYo
GOOD LUCK!
GOOD LUCK!
GOOD LUCK ON YOUR FINALS!
GOOD LUCK ON YOUR JOB HUNT!

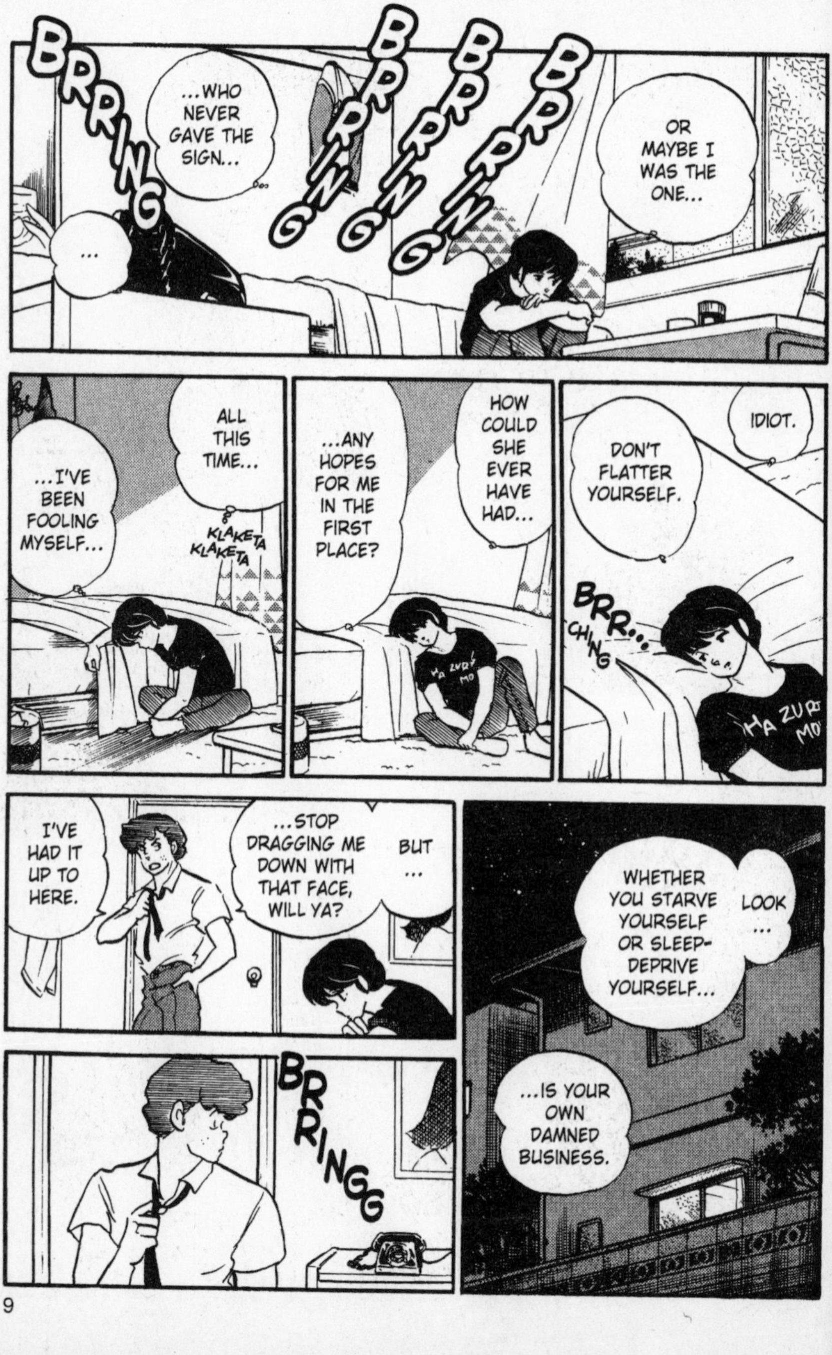
OR MAYBE I WAS THE ONE...
BRRRING
BRRRING
BRRRING
...WHO NEVER GAVE THE SIGN...
BRRRING
...
IDIOT.
DON'T FLATTER YOURSELF.
BRRR... CHING
HOW COULD SHE EVER HAVE HAD...
...ANY HOPES FOR ME IN THE FIRST PLACE?
ALL THIS TIME...
KLAKETA KLAKETA
...I'VE BEEN FOOLING MYSELF...
LOOK...
WHETHER YOU STARVE YOURSELF OR SLEEP-DEPRIVE YOURSELF...
...IS YOUR OWN DAMNED BUSINESS.
BUT...
...STOP DRAGGING ME DOWN WITH THAT FACE, WILL YA?
I'VE HAD IT UP TO HERE.
BRRINGG

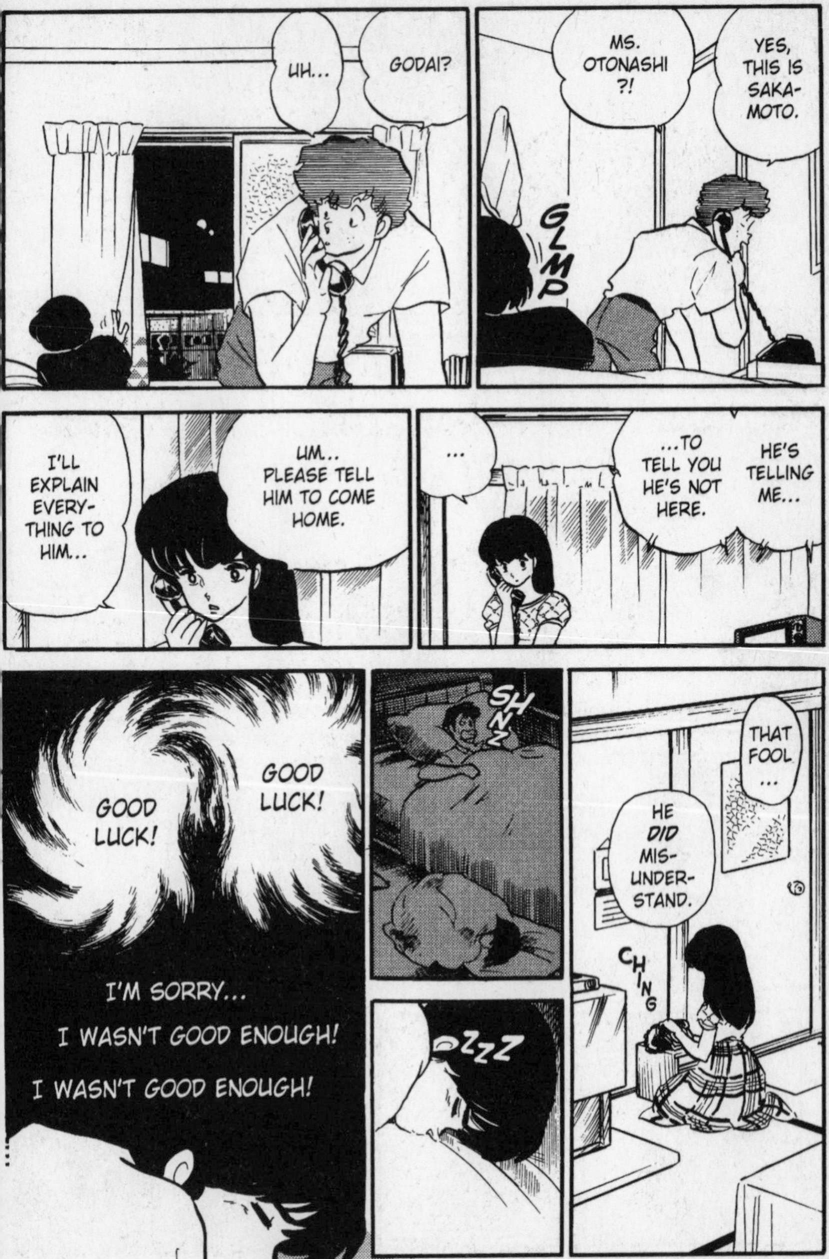
YES, THIS IS SAKA-MOTO.
MS. OTONASHI ?!
GLMP
GODAI?
UH...
HE'S TELLING ME...
...TO TELL YOU HE'S NOT HERE.
...
UM... PLEASE TELL HIM TO COME HOME.
I'LL EXPLAIN EVERY-THING TO HIM...
THAT FOOL ...
HE DID MIS-UNDER-STAND.
CHING
SHNZ
ZZZ
GOOD LUCK!
GOOD LUCK!
I'M SORRY...
I WASN'T GOOD ENOUGH!
I WASN'T GOOD ENOUGH!

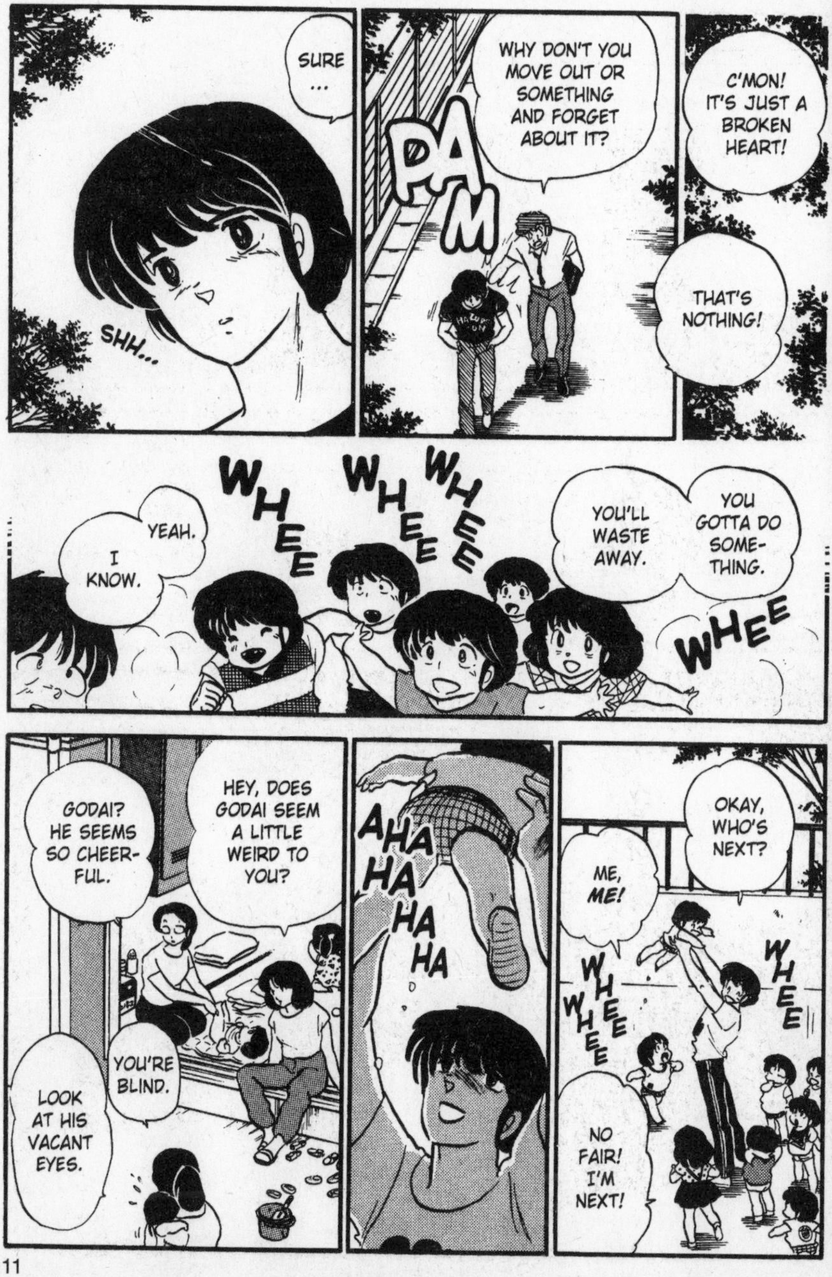
C'MON! IT'S JUST A BROKEN HEART!
THAT'S NOTHING!
WHY DON'T YOU MOVE OUT OR SOMETHING AND FORGET ABOUT IT?
PAM
SURE ...
SHH...
YOU GOTTA DO SOME-THING.
YOU'LL WASTE AWAY.
WHEE
WHEE
WHEE
WHEE
YEAH.
I KNOW.
OKAY, WHO'S NEXT?
ME, ME!
WHEE
WHEE
WHEE
NO FAIR! I'M NEXT!
AHA HA HA HA HA
HEY, DOES GODAI SEEM A LITTLE WEIRD TO YOU?
GODAI? HE SEEMS SO CHEER-FUL.
YOU'RE BLIND.
LOOK AT HIS VACANT EYES.

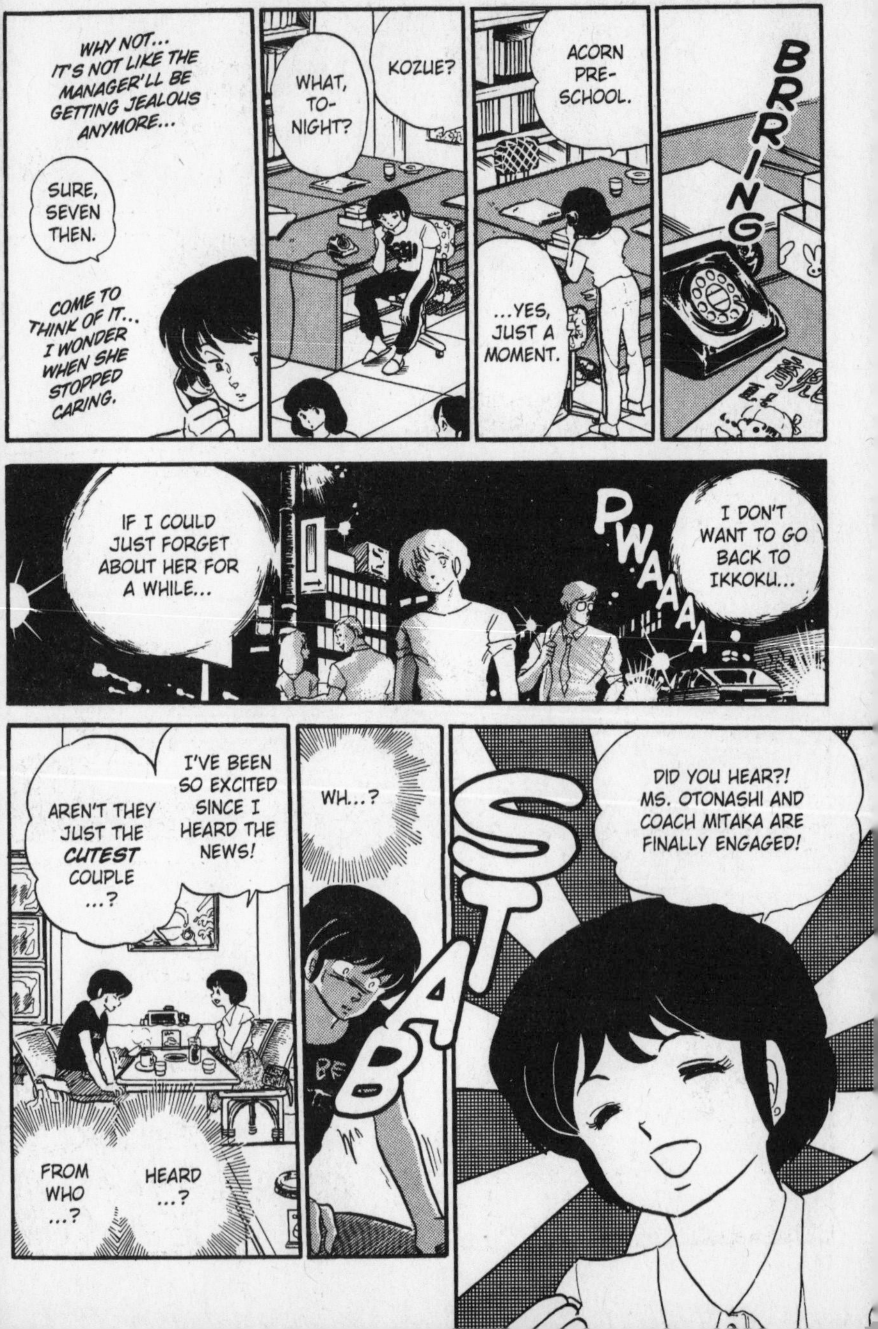
BRRRING
ACORN PRE-SCHOOL.
...YES, JUST A MOMENT.
KOZUE?
WHAT, TO-NIGHT?
WHY NOT... IT'S NOT LIKE THE MANAGER'LL BE GETTING JEALOUS ANYMORE...
SURE, SEVEN THEN.
COME TO THINK OF IT... I WONDER WHEN SHE STOPPED CARING.
I DON'T WANT TO GO BACK TO IKKOKU...
PWAAAAA
IF I COULD JUST FORGET ABOUT HER FOR A WHILE...
DID YOU HEAR?! MS. OTONASHI AND COACH MITAKA ARE FINALLY ENGAGED!
STAB
WH...?
I'VE BEEN SO EXCITED SINCE I HEARD THE NEWS!
AREN'T THEY JUST THE CUTEST COUPLE ...?
HEARD ...?
FROM WHO ...?

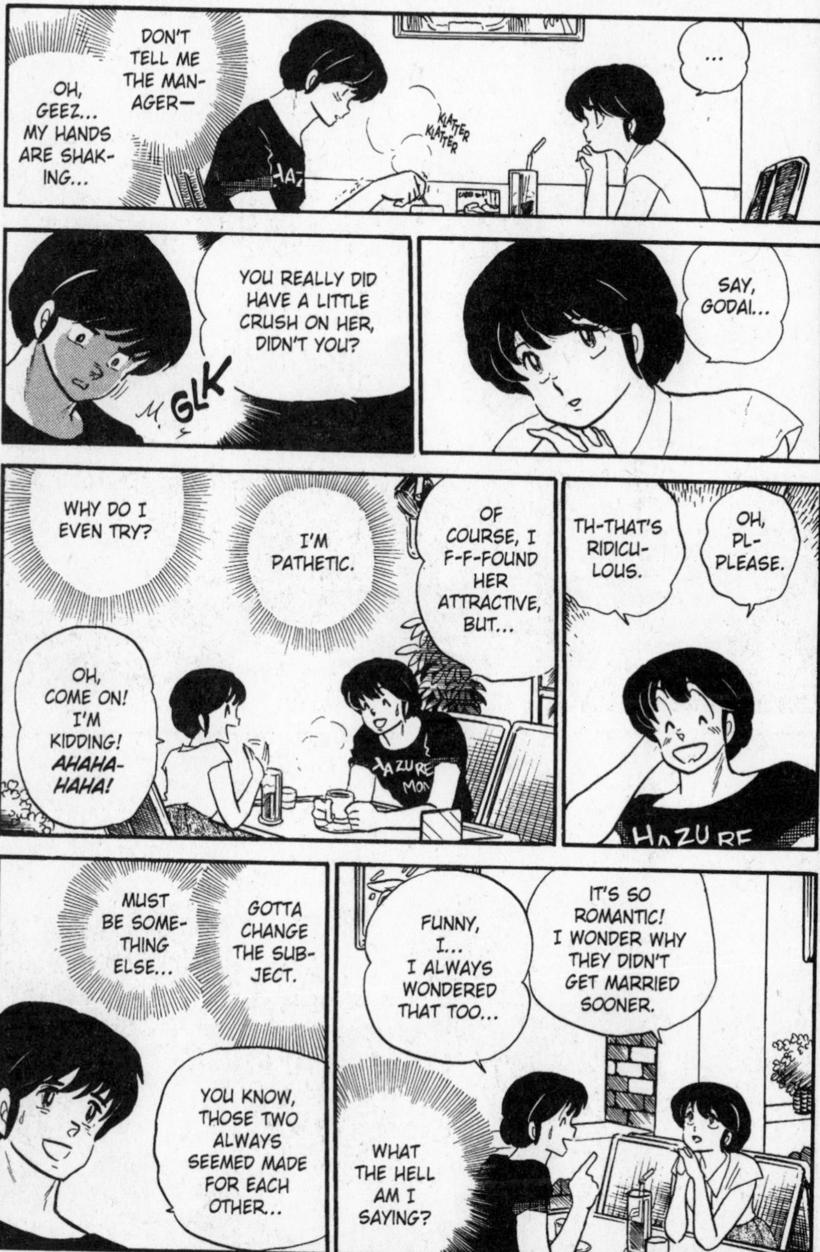
...
KLATTER KLATTER
DON'T TELL ME THE MANAGER—
OH, GEEZ... MY HANDS ARE SHAKING...
SAY, GODAI...
YOU REALLY DID HAVE A LITTLE CRUSH ON HER, DIDN'T YOU?
GLK
OH, PL-PLEASE.
TH-THAT'S RIDICULOUS.
OF COURSE, I F-F-FOUND HER ATTRACTIVE, BUT...
I'M PATHETIC.
WHY DO I EVEN TRY?
OH, COME ON! I'M KIDDING! ***AHAHAHAHA!***
IT'S SO ROMANTIC! I WONDER WHY THEY DIDN'T GET MARRIED SOONER.
FUNNY, I... I ALWAYS WONDERED THAT TOO...
WHAT THE HELL AM I SAYING?
GOTTA CHANGE THE SUBJECT.
MUST BE SOMETHING ELSE...
YOU KNOW, THOSE TWO ALWAYS SEEMED MADE FOR EACH OTHER...

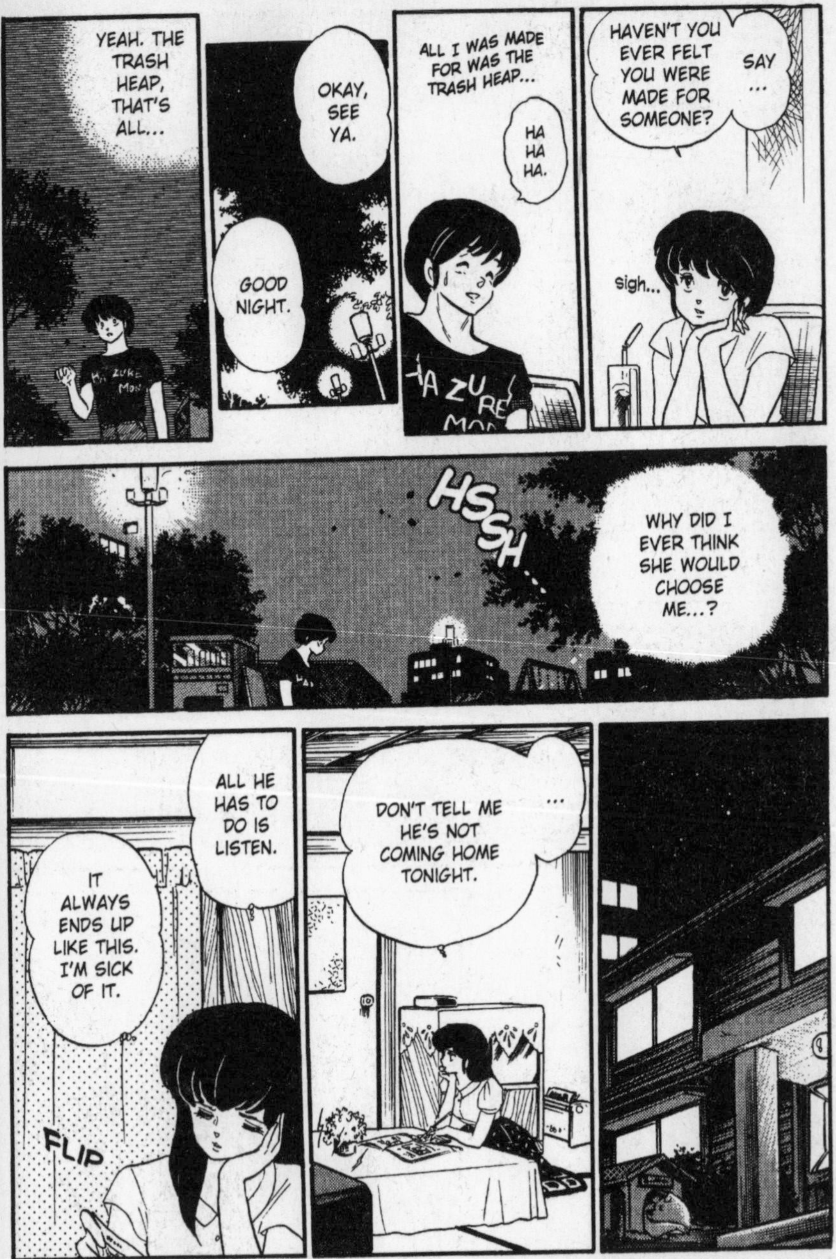
SAY ...
HAVEN'T YOU EVER FELT YOU WERE MADE FOR SOMEONE?
sigh...
ALL I WAS MADE FOR WAS THE TRASH HEAP...
HA HA HA.
OKAY, SEE YA.
GOOD NIGHT.
YEAH. THE TRASH HEAP, THAT'S ALL...
HSSH...
WHY DID I EVER THINK SHE WOULD CHOOSE ME...?
...
DON'T TELL ME HE'S NOT COMING HOME TONIGHT.
ALL HE HAS TO DO IS LISTEN.
IT ALWAYS ENDS UP LIKE THIS. I'M SICK OF IT.
FLIP

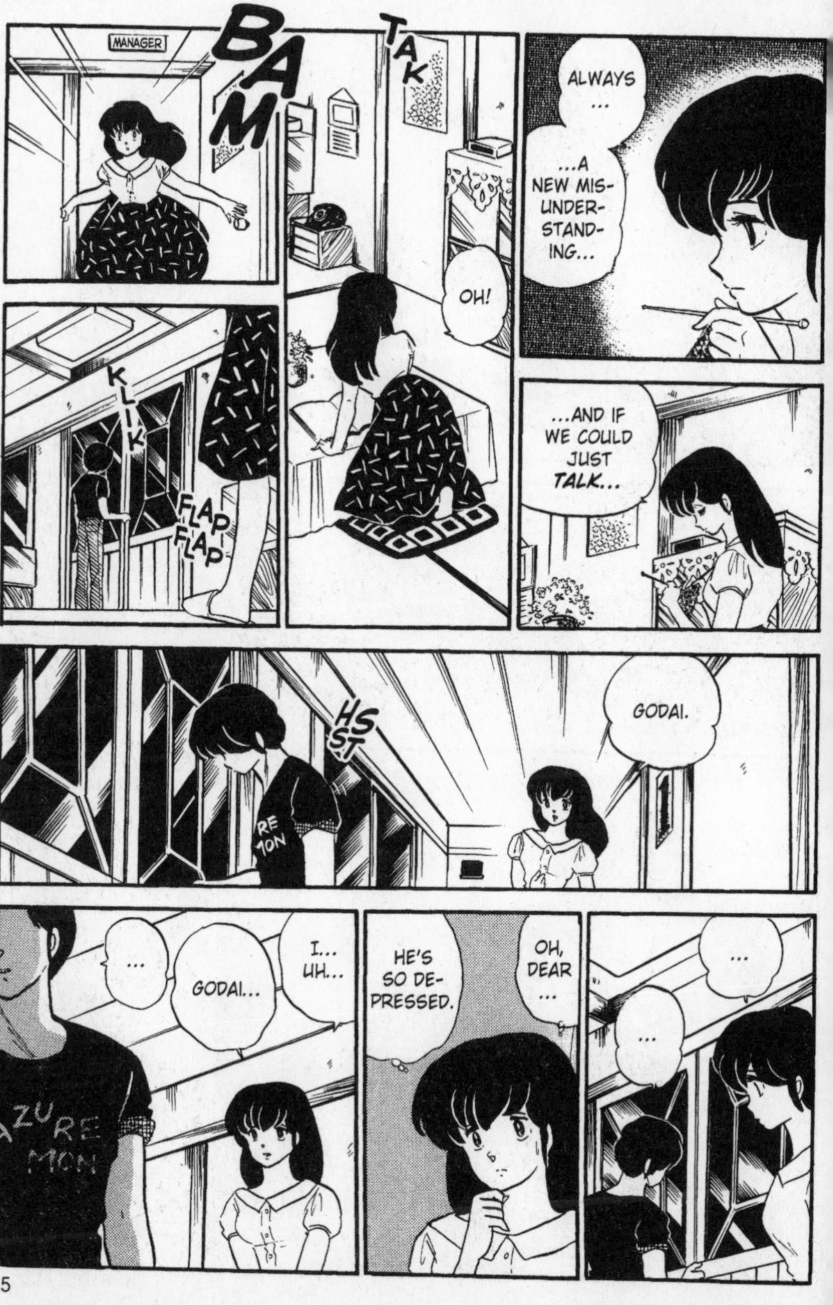
ALWAYS ...
...A NEW MIS-UNDER-STAND-ING...
...AND IF WE COULD JUST *TALK*...
TAK
OH!
BAM
MANAGER
KLIK
FLAP FLAP
GODAI.
HSST
...
...
OH, DEAR ...
HE'S SO DE-PRESSED.
I... UH...
GODAI...
...

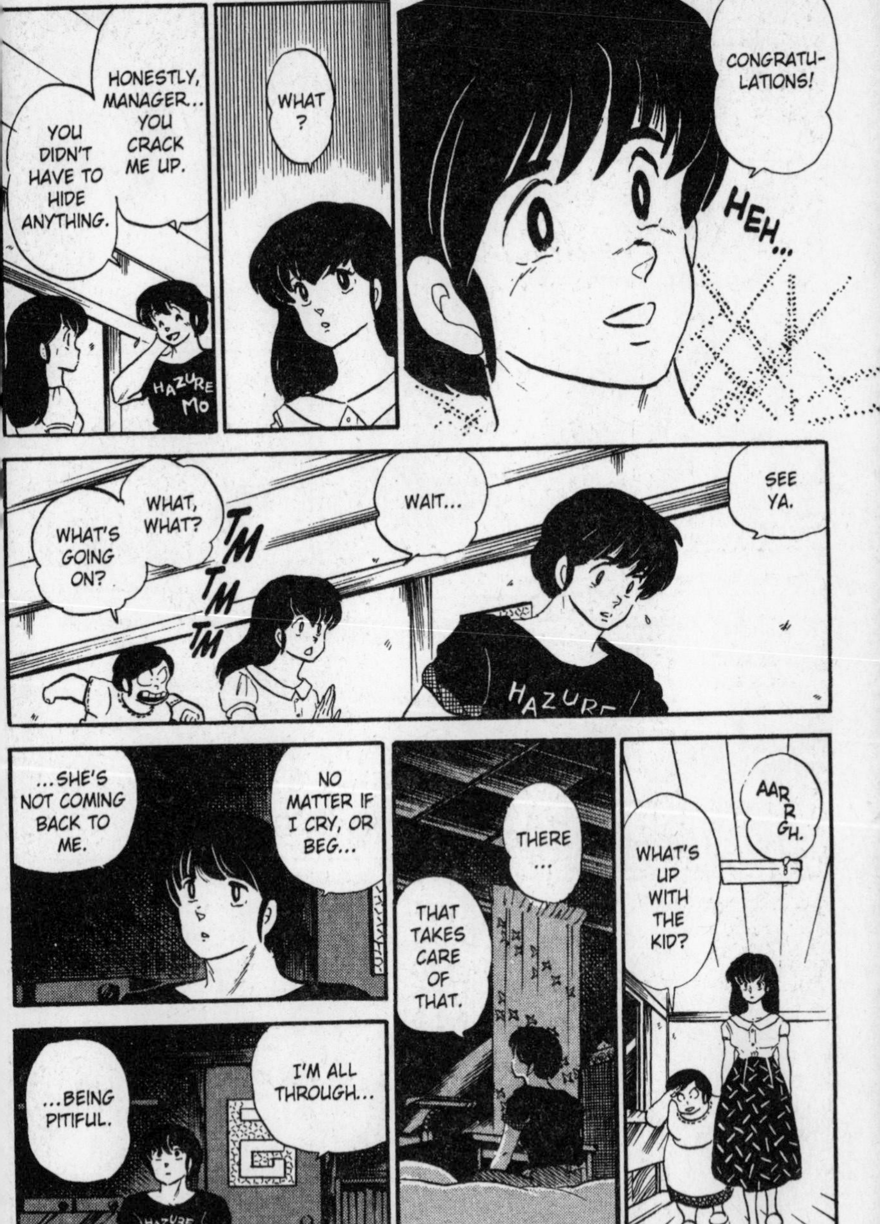
CONGRATULATIONS!
HEH...
WHAT?
HONESTLY, MANAGER... YOU CRACK ME UP.
YOU DIDN'T HAVE TO HIDE ANYTHING.
HAZURE MO
SEE YA.
WAIT...
TM TM TM
WHAT, WHAT?
WHAT'S GOING ON?
HAZURE
AARRGH.
WHAT'S UP WITH THE KID?
THERE...
THAT TAKES CARE OF THAT.
NO MATTER IF I CRY, OR BEG...
...SHE'S NOT COMING BACK TO ME.
I'M ALL THROUGH...
...BEING PITIFUL.
HAZURE MON

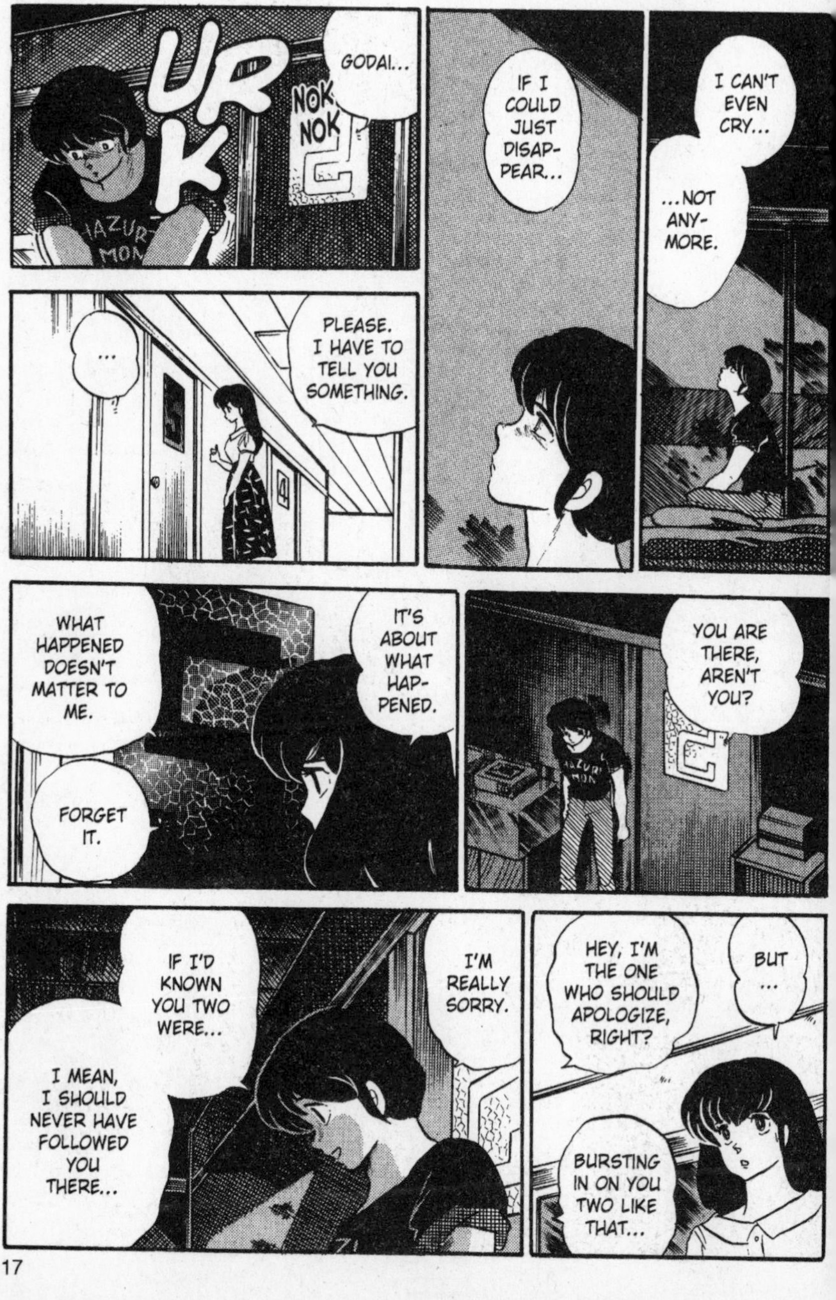
I CAN'T EVEN CRY...
...NOT ANYMORE.
IF I COULD JUST DISAPPEAR...
GODAI...
NOK NOK
URK
PLEASE. I HAVE TO TELL YOU SOMETHING.
...
YOU ARE THERE, AREN'T YOU?
IT'S ABOUT WHAT HAPPENED.
WHAT HAPPENED DOESN'T MATTER TO ME.
FORGET IT.
BUT...
HEY, I'M THE ONE WHO SHOULD APOLOGIZE, RIGHT?
BURSTING IN ON YOU TWO LIKE THAT...
I'M REALLY SORRY.
IF I'D KNOWN YOU TWO WERE...
I MEAN, I SHOULD NEVER HAVE FOLLOWED YOU THERE...

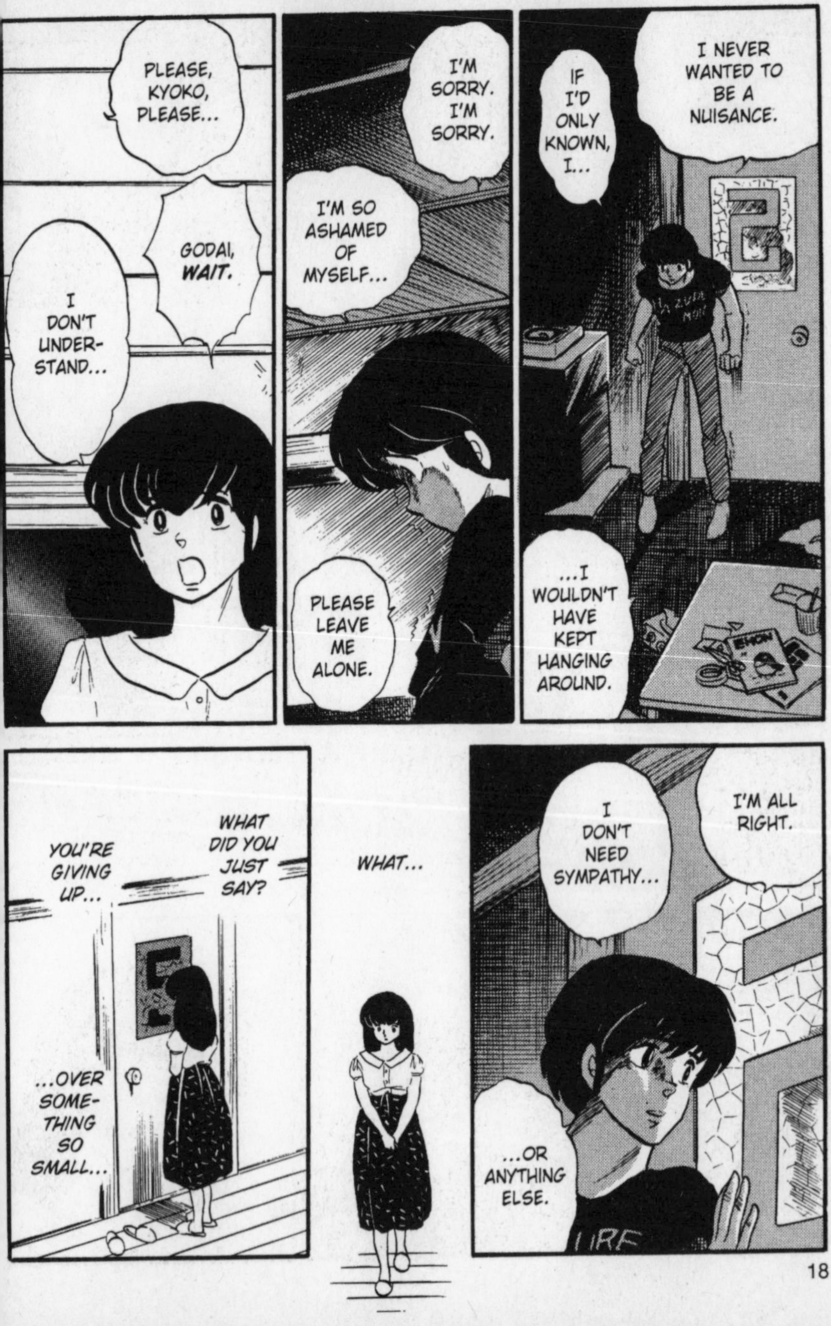
I NEVER WANTED TO BE A NUISANCE.
IF I'D ONLY KNOWN, I...
...I WOULDN'T HAVE KEPT HANGING AROUND.
I'M SORRY. I'M SORRY.
I'M SO ASHAMED OF MYSELF...
PLEASE LEAVE ME ALONE.
PLEASE, KYOKO, PLEASE...
GODAI, *WAIT.*
I DON'T UNDER-STAND...
I'M ALL RIGHT.
I DON'T NEED SYMPATHY...
...OR ANYTHING ELSE.
WHAT...
WHAT DID YOU JUST SAY?
YOU'RE GIVING UP...
...OVER SOME-THING SO SMALL...

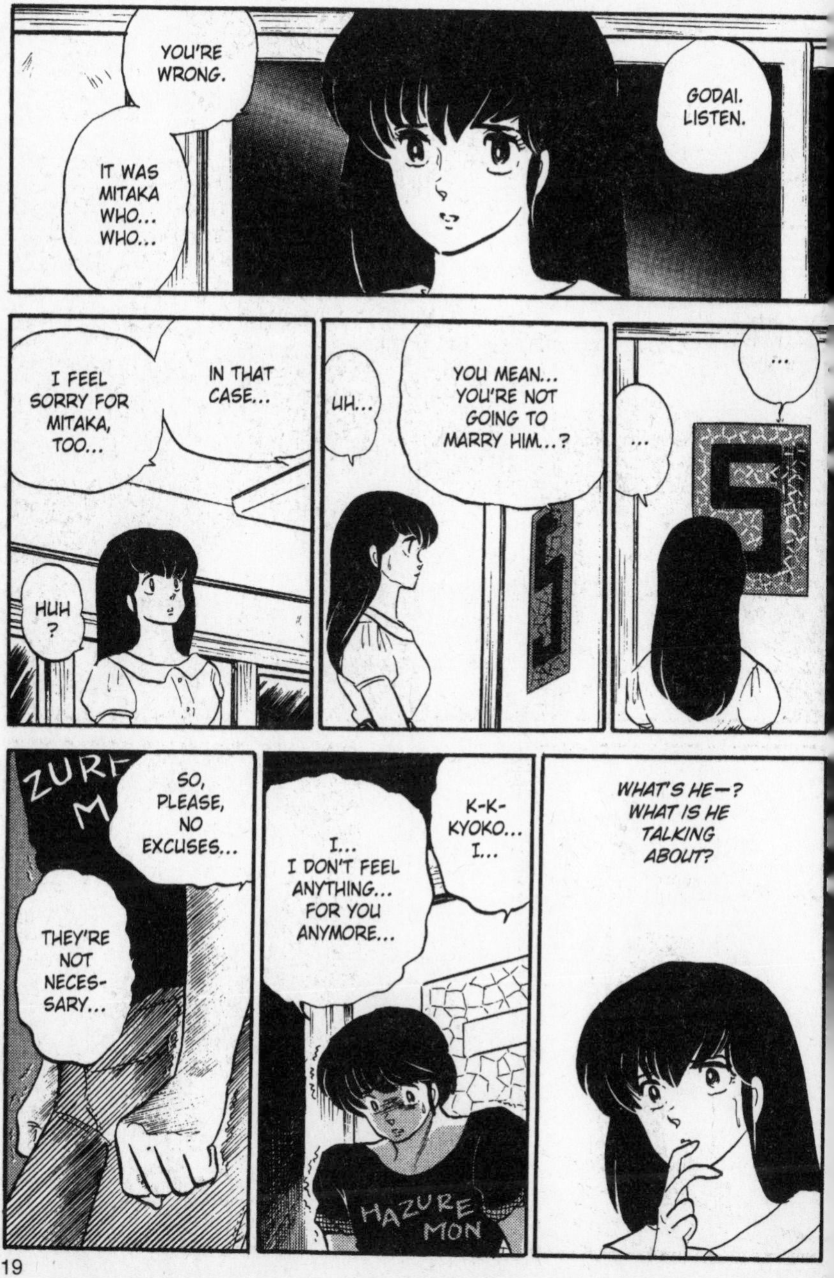
GODAI. LISTEN.
YOU'RE WRONG.
IT WAS MITAKA WHO... WHO...
...
...
YOU MEAN... YOU'RE NOT GOING TO MARRY HIM...?
UH...
IN THAT CASE...
I FEEL SORRY FOR MITAKA, TOO...
HUH?
WHAT'S HE—? WHAT IS HE TALKING ABOUT?
K-K-KYOKO... I...
I... I DON'T FEEL ANYTHING... FOR YOU ANYMORE...
HAZURE MON
SO, PLEASE, NO EXCUSES...
THEY'RE NOT NECES-SARY...

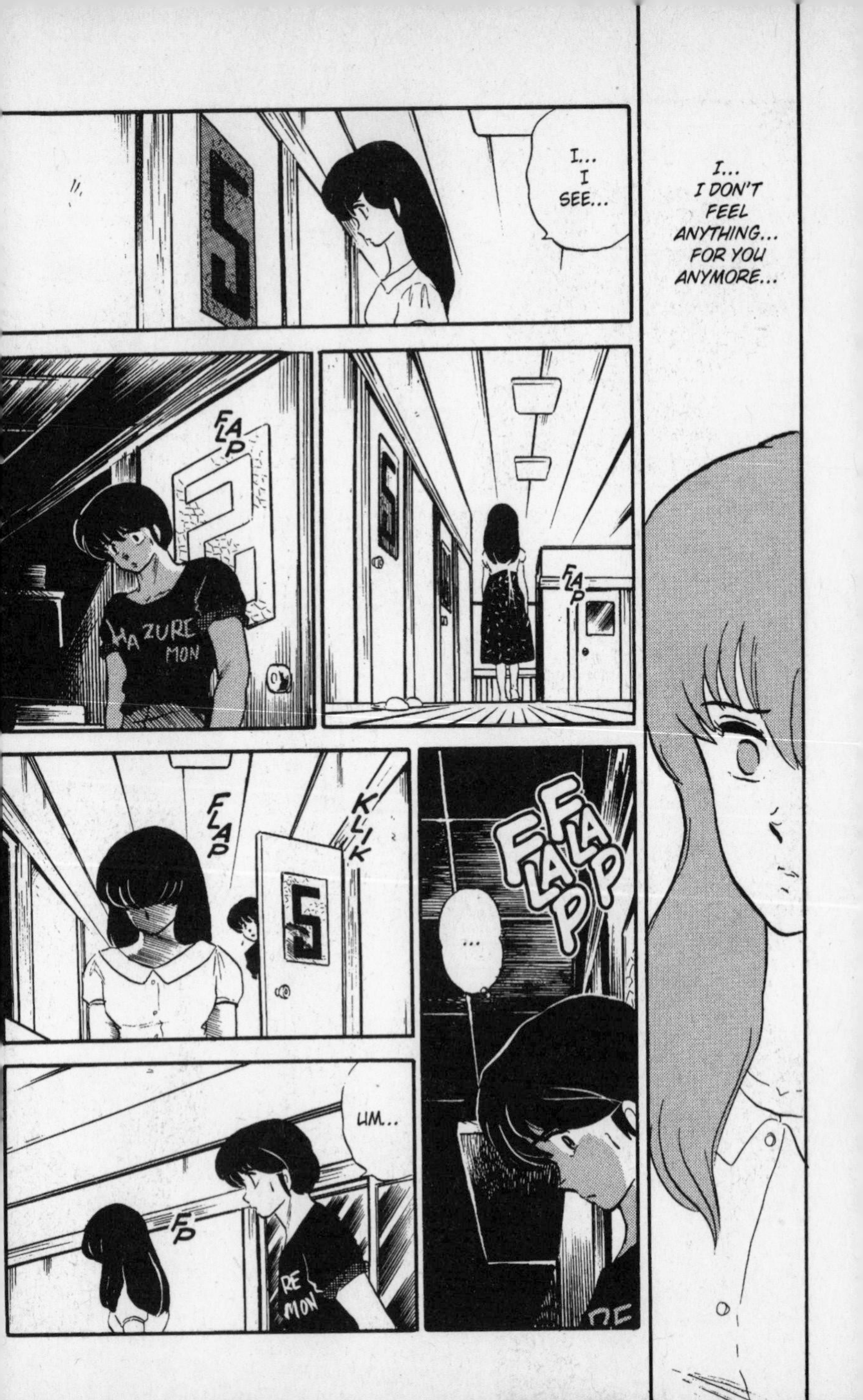
I... I DON'T FEEL ANYTHING... FOR YOU ANYMORE...
!!
I... I SEE...
FLAP
FLAP
HAZURE MON
FLAP FLAP
...
FLAP
KLIK
UM...
FP
RE MON

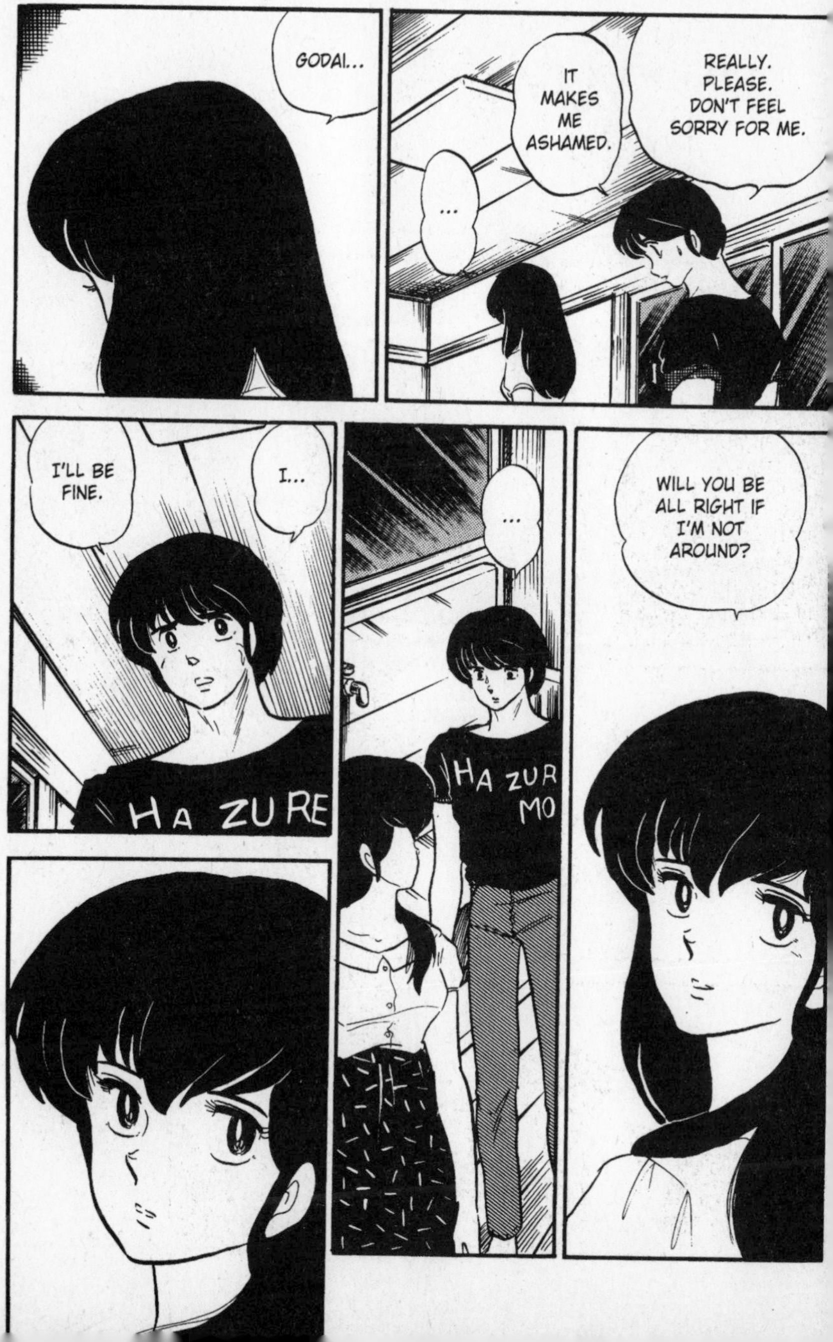
REALLY. PLEASE. DON'T FEEL SORRY FOR ME.
IT MAKES ME ASHAMED.
...
GODAI...
WILL YOU BE ALL RIGHT IF I'M NOT AROUND?
...
HA ZUR MO
I...
I'LL BE FINE.
HA ZURE

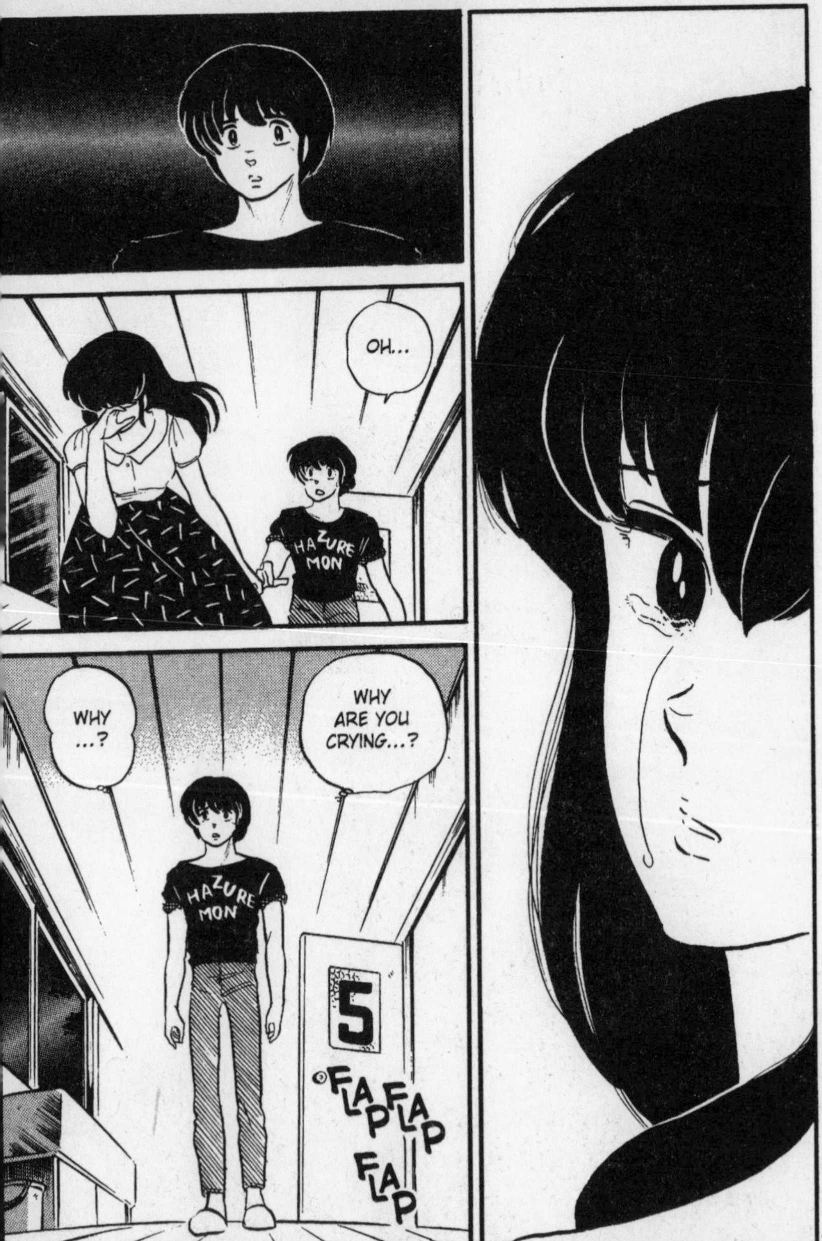
OH...
HAZURE MON
WHY ARE YOU CRYING...?
WHY ...?
HAZURE MON
5
FLAP FLAP
FLAP

PART TWO

TWIN JOURNEYS

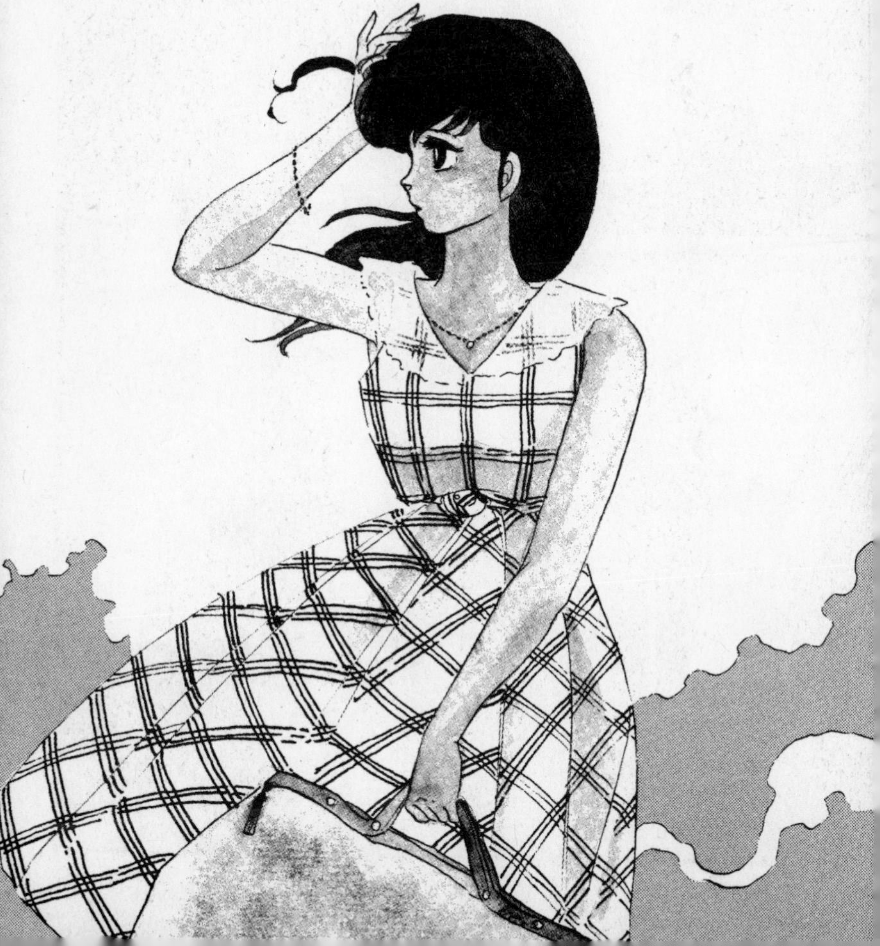

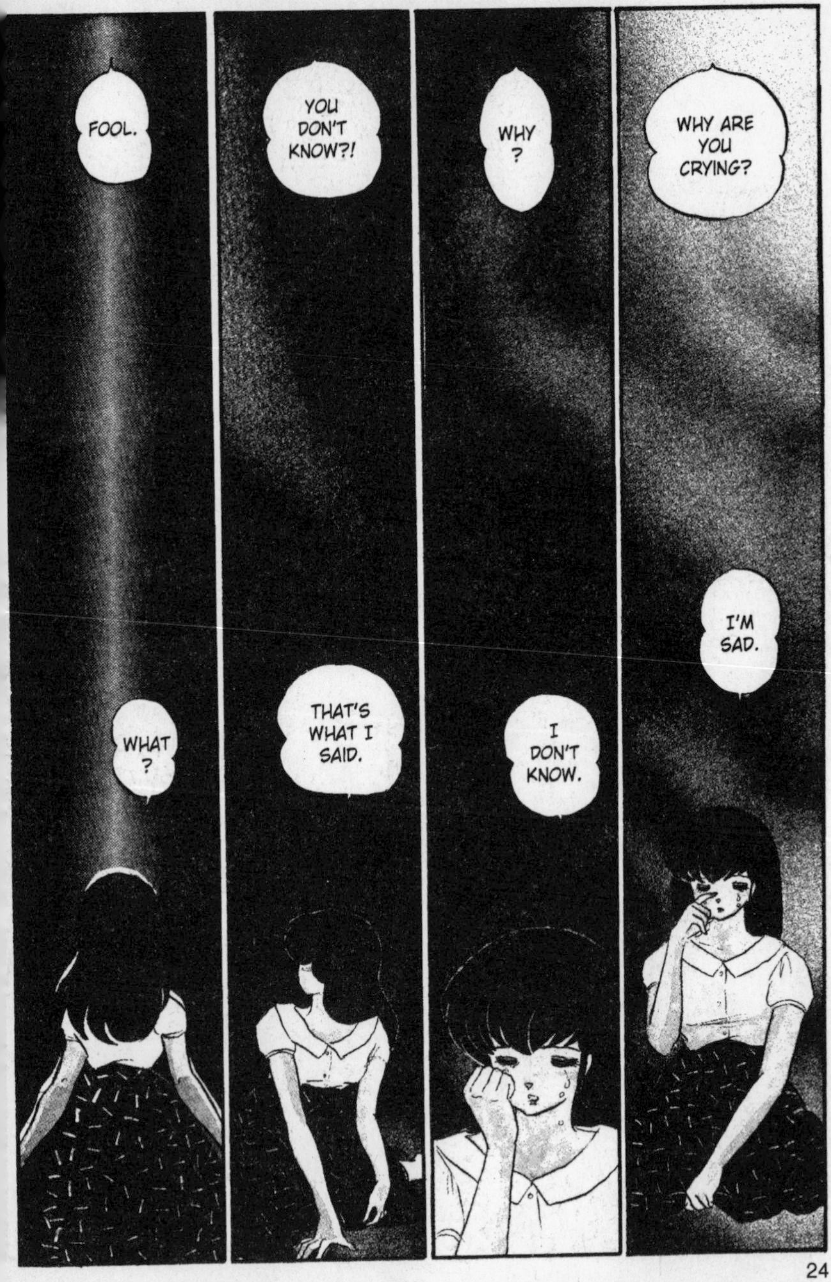
WHY ARE YOU CRYING?
I'M SAD.
WHY?
I DON'T KNOW.
YOU DON'T KNOW?!
THAT'S WHAT I SAID.
FOOL.
WHAT?

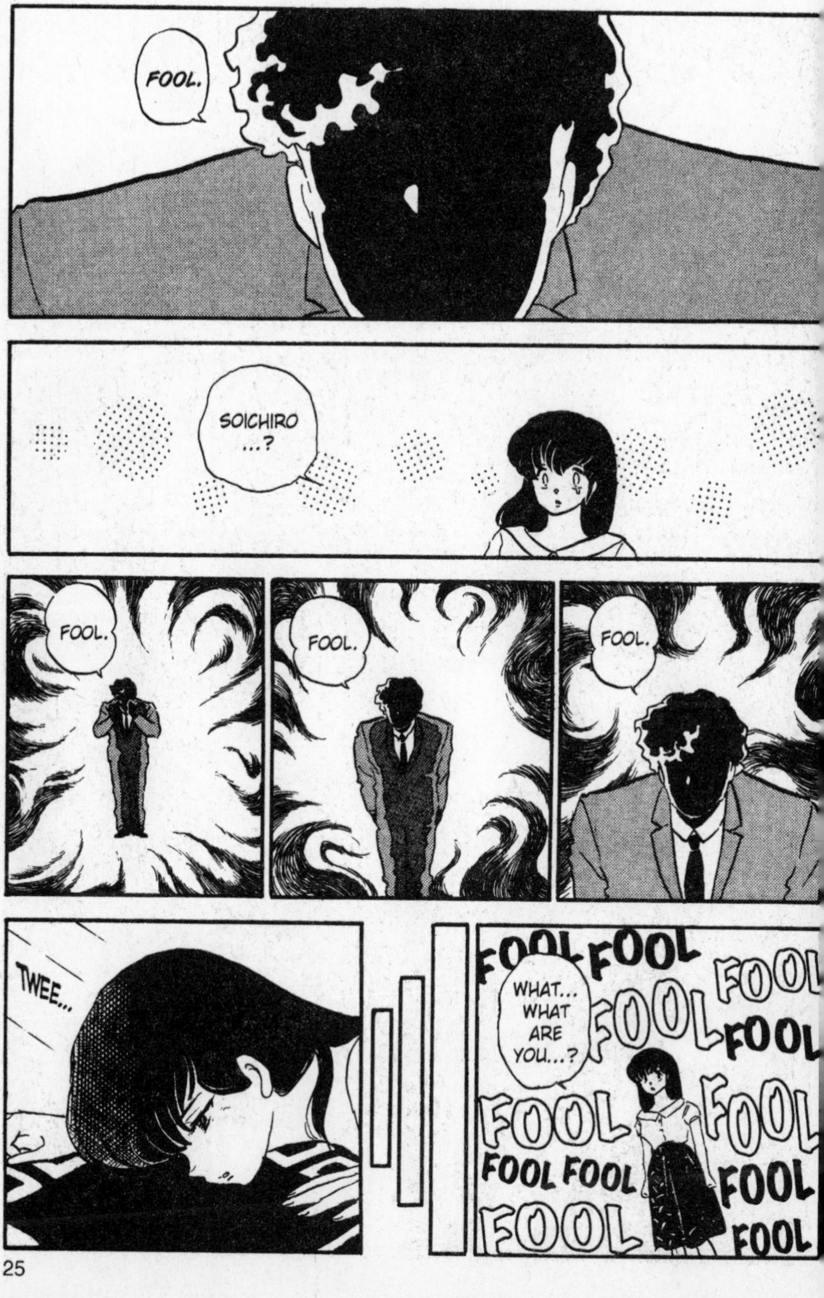
FOOL.
SOICHIRO ...?
FOOL.
FOOL.
FOOL.
FOOL FOOL FOOL FOOL FOOL FOOL FOOL FOOL FOOL FOOL FOOL FOOL FOOL
WHAT... WHAT ARE YOU...?
TWEE...

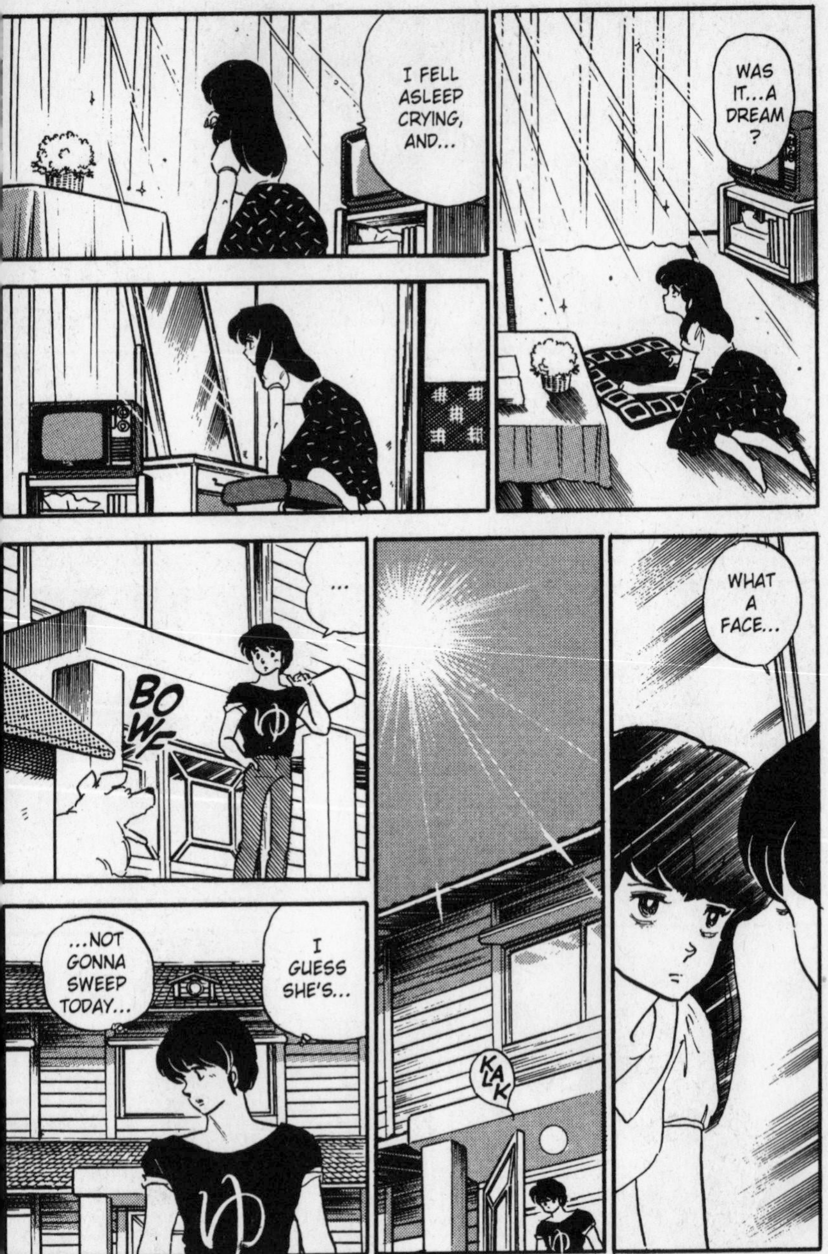
WAS IT...A DREAM ?
I FELL ASLEEP CRYING, AND...
WHAT A FACE...
KALK
...
BOWF
I GUESS SHE'S...
...NOT GONNA SWEEP TODAY...

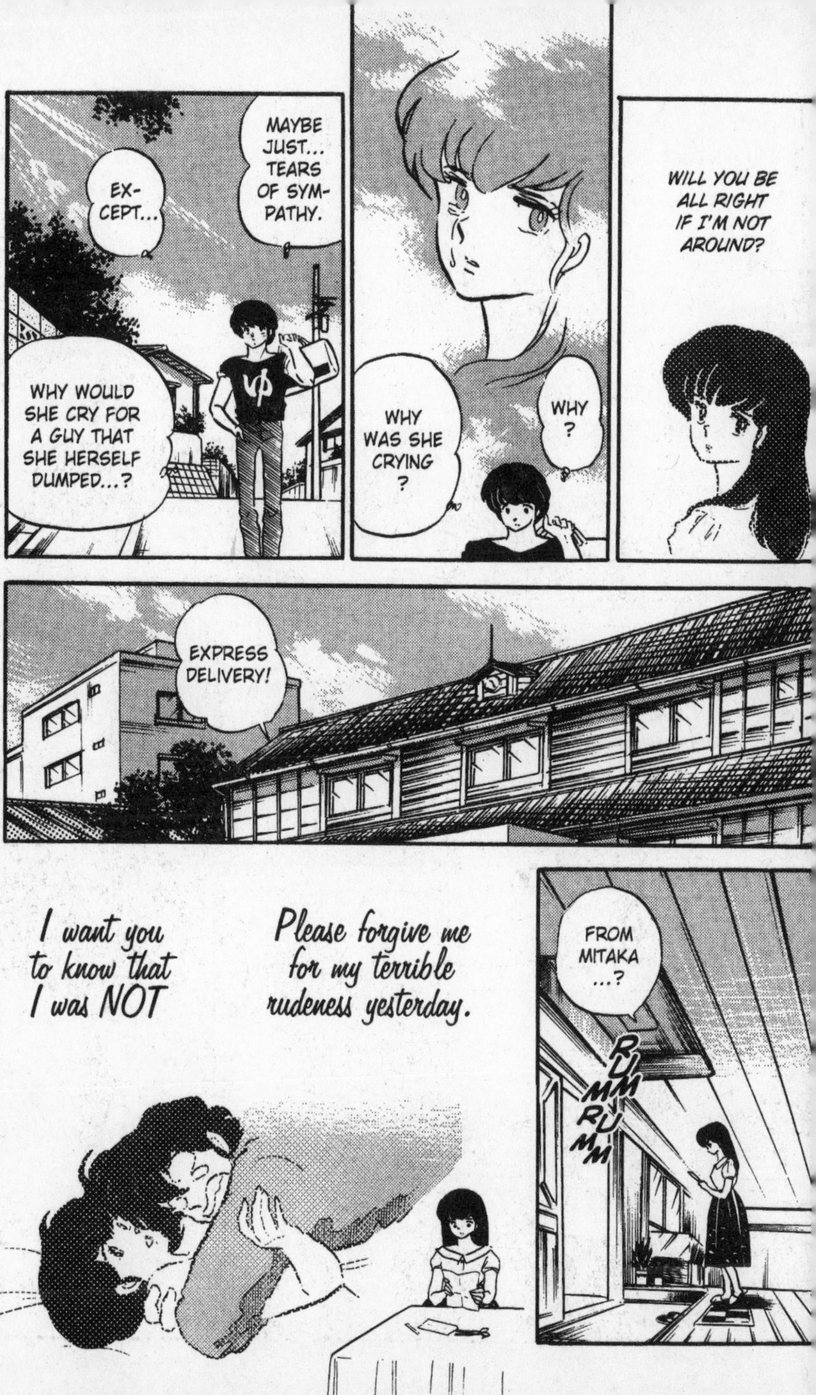
WILL YOU BE ALL RIGHT IF I'M NOT AROUND?
WHY?
WHY WAS SHE CRYING?
MAYBE JUST... TEARS OF SYMPATHY.
EX-CEPT...
WHY WOULD SHE CRY FOR A GUY THAT SHE HERSELF DUMPED...?
EXPRESS DELIVERY!
FROM MITAKA...?
RUMM RUMM
Please forgive me for my terrible rudeness yesterday.
I want you to know that I was NOT

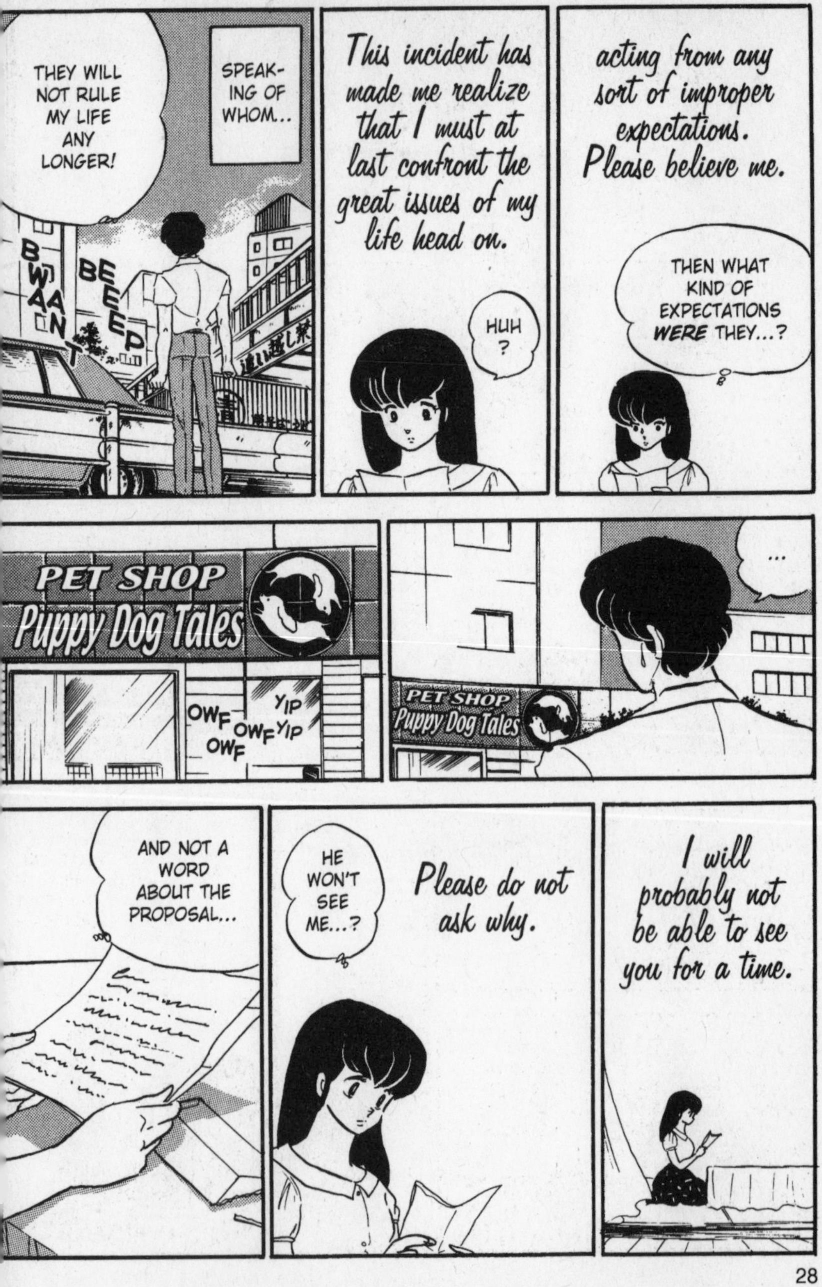
acting from any sort of improper expectations. Please believe me.
THEN WHAT KIND OF EXPECTATIONS WERE THEY...?
This incident has made me realize that I must at last confront the great issues of my life head on.
HUH ?
SPEAK-ING OF WHOM...
THEY WILL NOT RULE MY LIFE ANY LONGER!
BEEEEP
BWAAANT
...
PET SHOP Puppy Dog Tales
PET SHOP Puppy Dog Tales
YIP YIP
OWF OWF OWF
I will probably not be able to see you for a time.
Please do not ask why.
HE WON'T SEE ME...?
AND NOT A WORD ABOUT THE PROPOSAL...

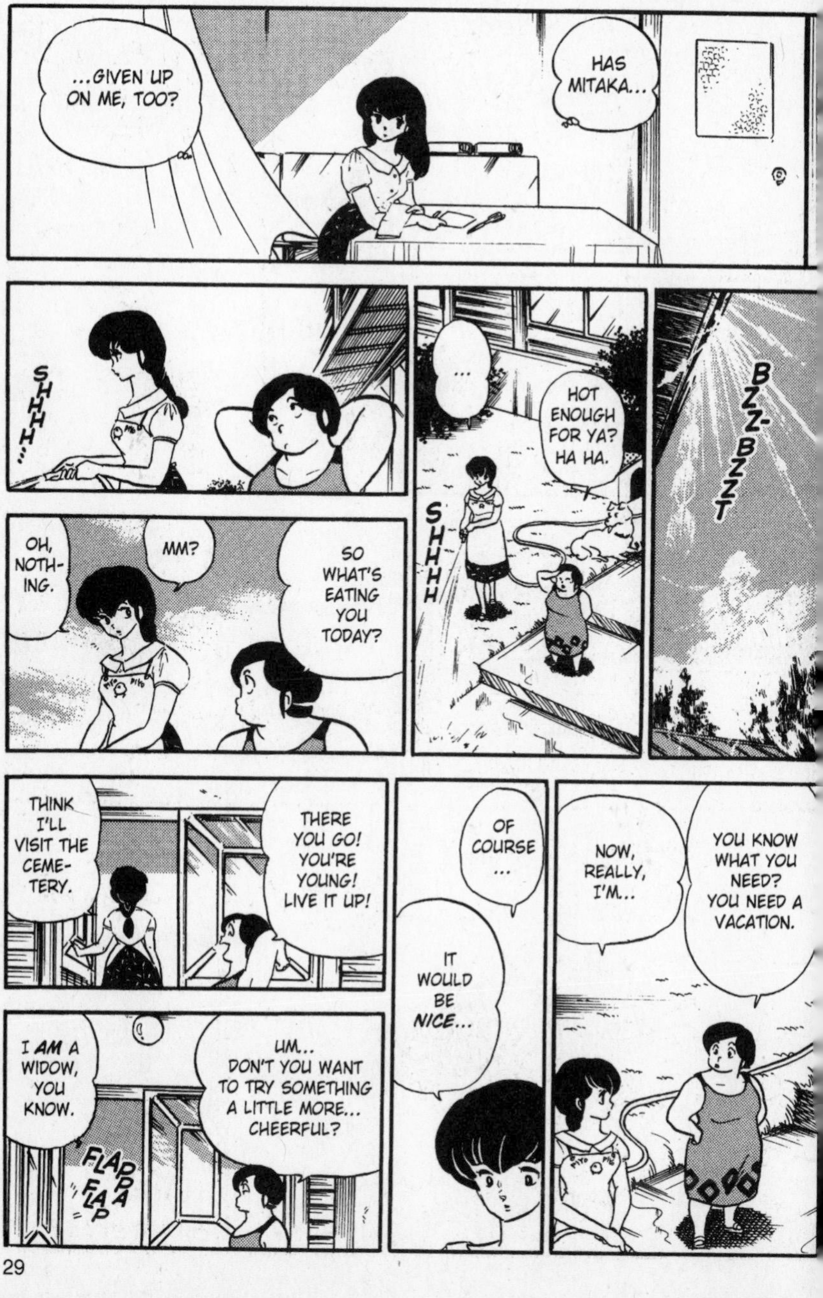
HAS MITAKA...
...GIVEN UP ON ME, TOO?
BZZ-BZZT
HOT ENOUGH FOR YA? HA HA.
...
SHHHH
SHHHH...
SO WHAT'S EATING YOU TODAY?
MM?
OH, NOTHING.
YOU KNOW WHAT YOU NEED? YOU NEED A VACATION.
NOW, REALLY, I'M...
OF COURSE...
IT WOULD BE NICE...
THERE YOU GO! YOU'RE YOUNG! LIVE IT UP!
THINK I'LL VISIT THE CEMETERY.
UM... DON'T YOU WANT TO TRY SOMETHING A LITTLE MORE... CHEERFUL?
I AM A WIDOW, YOU KNOW.
FLAPPA FLAP

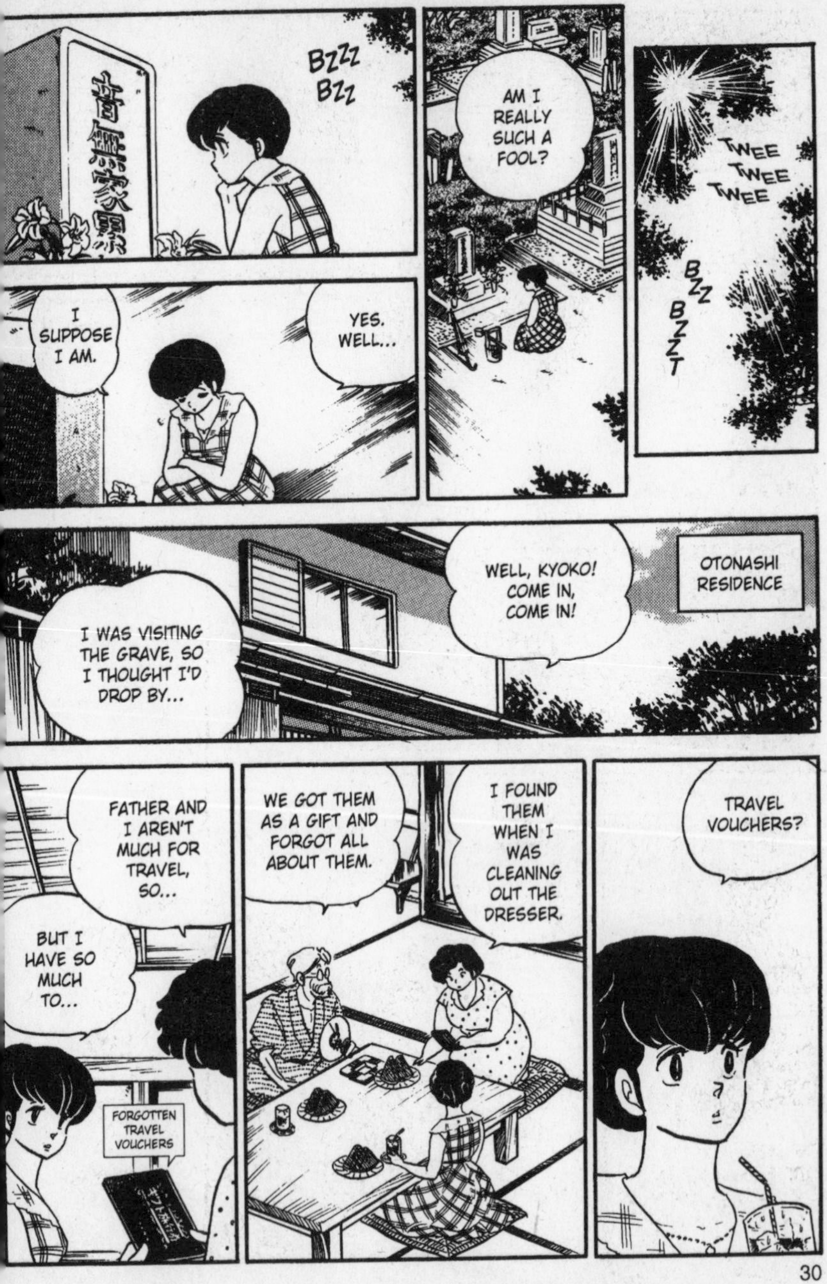
TWEE TWEE TWEE
BZZ BZZT
AM I REALLY SUCH A FOOL?
BZZZ BZZ
YES. WELL...
I SUPPOSE I AM.
OTONASHI RESIDENCE
WELL, KYOKO! COME IN, COME IN!
I WAS VISITING THE GRAVE, SO I THOUGHT I'D DROP BY...
TRAVEL VOUCHERS?
I FOUND THEM WHEN I WAS CLEANING OUT THE DRESSER.
WE GOT THEM AS A GIFT AND FORGOT ALL ABOUT THEM.
FATHER AND I AREN'T MUCH FOR TRAVEL, SO...
BUT I HAVE SO MUCH TO...
FORGOTTEN TRAVEL VOUCHERS

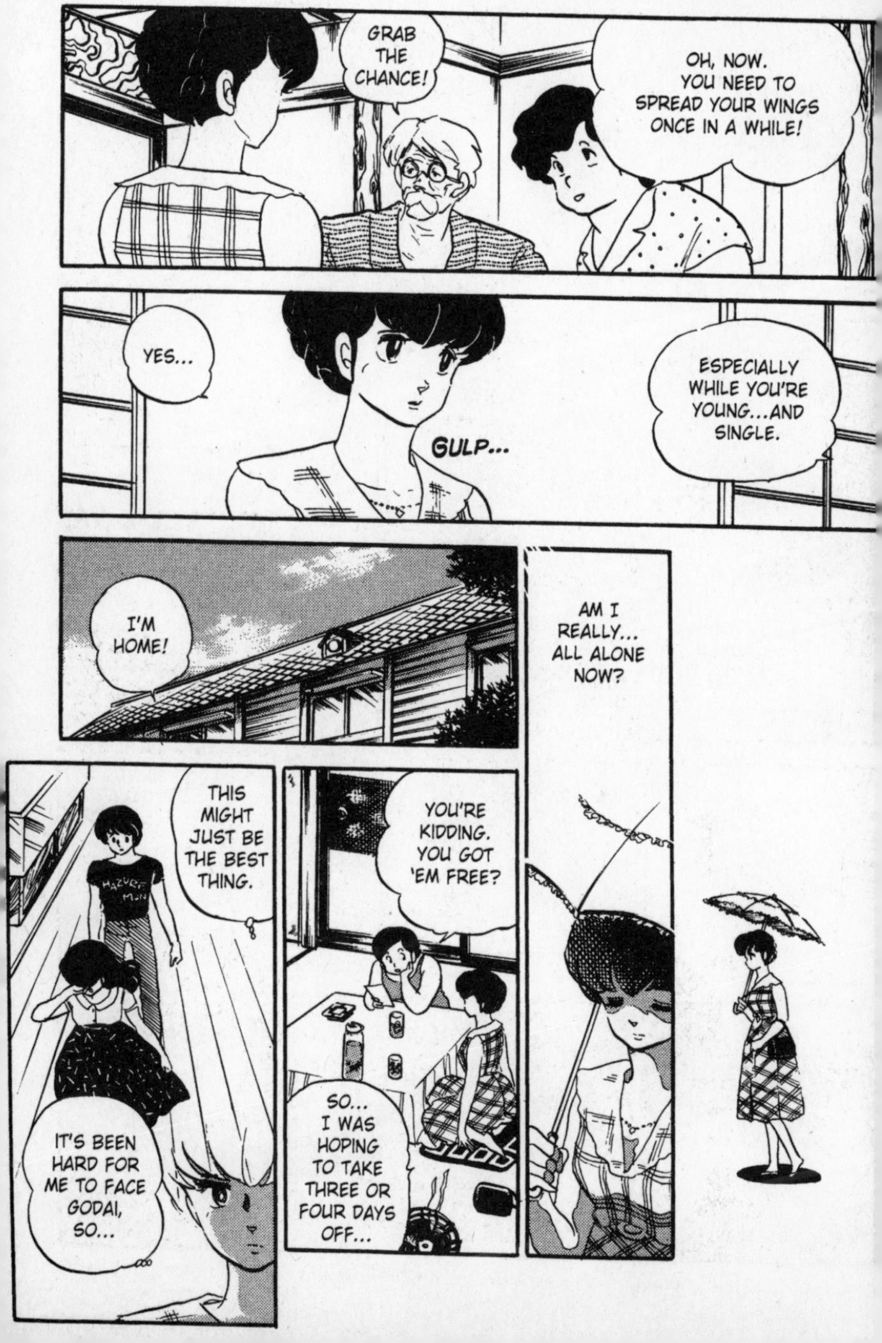
OH, NOW. YOU NEED TO SPREAD YOUR WINGS ONCE IN A WHILE!
GRAB THE CHANCE!
ESPECIALLY WHILE YOU'RE YOUNG...AND SINGLE.
GULP...
YES...
AM I REALLY... ALL ALONE NOW?
I'M HOME!
YOU'RE KIDDING. YOU GOT 'EM FREE?
SO... I WAS HOPING TO TAKE THREE OR FOUR DAYS OFF...
THIS MIGHT JUST BE THE BEST THING.
HAZURE MAN
IT'S BEEN HARD FOR ME TO FACE GODAI, SO...

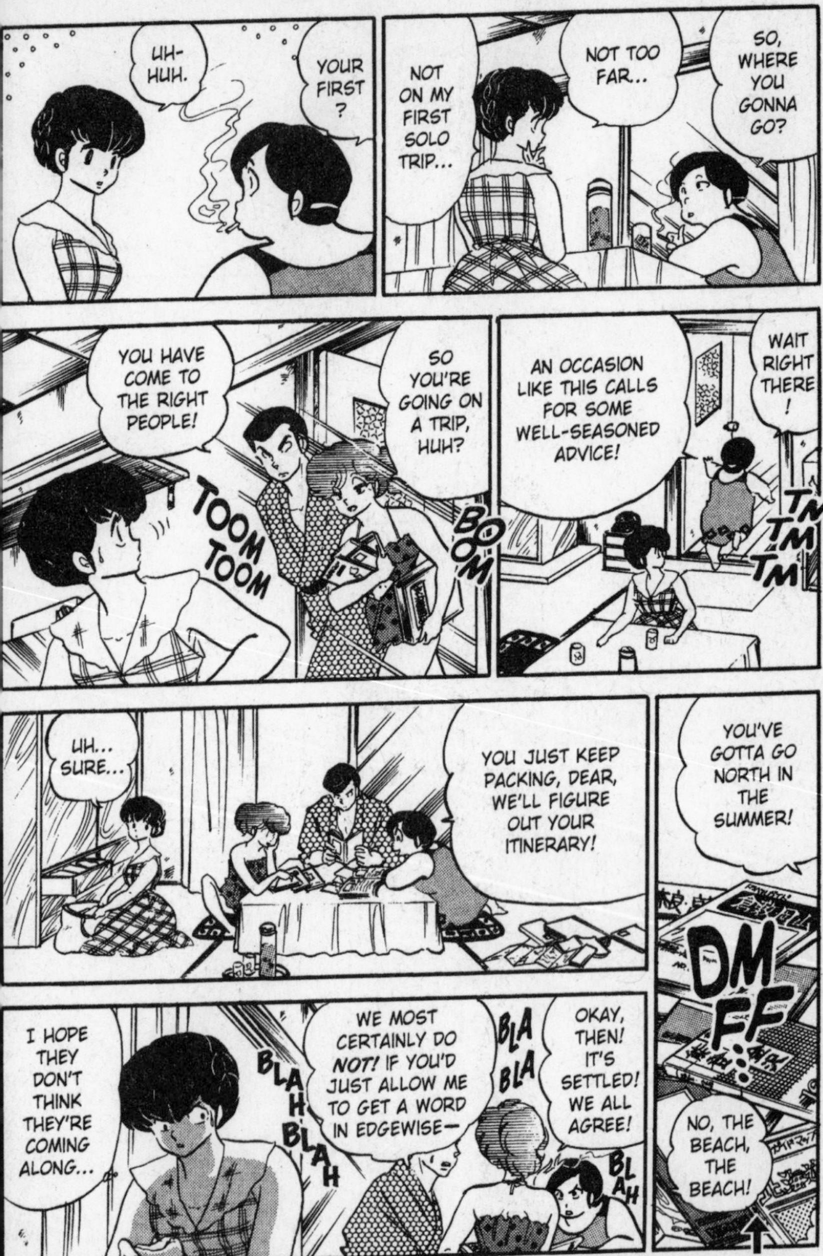

SO, WHERE YOU GONNA GO?
NOT TOO FAR...
NOT ON MY FIRST SOLO TRIP...
YOUR FIRST ?
UH-HUH.
WAIT RIGHT THERE!
AN OCCASION LIKE THIS CALLS FOR SOME WELL-SEASONED ADVICE!
TM TM TM
SO YOU'RE GOING ON A TRIP, HUH?
BOOOM
YOU HAVE COME TO THE RIGHT PEOPLE!
TOOM TOOM
YOU'VE GOTTA GO NORTH IN THE SUMMER!
DMFF
NO, THE BEACH, THE BEACH!
YOU JUST KEEP PACKING, DEAR, WE'LL FIGURE OUT YOUR ITINERARY!
UH... SURE...
OKAY, THEN! IT'S SETTLED! WE ALL AGREE!
BLAH
BLA BLA
WE MOST CERTAINLY DO *NOT!* IF YOU'D JUST ALLOW ME TO GET A WORD IN EDGEWISE—
BLAH BLAH
I HOPE THEY DON'T THINK THEY'RE COMING ALONG...

Travel Rustic Japan Holiday Nihon for Novices Unknown Japan Map of Japan Go Japan

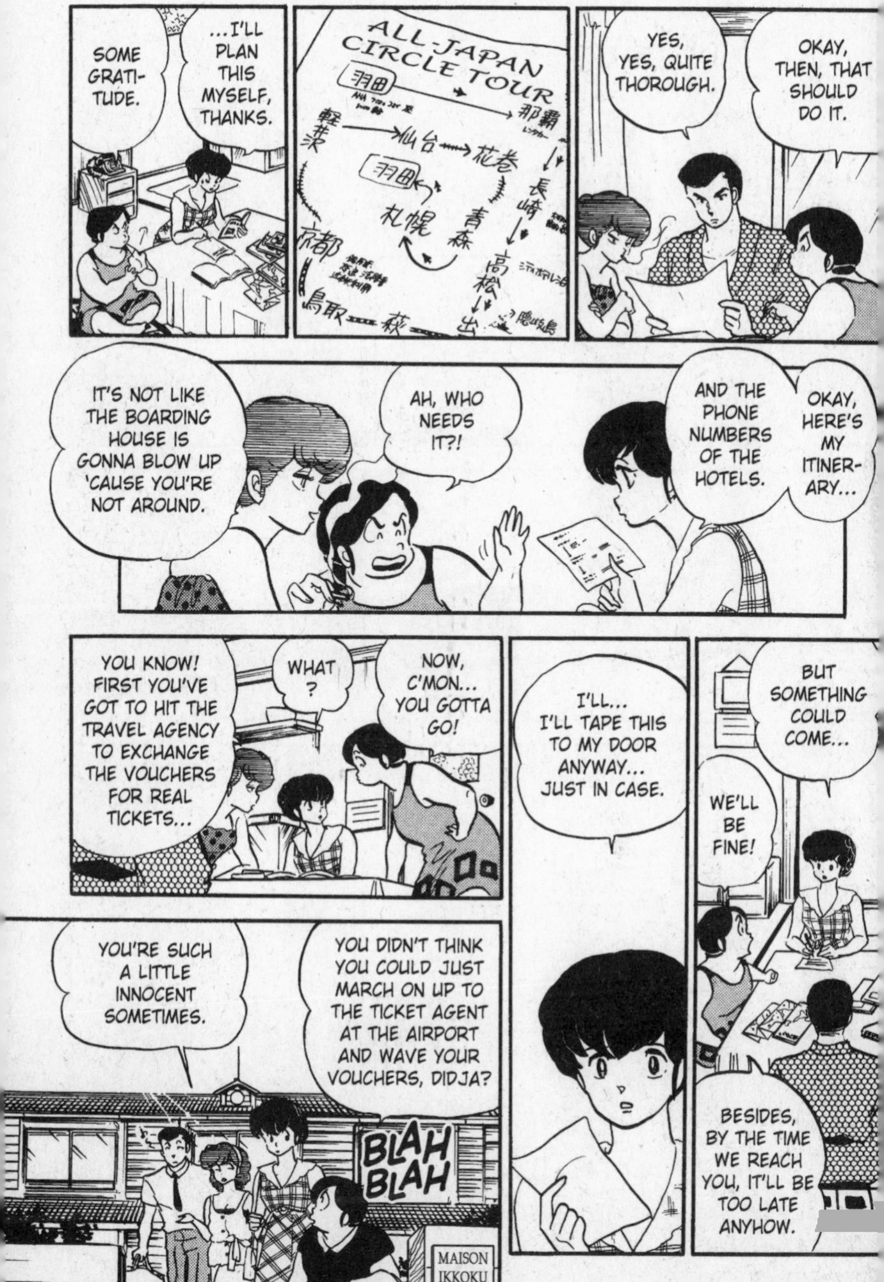
OKAY, THEN, THAT SHOULD DO IT.
YES, YES, QUITE THOROUGH.
ALL-JAPAN CIRCLE TOUR
羽田
那覇
仙台
花巻
長崎
羽田
青森
京都
高松
鳥取
萩
...I'LL PLAN THIS MYSELF, THANKS.
SOME GRATITUDE.
OKAY, HERE'S MY ITINERARY...
AND THE PHONE NUMBERS OF THE HOTELS.
AH, WHO NEEDS IT?!
IT'S NOT LIKE THE BOARDING HOUSE IS GONNA BLOW UP 'CAUSE YOU'RE NOT AROUND.
BUT SOMETHING COULD COME...
WE'LL BE FINE!
BESIDES, BY THE TIME WE REACH YOU, IT'LL BE TOO LATE ANYHOW.
I'LL... I'LL TAPE THIS TO MY DOOR ANYWAY... JUST IN CASE.
NOW, C'MON... YOU GOTTA GO!
WHAT?
YOU KNOW! FIRST YOU'VE GOT TO HIT THE TRAVEL AGENCY TO EXCHANGE THE VOUCHERS FOR REAL TICKETS...
YOU DIDN'T THINK YOU COULD JUST MARCH ON UP TO THE TICKET AGENT AT THE AIRPORT AND WAVE YOUR VOUCHERS, DIDJA?
YOU'RE SUCH A LITTLE INNOCENT SOMETIMES.
BLAH BLAH
MAISON IKKOKU

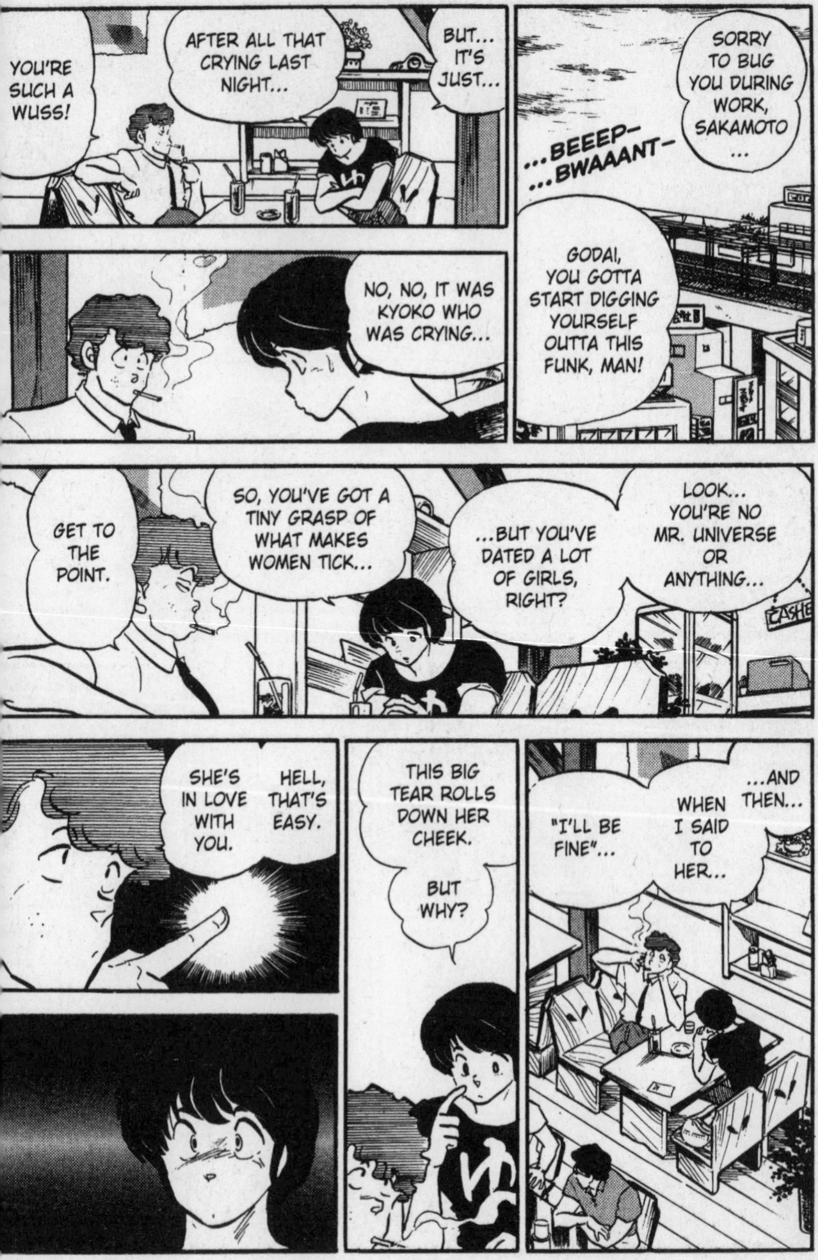
SORRY TO BUG YOU DURING WORK, SAKAMOTO ...
...BEEEP- ...BWAAANT-
GODAI, YOU GOTTA START DIGGING YOURSELF OUTTA THIS FUNK, MAN!
BUT... IT'S JUST...
AFTER ALL THAT CRYING LAST NIGHT...
YOU'RE SUCH A WUSS!
NO, NO, IT WAS KYOKO WHO WAS CRYING...
LOOK... YOU'RE NO MR. UNIVERSE OR ANYTHING...
...BUT YOU'VE DATED A LOT OF GIRLS, RIGHT?
SO, YOU'VE GOT A TINY GRASP OF WHAT MAKES WOMEN TICK...
GET TO THE POINT.
...AND THEN...
WHEN I SAID TO HER...
"I'LL BE FINE"...
THIS BIG TEAR ROLLS DOWN HER CHEEK.
BUT WHY?
HELL, THAT'S EASY.
SHE'S IN LOVE WITH YOU.

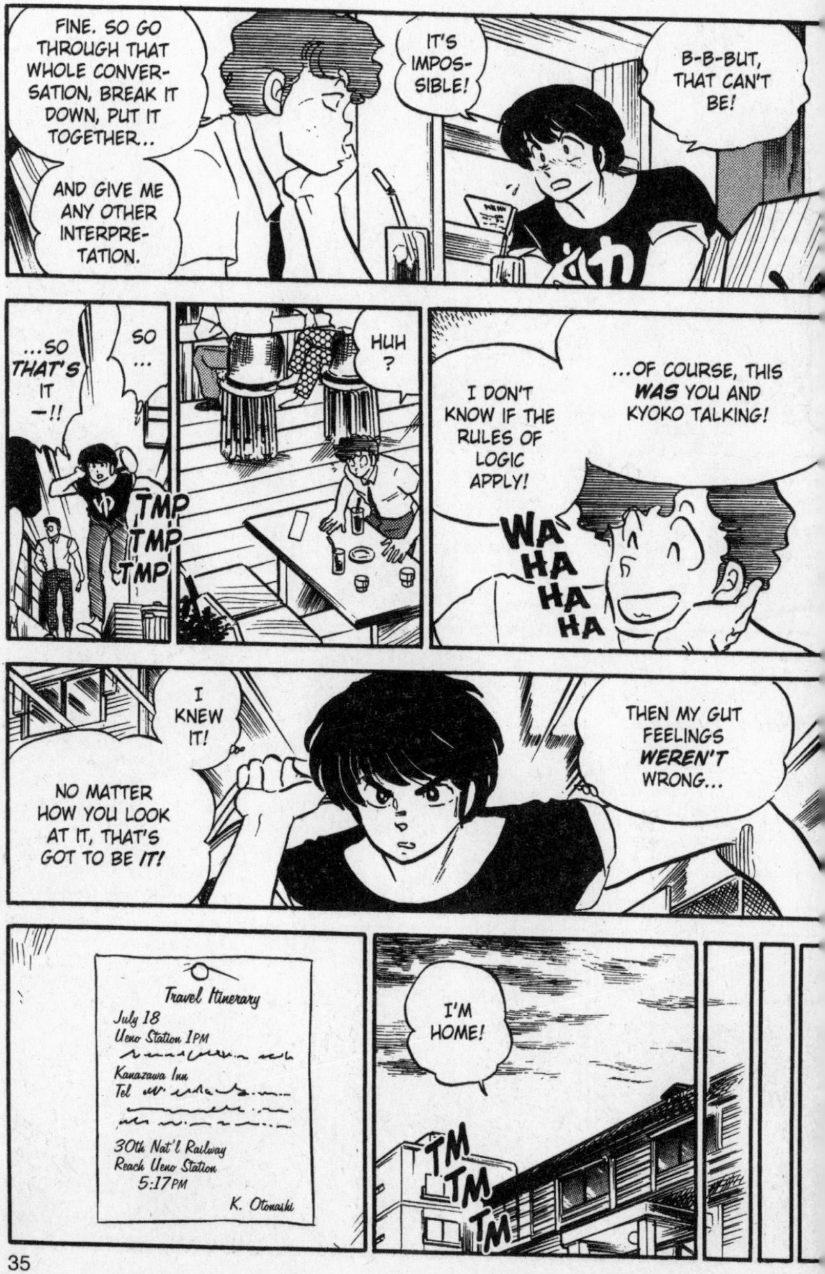
B-B-BUT, THAT CAN'T BE!
IT'S IMPOSSIBLE!
FINE. SO GO THROUGH THAT WHOLE CONVERSATION, BREAK IT DOWN, PUT IT TOGETHER...
AND GIVE ME ANY OTHER INTERPRETATION.
...OF COURSE, THIS WAS YOU AND KYOKO TALKING!
I DON'T KNOW IF THE RULES OF LOGIC APPLY!
WA HA HA HA HA
HUH?
SO ...
...SO THAT'S IT —!!
TMP TMP TMP
THEN MY GUT FEELINGS WEREN'T WRONG...
I KNEW IT!
NO MATTER HOW YOU LOOK AT IT, THAT'S GOT TO BE IT!
I'M HOME!
TM TM TM
Travel Itinerary
July 18
Ueno Station 1PM
Kanazawa Inn
Tel
30th Nat'l Railway
Reach Ueno Station
5:17PM
K. Otonashi

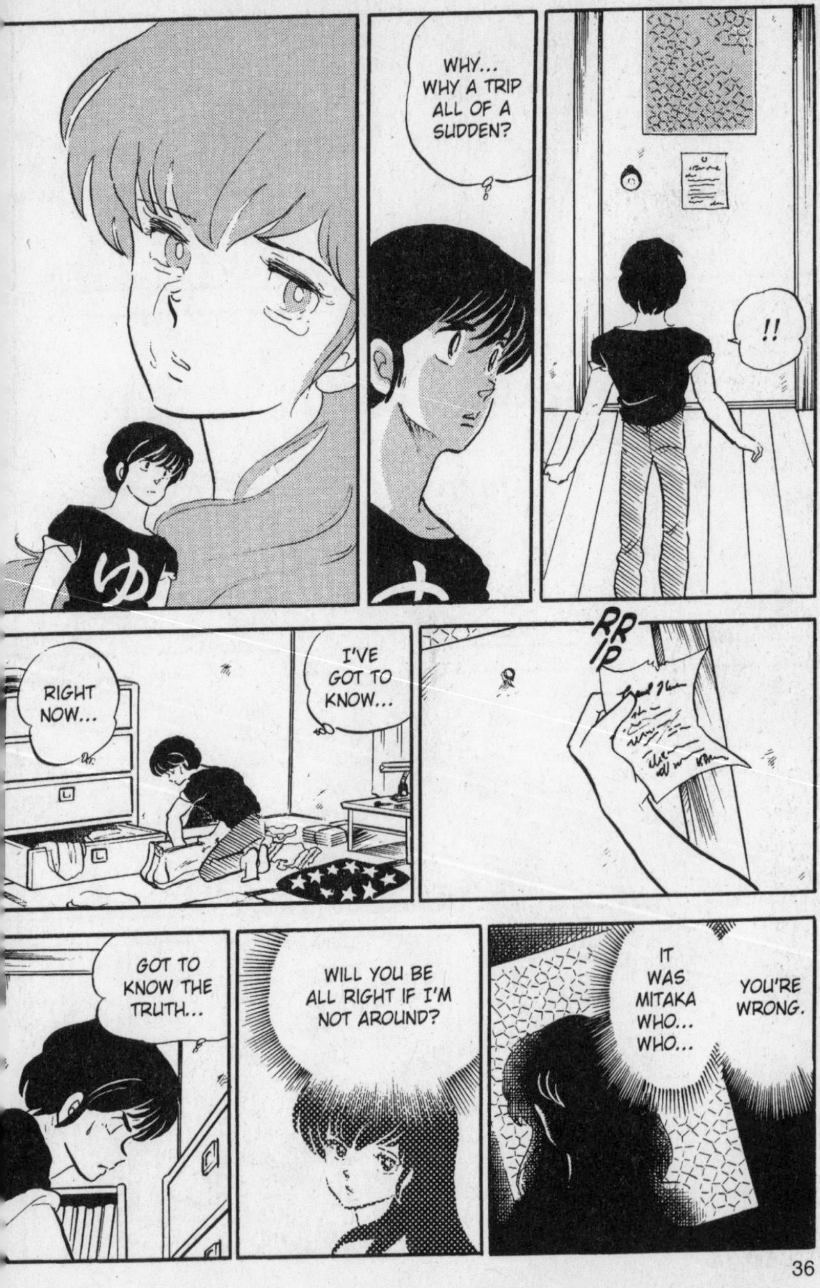
!!
WHY... WHY A TRIP ALL OF A SUDDEN?
RR IP
I'VE GOT TO KNOW...
RIGHT NOW...
YOU'RE WRONG.
IT WAS MITAKA WHO... WHO...
WILL YOU BE ALL RIGHT IF I'M NOT AROUND?
GOT TO KNOW THE TRUTH...

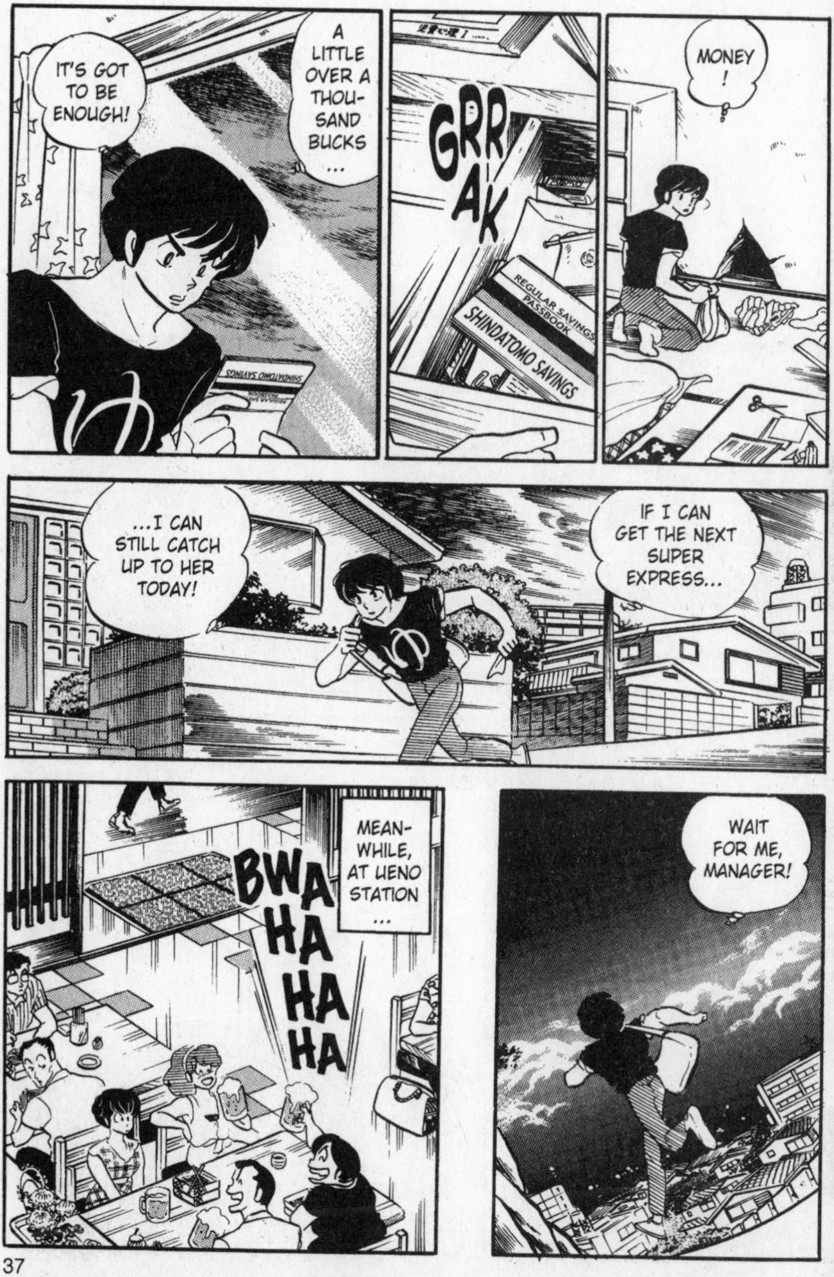
MONEY !
GRR AK
REGULAR SAVINGS PASSBOOK
SHINDATOMO SAVINGS
A LITTLE OVER A THOUSAND BUCKS ...
IT'S GOT TO BE ENOUGH!
IF I CAN GET THE NEXT SUPER EXPRESS...
...I CAN STILL CATCH UP TO HER TODAY!
WAIT FOR ME, MANAGER!
MEAN-WHILE, AT UENO STATION ...
BWAHAHAHAHA

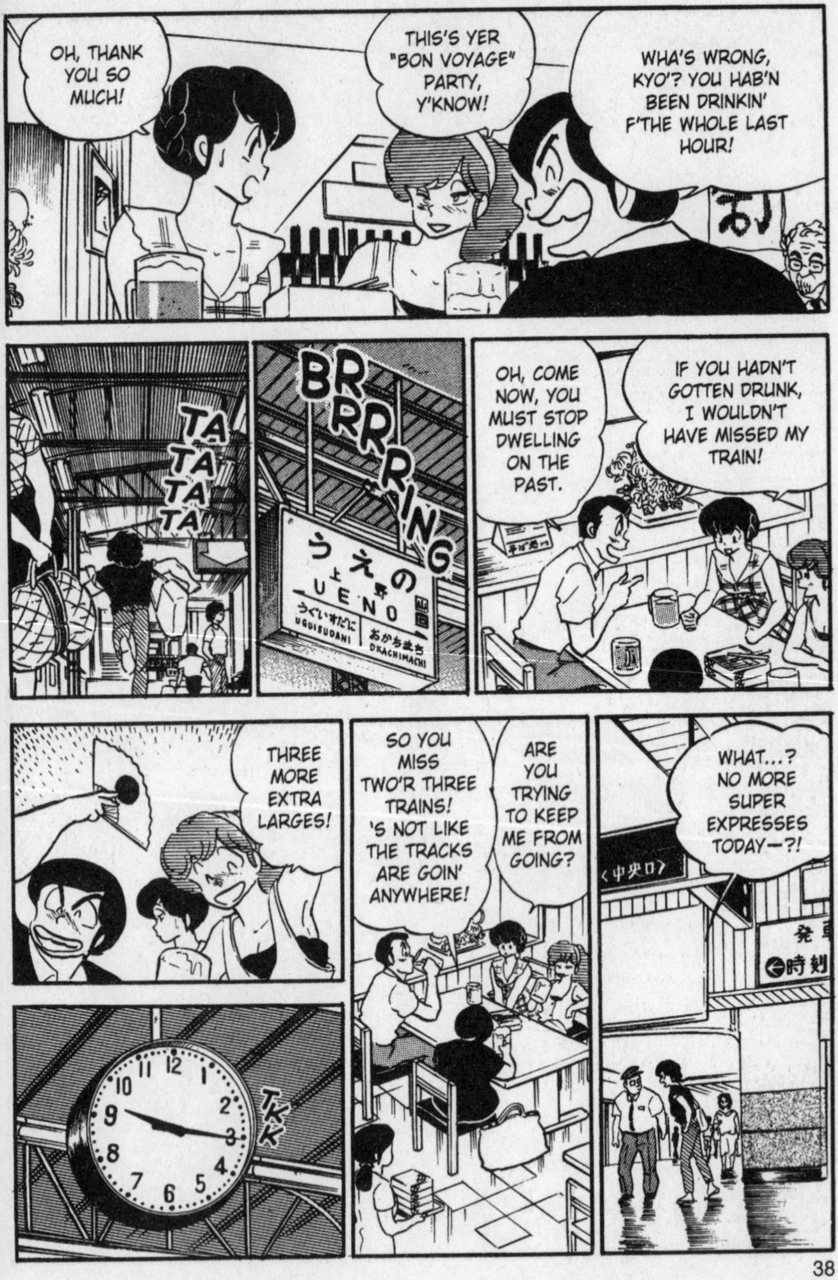
WHA'S WRONG, KYO'? YOU HAB'N BEEN DRINKIN' F'THE WHOLE LAST HOUR!
THIS'S YER "BON VOYAGE" PARTY, Y'KNOW!
OH, THANK YOU SO MUCH!
IF YOU HADN'T GOTTEN DRUNK, I WOULDN'T HAVE MISSED MY TRAIN!
OH, COME NOW, YOU MUST STOP DWELLING ON THE PAST.
BRRRRRING
うえの
上野
UENO
うぐいすだに
UGUISUDANI
おかちまち
OKACHIMACHI
TA TA TA TA
WHAT...? NO MORE SUPER EXPRESSES TODAY—?!
<中央口>
発車時刻
ARE YOU TRYING TO KEEP ME FROM GOING?
SO YOU MISS TWO'R THREE TRAINS! 'S NOT LIKE THE TRACKS ARE GOIN' ANYWHERE!
THREE MORE EXTRA LARGES!
TKK

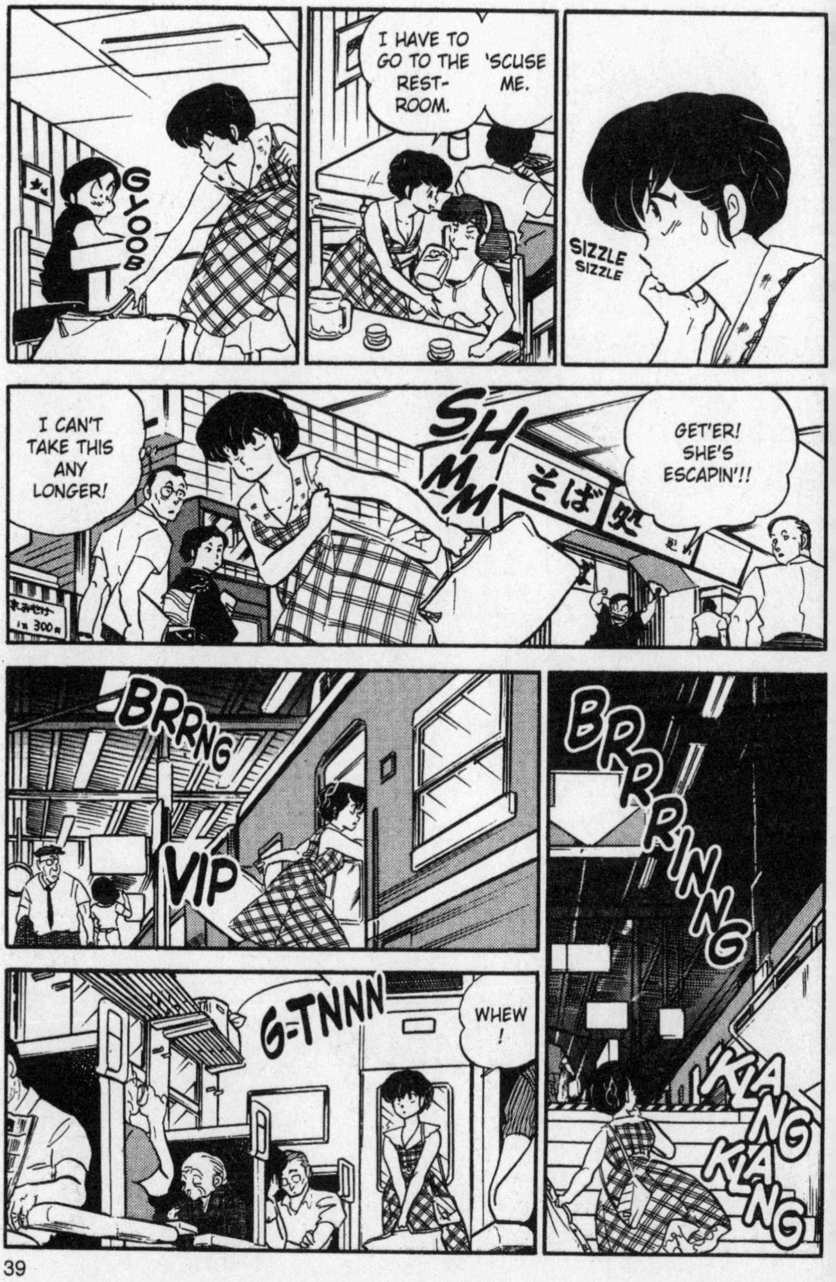
SIZZLE SIZZLE
'SCUSE ME.
I HAVE TO GO TO THE REST-ROOM.
GYOOB
GET'ER! SHE'S ESCAPIN'!!
SHMMM
そば
I CAN'T TAKE THIS ANY LONGER!
BRRRRINNNG
KLANG KLANG
BRRNG
VIP
WHEW!
G-TNNN

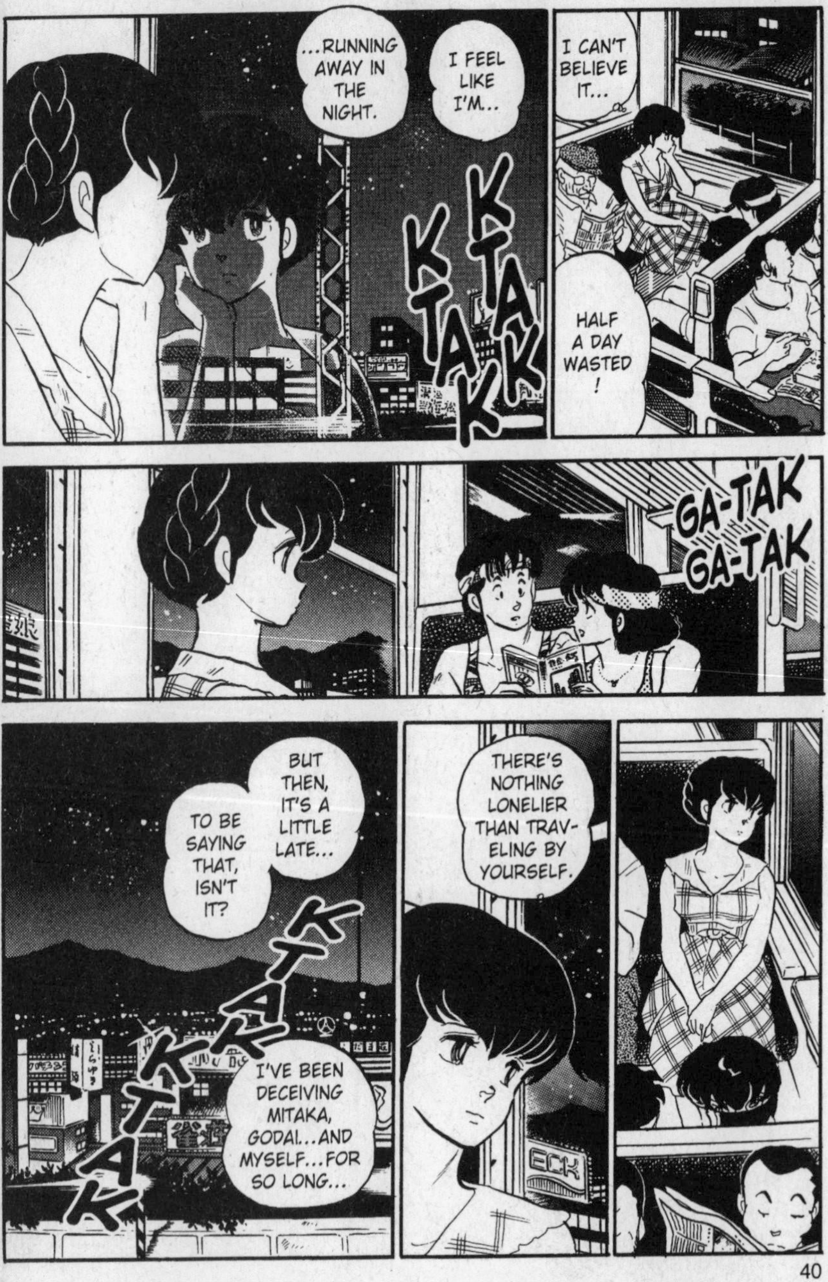
I CAN'T BELIEVE IT...
HALF A DAY WASTED!
I FEEL LIKE I'M...
...RUNNING AWAY IN THE NIGHT.
KTAK KTAK
GA-TAK GA-TAK
THERE'S NOTHING LONELIER THAN TRAVELING BY YOURSELF.
BUT THEN, IT'S A LITTLE LATE...
TO BE SAYING THAT, ISN'T IT?
KTAK KTAK
I'VE BEEN DECEIVING MITAKA, GODAI...AND MYSELF...FOR SO LONG...

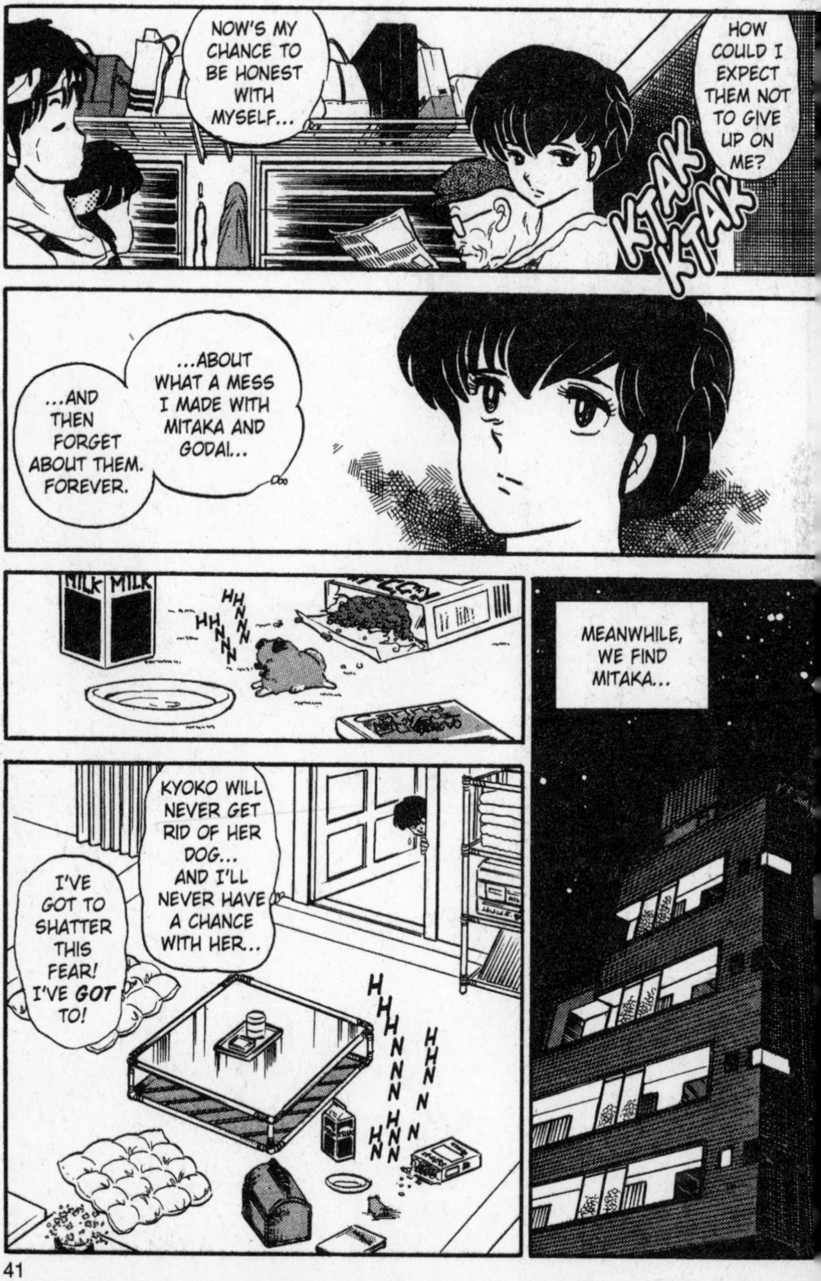
HOW COULD I EXPECT THEM NOT TO GIVE UP ON ME?
KTAK KTAK
NOW'S MY CHANCE TO BE HONEST WITH MYSELF...
...ABOUT WHAT A MESS I MADE WITH MITAKA AND GODAI...
...AND THEN FORGET ABOUT THEM. FOREVER.
MEANWHILE, WE FIND MITAKA...
MILK
MILK
HHNNN
HHNNN
KYOKO WILL NEVER GET RID OF HER DOG... AND I'LL NEVER HAVE A CHANCE WITH HER...
I'VE GOT TO SHATTER THIS FEAR! I'VE *GOT* TO!
HHHNNNN
HHNNNN

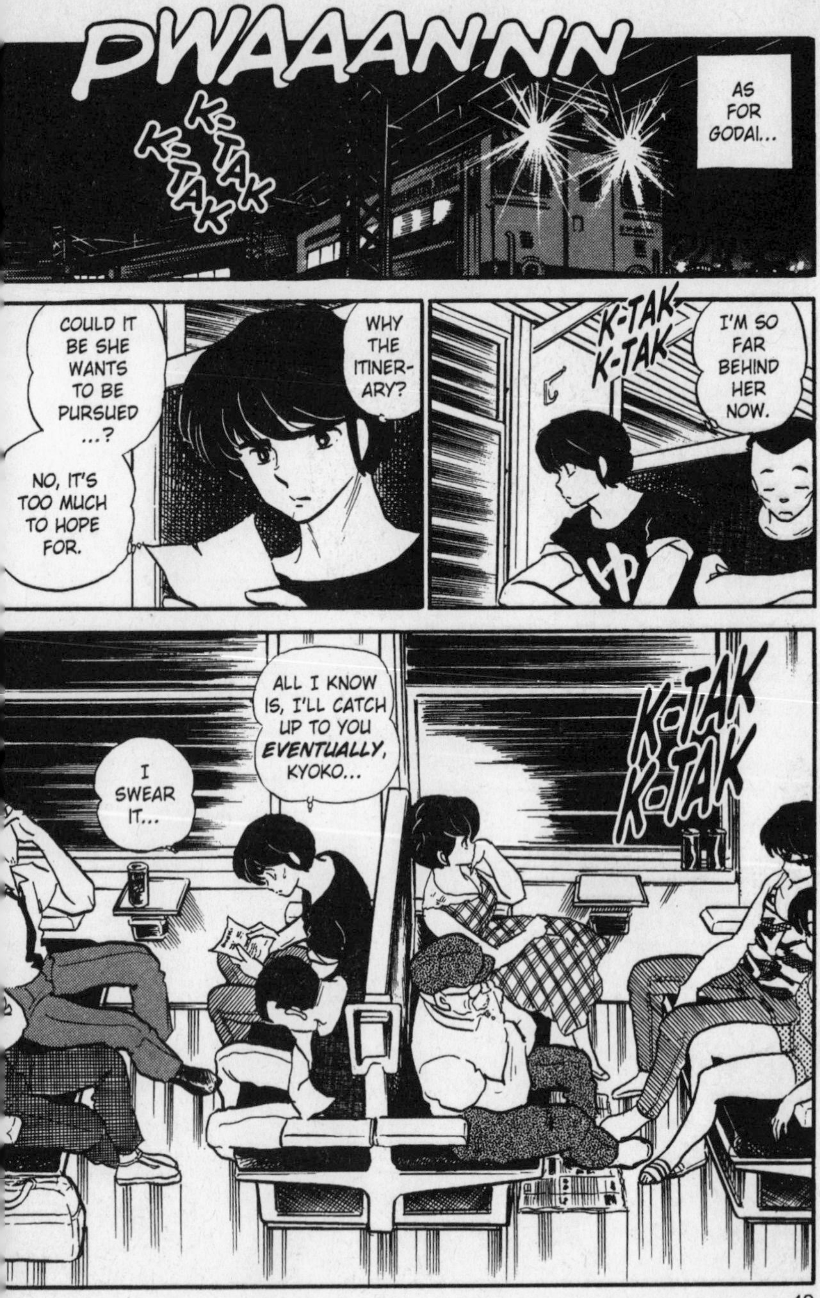
AS FOR GODAI...
PWAAANNN
K-TAK K-TAK
K-TAK K-TAK
I'M SO FAR BEHIND HER NOW.
WHY THE ITINER-ARY?
COULD IT BE SHE WANTS TO BE PURSUED ...?
NO, IT'S TOO MUCH TO HOPE FOR.
K-TAK K-TAK
ALL I KNOW IS, I'LL CATCH UP TO YOU *EVENTUALLY*, KYOKO...
I SWEAR IT...

PART THREE
PARTY OF TWO

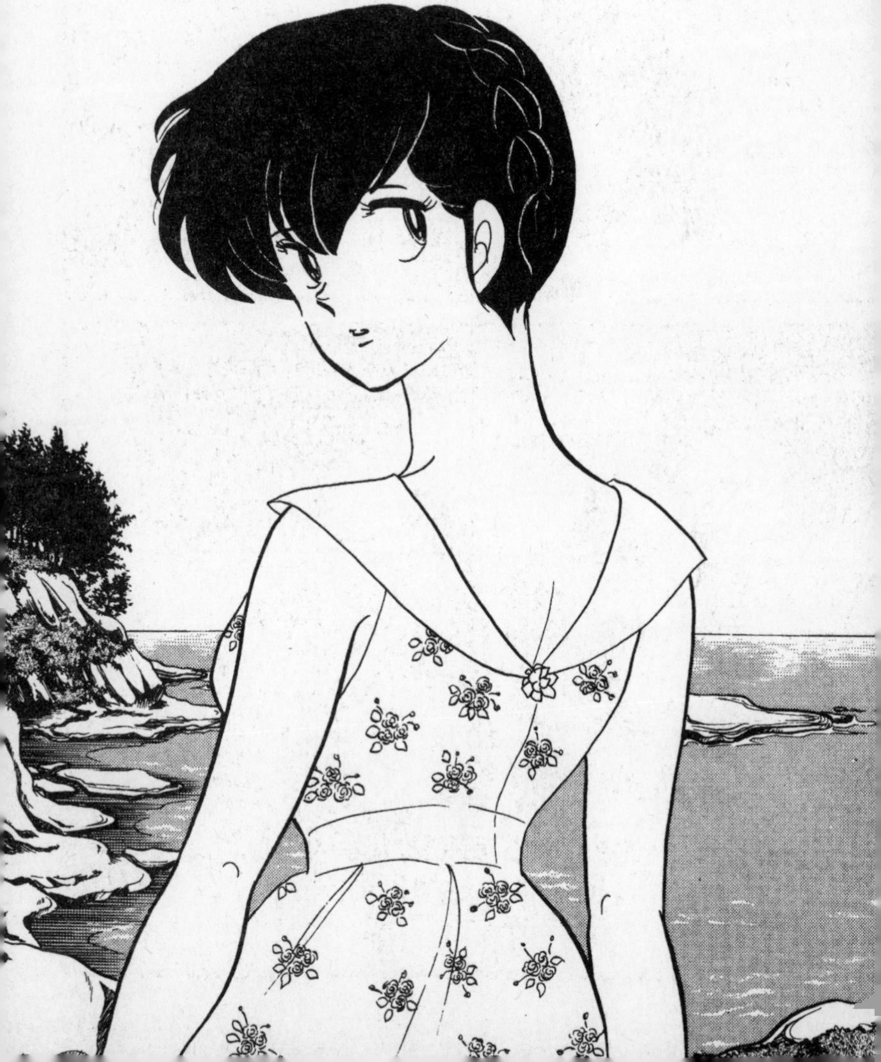

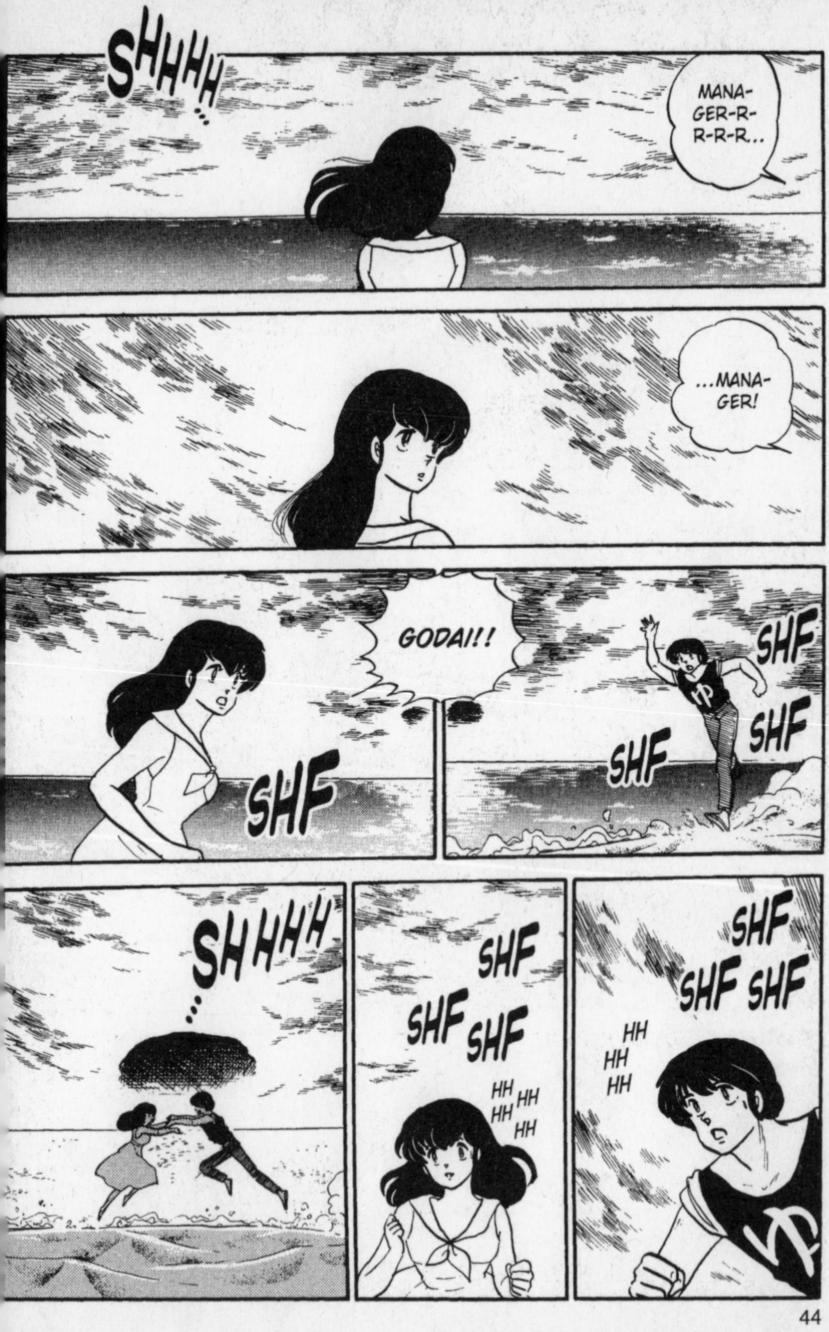

MANA-GER-R-R-R-R...
SHHHH...
...MANA-GER!
SHF
SHF
SHF
GODAI!!
SHF
SHF
SHF SHF
HH HH HH
SHF
SHF SHF
HH HH HH HH
SHHHH...

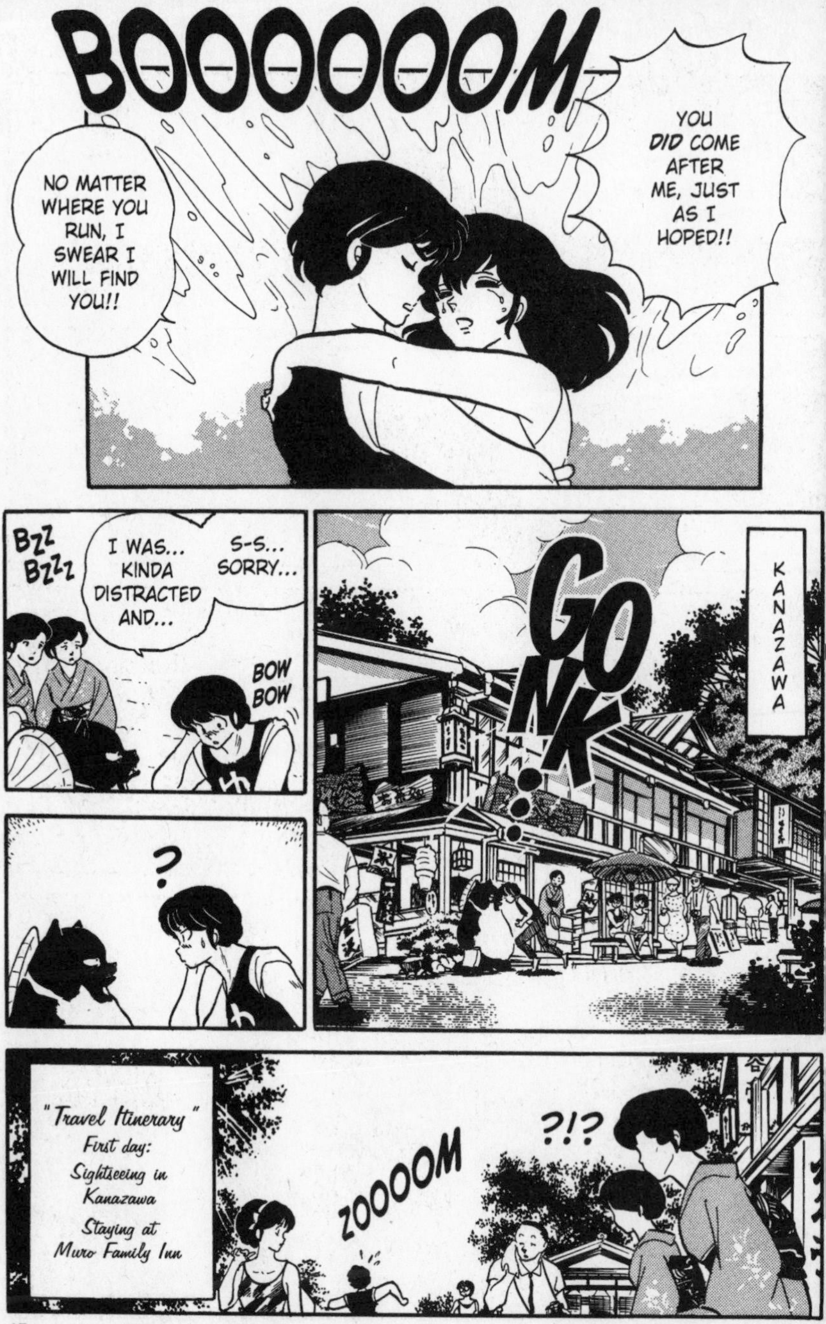
BOOOOOOM
YOU DID COME AFTER ME, JUST AS I HOPED!!
NO MATTER WHERE YOU RUN, I SWEAR I WILL FIND YOU!!
KANAZAWA
GONK
S-S... SORRY...
I WAS... KINDA DISTRACTED AND...
BZZZ BZZZ
BOW BOW
?
?!?
ZOOOOM
"Travel Itinerary"
First day:
Sightseeing in Kanazawa
Staying at Muro Family Inn

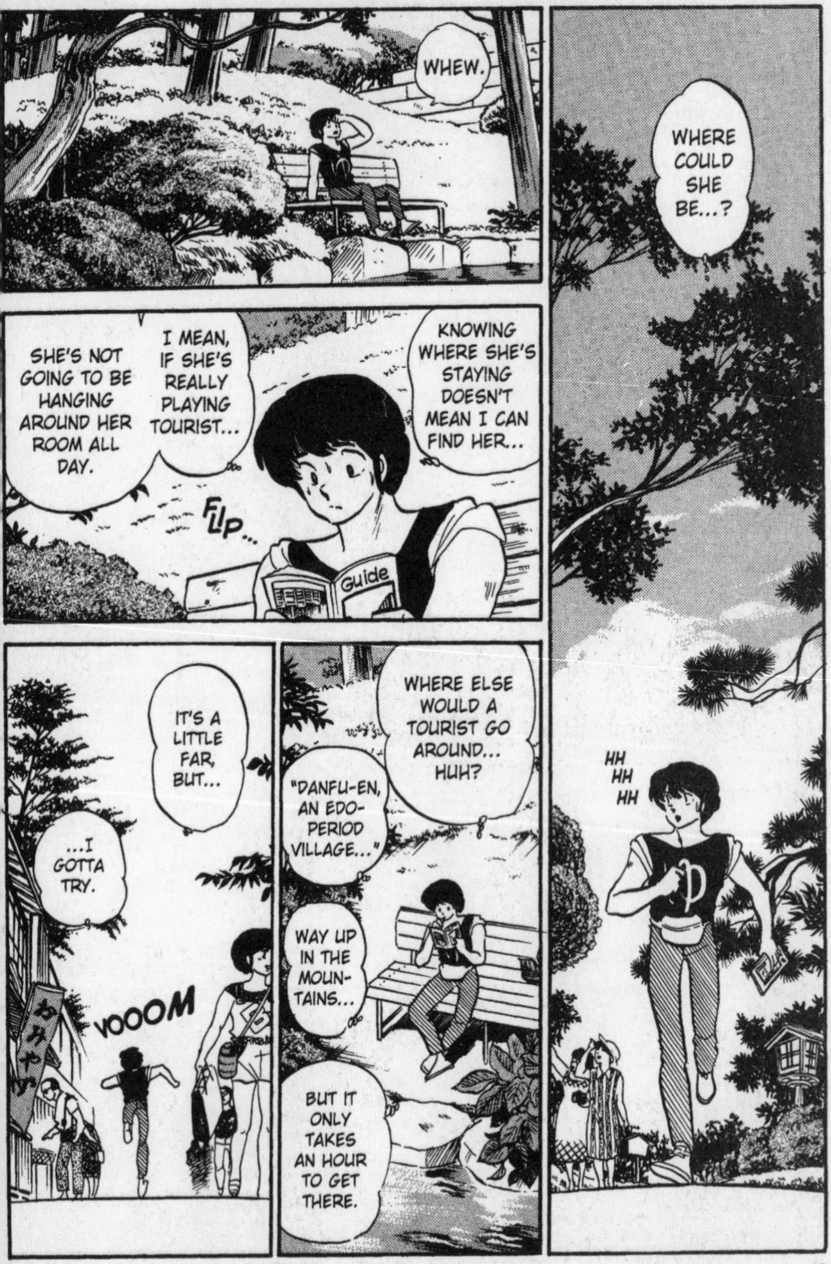
WHERE COULD SHE BE...?
HH HH HH
WHEW.
KNOWING WHERE SHE'S STAYING DOESN'T MEAN I CAN FIND HER...
I MEAN, IF SHE'S REALLY PLAYING TOURIST...
SHE'S NOT GOING TO BE HANGING AROUND HER ROOM ALL DAY.
FLIP...
Guide
WHERE ELSE WOULD A TOURIST GO AROUND... HUH?
"DANFU-EN, AN EDO-PERIOD VILLAGE..."
WAY UP IN THE MOUN-TAINS...
BUT IT ONLY TAKES AN HOUR TO GET THERE.
IT'S A LITTLE FAR, BUT...
...I GOTTA TRY.
VOOOM

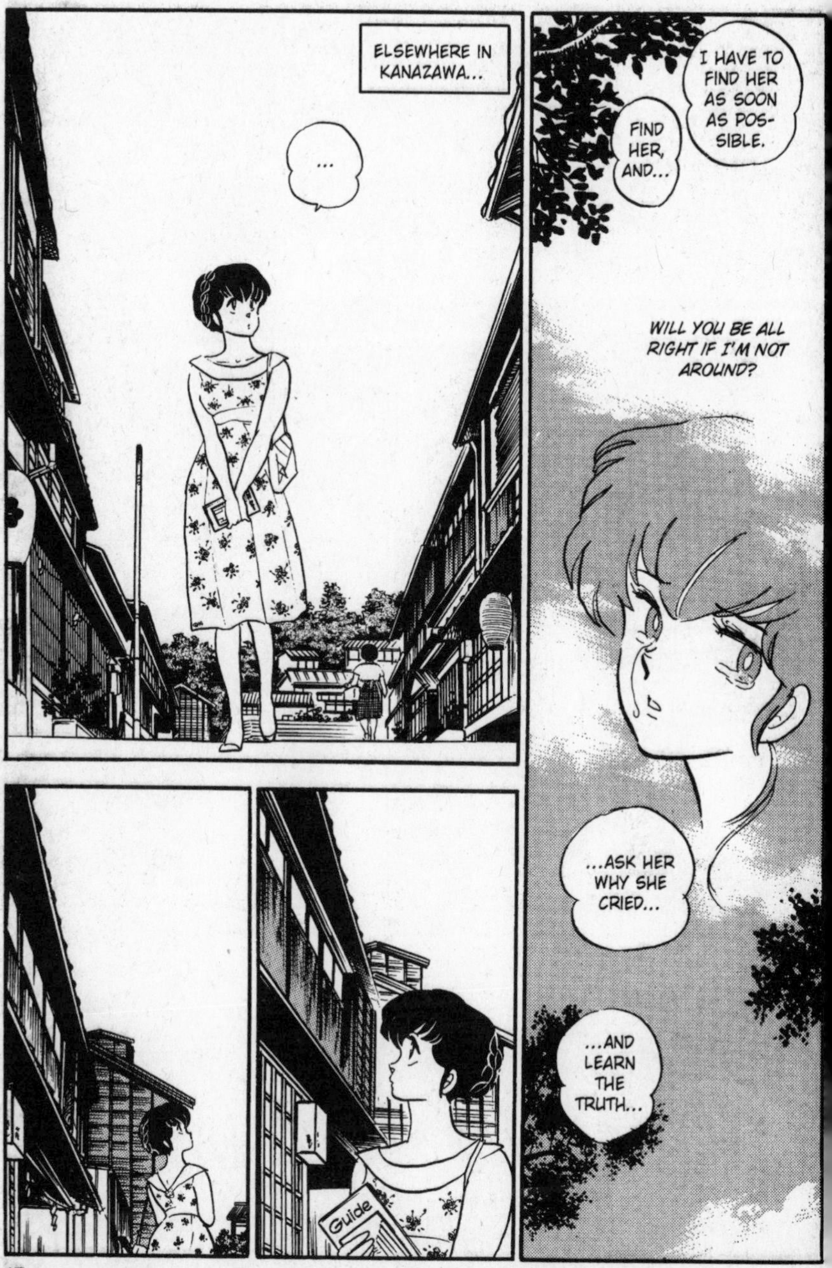
I HAVE TO FIND HER AS SOON AS POS-SIBLE.
FIND HER, AND...
WILL YOU BE ALL RIGHT IF I'M NOT AROUND?
...ASK HER WHY SHE CRIED...
...AND LEARN THE TRUTH...
ELSEWHERE IN KANAZAWA...
...
Guide

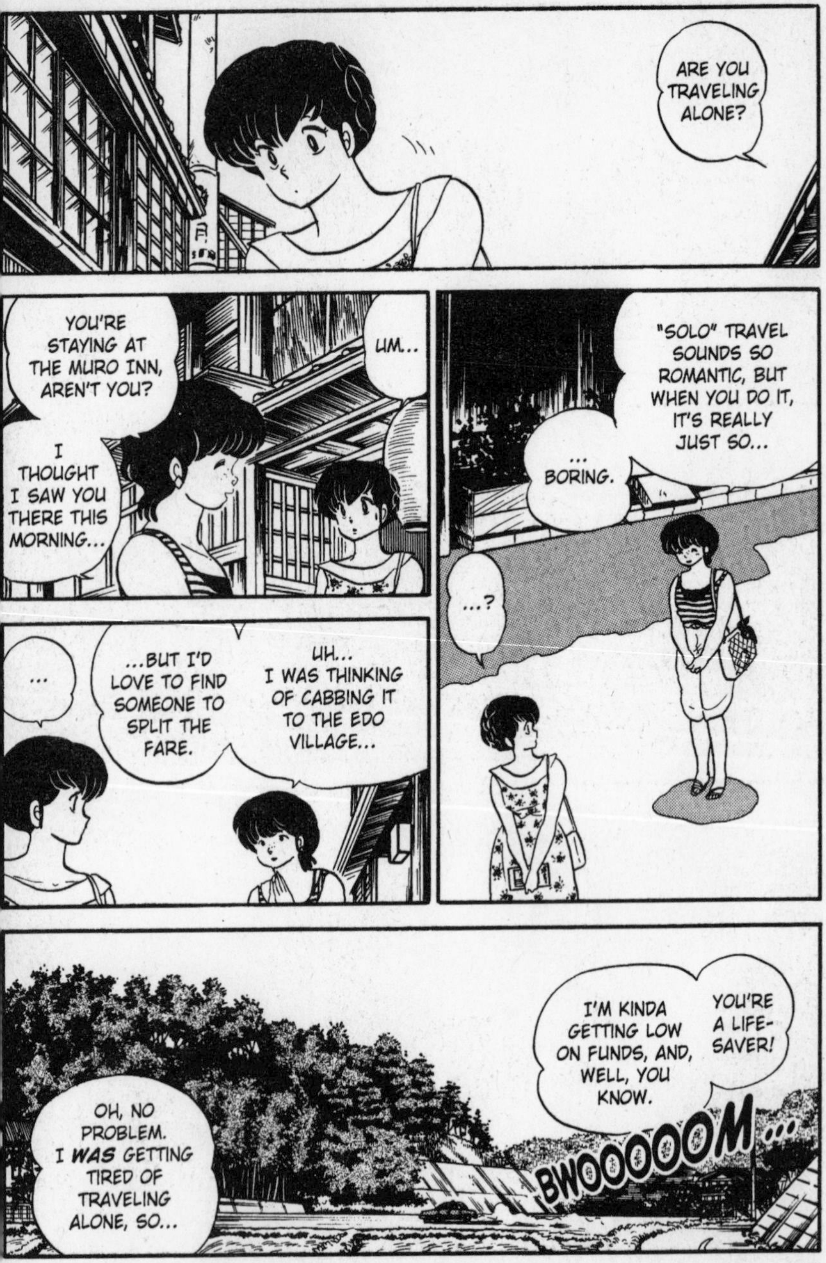
ARE YOU TRAVELING ALONE?
"SOLO" TRAVEL SOUNDS SO ROMANTIC, BUT WHEN YOU DO IT, IT'S REALLY JUST SO...
... BORING.
...?
UM...
YOU'RE STAYING AT THE MURO INN, AREN'T YOU?
I THOUGHT I SAW YOU THERE THIS MORNING...
UH... I WAS THINKING OF CABBING IT TO THE EDO VILLAGE...
...BUT I'D LOVE TO FIND SOMEONE TO SPLIT THE FARE.
...
YOU'RE A LIFE-SAVER!
I'M KINDA GETTING LOW ON FUNDS, AND, WELL, YOU KNOW.
BWOOOOOM...
OH, NO PROBLEM. I *WAS* GETTING TIRED OF TRAVELING ALONE, SO...

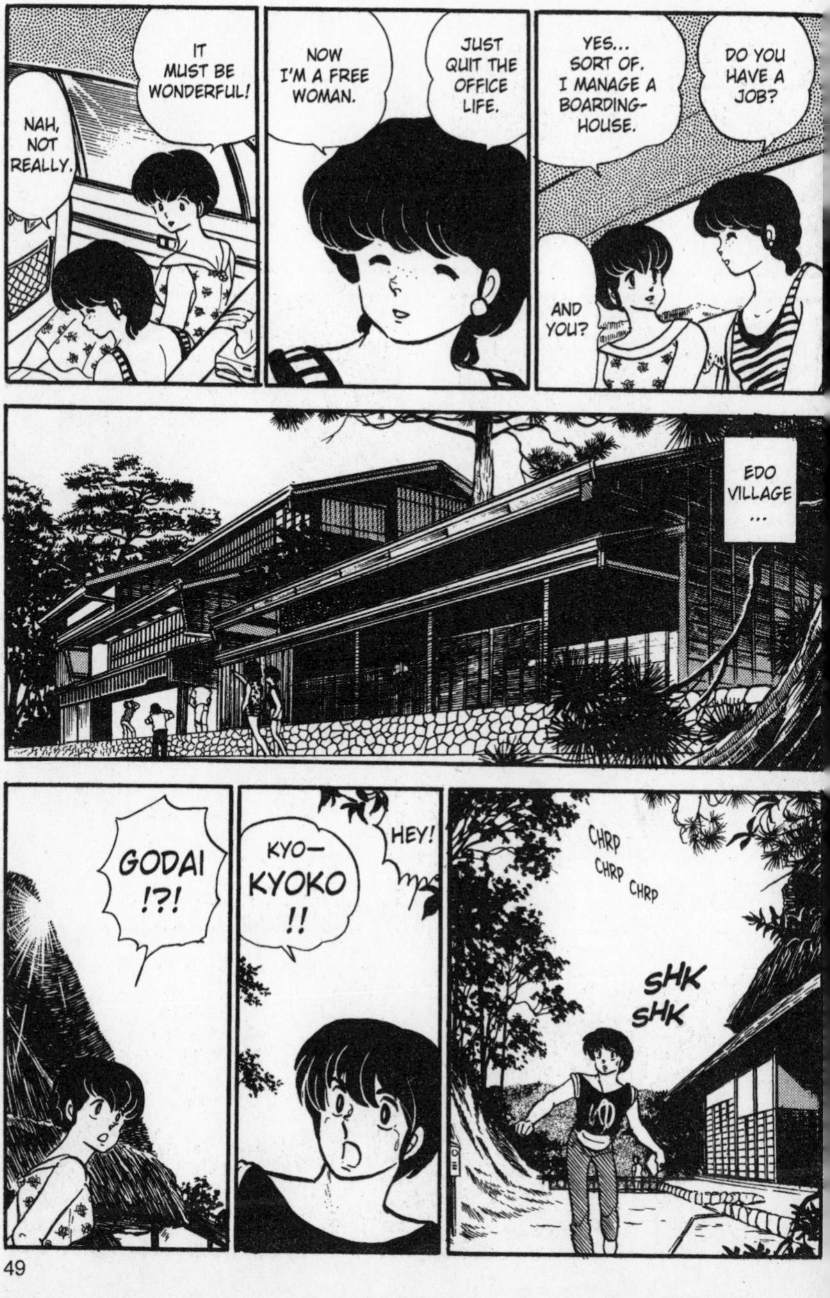
DO YOU HAVE A JOB?
YES... SORT OF. I MANAGE A BOARDING-HOUSE.
AND YOU?
JUST QUIT THE OFFICE LIFE.
NOW I'M A FREE WOMAN.
IT MUST BE WONDERFUL!
NAH, NOT REALLY.
EDO VILLAGE ...
CHRP
CHRP CHRP
SHK SHK
HEY!
KYO— KYOKO !!
GODAI !?!

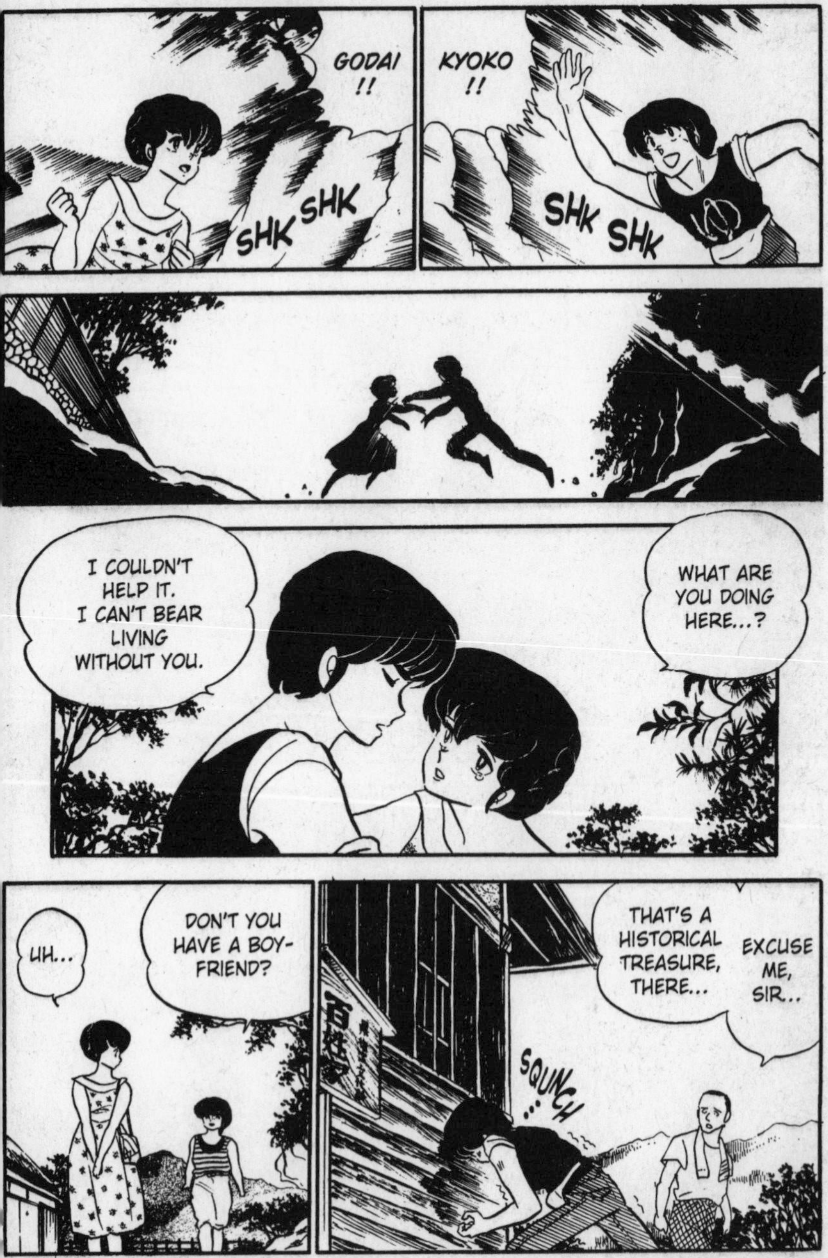
KYOKO !!
SHK SHK
GODAI !!
SHK SHK
WHAT ARE YOU DOING HERE...?
I COULDN'T HELP IT. I CAN'T BEAR LIVING WITHOUT YOU.
EXCUSE ME, SIR...
THAT'S A HISTORICAL TREASURE, THERE...
SQUNCH...
DON'T YOU HAVE A BOY-FRIEND?
UH...

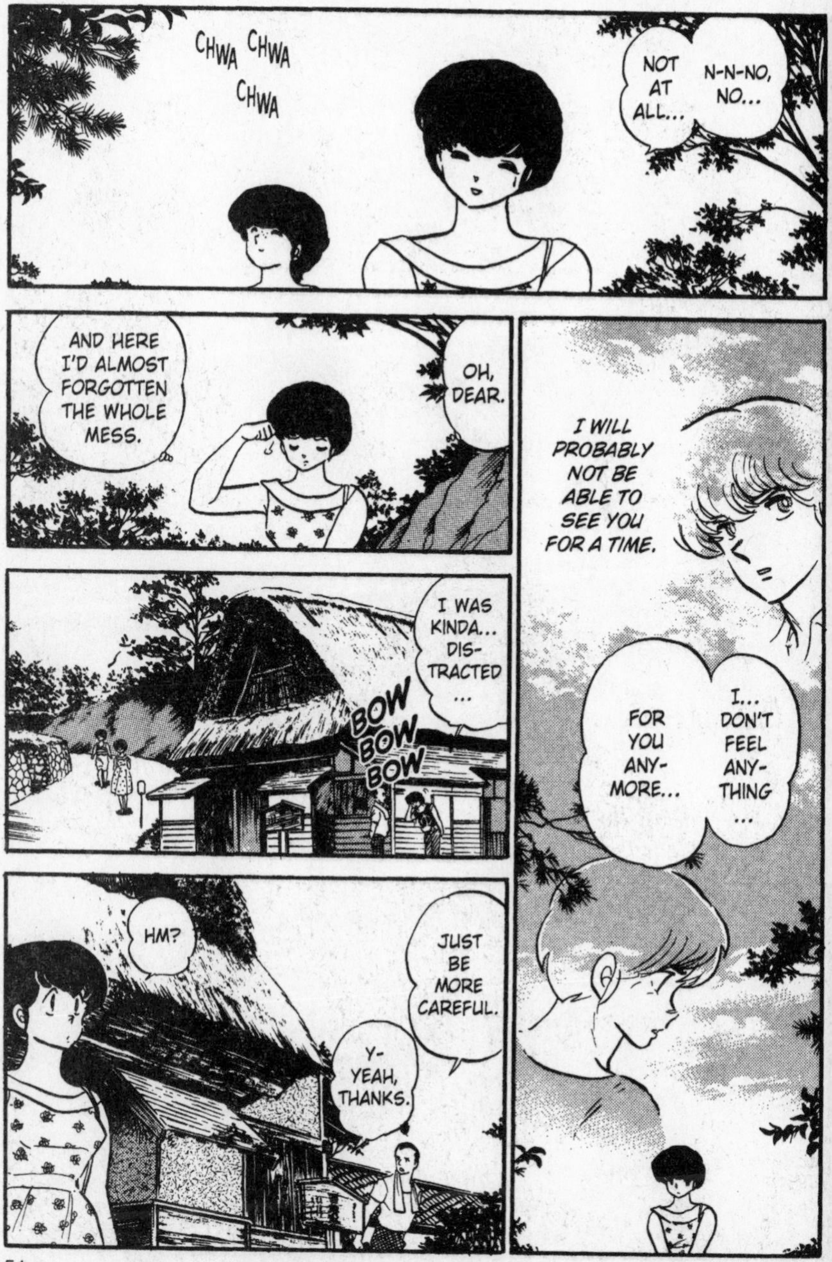

N-N-NO, NO...
NOT AT ALL...
CHWA CHWA CHWA
I WILL PROBABLY NOT BE ABLE TO SEE YOU FOR A TIME.
I... DON'T FEEL ANYTHING...
FOR YOU ANYMORE...
OH, DEAR.
AND HERE I'D ALMOST FORGOTTEN THE WHOLE MESS.
I WAS KINDA... DIS-TRACTED...
BOW BOW BOW
JUST BE MORE CAREFUL.
HM?
Y-YEAH, THANKS.

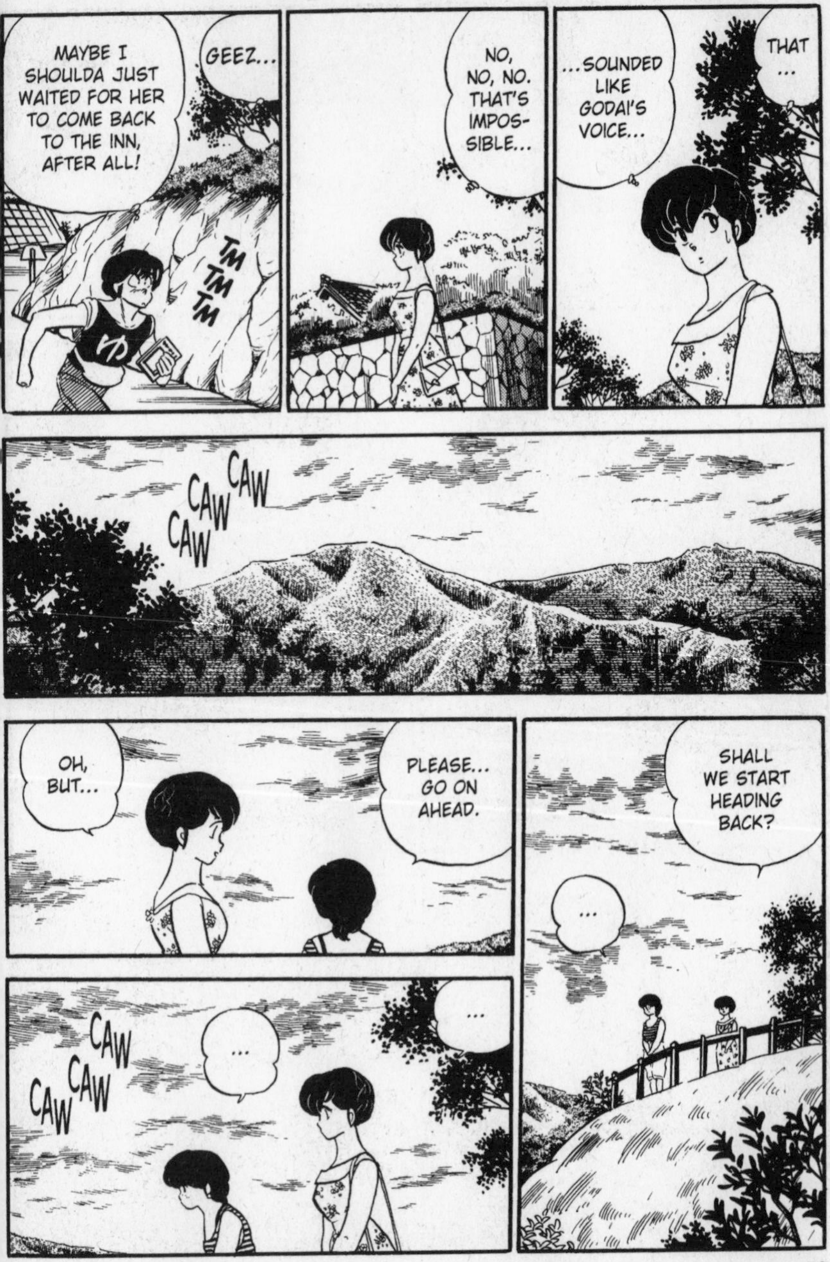
THAT ...
...SOUNDED LIKE GODAI'S VOICE...
NO, NO, NO. THAT'S IMPOS-SIBLE...
GEEZ...
MAYBE I SHOULDA JUST WAITED FOR HER TO COME BACK TO THE INN, AFTER ALL!
TM TM TM
CAW CAW CAW
SHALL WE START HEADING BACK?
...
PLEASE... GO ON AHEAD.
OH, BUT...
...
...
CAW CAW CAW

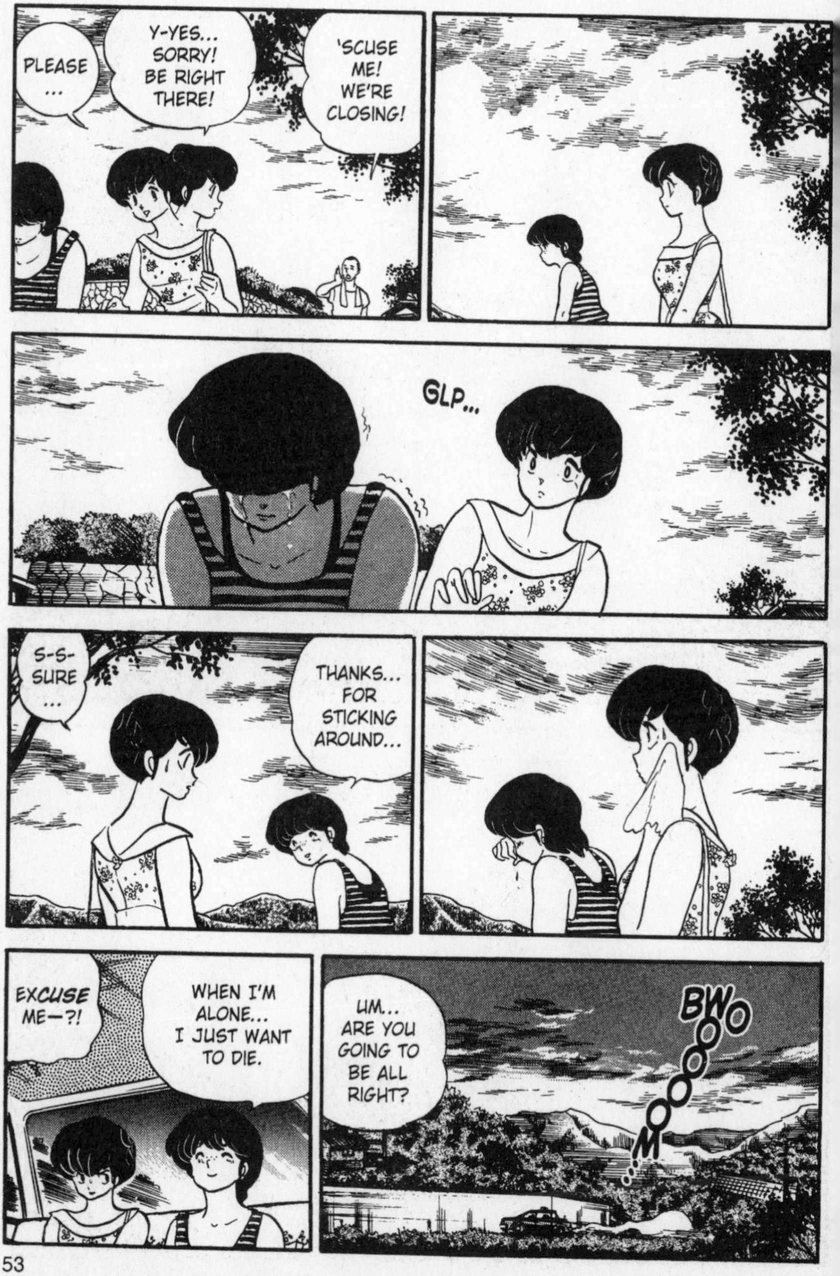
'SCUSE ME! WE'RE CLOSING!
Y-YES... SORRY! BE RIGHT THERE!
PLEASE ...
GLP...
THANKS... FOR STICKING AROUND...
S-S-SURE ...
UM... ARE YOU GOING TO BE ALL RIGHT?
BWOOOOOM...
WHEN I'M ALONE... I JUST WANT TO DIE.
EXCUSE ME—?!

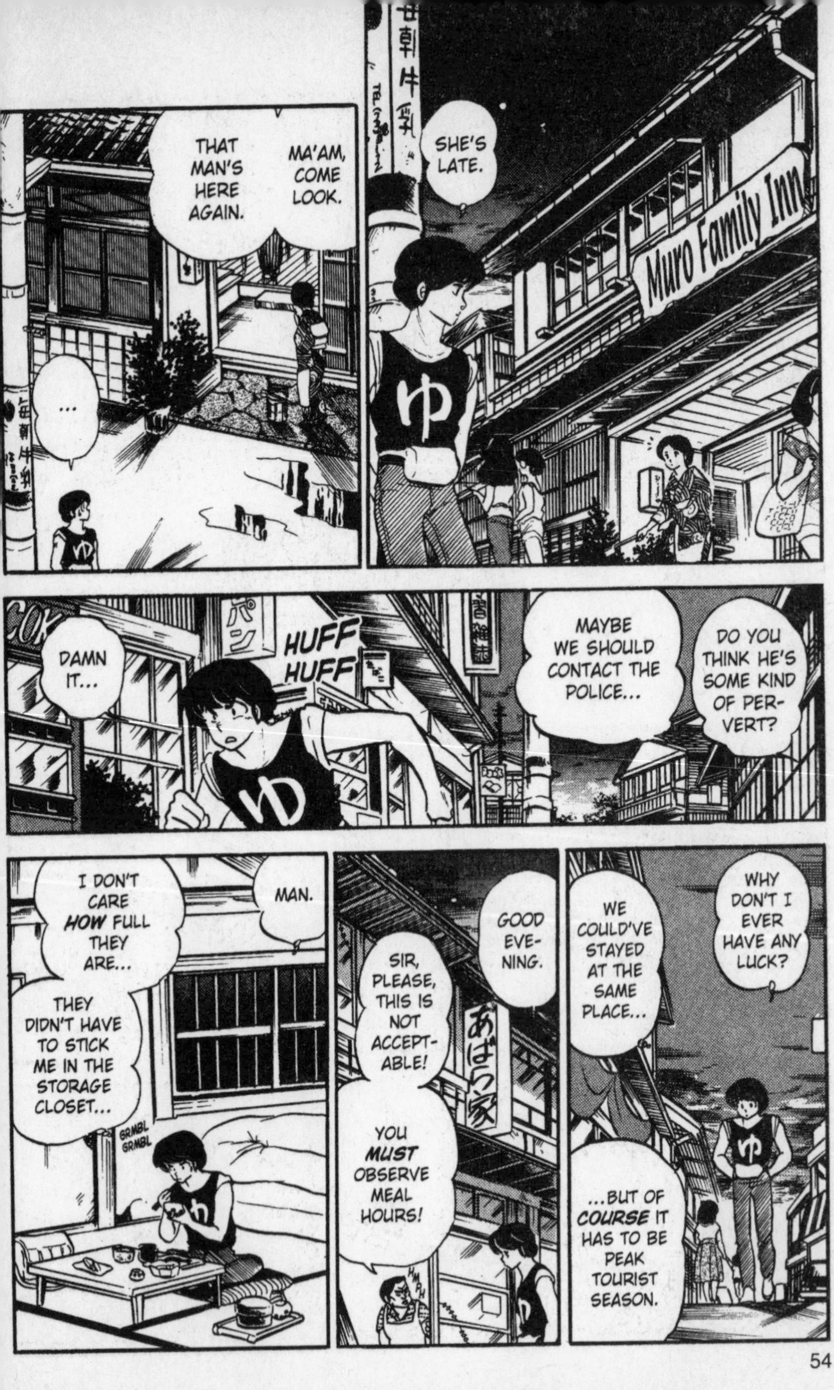
Muro Family Inn
SHE'S LATE.
MA'AM, COME LOOK.
THAT MAN'S HERE AGAIN.
...
DO YOU THINK HE'S SOME KIND OF PER-VERT?
MAYBE WE SHOULD CONTACT THE POLICE...
HUFF HUFF
DAMN IT...
WHY DON'T I EVER HAVE ANY LUCK?
WE COULD'VE STAYED AT THE SAME PLACE...
...BUT OF COURSE IT HAS TO BE PEAK TOURIST SEASON.
GOOD EVE-NING.
SIR, PLEASE, THIS IS NOT ACCEPT-ABLE!
YOU MUST OBSERVE MEAL HOURS!
HMPH
MAN.
I DON'T CARE HOW FULL THEY ARE...
THEY DIDN'T HAVE TO STICK ME IN THE STORAGE CLOSET...
GRMBL GRMBL

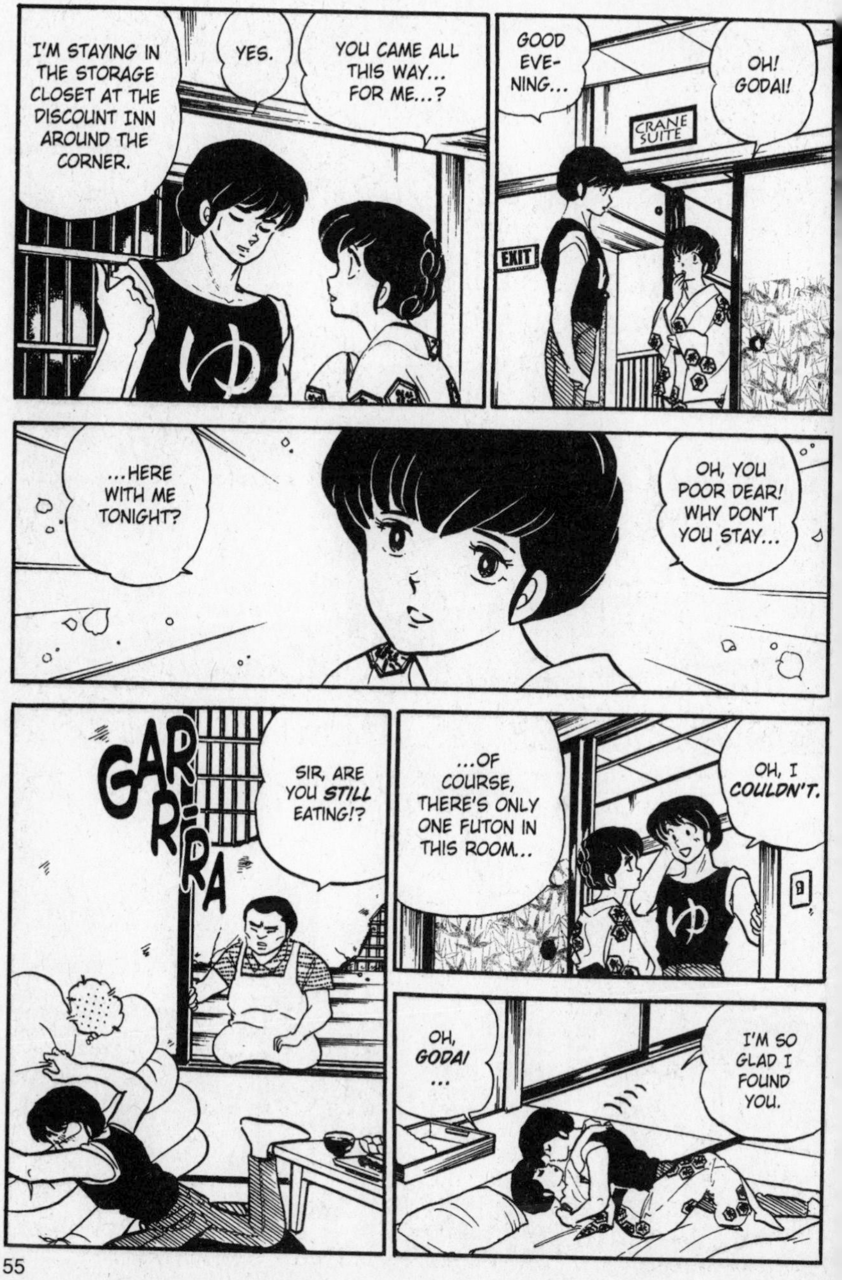
OH! GODAI!
GOOD EVE- NING...
CRANE SUITE
EXIT
YOU CAME ALL THIS WAY... FOR ME...?
YES.
I'M STAYING IN THE STORAGE CLOSET AT THE DISCOUNT INN AROUND THE CORNER.
OH, YOU POOR DEAR! WHY DON'T YOU STAY...
...HERE WITH ME TONIGHT?
OH, I *COULDN'T.*
...OF COURSE, THERE'S ONLY ONE FUTON IN THIS ROOM...
I'M SO GLAD I FOUND YOU.
OH, *GODAI* ...
SIR, ARE YOU *STILL* EATING!?
GAR-RI-RA

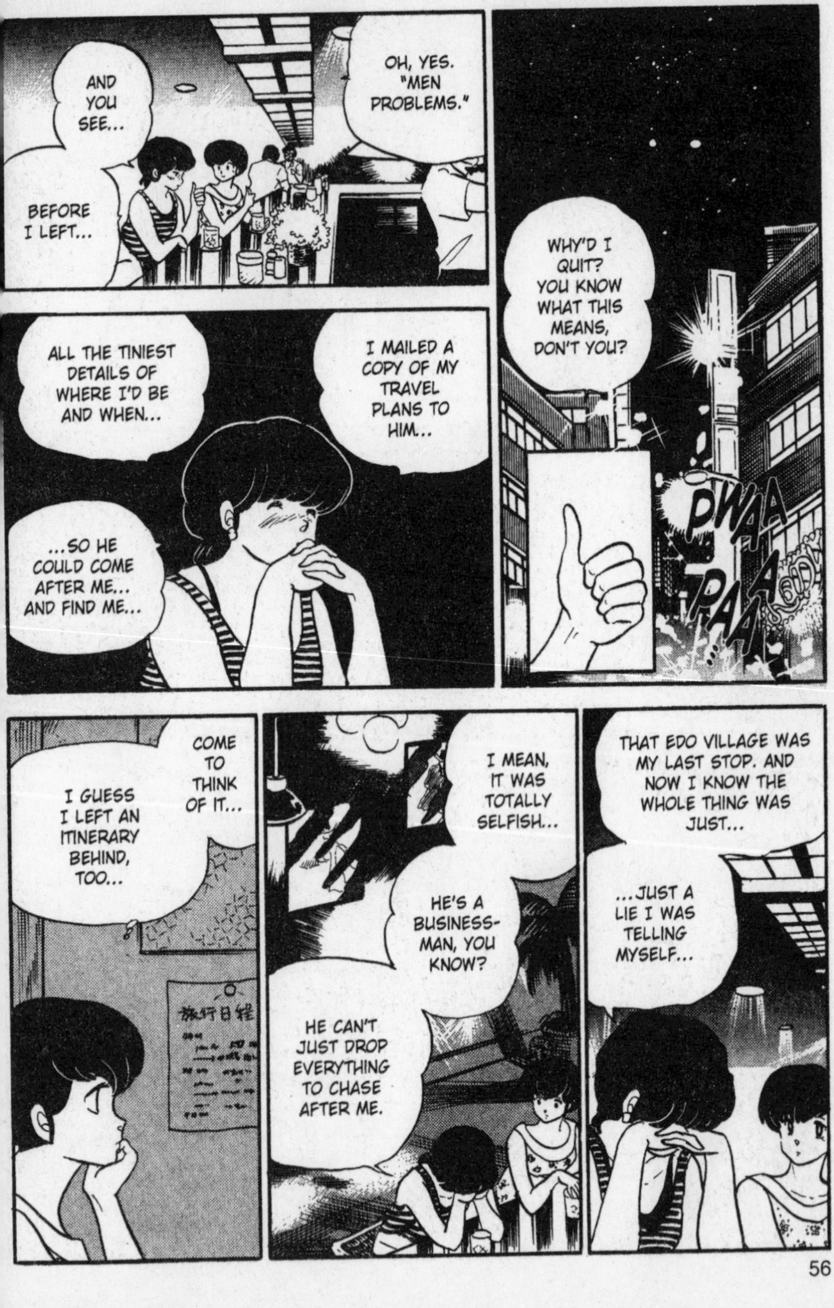
WHY'D I QUIT? YOU KNOW WHAT THIS MEANS, DON'T YOU?
PWAA PAA...
OH, YES. "MEN PROBLEMS."
AND YOU SEE...
BEFORE I LEFT...
I MAILED A COPY OF MY TRAVEL PLANS TO HIM...
ALL THE TINIEST DETAILS OF WHERE I'D BE AND WHEN...
...SO HE COULD COME AFTER ME... AND FIND ME...
THAT EDO VILLAGE WAS MY LAST STOP. AND NOW I KNOW THE WHOLE THING WAS JUST...
...JUST A LIE I WAS TELLING MYSELF...
I MEAN, IT WAS TOTALLY SELFISH...
HE'S A BUSINESS-MAN, YOU KNOW?
HE CAN'T JUST DROP EVERYTHING TO CHASE AFTER ME.
COME TO THINK OF IT...
I GUESS I LEFT AN ITINERARY BEHIND, TOO...
旅行日程

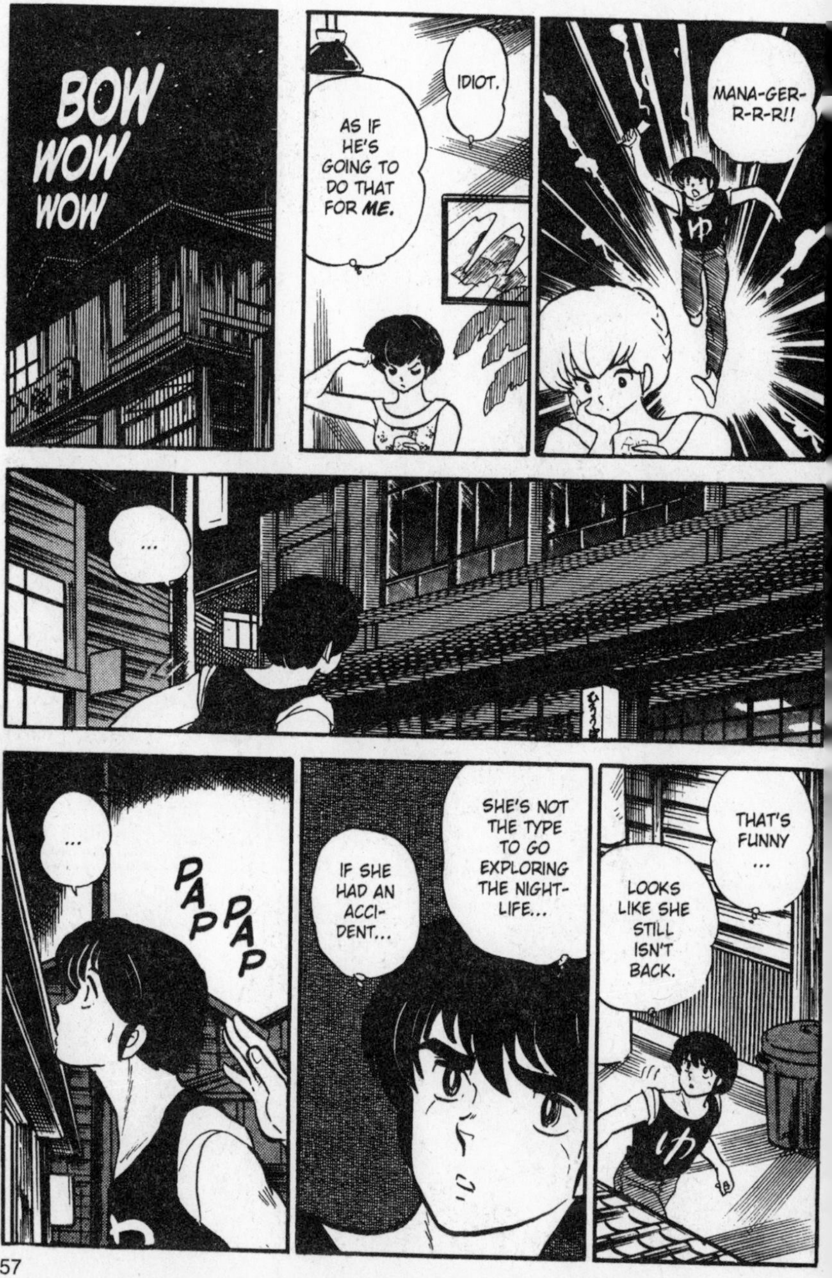
MANA-GER-R-R-R!!
IDIOT.
AS IF HE'S GOING TO DO THAT FOR **ME.**
BOW WOW WOW
...
THAT'S FUNNY ...
LOOKS LIKE SHE STILL ISN'T BACK.
SHE'S NOT THE TYPE TO GO EXPLORING THE NIGHT-LIFE...
IF SHE HAD AN ACCI-DENT...
...
PAP PAP

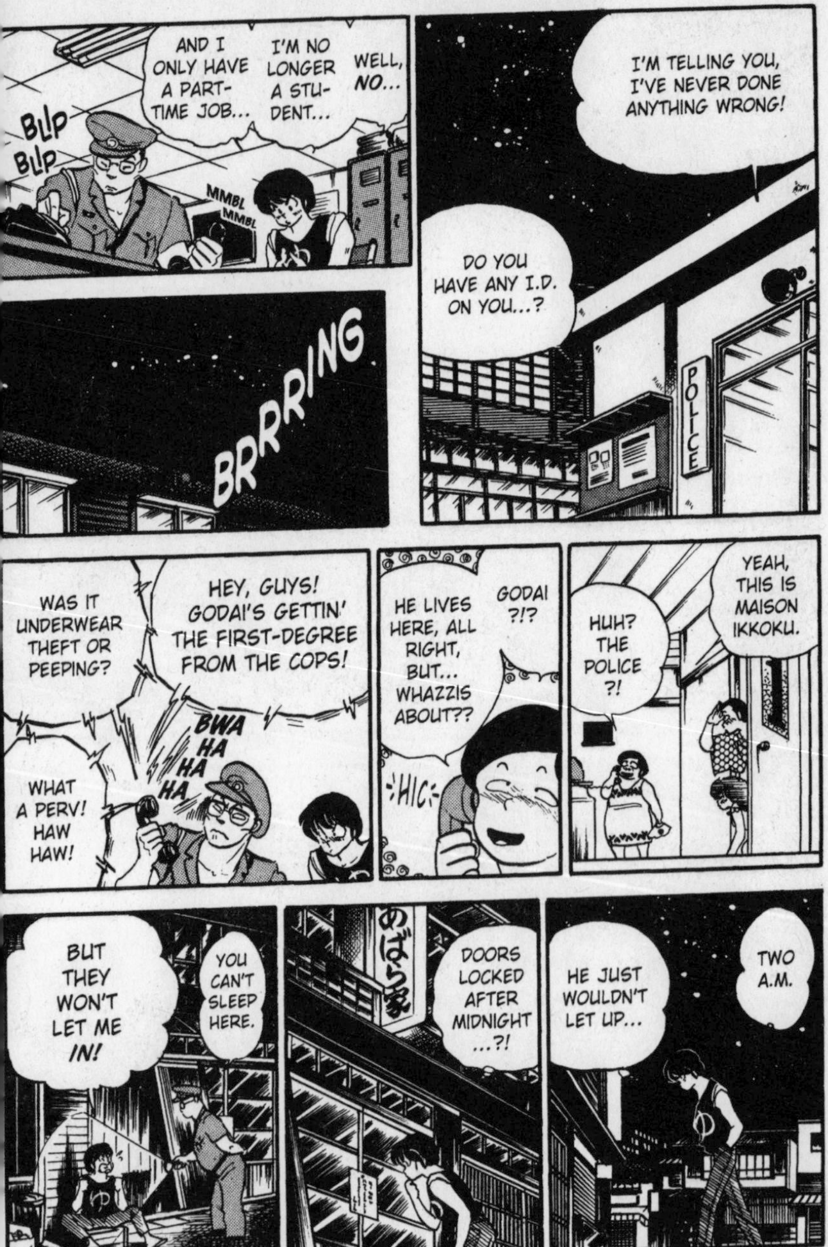
I'M TELLING YOU, I'VE NEVER DONE ANYTHING WRONG!
DO YOU HAVE ANY I.D. ON YOU...?
POLICE
WELL, NO...
I'M NO LONGER A STU-DENT...
AND I ONLY HAVE A PART-TIME JOB...
BLIP BLIP
MMBL MMBL
BRRRING
YEAH, THIS IS MAISON IKKOKU.
HUH? THE POLICE ?!
GODAI ?!?
HE LIVES HERE, ALL RIGHT, BUT... WHAZZIS ABOUT??
HIC
HEY, GUYS! GODAI'S GETTIN' THE FIRST-DEGREE FROM THE COPS!
WAS IT UNDERWEAR THEFT OR PEEPING?
BWA HA HA HA
WHAT A PERV! HAW HAW!
TWO A.M.
HE JUST WOULDN'T LET UP...
DOORS LOCKED AFTER MIDNIGHT ...?!
YOU CAN'T SLEEP HERE.
BUT THEY WON'T LET ME IN!

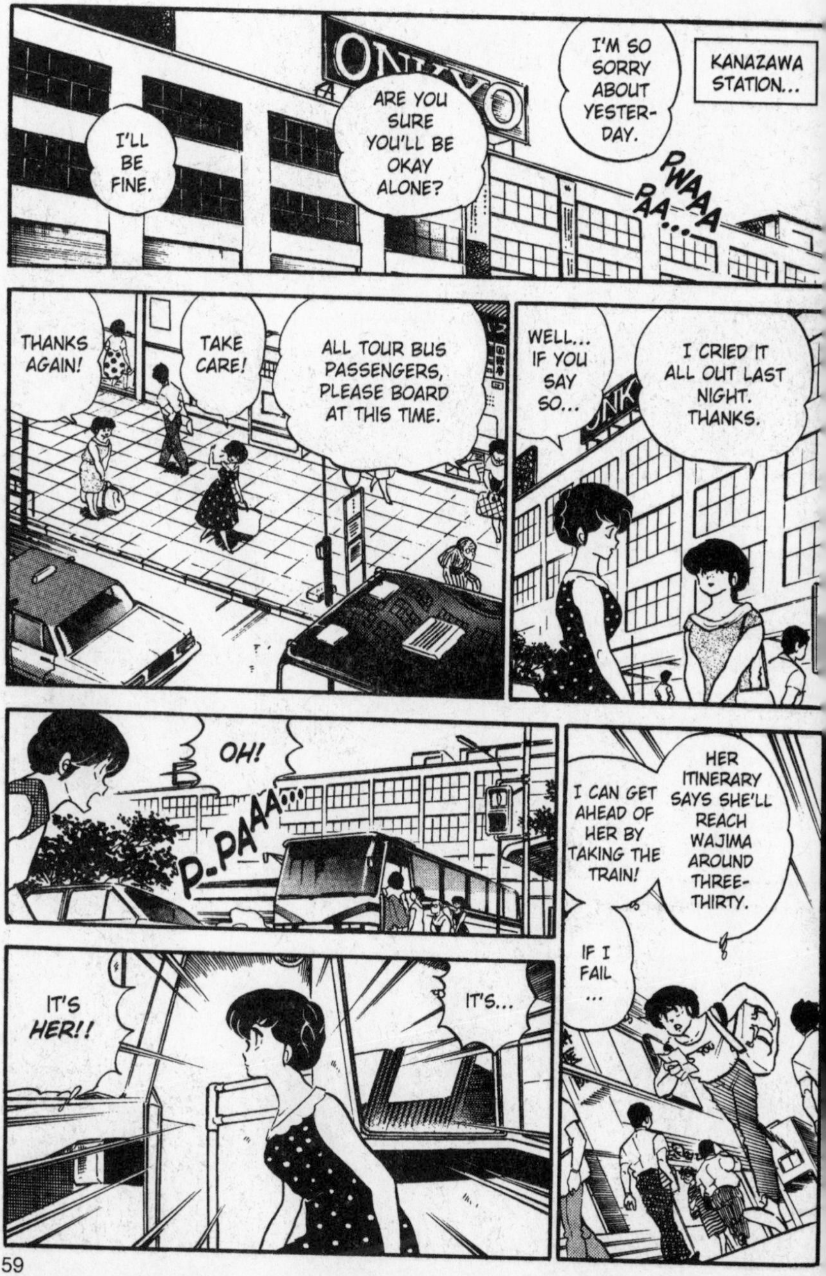
KANAZAWA STATION...
I'M SO SORRY ABOUT YESTER-DAY.
PWAAA AA...
ARE YOU SURE YOU'LL BE OKAY ALONE?
I'LL BE FINE.
I CRIED IT ALL OUT LAST NIGHT. THANKS.
WELL... IF YOU SAY SO...
ALL TOUR BUS PASSENGERS, PLEASE BOARD AT THIS TIME.
TAKE CARE!
THANKS AGAIN!
HER ITINERARY SAYS SHE'LL REACH WAJIMA AROUND THREE-THIRTY.
I CAN GET AHEAD OF HER BY TAKING THE TRAIN!
IF I FAIL ...
OH!
P-PAAA...
IT'S...
IT'S HER!!

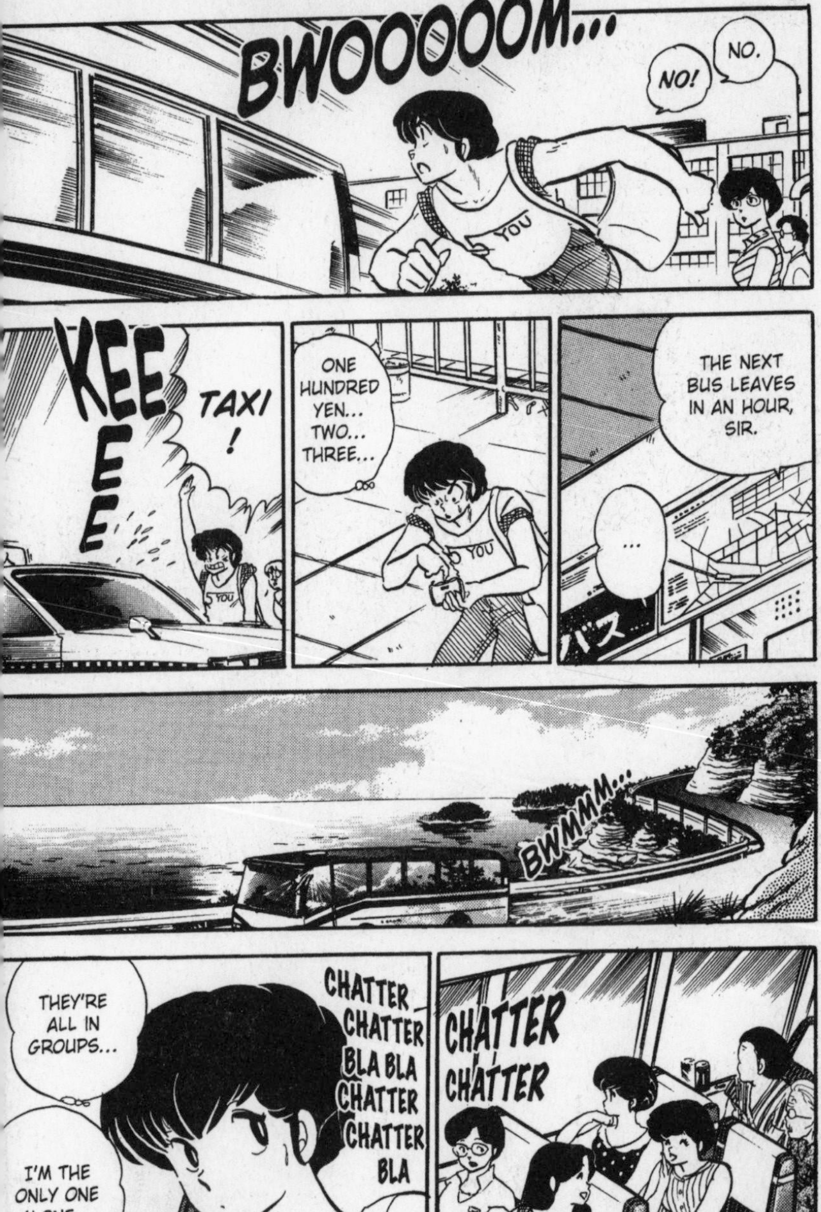
NO.
NO!
BWOOOOOM...
THE NEXT BUS LEAVES IN AN HOUR, SIR.
...
バス
ONE HUNDRED YEN... TWO... THREE...
TAXI !
KEEEE
BWMMM...
CHATTER CHATTER
CHATTER CHATTER BLA BLA CHATTER CHATTER BLA
THEY'RE ALL IN GROUPS...
I'M THE ONLY ONE ALONE...

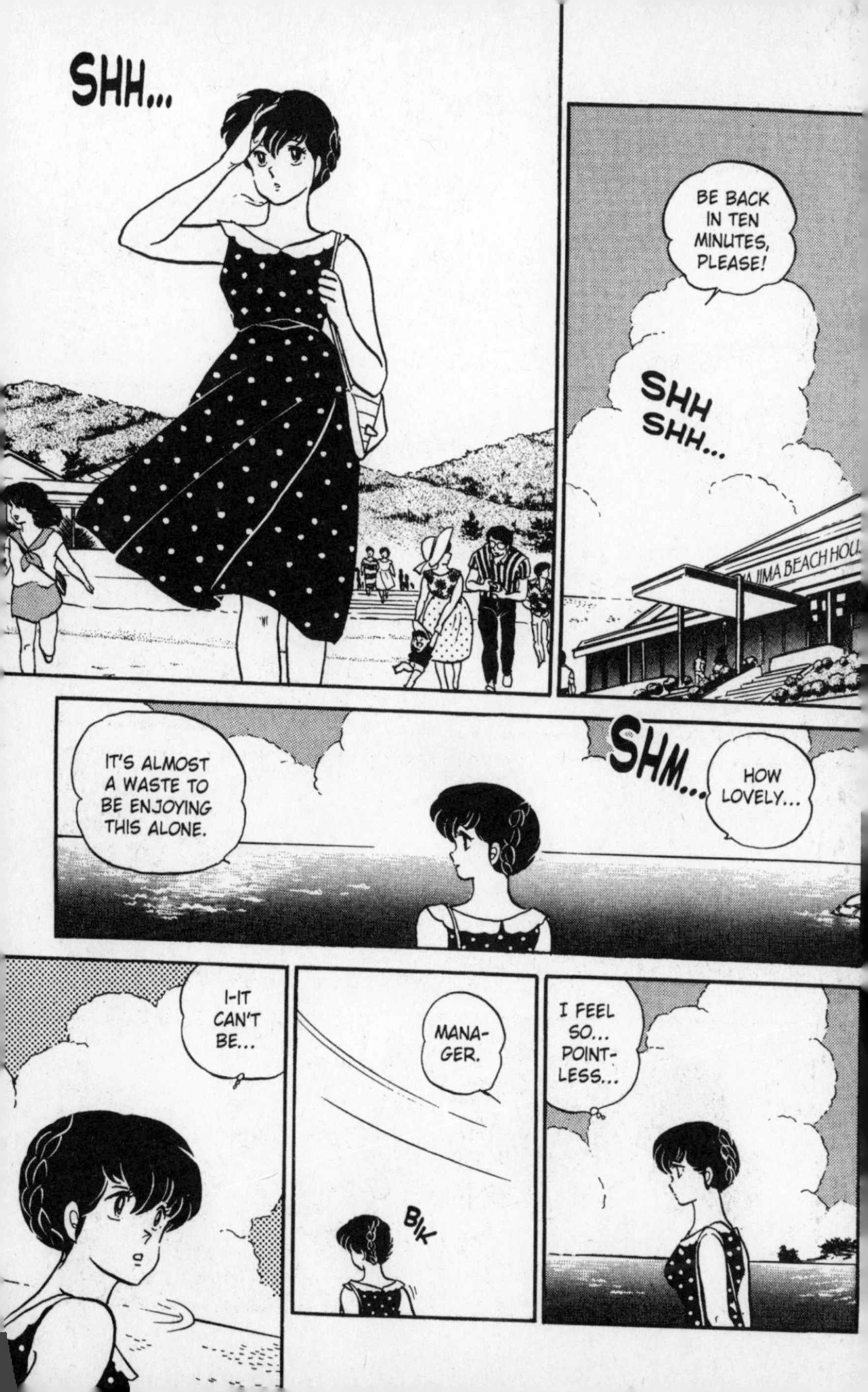
BE BACK IN TEN MINUTES, PLEASE!
SHH SHH...
SHH...
SHM...
HOW LOVELY...
IT'S ALMOST A WASTE TO BE ENJOYING THIS ALONE.
I FEEL SO... POINTLESS...
MANAGER.
BIK
I-IT CAN'T BE...

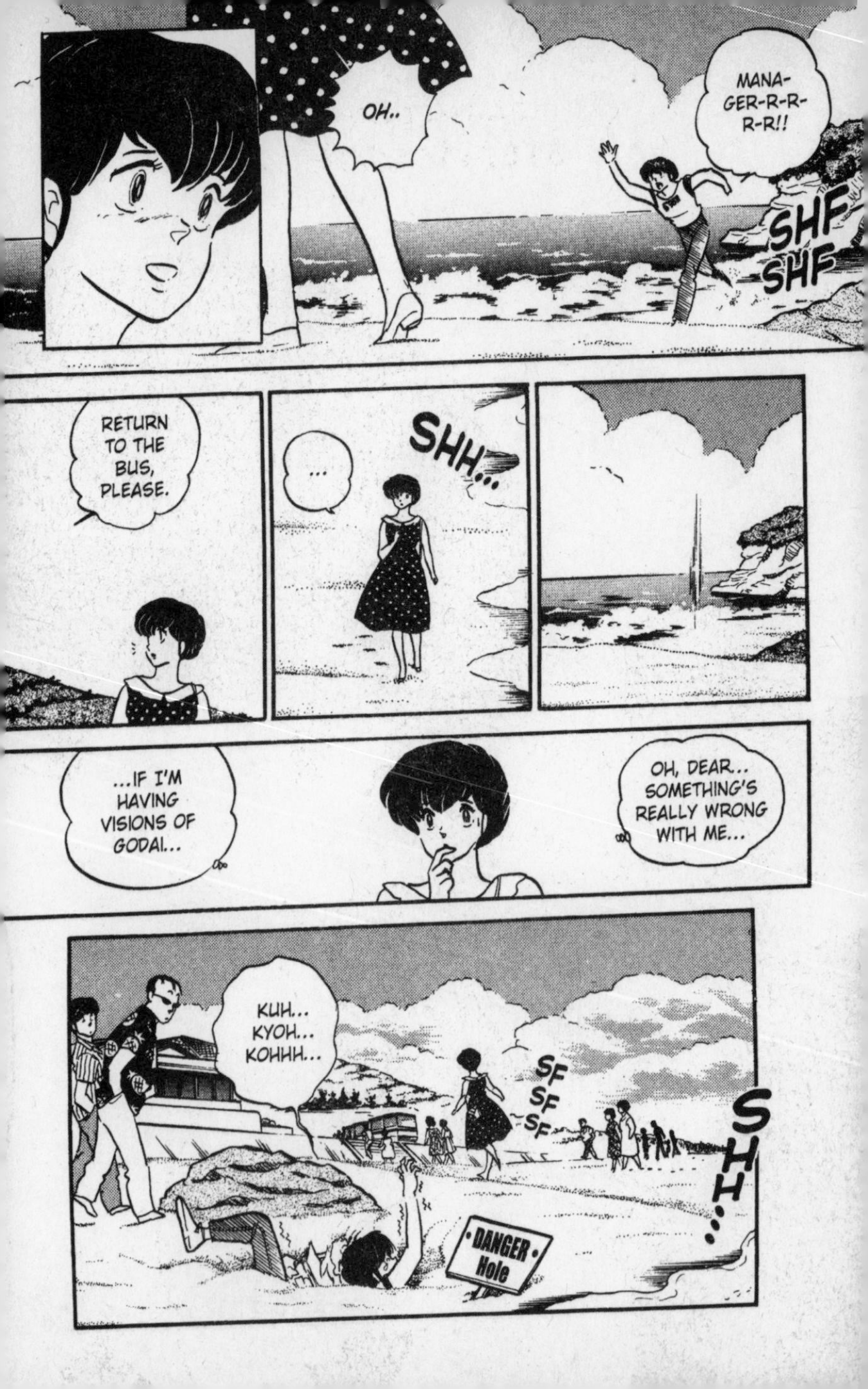

MANA-GER-R-R-R-R!!
SHF SHF
OH..
SHH...
...
RETURN TO THE BUS, PLEASE.
OH, DEAR... SOMETHING'S REALLY WRONG WITH ME...
...IF I'M HAVING VISIONS OF GODAI...
SHH...
SF SF SF
KUH... KYOH... KOHHH...
DANGER Hole

PART FOUR
STEAMY LOVE

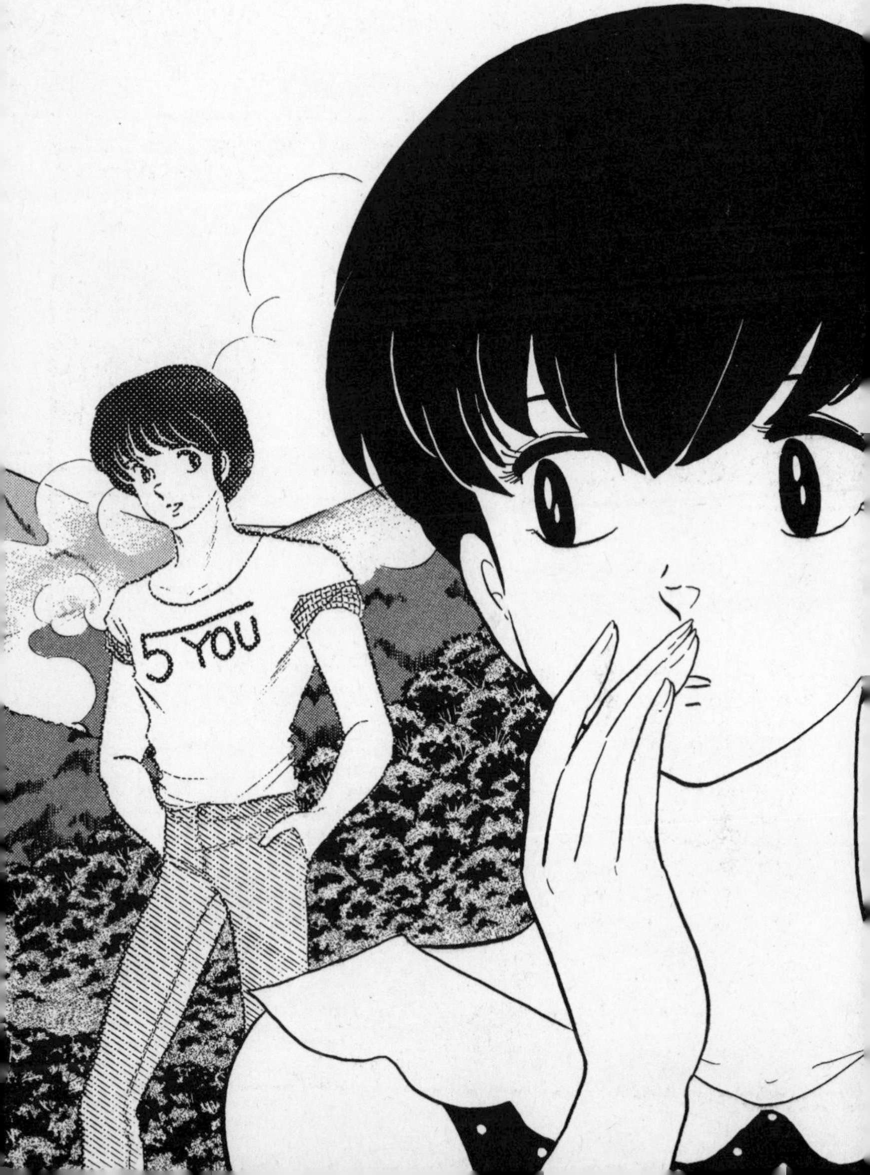
5 YOU

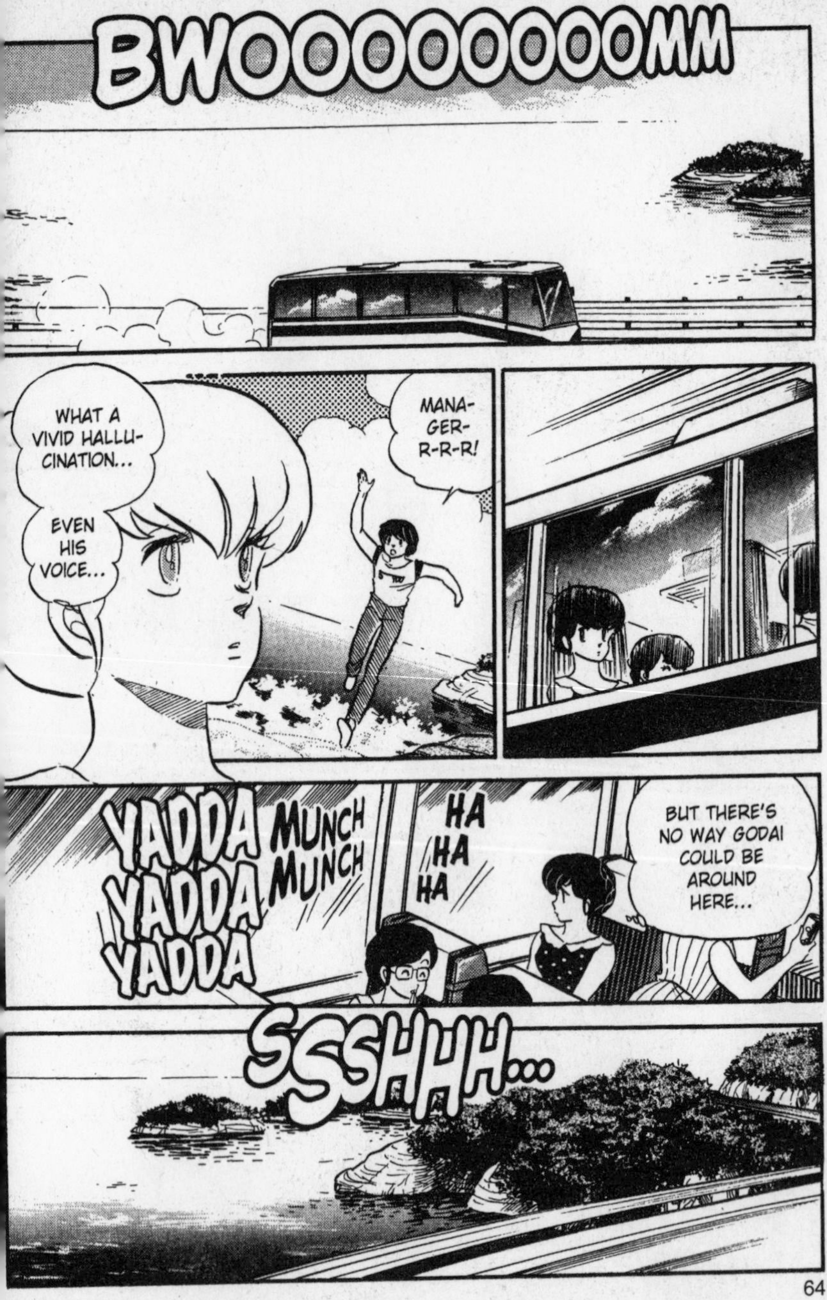
BWOOOOOOOOMM
MANA-GER-R-R-R!
WHAT A VIVID HALLU-CINATION...
EVEN HIS VOICE...
BUT THERE'S NO WAY GODAI COULD BE AROUND HERE...
HA HA HA
MUNCH MUNCH
YADDA YADDA YADDA
SSSHHH...

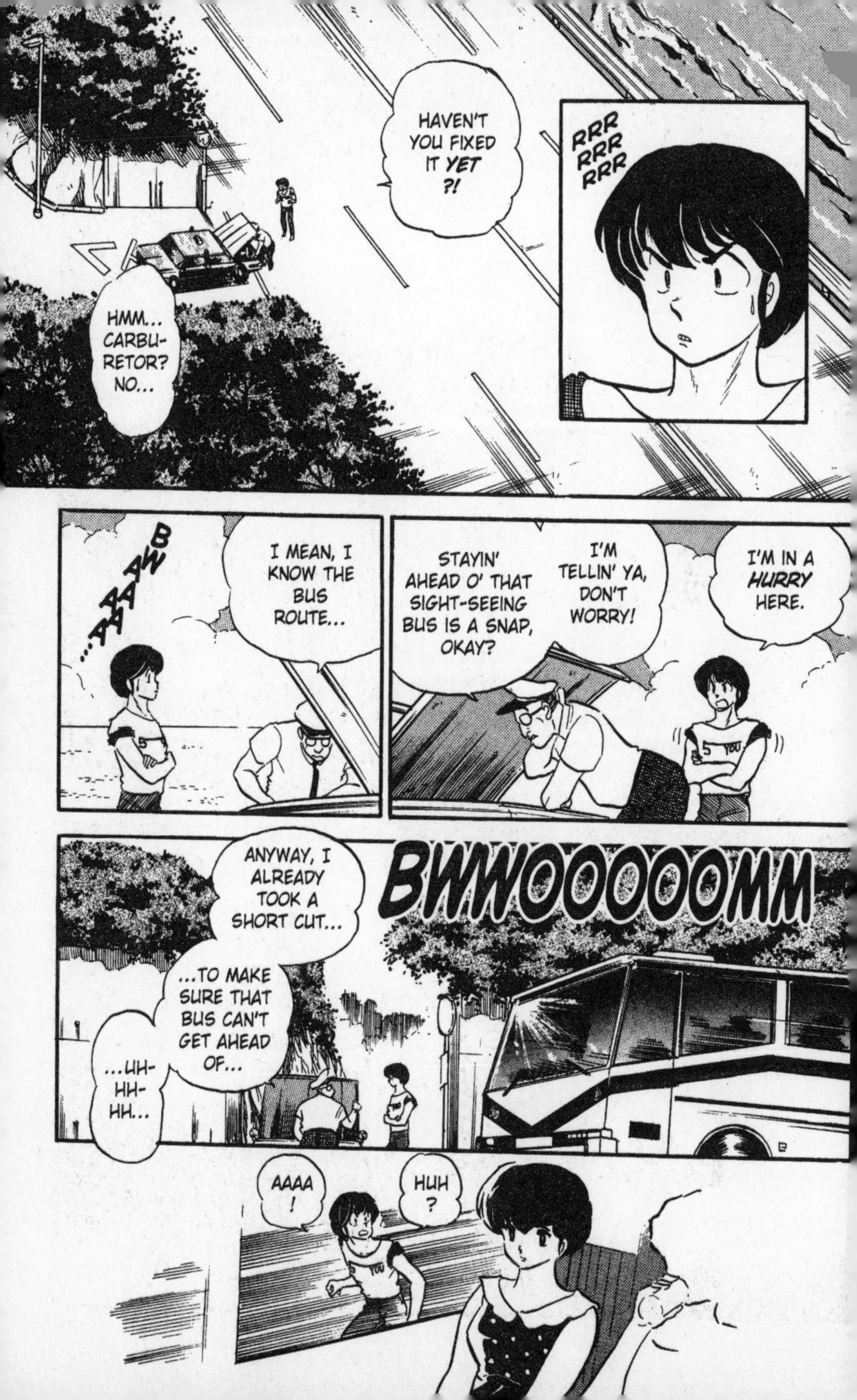
RRR RRR RRR
HAVEN'T YOU FIXED IT *YET* ?!
HMM... CARBU-RETOR? NO...
I'M IN A *HURRY* HERE.
I'M TELLIN' YA, DON'T WORRY!
STAYIN' AHEAD O' THAT SIGHT-SEEING BUS IS A SNAP, OKAY?
I MEAN, I KNOW THE BUS ROUTE...
BWAAAAA...
BWWOOOOOMM
ANYWAY, I ALREADY TOOK A SHORT CUT...
...TO MAKE SURE THAT BUS CAN'T GET AHEAD OF...
...UH-HH-HH...
HUH ?
AAAA !

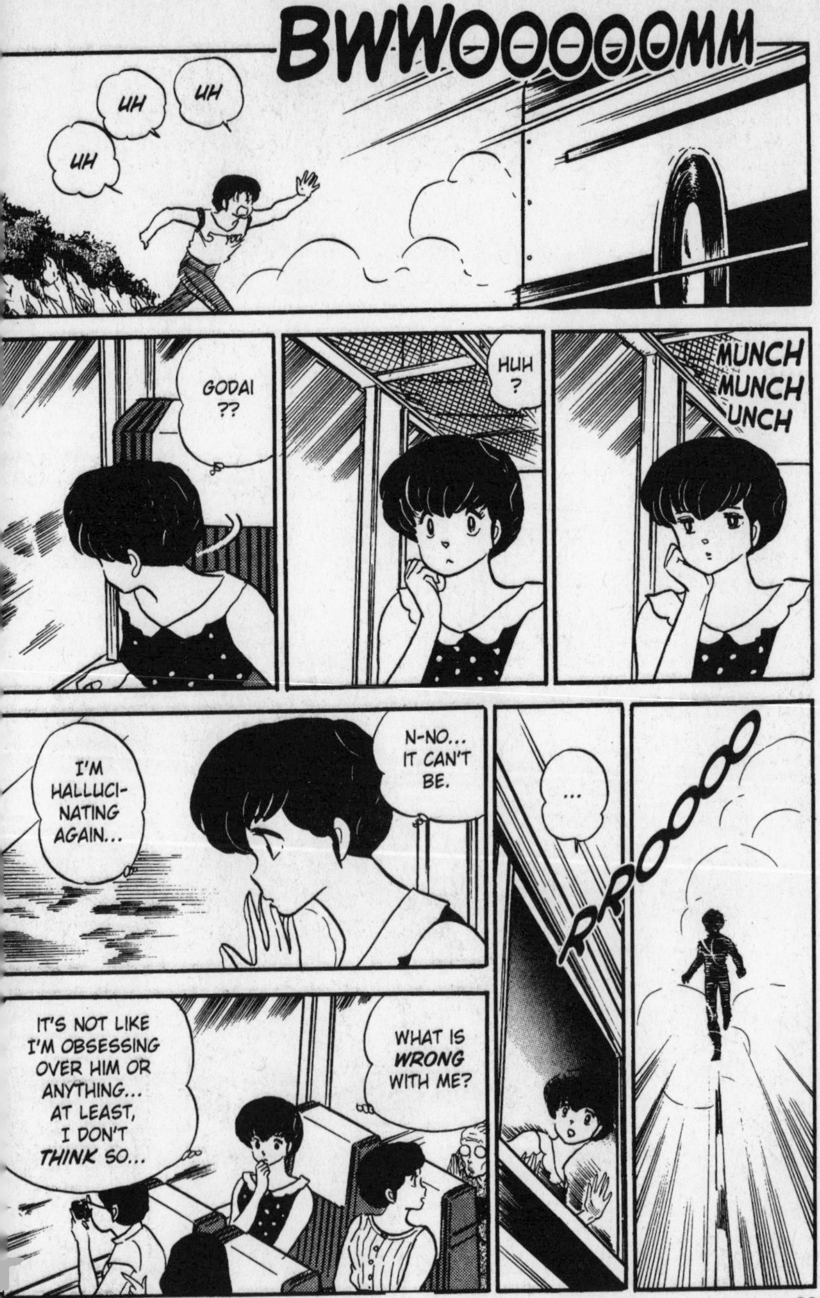
BWWOOOOOMM
UH
UH
UH
MUNCH MUNCH UNCH
HUH ?
GODAI ??
PROOOOO
...
N-NO... IT CAN'T BE.
I'M HALLUCINATING AGAIN...
WHAT IS WRONG WITH ME?
IT'S NOT LIKE I'M OBSESSING OVER HIM OR ANYTHING... AT LEAST, I DON'T THINK SO...

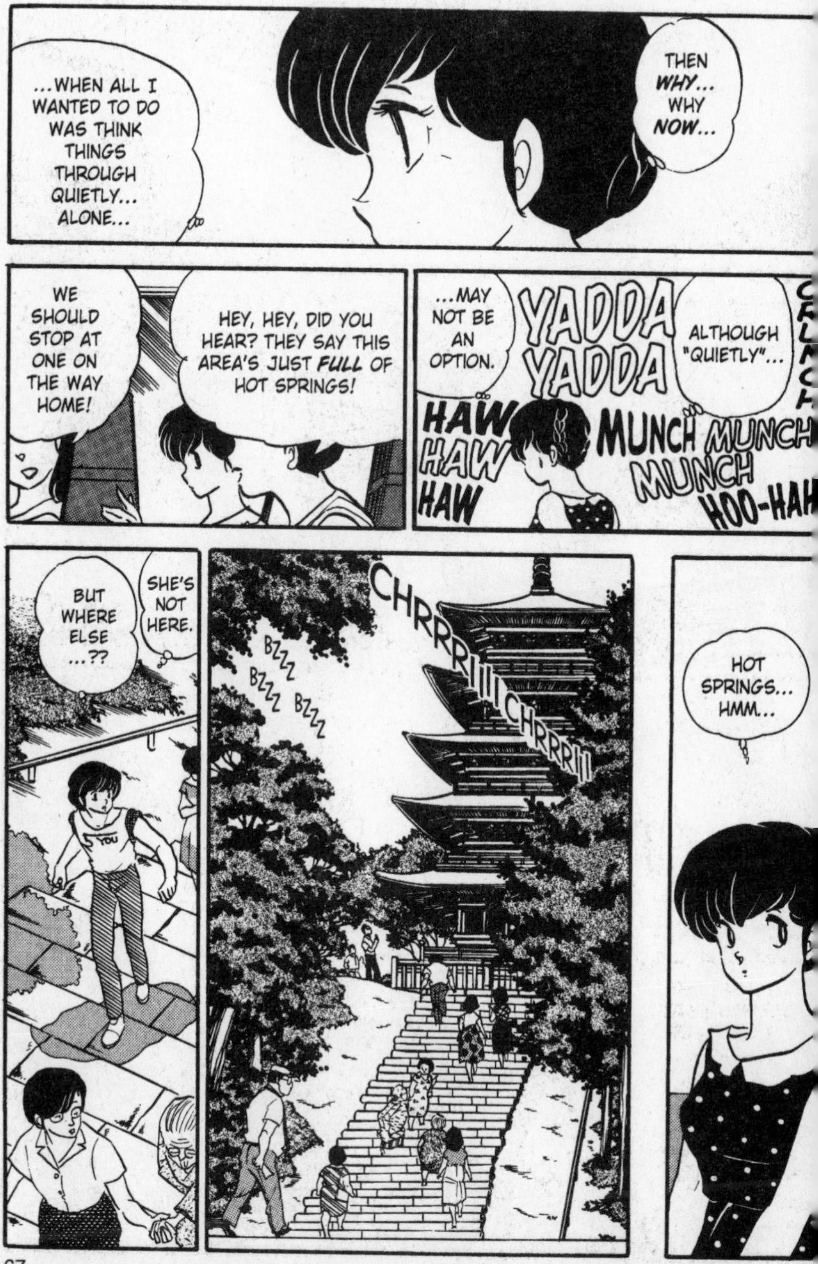
THEN WHY... WHY NOW...
...WHEN ALL I WANTED TO DO WAS THINK THINGS THROUGH QUIETLY... ALONE...
CRUNCH
ALTHOUGH "QUIETLY"...
YADDA YADDA
...MAY NOT BE AN OPTION.
MUNCH MUNCH MUNCH
HOO-HAH
HAW HAW HAW
HEY, HEY, DID YOU HEAR? THEY SAY THIS AREA'S JUST FULL OF HOT SPRINGS!
WE SHOULD STOP AT ONE ON THE WAY HOME!
HOT SPRINGS... HMM...
CHRRRIIII CHRRRIII
BZZZ BZZZ BZZZ
SHE'S NOT HERE.
BUT WHERE ELSE ...??

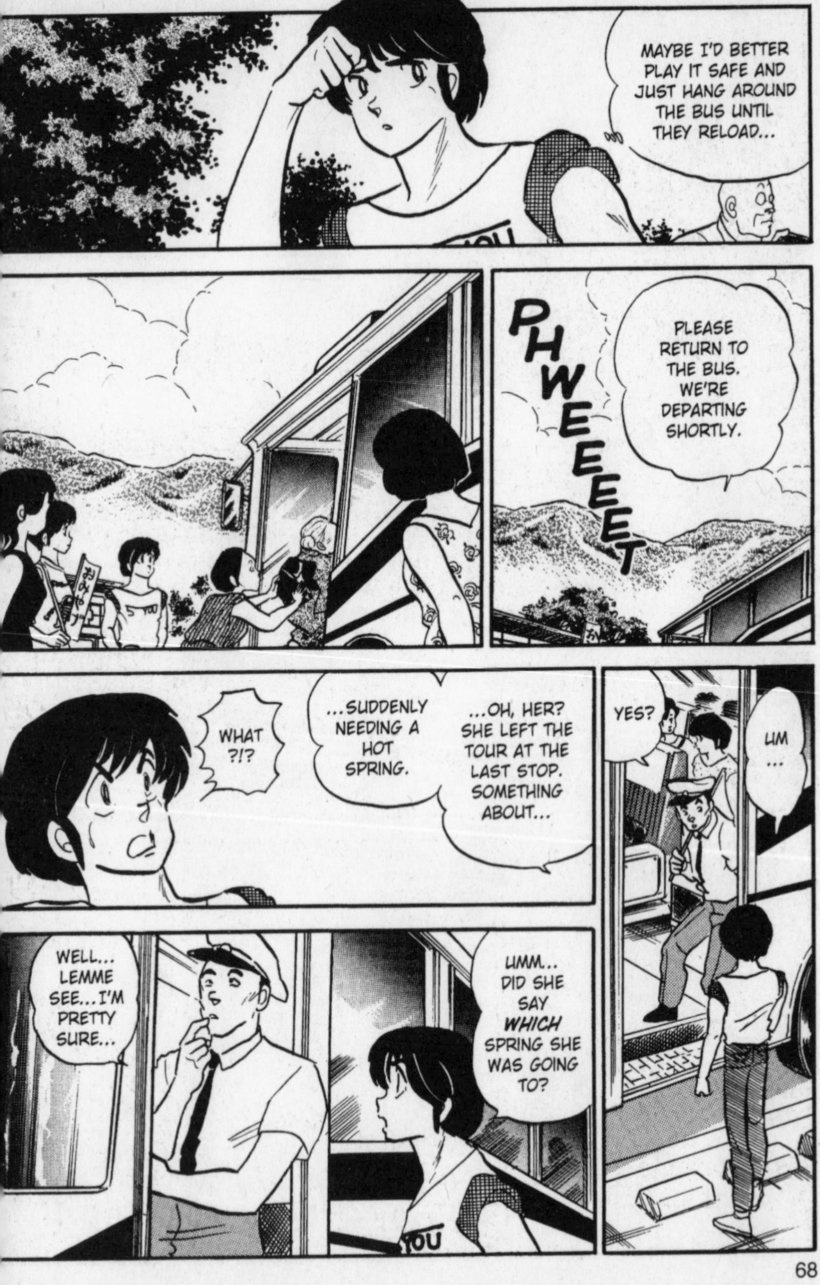
MAYBE I'D BETTER PLAY IT SAFE AND JUST HANG AROUND THE BUS UNTIL THEY RELOAD...
PLEASE RETURN TO THE BUS. WE'RE DEPARTING SHORTLY.
PHWEEEEET
UM ...
YES?
...OH, HER? SHE LEFT THE TOUR AT THE LAST STOP. SOMETHING ABOUT...
...SUDDENLY NEEDING A HOT SPRING.
WHAT ?!?
UMM... DID SHE SAY *WHICH* SPRING SHE WAS GOING TO?
WELL... LEMME SEE... I'M PRETTY SURE...

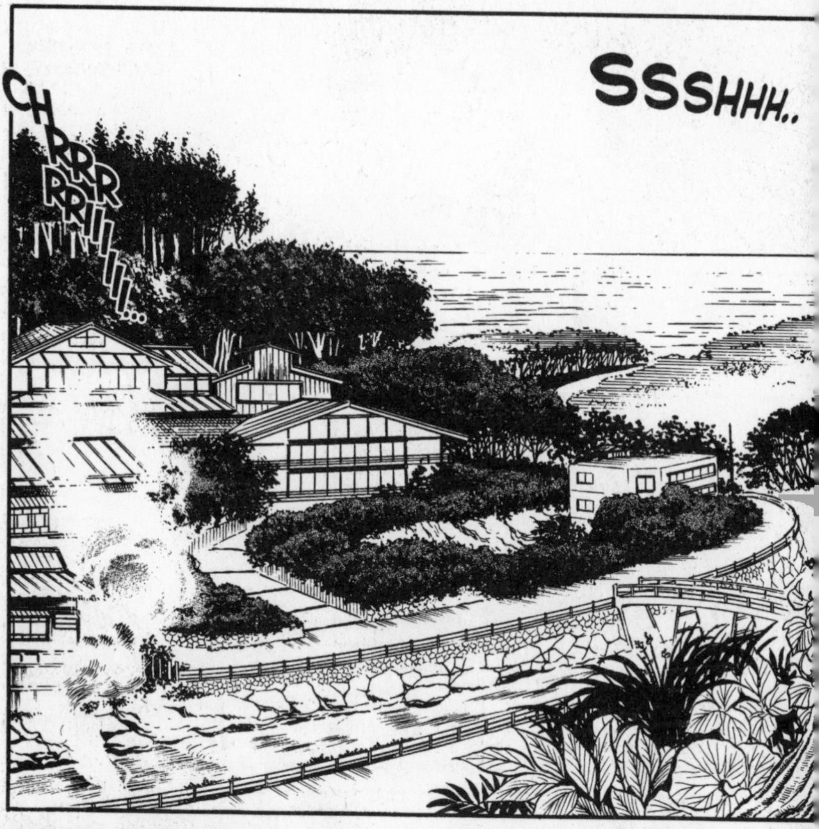
SSSHHH..
CHRRRRRRIIIIII...

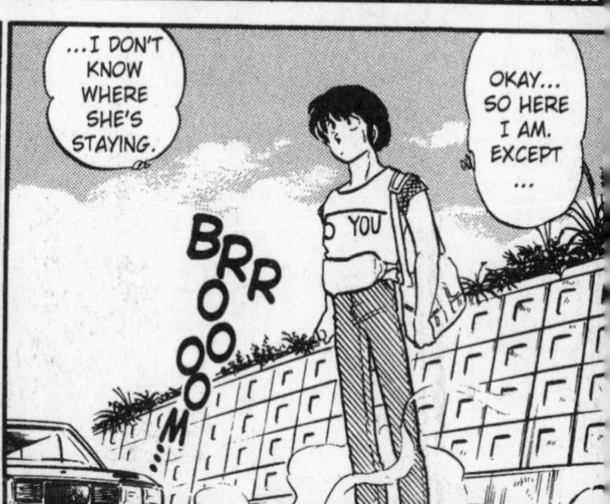
OKAY... SO HERE I AM. EXCEPT ...
...I DON'T KNOW WHERE SHE'S STAYING.
YOU
BRROOOOM...

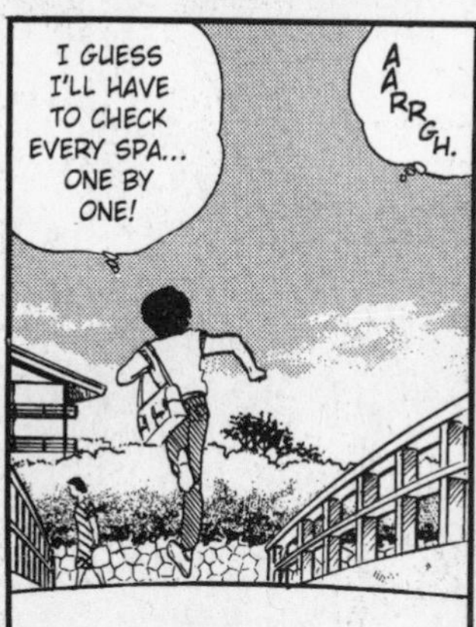
AARRGH.
I GUESS I'LL HAVE TO CHECK EVERY SPA... ONE BY ONE!

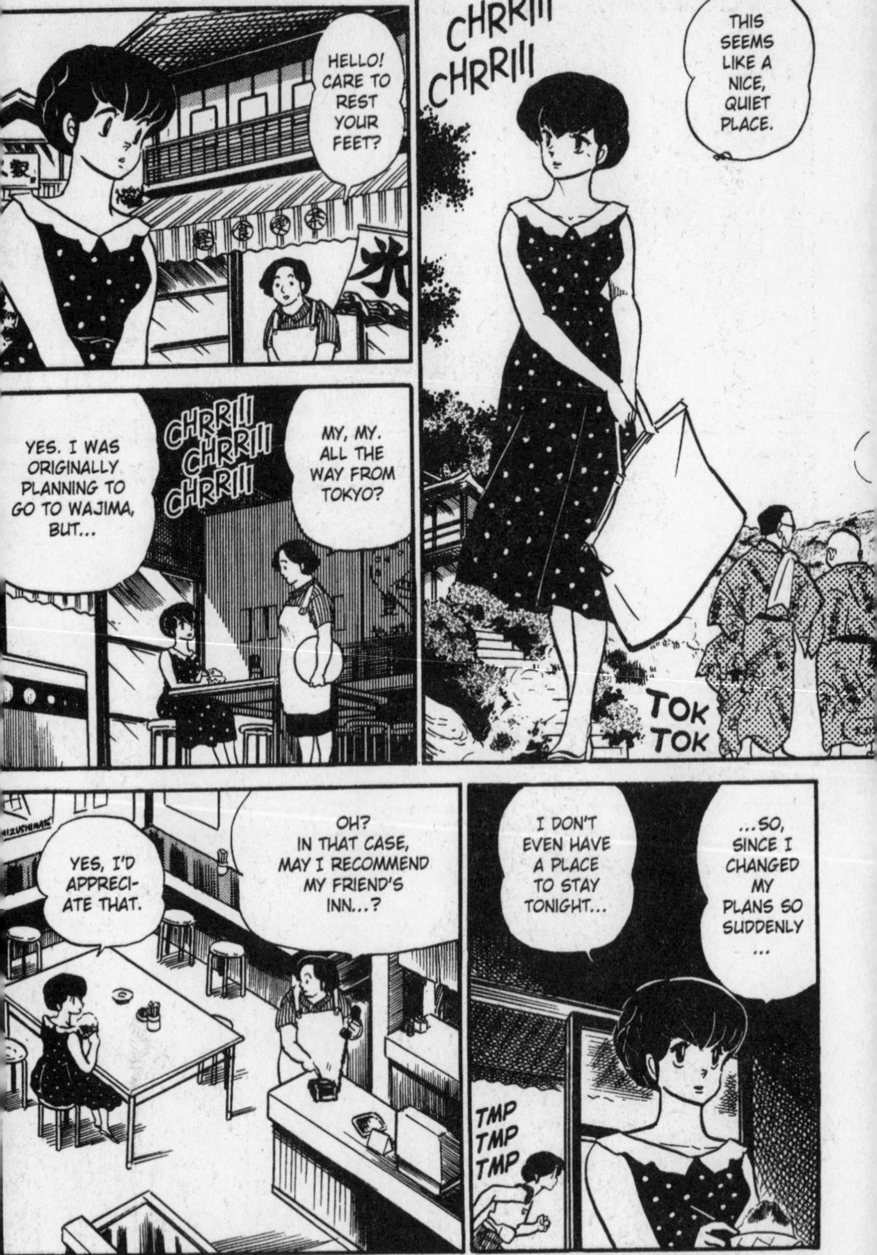
CHRRIII
CHRRIII
THIS SEEMS LIKE A NICE, QUIET PLACE.
TOK TOK
HELLO! CARE TO REST YOUR FEET?
MY, MY. ALL THE WAY FROM TOKYO?
CHRRIII CHRRIII CHRRIII
YES. I WAS ORIGINALLY PLANNING TO GO TO WAJIMA, BUT...
...SO, SINCE I CHANGED MY PLANS SO SUDDENLY ...
I DON'T EVEN HAVE A PLACE TO STAY TONIGHT...
TMP TMP TMP
OH? IN THAT CASE, MAY I RECOMMEND MY FRIEND'S INN...?
YES, I'D APPRECIATE THAT.

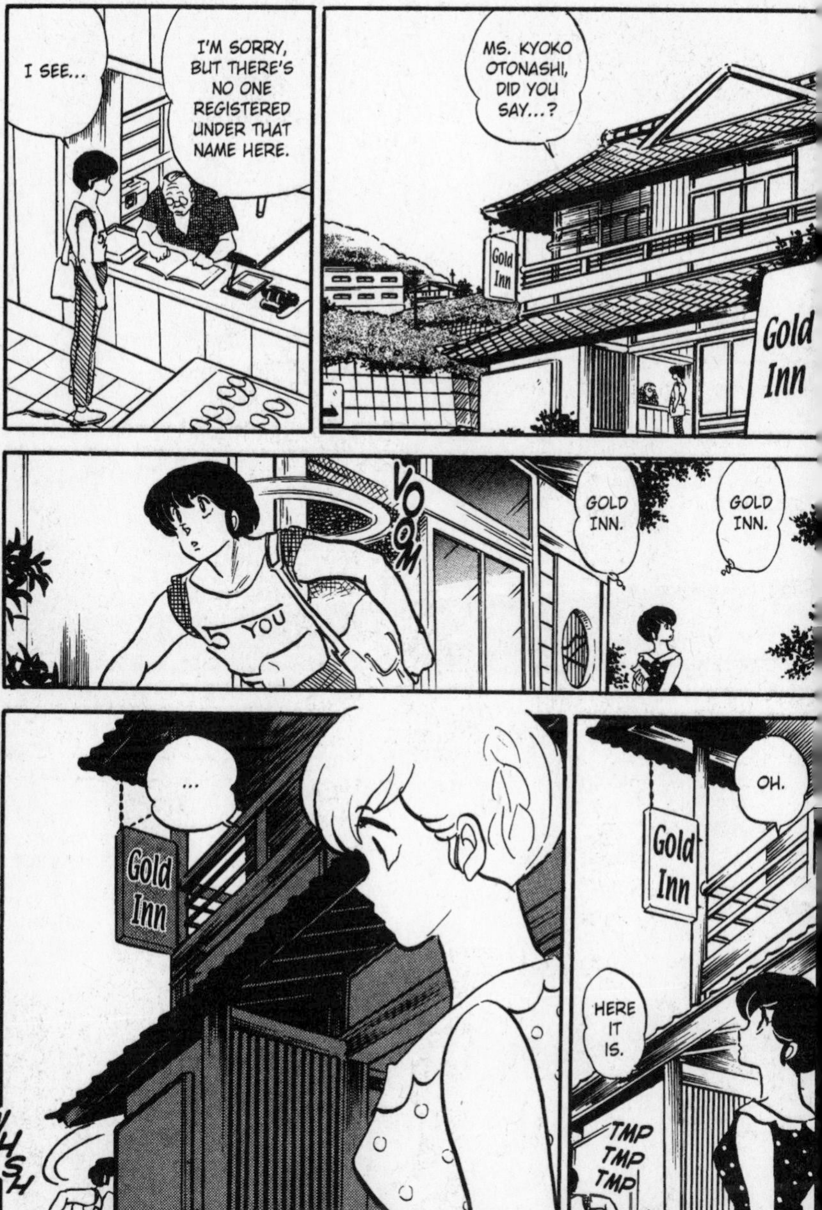
MS. KYOKO OTONASHI, DID YOU SAY...?
Gold Inn
Gold Inn
I'M SORRY, BUT THERE'S NO ONE REGISTERED UNDER THAT NAME HERE.
I SEE...
GOLD INN.
GOLD INN.
VOOM
YOU
OH.
Gold Inn
HERE IT IS.
TMP TMP TMP
...
Gold Inn
WHSH

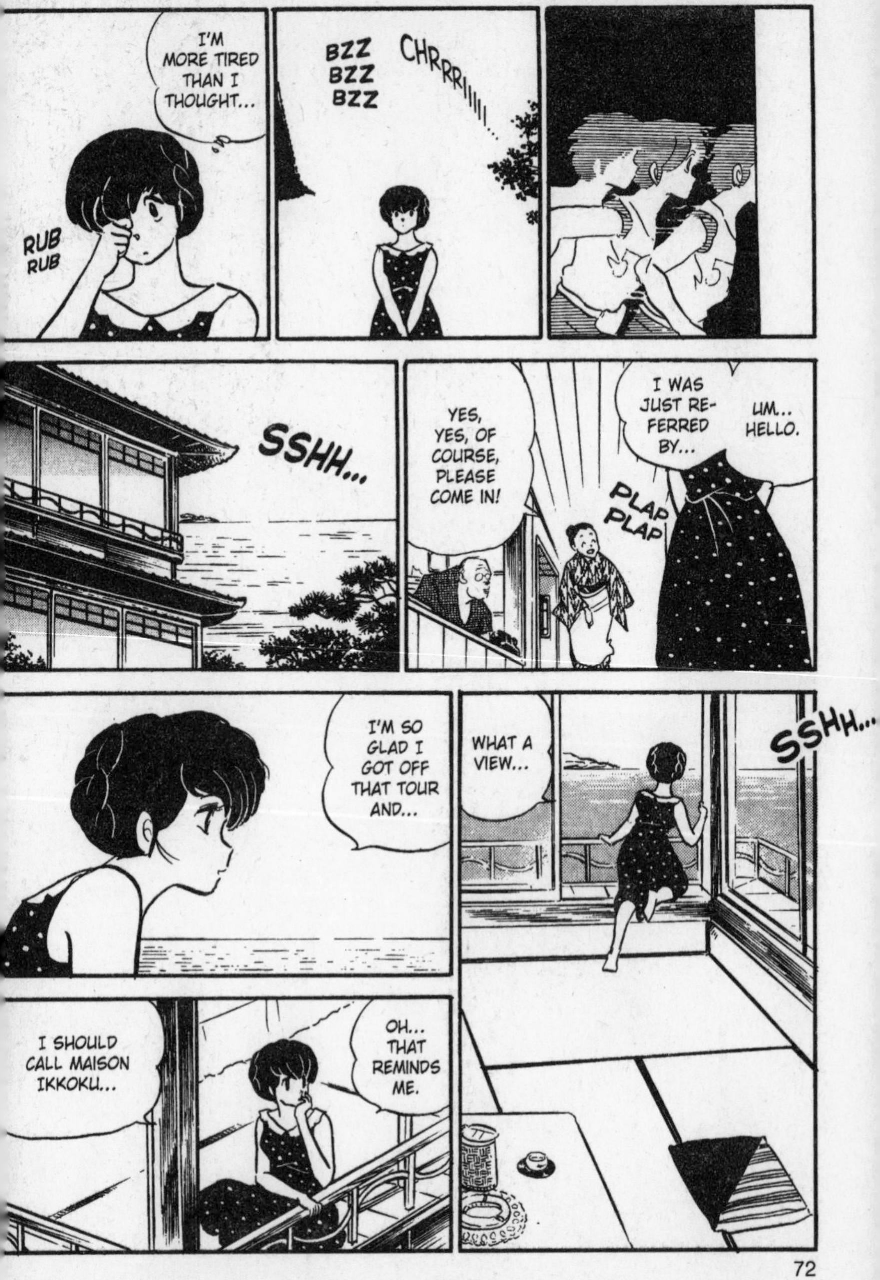
BZZ BZZ BZZ
CHRRRIIIII...
I'M MORE TIRED THAN I THOUGHT...
RUB RUB
UM... HELLO.
I WAS JUST RE-FERRED BY...
PLAP PLAP
YES, YES, OF COURSE, PLEASE COME IN!
SSHH...
SSHH...
WHAT A VIEW...
I'M SO GLAD I GOT OFF THAT TOUR AND...
OH... THAT REMINDS ME.
I SHOULD CALL MAISON IKKOKU...

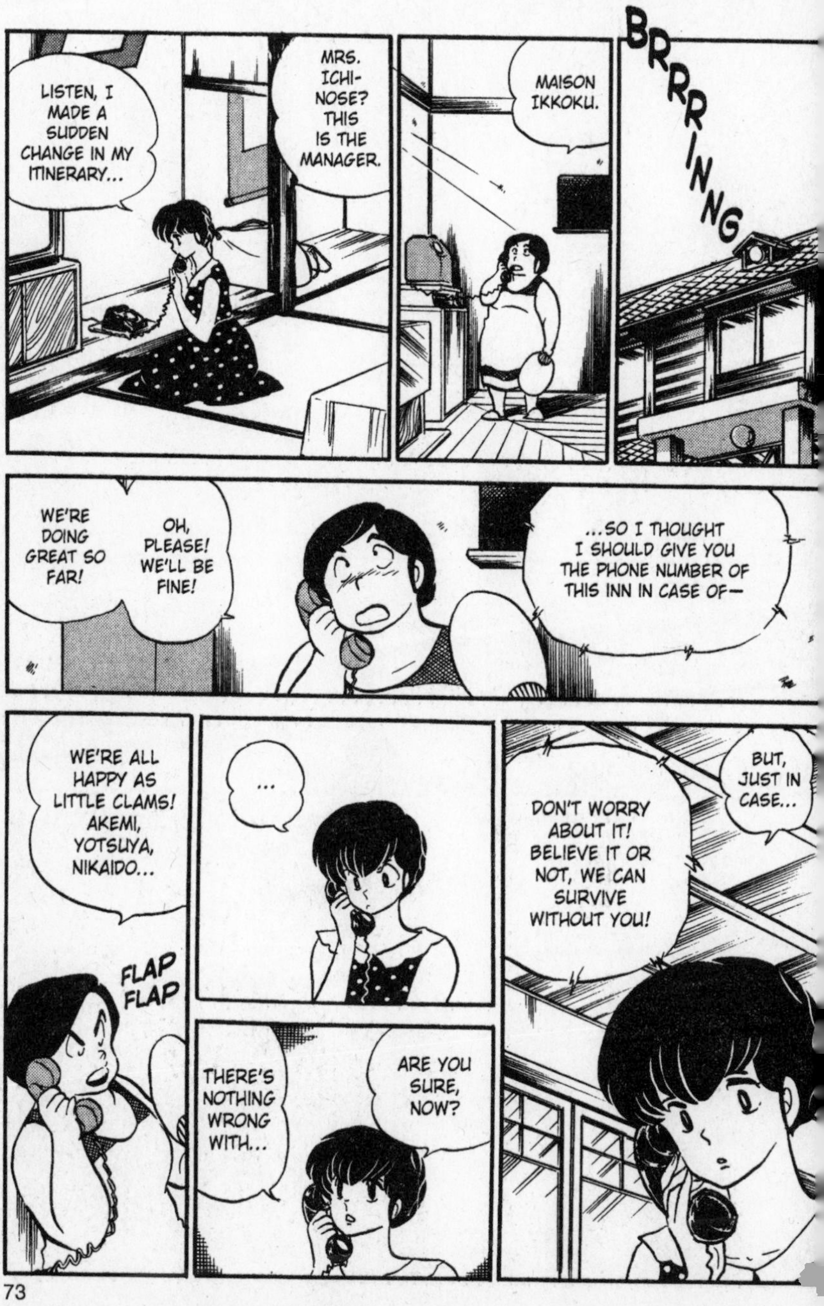
BRRRINNNG
MAISON IKKOKU.
MRS. ICHI-NOSE? THIS IS THE MANAGER.
LISTEN, I MADE A SUDDEN CHANGE IN MY ITINERARY...
...SO I THOUGHT I SHOULD GIVE YOU THE PHONE NUMBER OF THIS INN IN CASE OF—
OH, PLEASE! WE'LL BE FINE!
WE'RE DOING GREAT SO FAR!
BUT, JUST IN CASE...
DON'T WORRY ABOUT IT! BELIEVE IT OR NOT, WE CAN SURVIVE WITHOUT YOU!
...
ARE YOU SURE, NOW?
THERE'S NOTHING WRONG WITH...
WE'RE ALL HAPPY AS LITTLE CLAMS! AKEMI, YOTSUYA, NIKAIDO...
FLAP FLAP

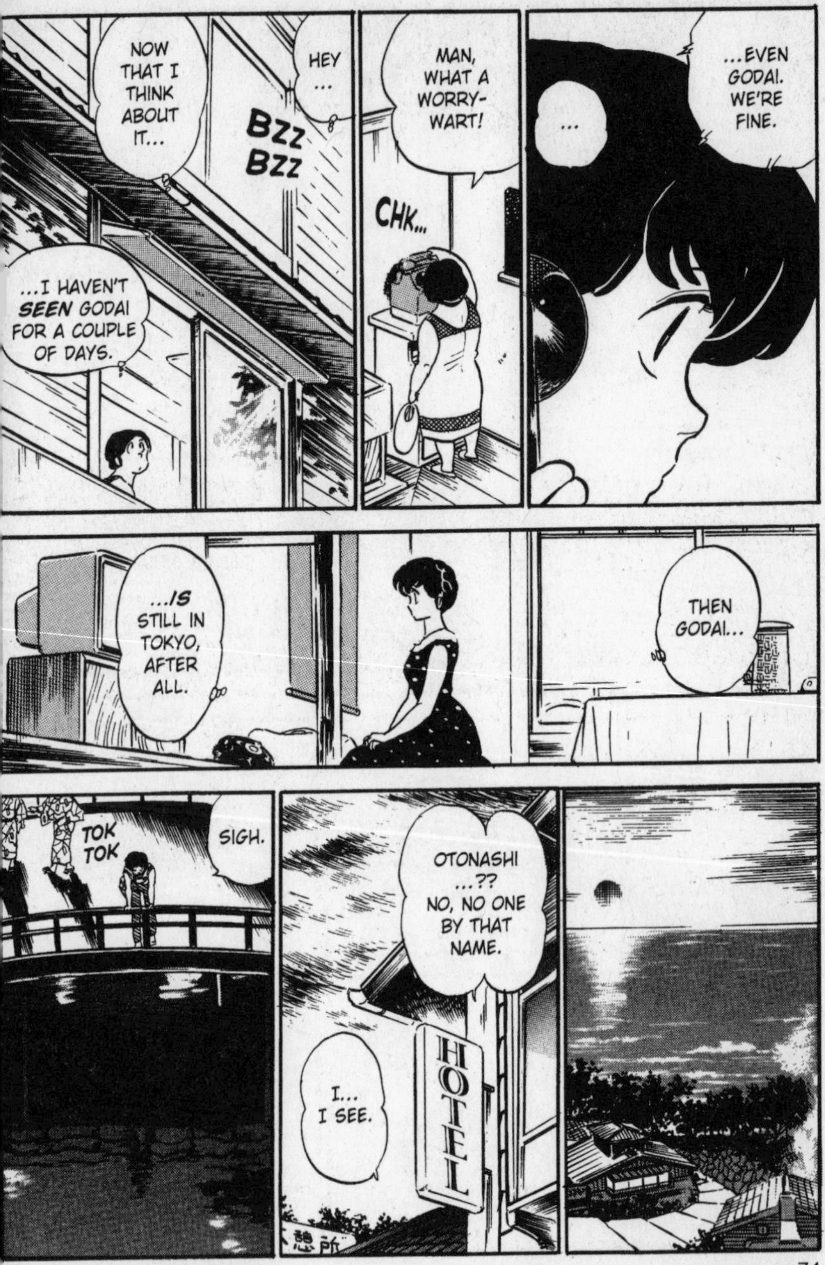
...EVEN GODAI. WE'RE FINE.
...
MAN, WHAT A WORRY-WART!
CHK...
HEY ...
NOW THAT I THINK ABOUT IT...
BZZ BZZ
...I HAVEN'T *SEEN* GODAI FOR A COUPLE OF DAYS.
THEN GODAI...
...*IS* STILL IN TOKYO, AFTER ALL.
OTONASHI ...?? NO, NO ONE BY THAT NAME.
HOTEL
I... I SEE.
SIGH.
TOK TOK

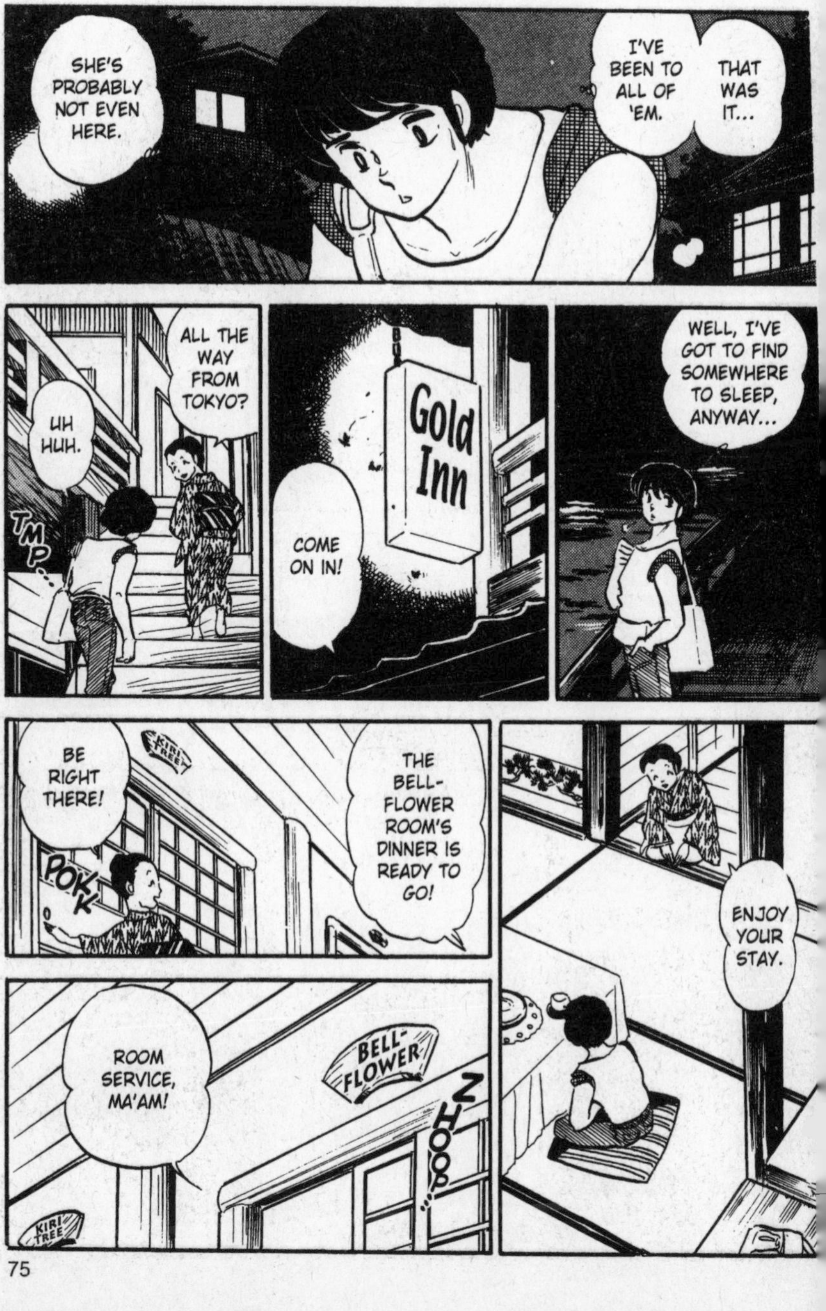
THAT WAS IT...
I'VE BEEN TO ALL OF 'EM.
SHE'S PROBABLY NOT EVEN HERE.
WELL, I'VE GOT TO FIND SOMEWHERE TO SLEEP, ANYWAY...
Gold Inn
COME ON IN!
ALL THE WAY FROM TOKYO?
UH HUH.
TMP...
ENJOY YOUR STAY.
THE BELL-FLOWER ROOM'S DINNER IS READY TO GO!
KIRI TREE
BE RIGHT THERE!
POKK
BELL-FLOWER
ZHOOP...
ROOM SERVICE, MA'AM!
KIRI TREE

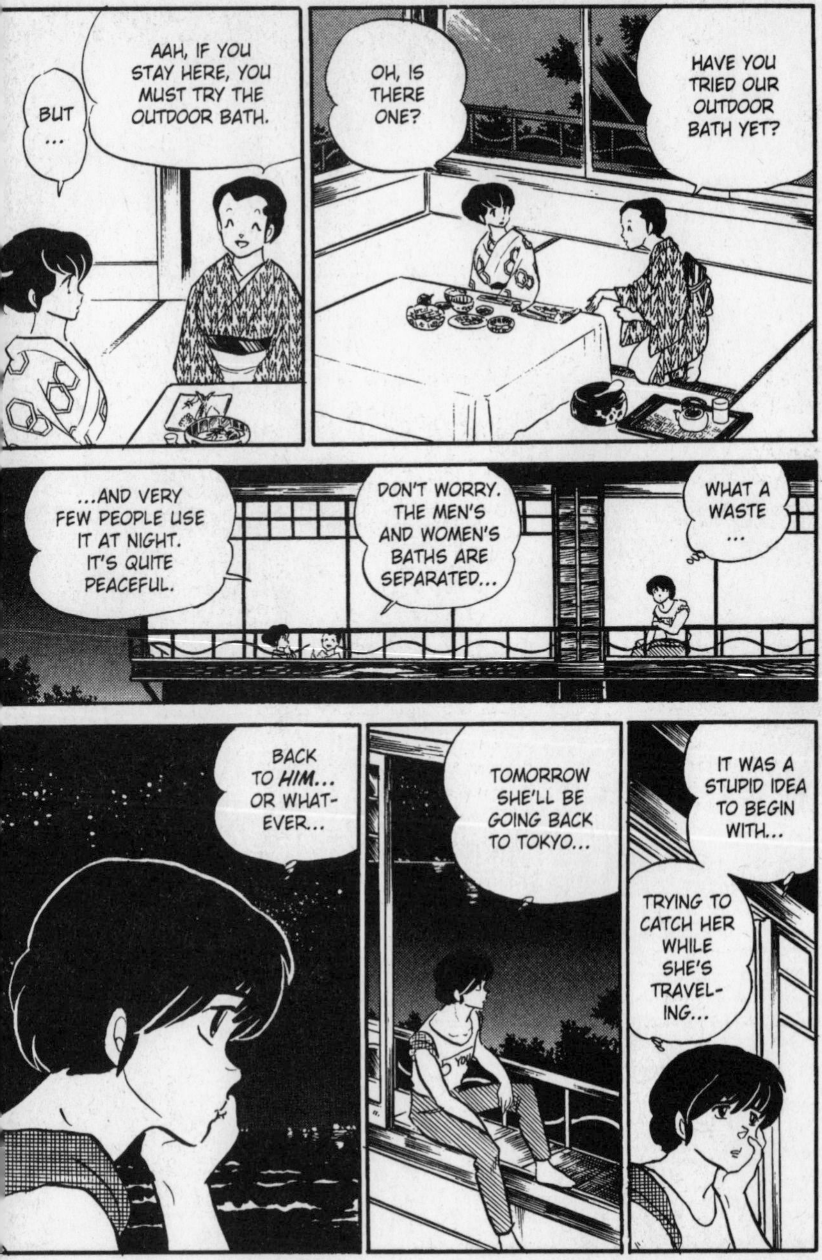
HAVE YOU TRIED OUR OUTDOOR BATH YET?
OH, IS THERE ONE?
AAH, IF YOU STAY HERE, YOU MUST TRY THE OUTDOOR BATH.
BUT ...
WHAT A WASTE ...
DON'T WORRY. THE MEN'S AND WOMEN'S BATHS ARE SEPARATED...
...AND VERY FEW PEOPLE USE IT AT NIGHT. IT'S QUITE PEACEFUL.
IT WAS A STUPID IDEA TO BEGIN WITH...
TRYING TO CATCH HER WHILE SHE'S TRAVELING...
TOMORROW SHE'LL BE GOING BACK TO TOKYO...
BACK TO *HIM*... OR WHATEVER...

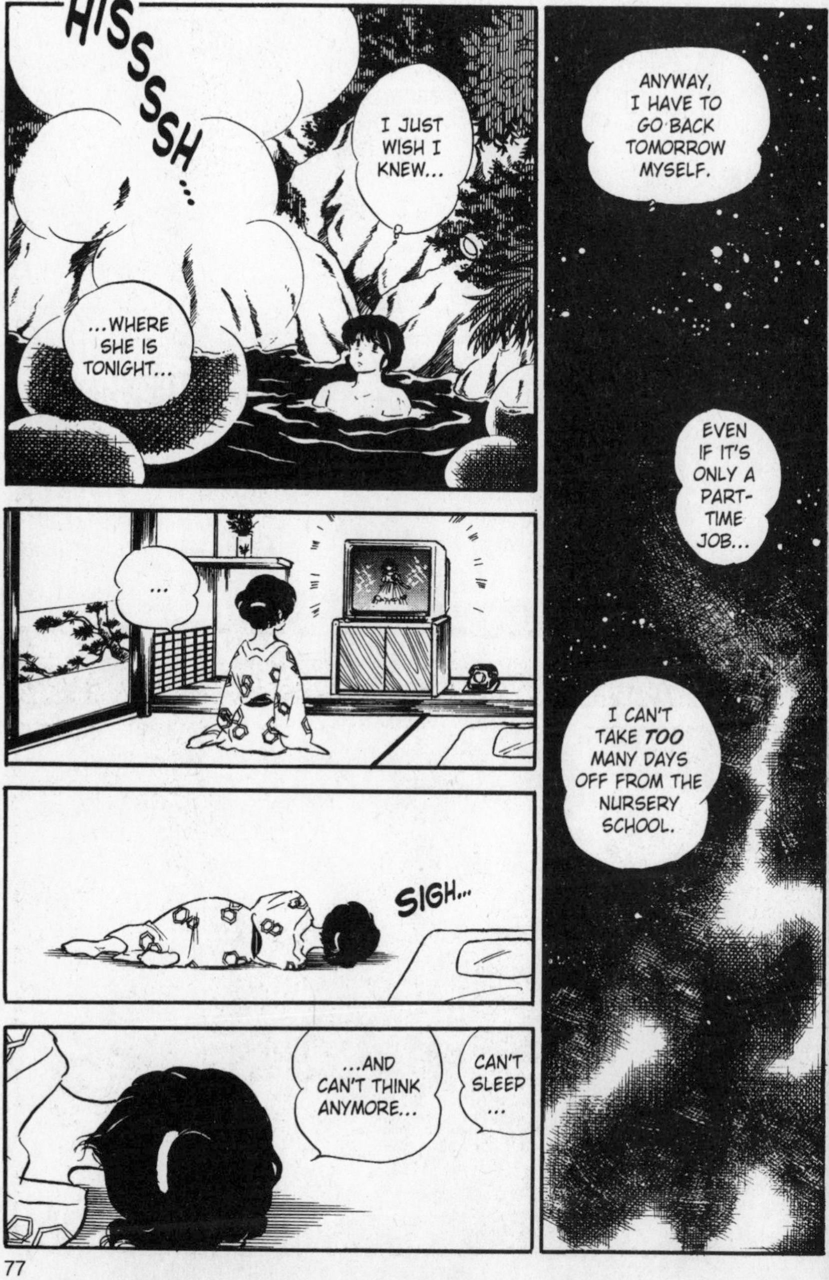
ANYWAY, I HAVE TO GO BACK TOMORROW MYSELF.
EVEN IF IT'S ONLY A PART-TIME JOB...
I CAN'T TAKE *TOO* MANY DAYS OFF FROM THE NURSERY SCHOOL.
I JUST WISH I KNEW...
HISSSSH...
...WHERE SHE IS TONIGHT...
...
SIGH...
CAN'T SLEEP...
...AND CAN'T THINK ANYMORE...

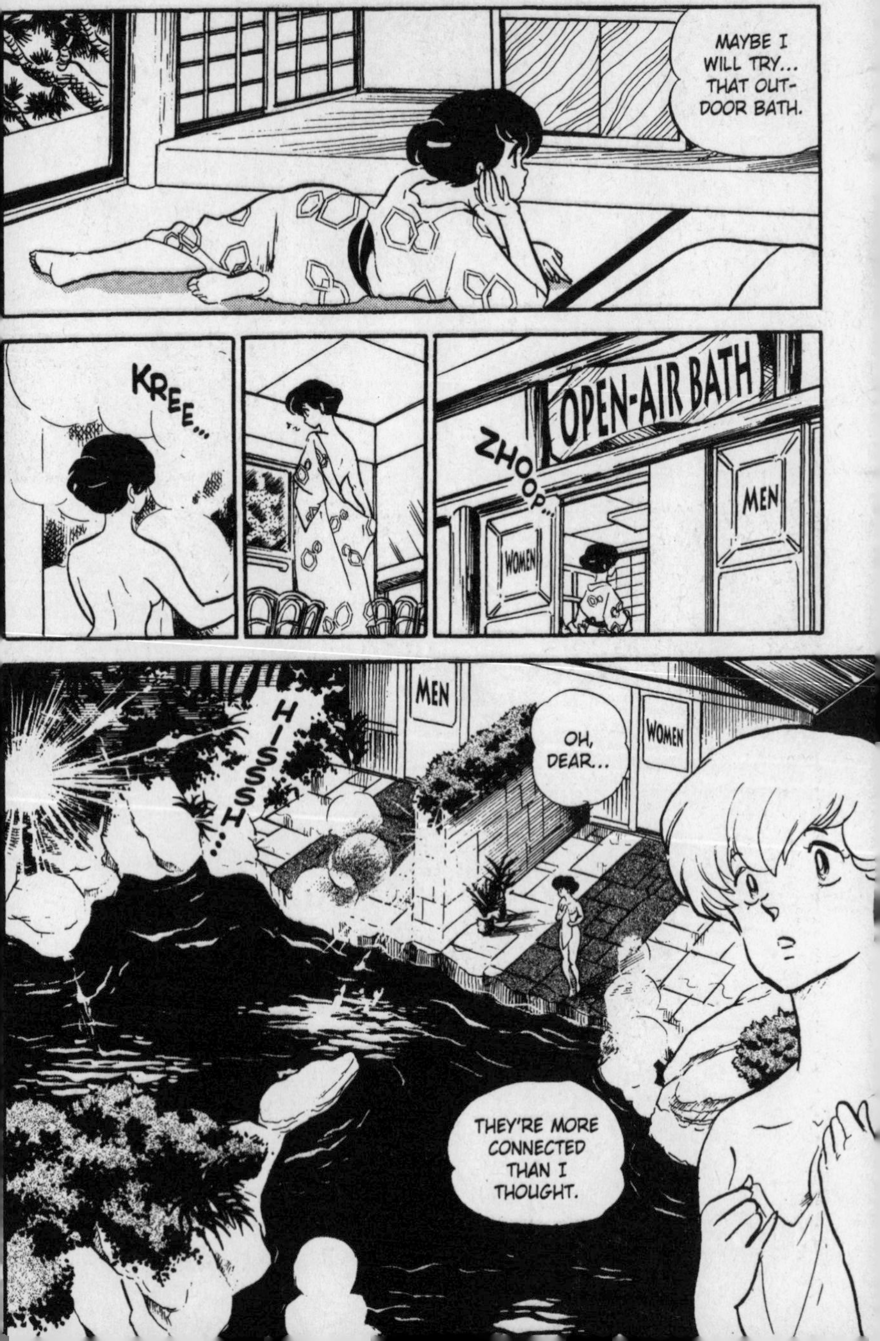
MAYBE I WILL TRY... THAT OUT-DOOR BATH.
OPEN-AIR BATH
MEN
ZHOOP...
WOMEN
KREE...
WOMEN
OH, DEAR...
MEN
HISSSH...
THEY'RE MORE CONNECTED THAN I THOUGHT.

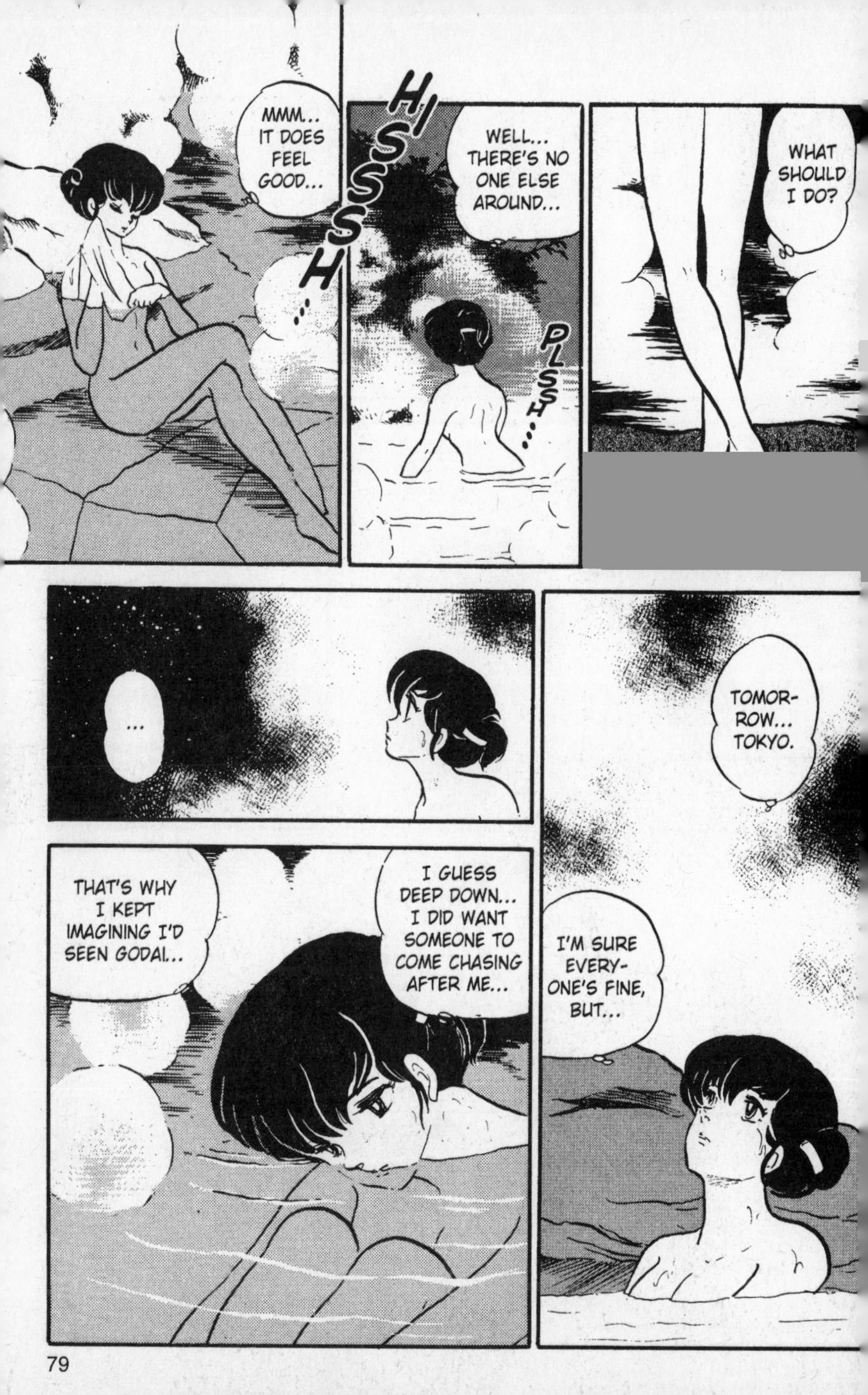
WHAT SHOULD I DO?
WELL... THERE'S NO ONE ELSE AROUND...
HISSSH...
PLSSH...
MMM... IT DOES FEEL GOOD...
TOMOR-ROW... TOKYO.
I'M SURE EVERY-ONE'S FINE, BUT...
...
I GUESS DEEP DOWN... I DID WANT SOMEONE TO COME CHASING AFTER ME...
THAT'S WHY I KEPT IMAGINING I'D SEEN GODAI...

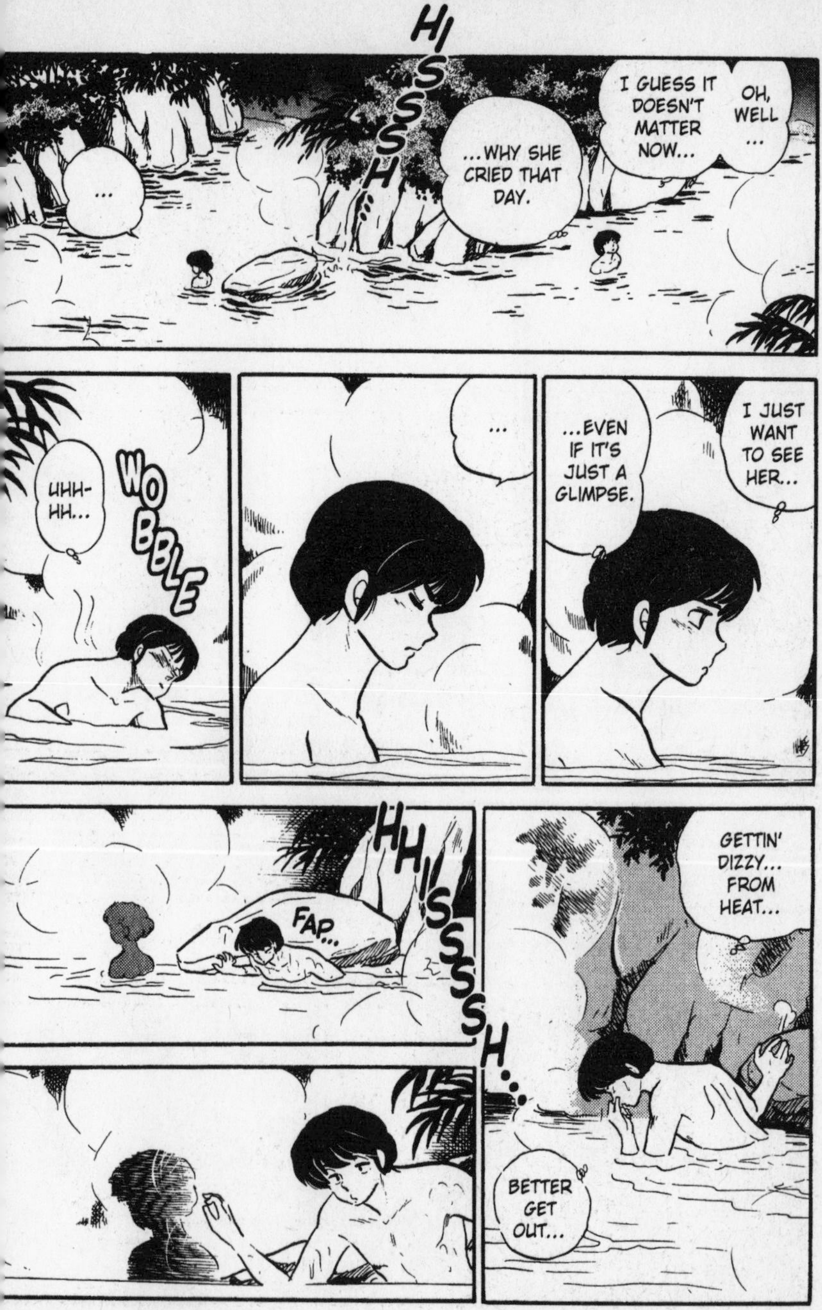
OH, WELL ...
I GUESS IT DOESN'T MATTER NOW...
...WHY SHE CRIED THAT DAY.
HISSSH...
...
I JUST WANT TO SEE HER...
...EVEN IF IT'S JUST A GLIMPSE.
...
UHH-HH...
WOBBLE
GETTIN' DIZZY... FROM HEAT...
BETTER GET OUT...
HHISSSSH...
FAP...

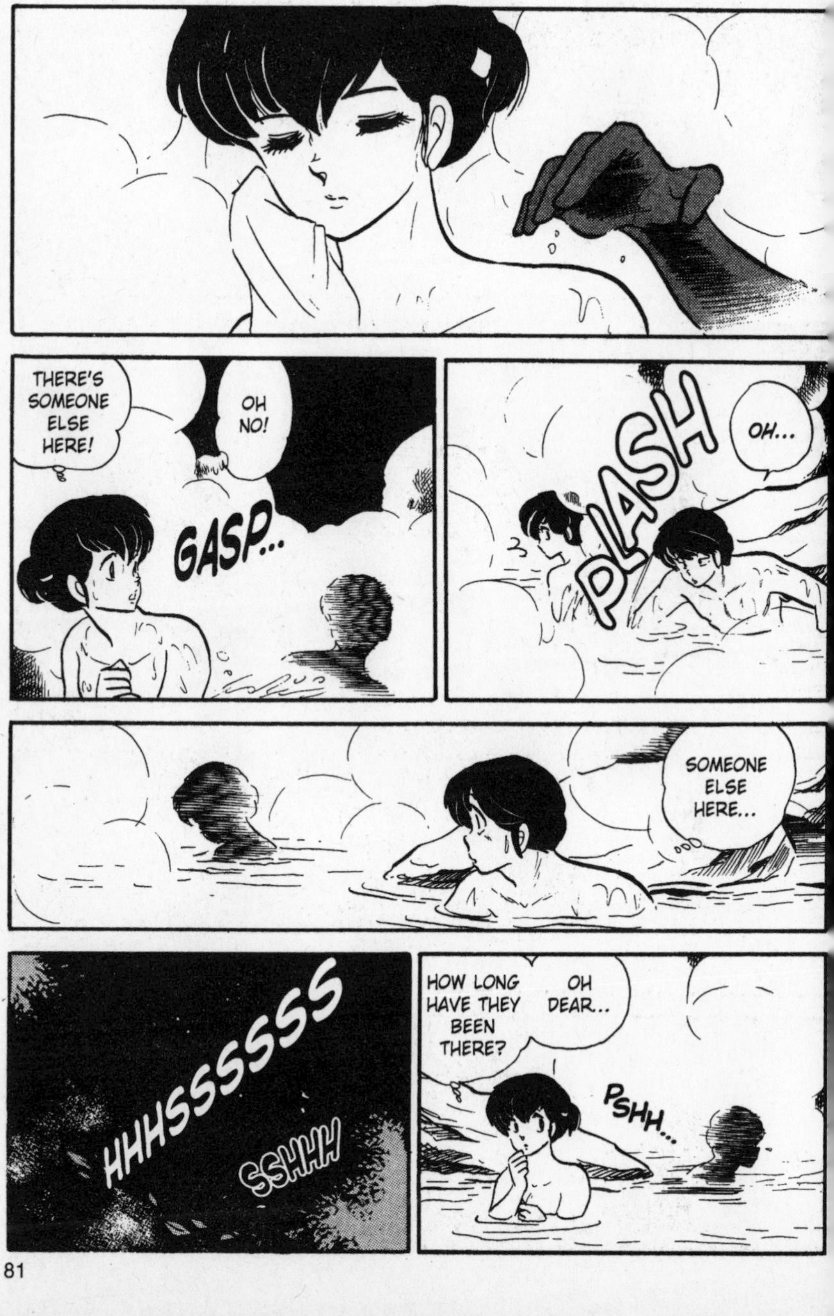
OH...
PLASH
OH NO!
THERE'S SOMEONE ELSE HERE!
GASP...
SOMEONE ELSE HERE...
OH DEAR...
HOW LONG HAVE THEY BEEN THERE?
PSHH...
HHHSSSSSS
SSHHH

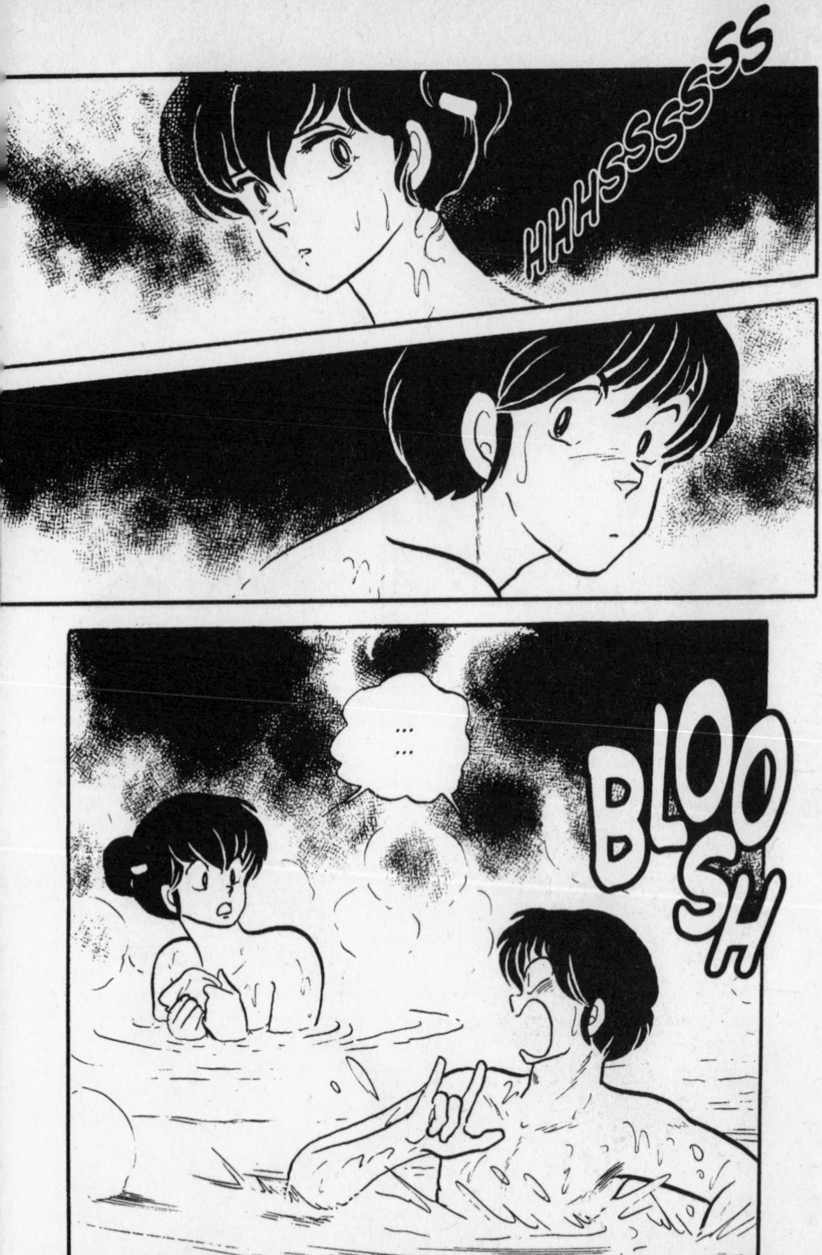
HHHSSSSSSS
BLOOSH
...
...

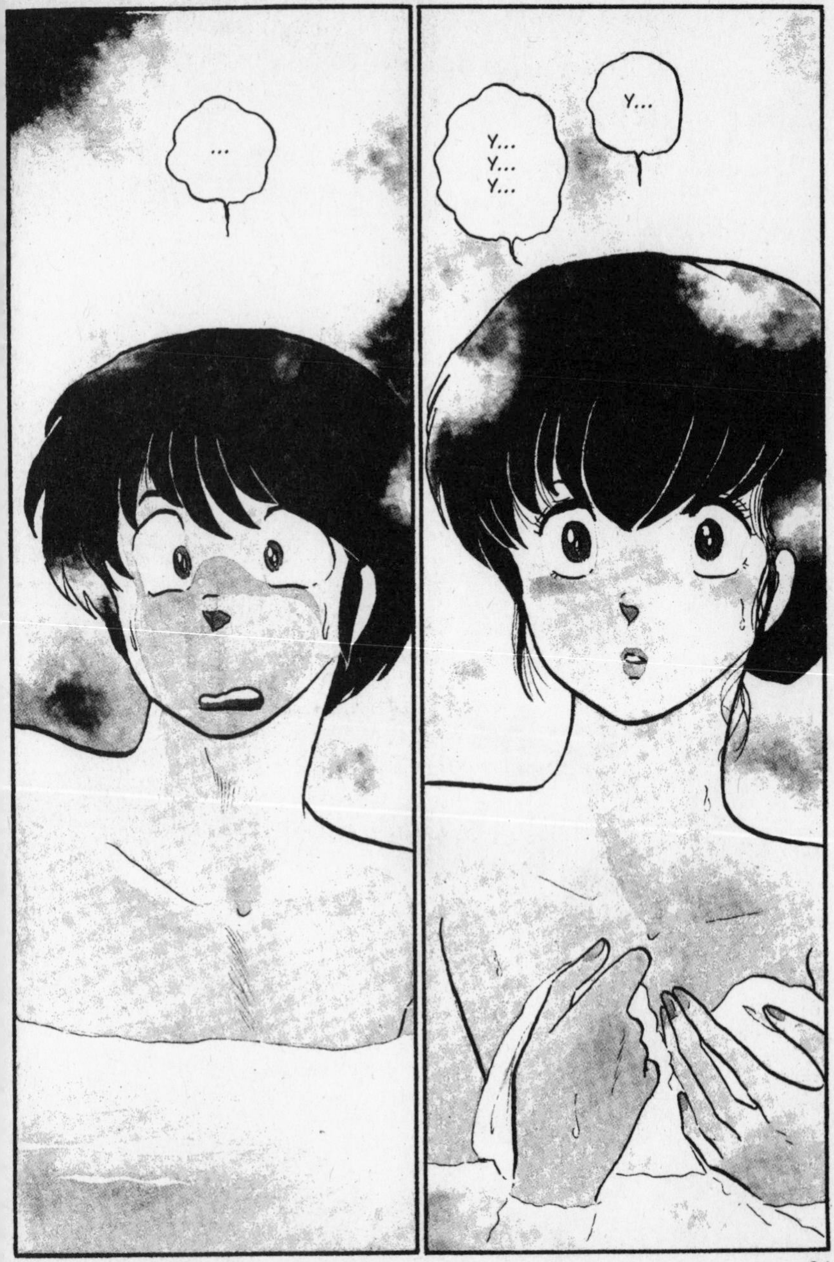
Y...
Y...
Y...
Y...
...

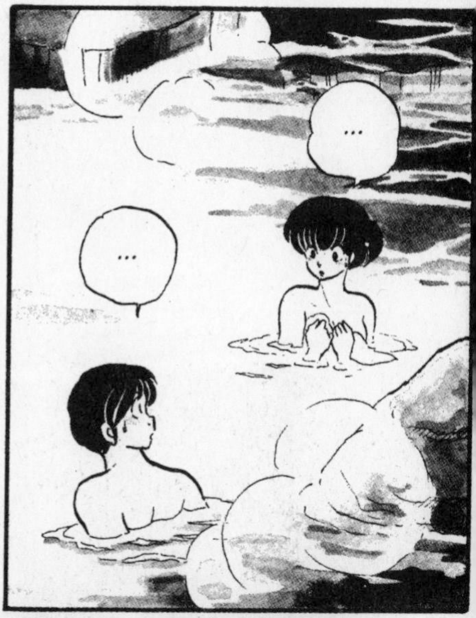
...
...

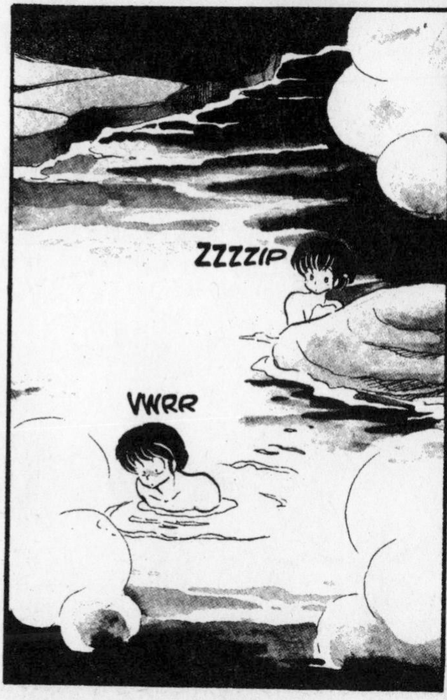
ZZZZIP
VWRR

PART FIVE

ONE NIGHT DREAM

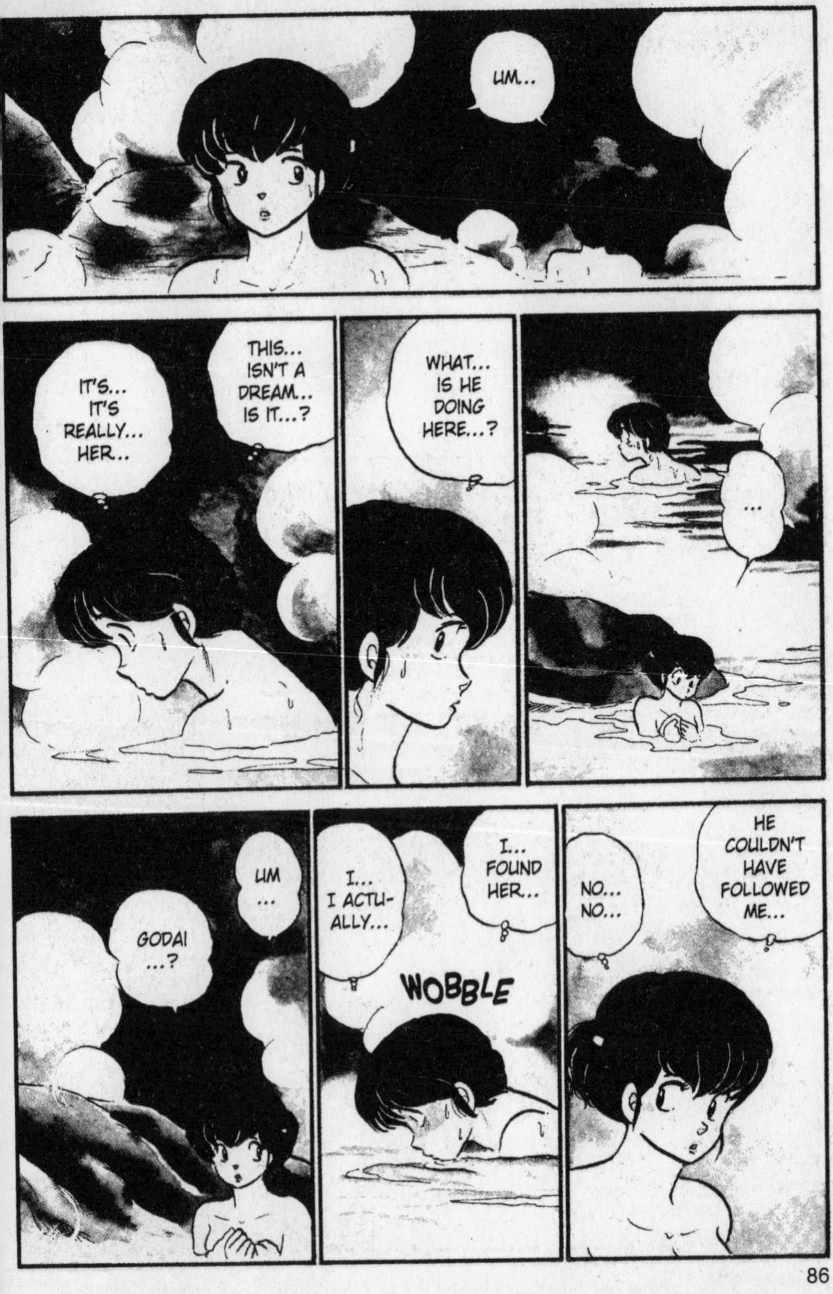
UM...
...
WHAT... IS HE DOING HERE...?
THIS... ISN'T A DREAM... IS IT...?
IT'S... IT'S REALLY... HER...
HE COULDN'T HAVE FOLLOWED ME...
NO... NO...
I... FOUND HER...
I... I ACTU-ALLY...
WOBBLE
UM ...
GODAI ...?

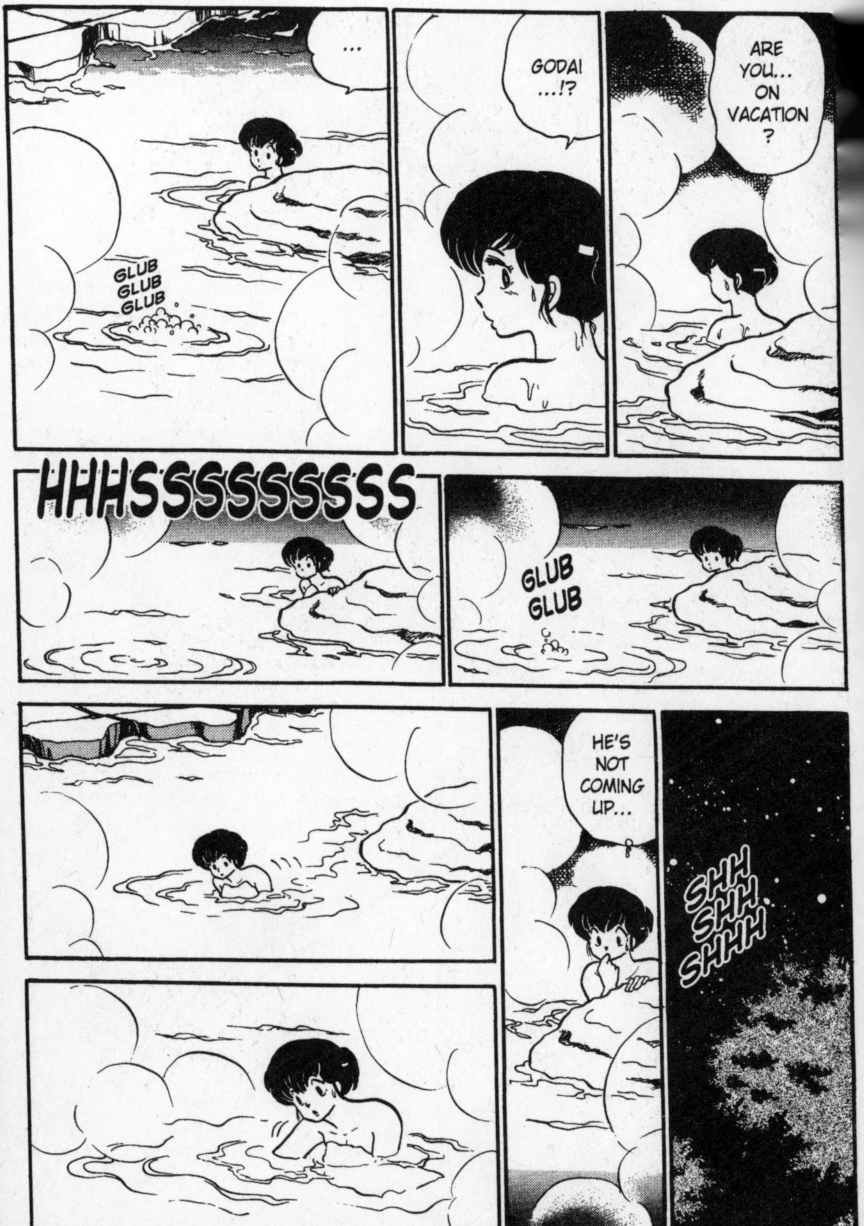
ARE YOU... ON VACATION ?
GODAI ...!?
...
GLUB GLUB GLUB
GLUB GLUB
HHHSSSSSSSSS
SHH SHH SHHH
HE'S NOT COMING UP...

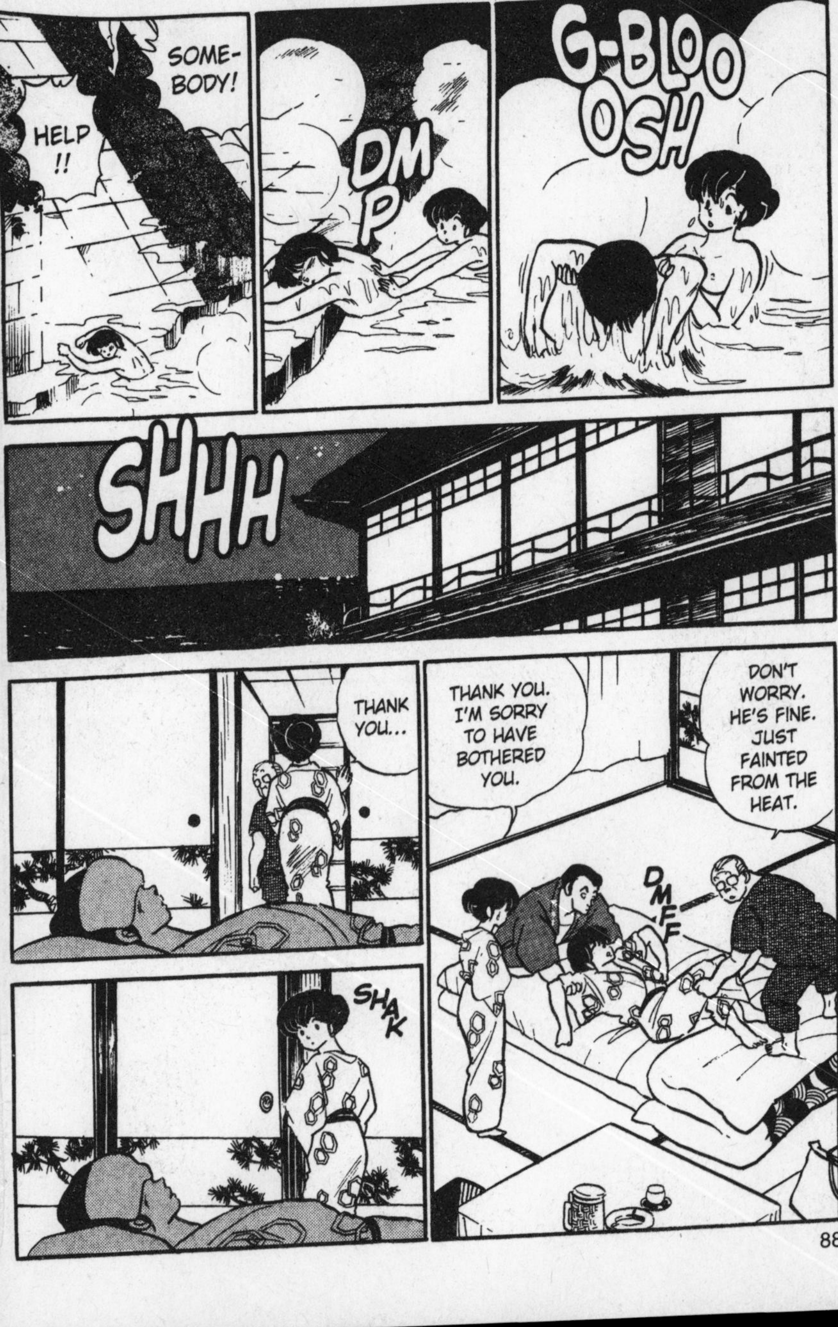
G-BLOO OSH
DMP
SOME-BODY!
HELP !!
SHHH
DON'T WORRY. HE'S FINE. JUST FAINTED FROM THE HEAT.
THANK YOU. I'M SORRY TO HAVE BOTHERED YOU.
DMFF
THANK YOU...
SHAK

SSHH...
...
WHAT DO I DO ...??
THEY CARRIED HIM INTO MY ROOM...
SS... SS...
HE'S SOUND ASLEEP ...
...
WHY ARE YOU HERE...??
COINCI-DENCE ??
OR WERE YOU REALLY...
...REALLY COMING AFTER ME...?
SSHHH...

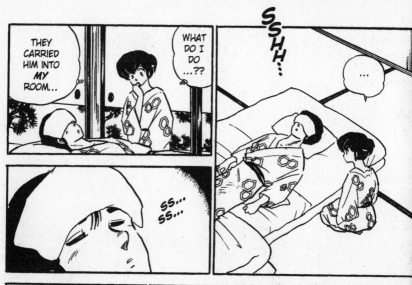

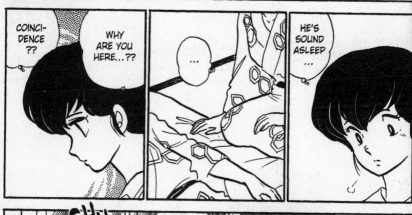

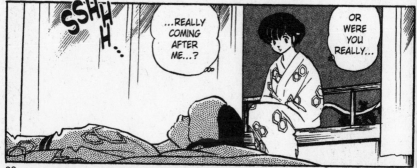

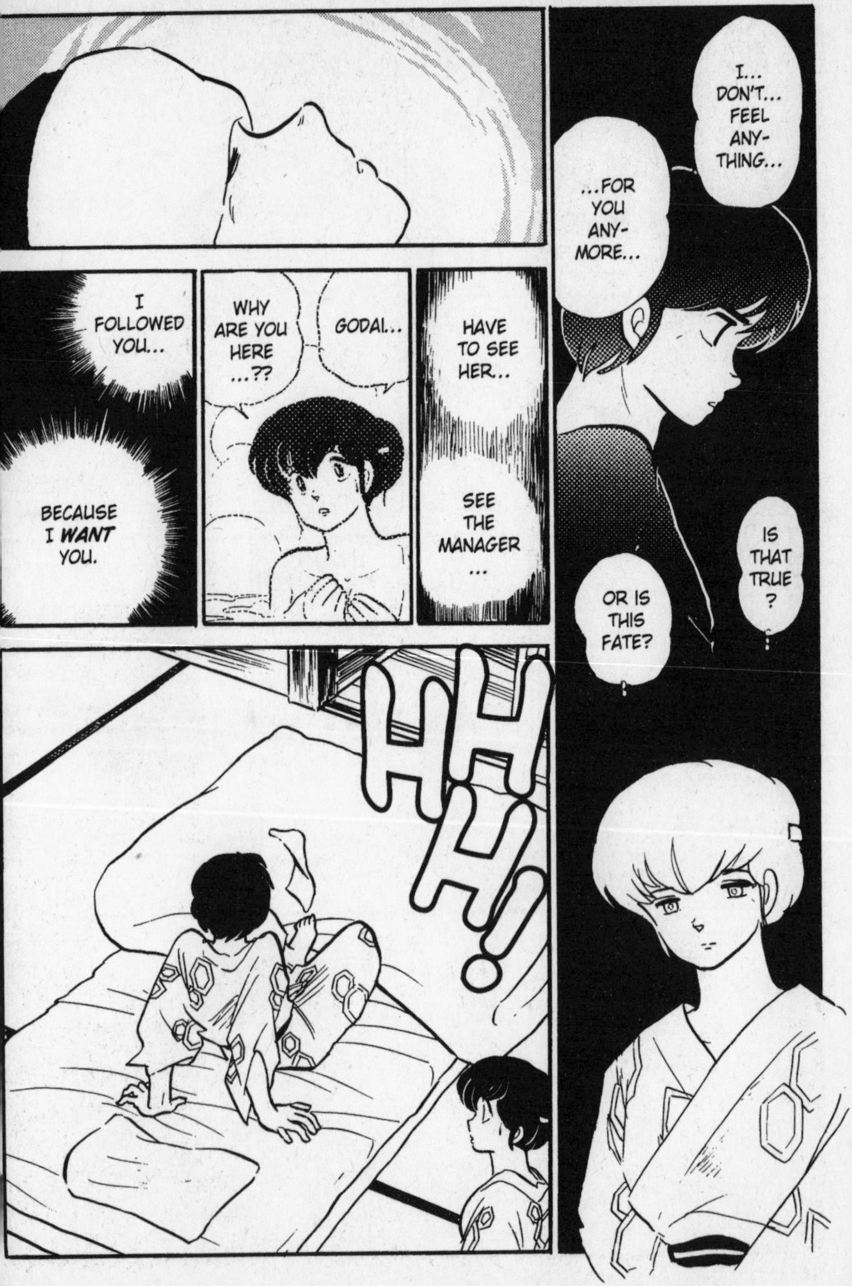
I... DON'T... FEEL ANY-THING...
...FOR YOU ANY-MORE...
IS THAT TRUE?
OR IS THIS FATE?
HAVE TO SEE HER...
SEE THE MANAGER...
GODAI...
WHY ARE YOU HERE...??
I FOLLOWED YOU...
BECAUSE I *WANT* YOU.
HHHH!!

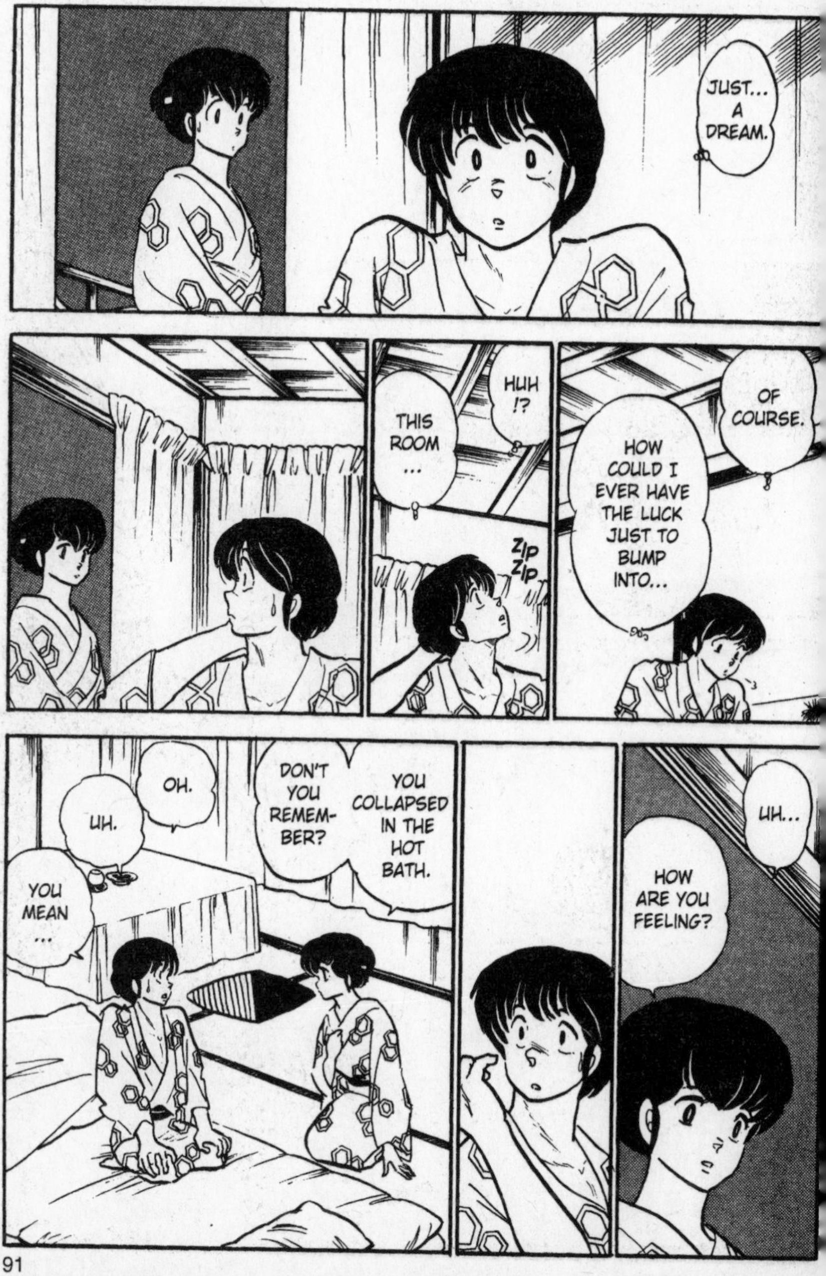
JUST... A DREAM.
OF COURSE.
HOW COULD I EVER HAVE THE LUCK JUST TO BUMP INTO...
HUH !?
THIS ROOM ...
ZIP ZIP
UH...
HOW ARE YOU FEELING?
YOU COLLAPSED IN THE HOT BATH.
DON'T YOU REMEMBER?
OH.
UH.
YOU MEAN ...

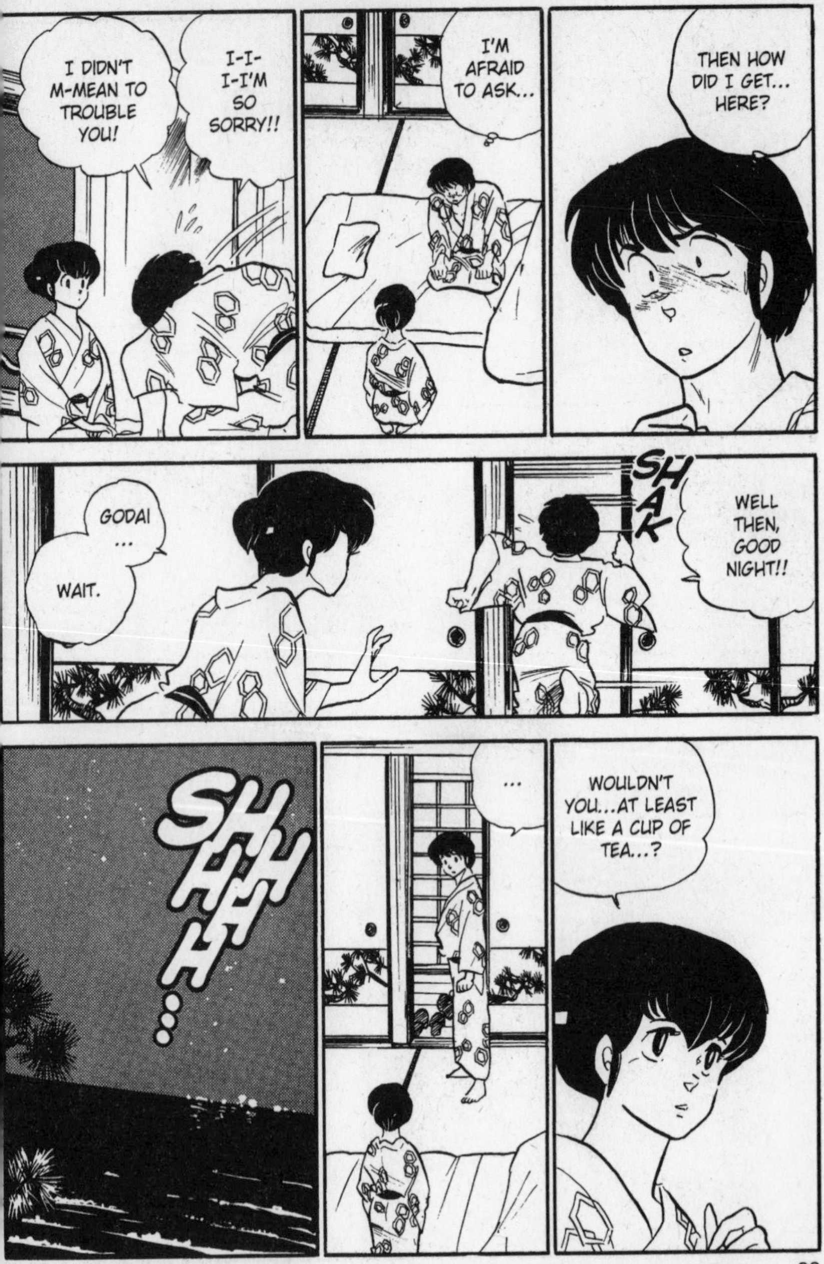
THEN HOW DID I GET... HERE?
I'M AFRAID TO ASK...
I-I-I-I'M SO SORRY!!
I DIDN'T M-MEAN TO TROUBLE YOU!
SHAK
WELL THEN, GOOD NIGHT!!
GODAI ...
WAIT.
WOULDN'T YOU...AT LEAST LIKE A CUP OF TEA...?
...
SHHHHH...

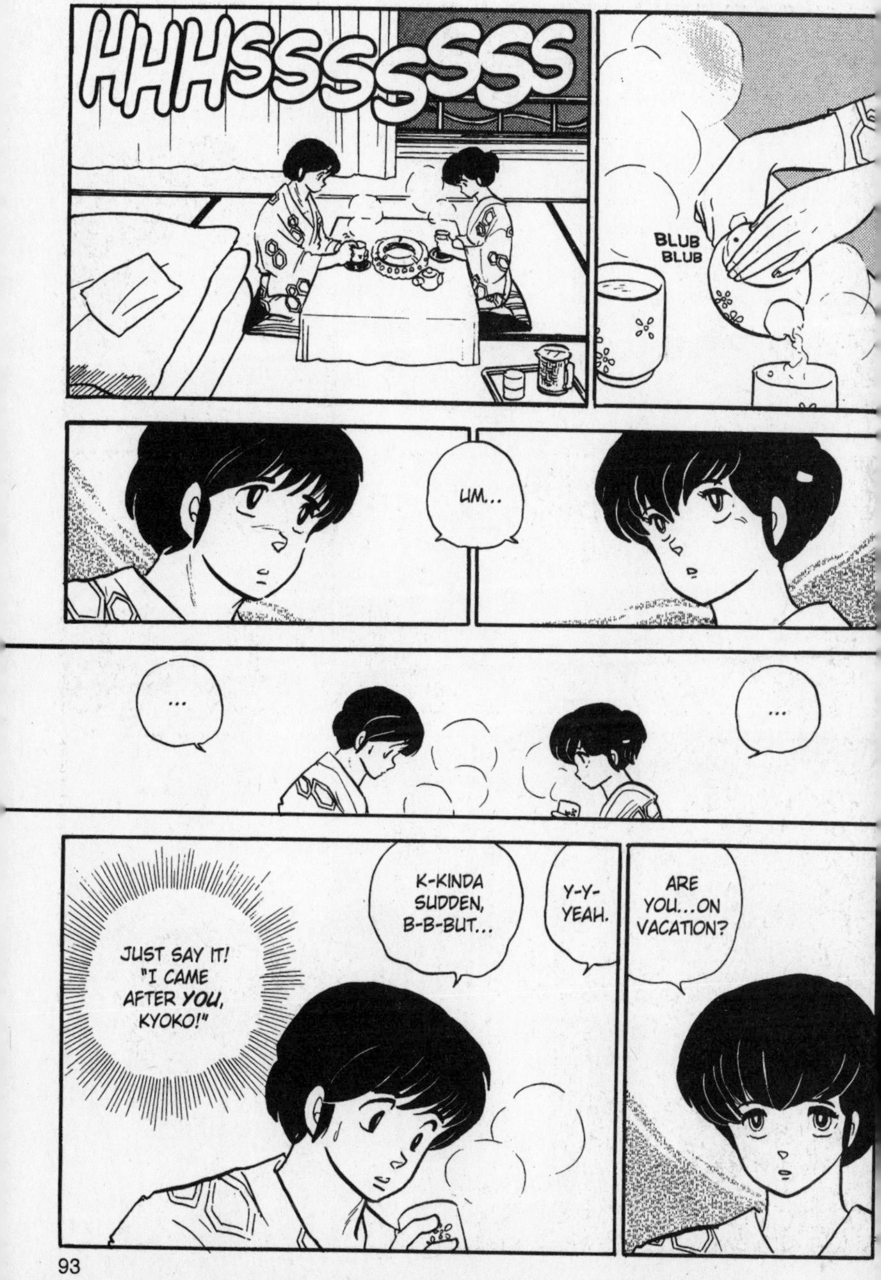
BLUB BLUB
HHHSSSSSSS
UM...
...
...
ARE YOU...ON VACATION?
Y-Y-YEAH.
K-KINDA SUDDEN, B-B-BUT...
JUST SAY IT! "I CAME AFTER YOU, KYOKO!"

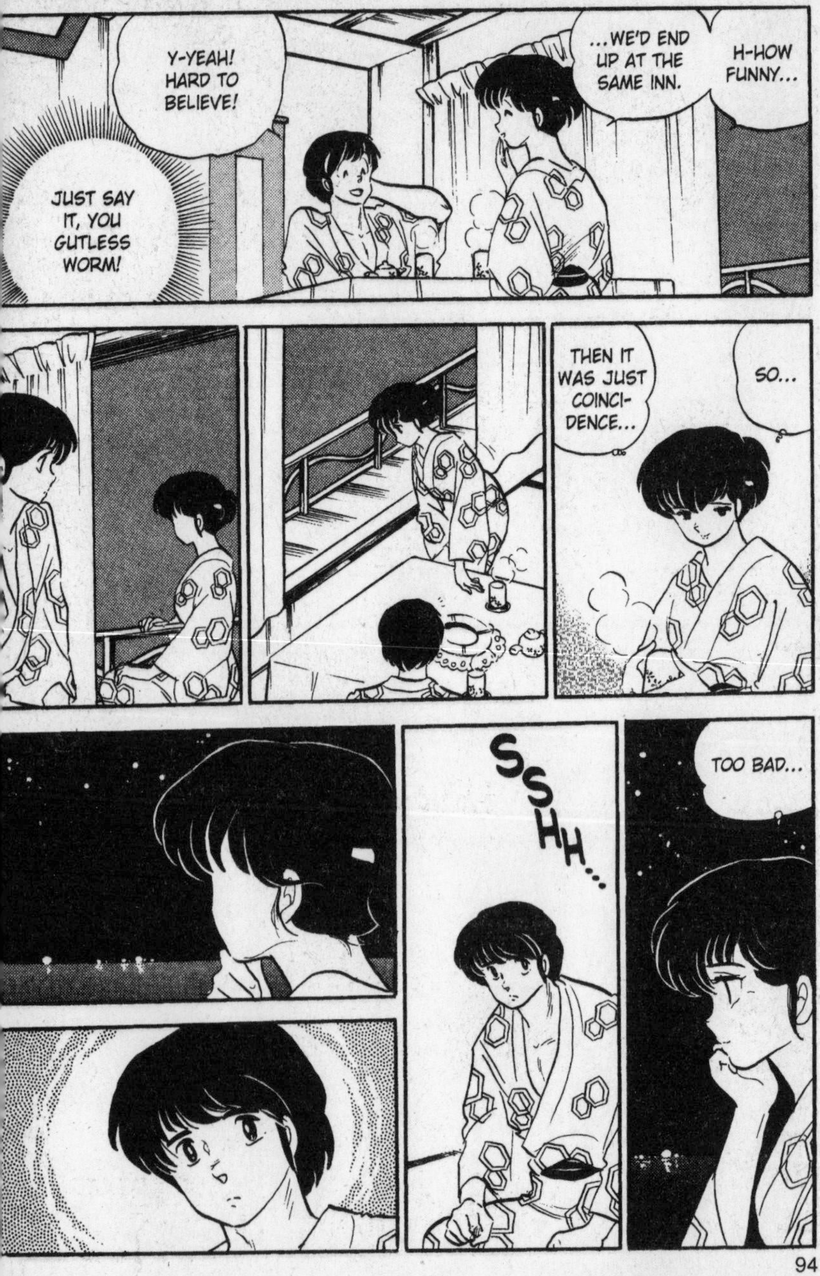
H-HOW FUNNY...
...WE'D END UP AT THE SAME INN.
Y-YEAH! HARD TO BELIEVE!
JUST SAY IT, YOU GUTLESS WORM!
SO...
THEN IT WAS JUST COINCI-DENCE...
TOO BAD...
SSHH...

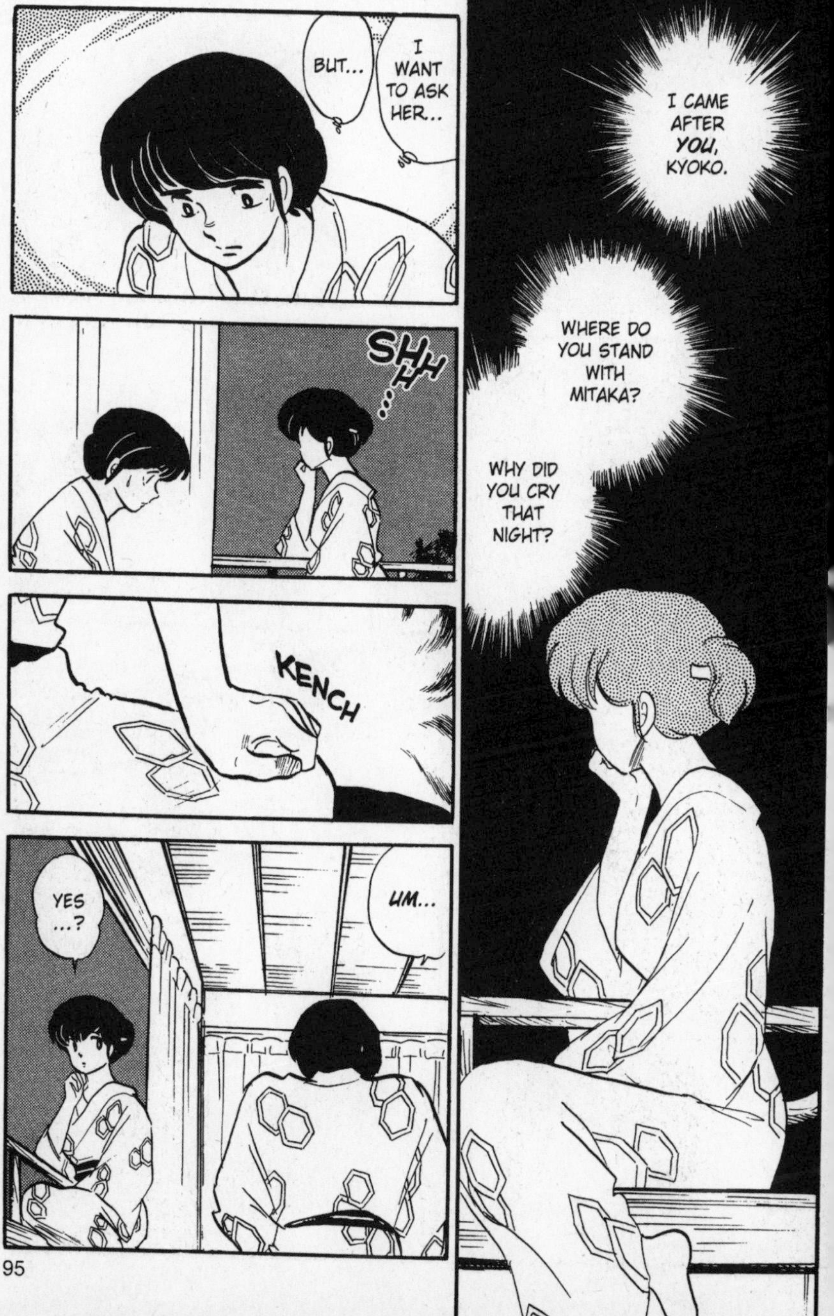
I CAME AFTER YOU, KYOKO.
WHERE DO YOU STAND WITH MITAKA?
WHY DID YOU CRY THAT NIGHT?
I WANT TO ASK HER...
BUT...
SHHH...
KENCH
UM...
YES ...?

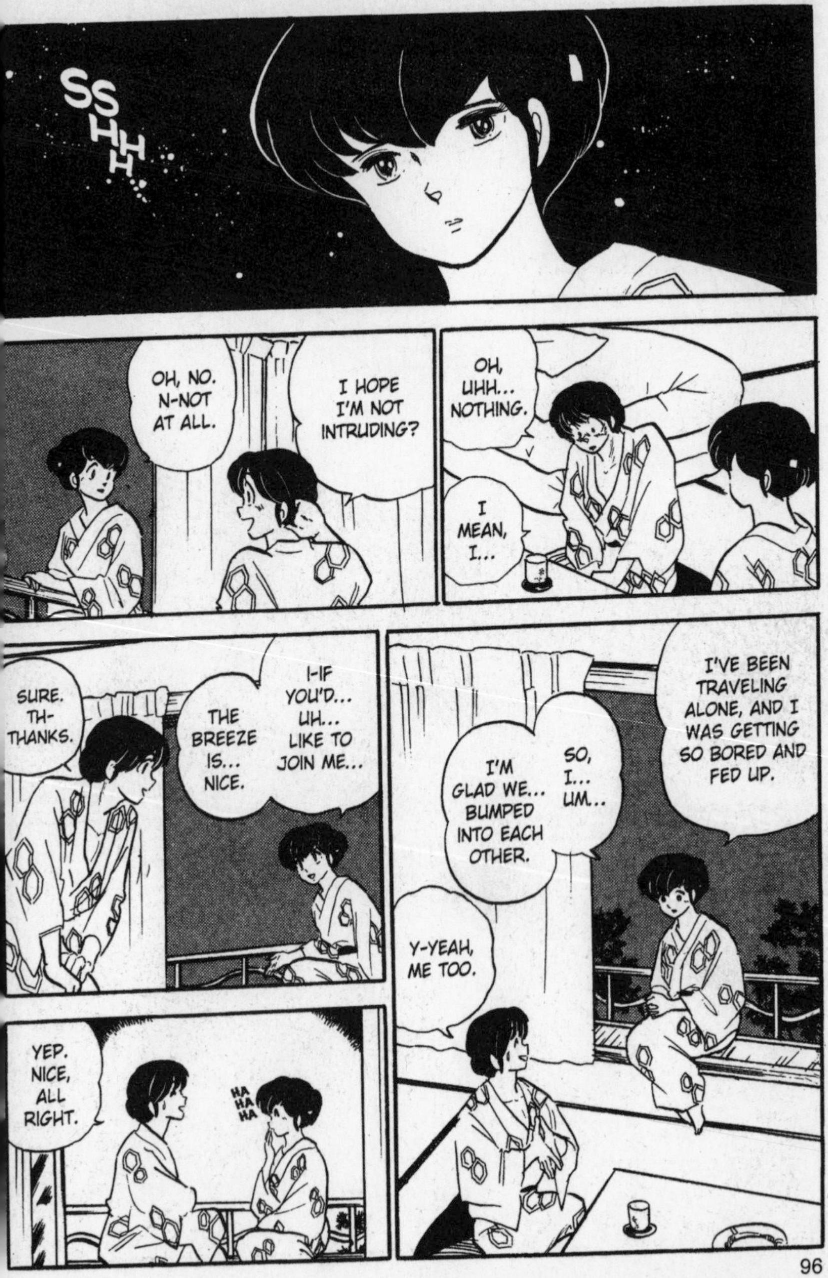
SSHHH
OH, UHH... NOTHING.
I MEAN, I...
I HOPE I'M NOT INTRUDING?
OH, NO. N-NOT AT ALL.
I'VE BEEN TRAVELING ALONE, AND I WAS GETTING SO BORED AND FED UP.
SO, I... UM...
I'M GLAD WE... BUMPED INTO EACH OTHER.
Y-YEAH, ME TOO.
I-IF YOU'D... UH... LIKE TO JOIN ME...
THE BREEZE IS... NICE.
SURE. TH-THANKS.
HA HA HA
YEP. NICE, ALL RIGHT.

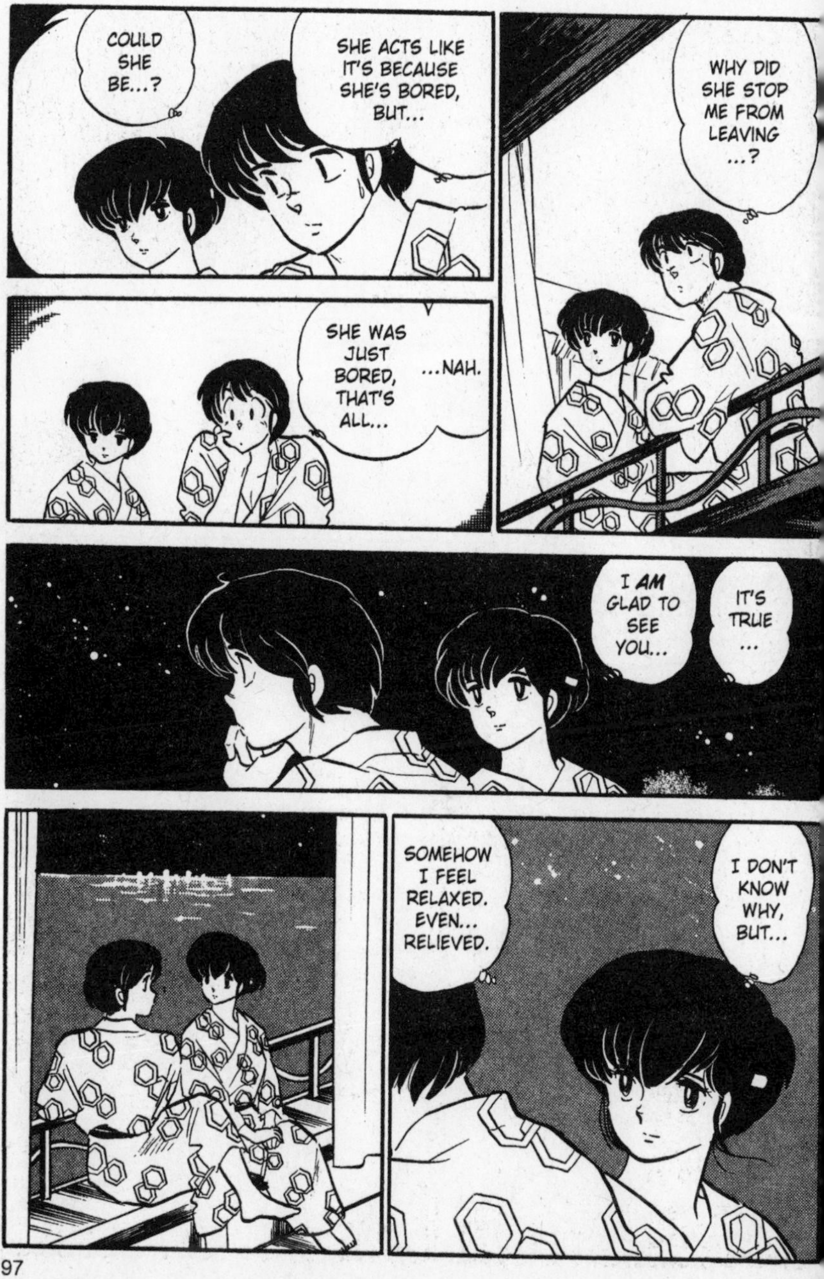
WHY DID SHE STOP ME FROM LEAVING ...?
SHE ACTS LIKE IT'S BECAUSE SHE'S BORED, BUT...
COULD SHE BE...?
...NAH.
SHE WAS JUST BORED, THAT'S ALL...
IT'S TRUE ...
I *AM* GLAD TO SEE YOU...
I DON'T KNOW WHY, BUT...
SOMEHOW I FEEL RELAXED. EVEN... RELIEVED.

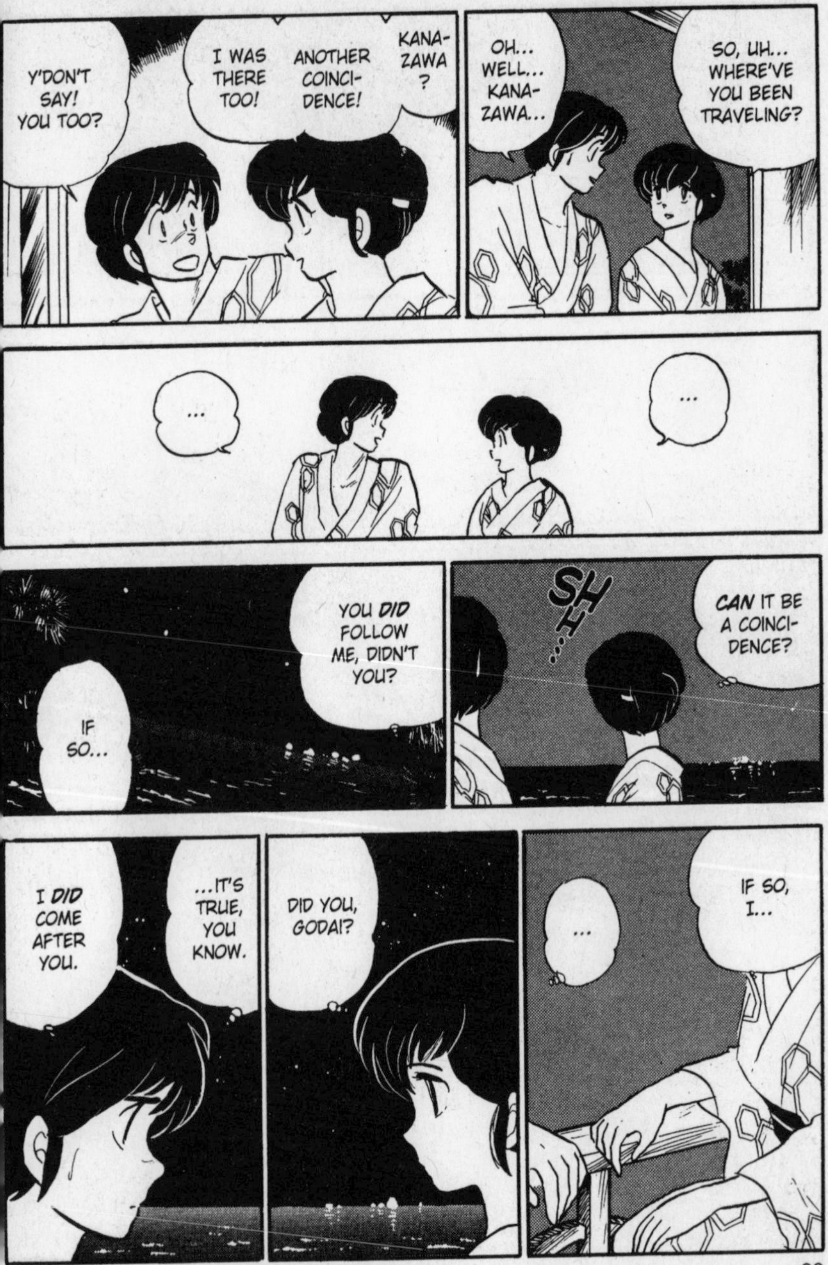
SO, UH... WHERE'VE YOU BEEN TRAVELING?
OH... WELL... KANA-ZAWA...
KANA-ZAWA?
ANOTHER COINCI-DENCE!
I WAS THERE TOO!
Y'DON'T SAY! YOU TOO?
...
...
CAN IT BE A COINCI-DENCE?
SHH...
YOU DID FOLLOW ME, DIDN'T YOU?
IF SO...
IF SO, I...
...
DID YOU, GODAI?
...IT'S TRUE, YOU KNOW.
I DID COME AFTER YOU.

OH, GODAI... DON'T APOLOGIZE...

I-I-I'M SORRY.

OH...

99

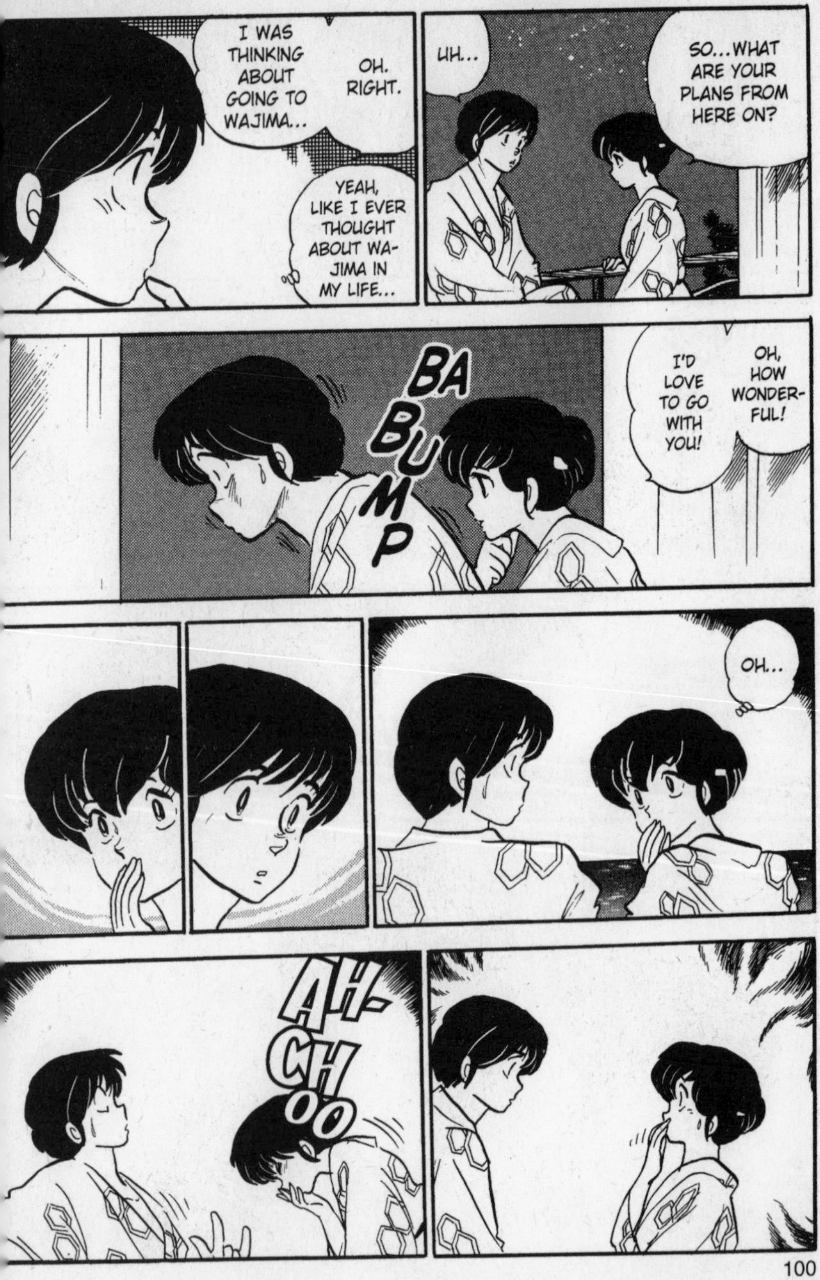
SO...WHAT ARE YOUR PLANS FROM HERE ON?
UH...
I WAS THINKING ABOUT GOING TO WAJIMA...
OH. RIGHT.
YEAH, LIKE I EVER THOUGHT ABOUT WA-JIMA IN MY LIFE...
OH, HOW WONDER-FUL!
I'D LOVE TO GO WITH YOU!
BA BUMP
OH...
AH-CHOO

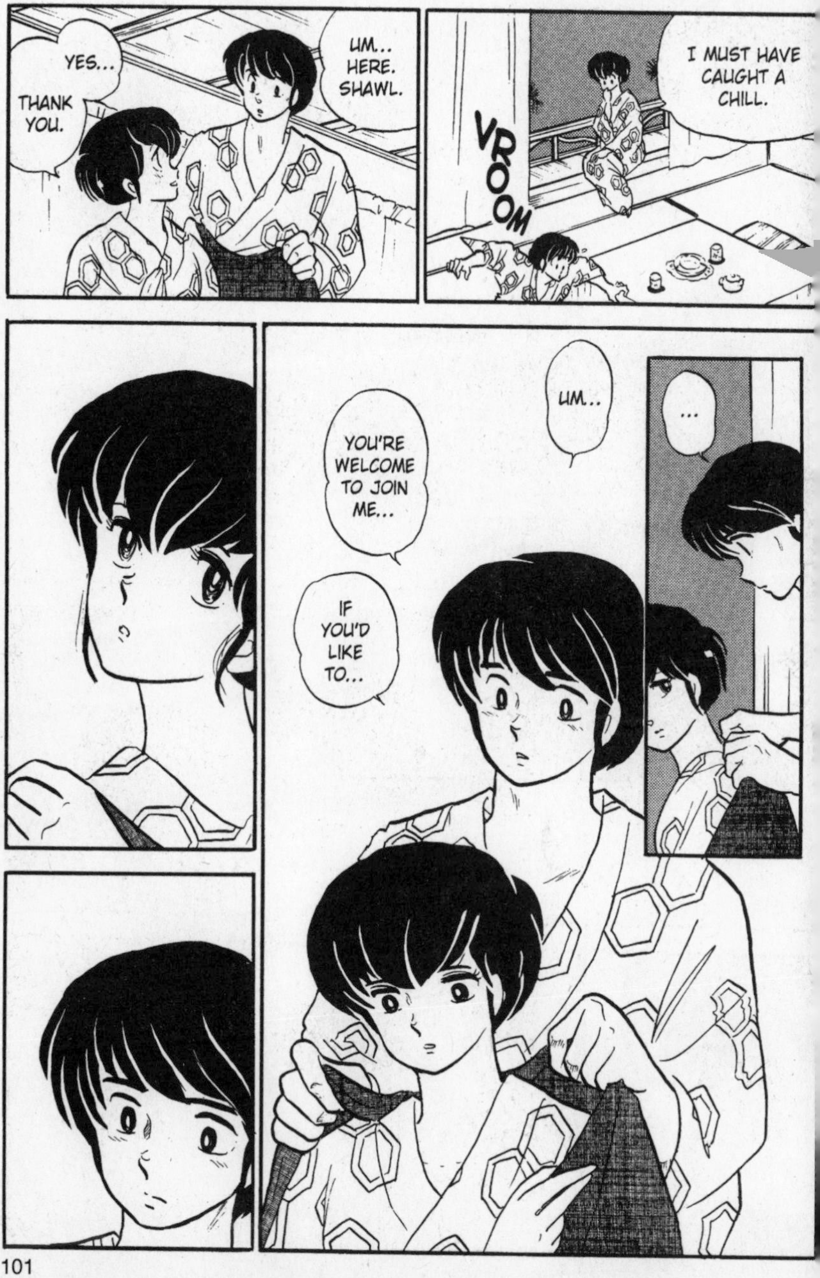
I MUST HAVE CAUGHT A CHILL.
VROOM
UM... HERE. SHAWL.
YES... THANK YOU.
...
UM...
YOU'RE WELCOME TO JOIN ME...
IF YOU'D LIKE TO...

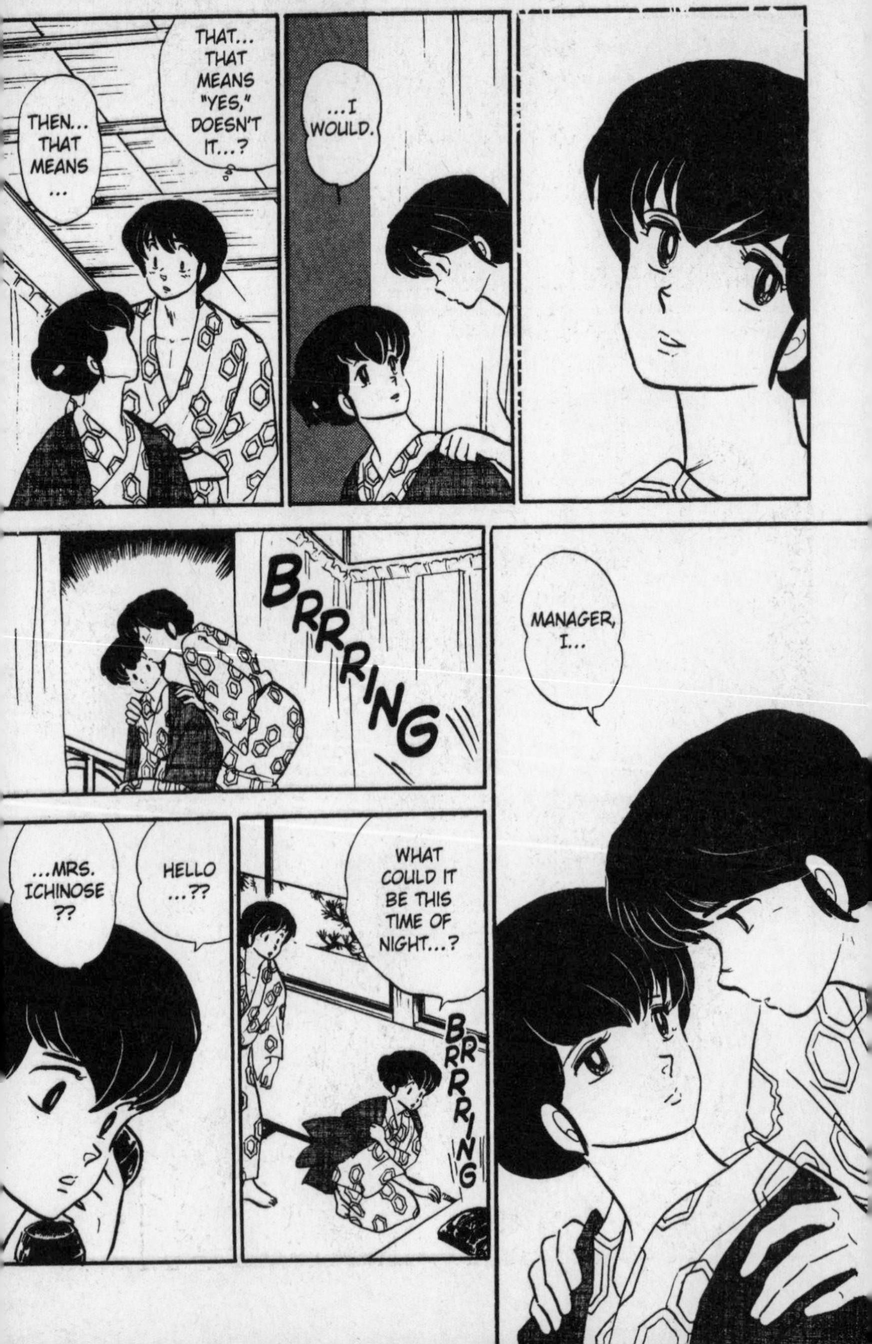
...I WOULD.
THAT... THAT MEANS "YES," DOESN'T IT...?
THEN... THAT MEANS ...
MANAGER, I...
BRRRING
WHAT COULD IT BE THIS TIME OF NIGHT...?
BRRRRING
HELLO ...??
...MRS. ICHINOSE ??

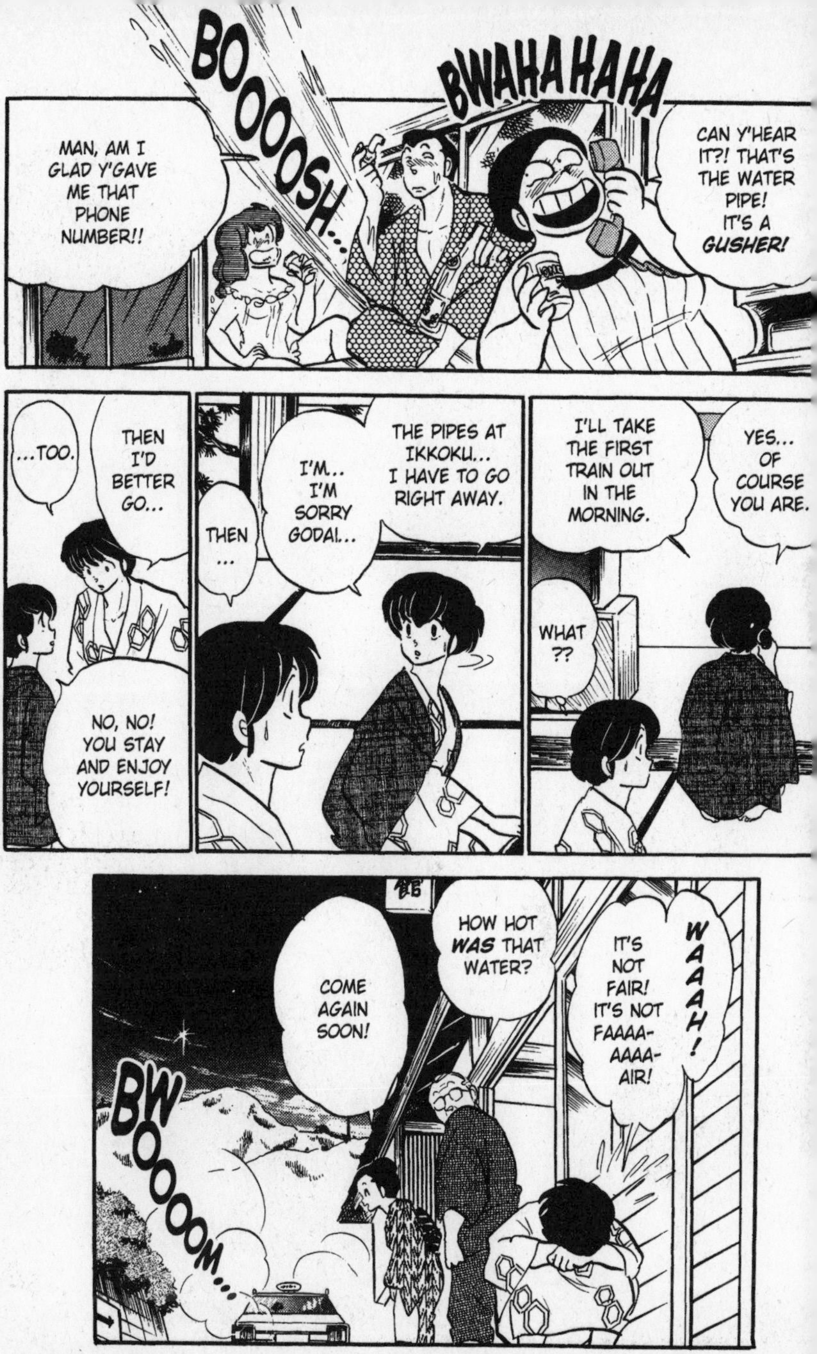
BWAHAHAHA
BOOOOSH...
CAN Y'HEAR IT?! THAT'S THE WATER PIPE! IT'S A *GUSHER!*
MAN, AM I GLAD Y'GAVE ME THAT PHONE NUMBER!!
YES... OF COURSE YOU ARE.
I'LL TAKE THE FIRST TRAIN OUT IN THE MORNING.
WHAT ??
THE PIPES AT IKKOKU... I HAVE TO GO RIGHT AWAY.
I'M.. I'M SORRY GODAI...
THEN ...
THEN I'D BETTER GO...
...TOO.
NO, NO! YOU STAY AND ENJOY YOURSELF!
WAAAH!
IT'S NOT FAIR! IT'S NOT FAAAA-AAAA-AIR!
HOW HOT *WAS* THAT WATER?
COME AGAIN SOON!
BWBOOOOOM...

PART SIX

BACK TO...SCHOOL?

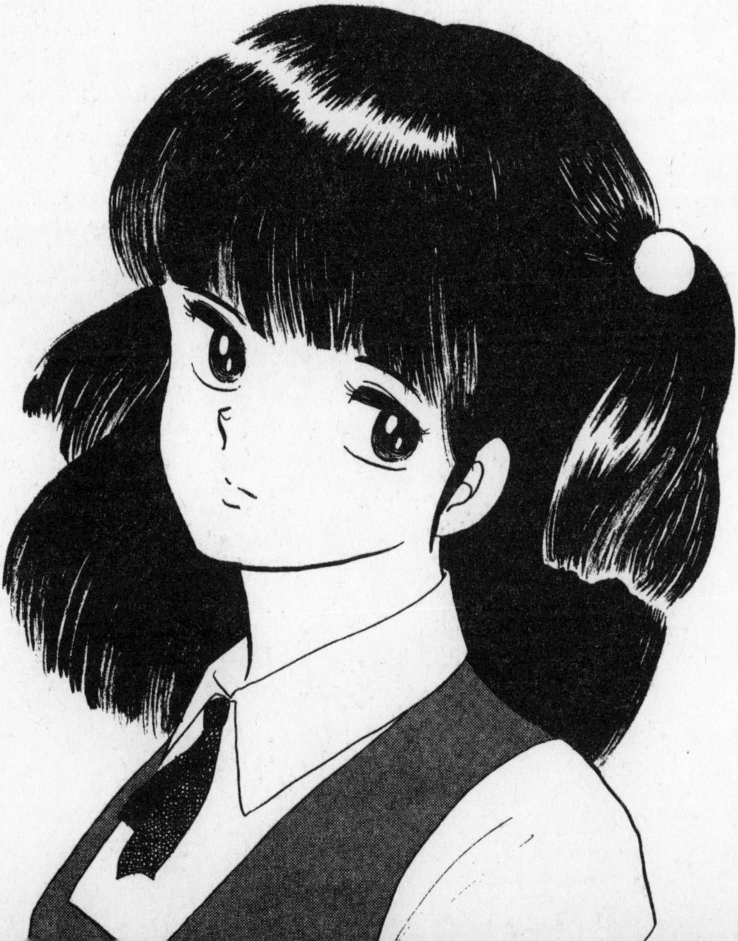

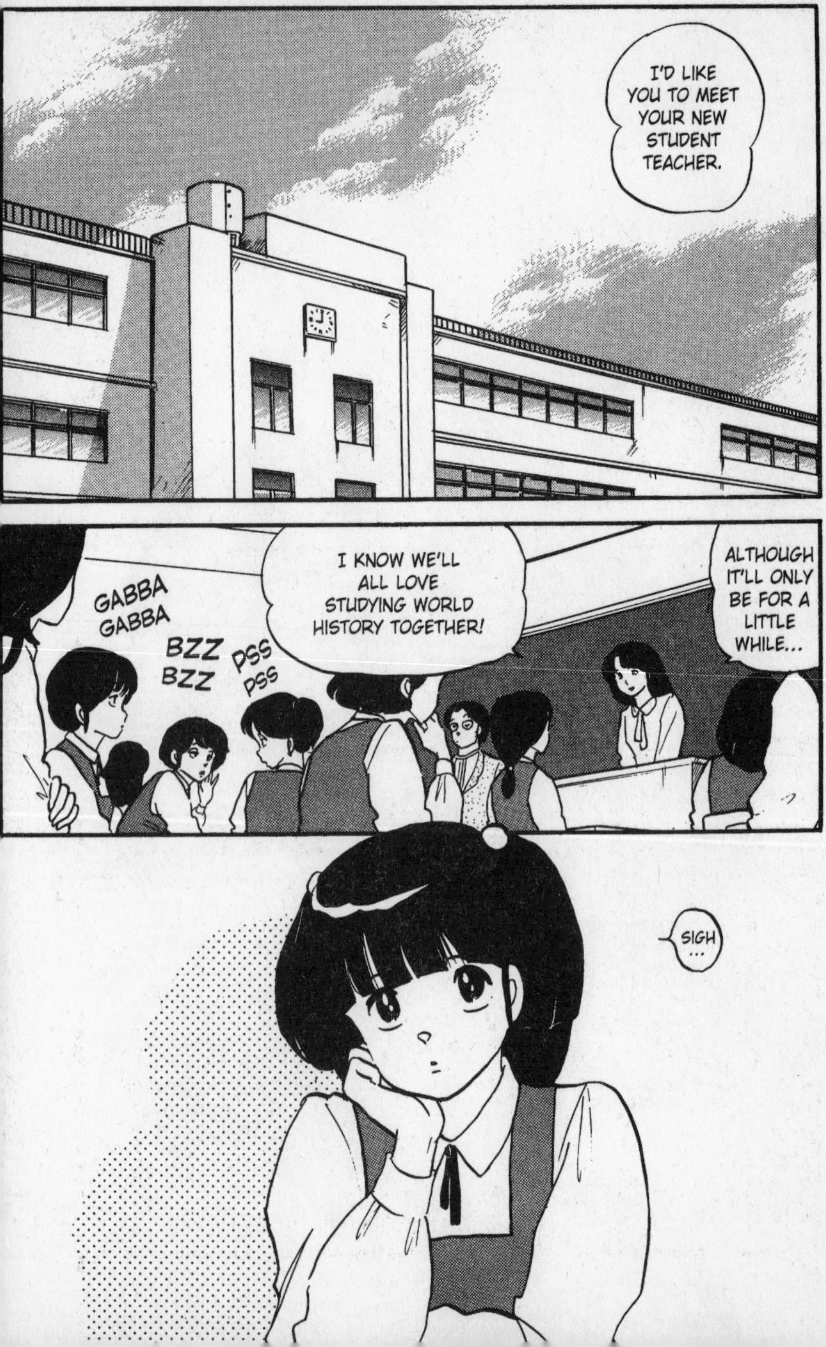
I'D LIKE YOU TO MEET YOUR NEW STUDENT TEACHER.
ALTHOUGH IT'LL ONLY BE FOR A LITTLE WHILE...
I KNOW WE'LL ALL LOVE STUDYING WORLD HISTORY TOGETHER!
PSS PSS
BZZ BZZ
GABBA GABBA
SIGH...

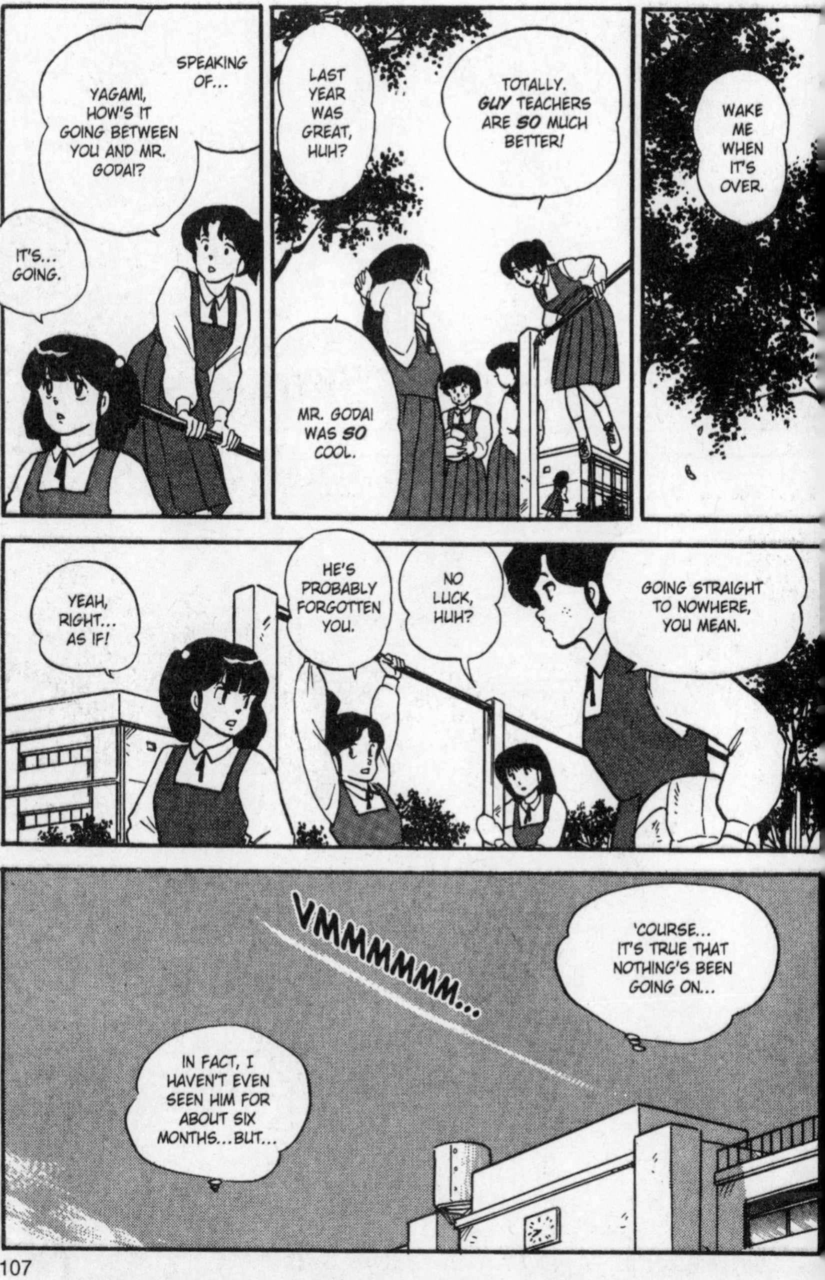
WAKE ME WHEN IT'S OVER.
TOTALLY. GUY TEACHERS ARE SO MUCH BETTER!
LAST YEAR WAS GREAT, HUH?
MR. GODAI WAS SO COOL.
SPEAKING OF...
YAGAMI, HOW'S IT GOING BETWEEN YOU AND MR. GODAI?
IT'S... GOING.
GOING STRAIGHT TO NOWHERE, YOU MEAN.
NO LUCK, HUH?
HE'S PROBABLY FORGOTTEN YOU.
YEAH, RIGHT... AS IF!
'COURSE... IT'S TRUE THAT NOTHING'S BEEN GOING ON...
VMMMMMMM...
IN FACT, I HAVEN'T EVEN SEEN HIM FOR ABOUT SIX MONTHS...BUT...

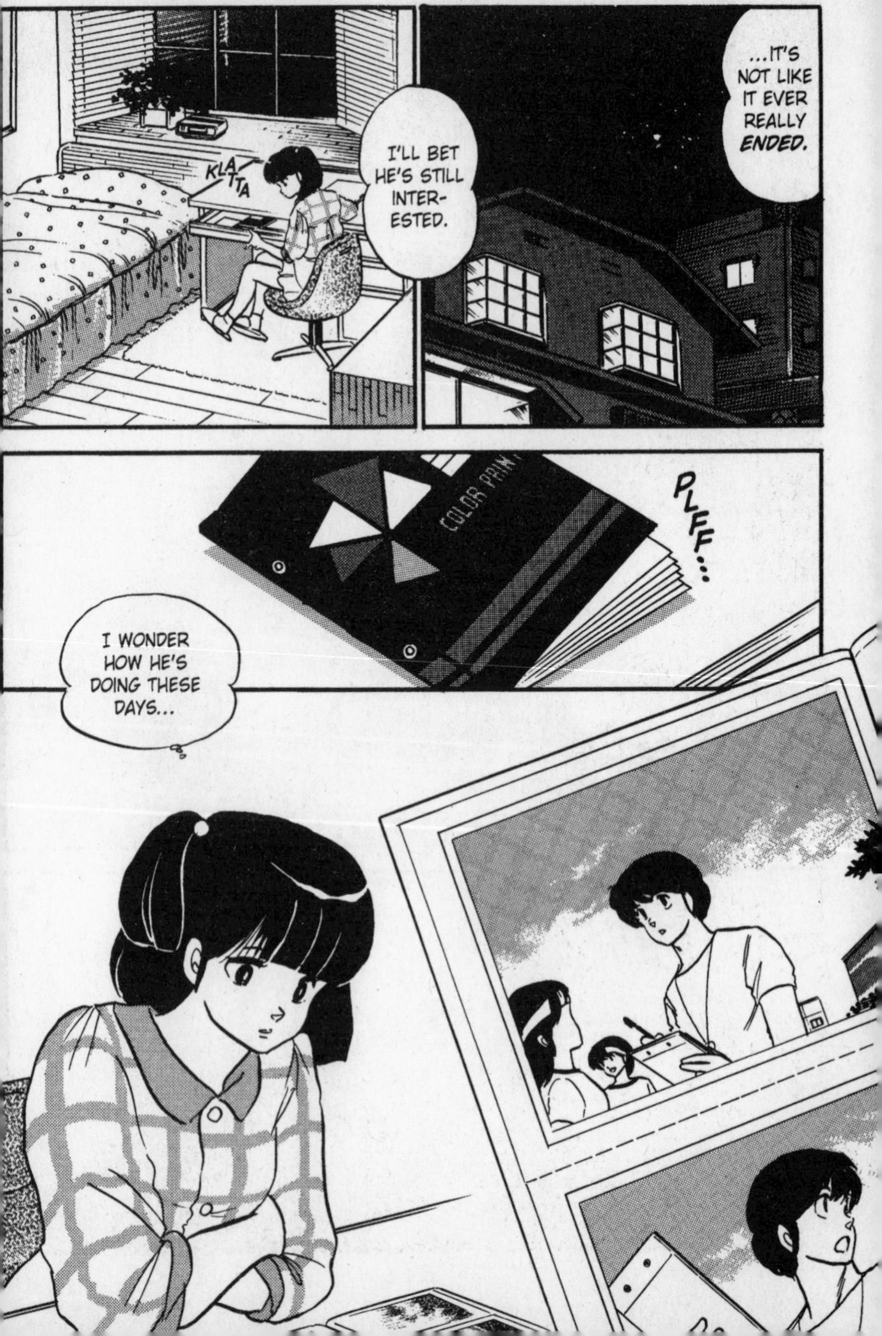
...IT'S NOT LIKE IT EVER REALLY ENDED.
I'LL BET HE'S STILL INTER-ESTED.
KLATTA
PLFF...
I WONDER HOW HE'S DOING THESE DAYS...

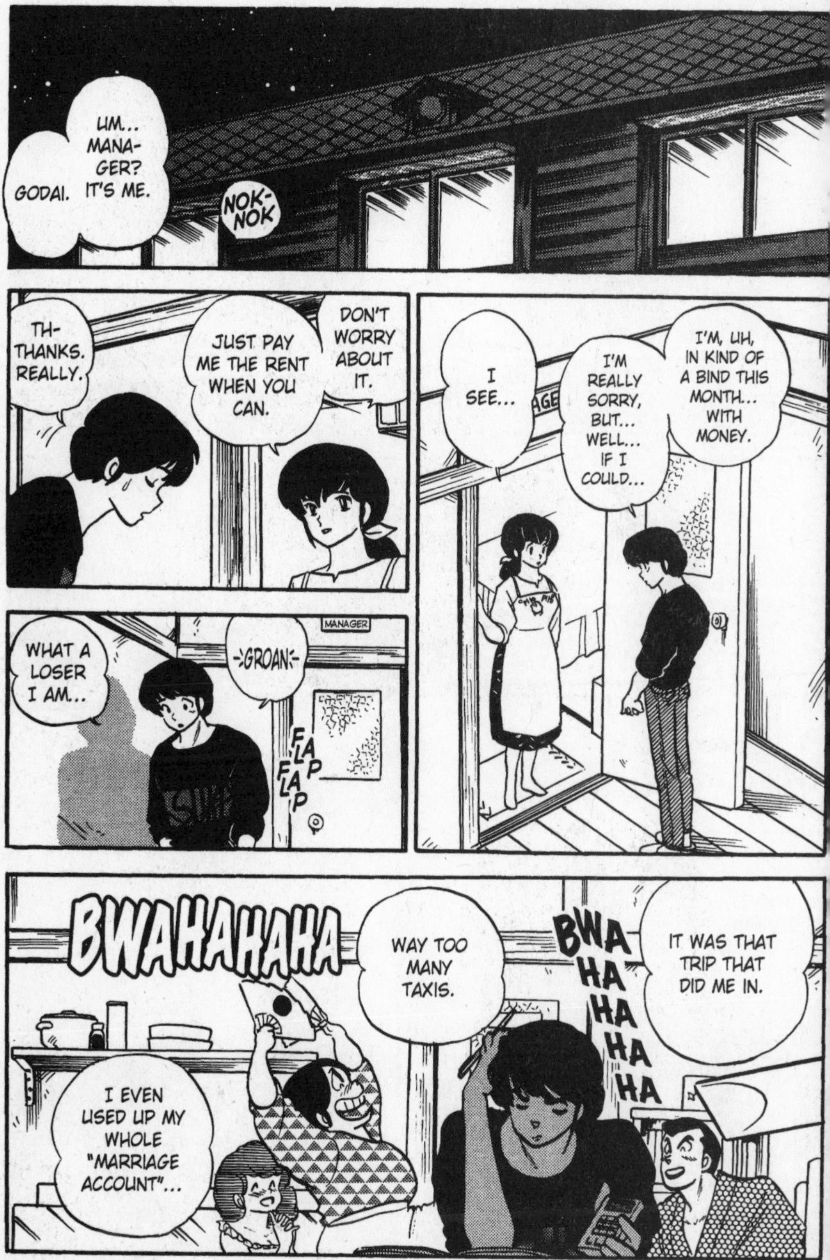

NOK-NOK
UM... MANA-GER? IT'S ME.
GODAI.
I'M, UH, IN KIND OF A BIND THIS MONTH... WITH MONEY.
I'M REALLY SORRY, BUT... WELL... IF I COULD...
I SEE...
MANAGER
DON'T WORRY ABOUT IT.
JUST PAY ME THE RENT WHEN YOU CAN.
TH-THANKS. REALLY.
MANAGER
-GROAN-
WHAT A LOSER I AM...
FLAP FLAP
IT WAS THAT TRIP THAT DID ME IN.
BWAHAHAHAHA
WAY TOO MANY TAXIS.
BWAHAHAHA
I EVEN USED UP MY WHOLE "MARRIAGE ACCOUNT"...

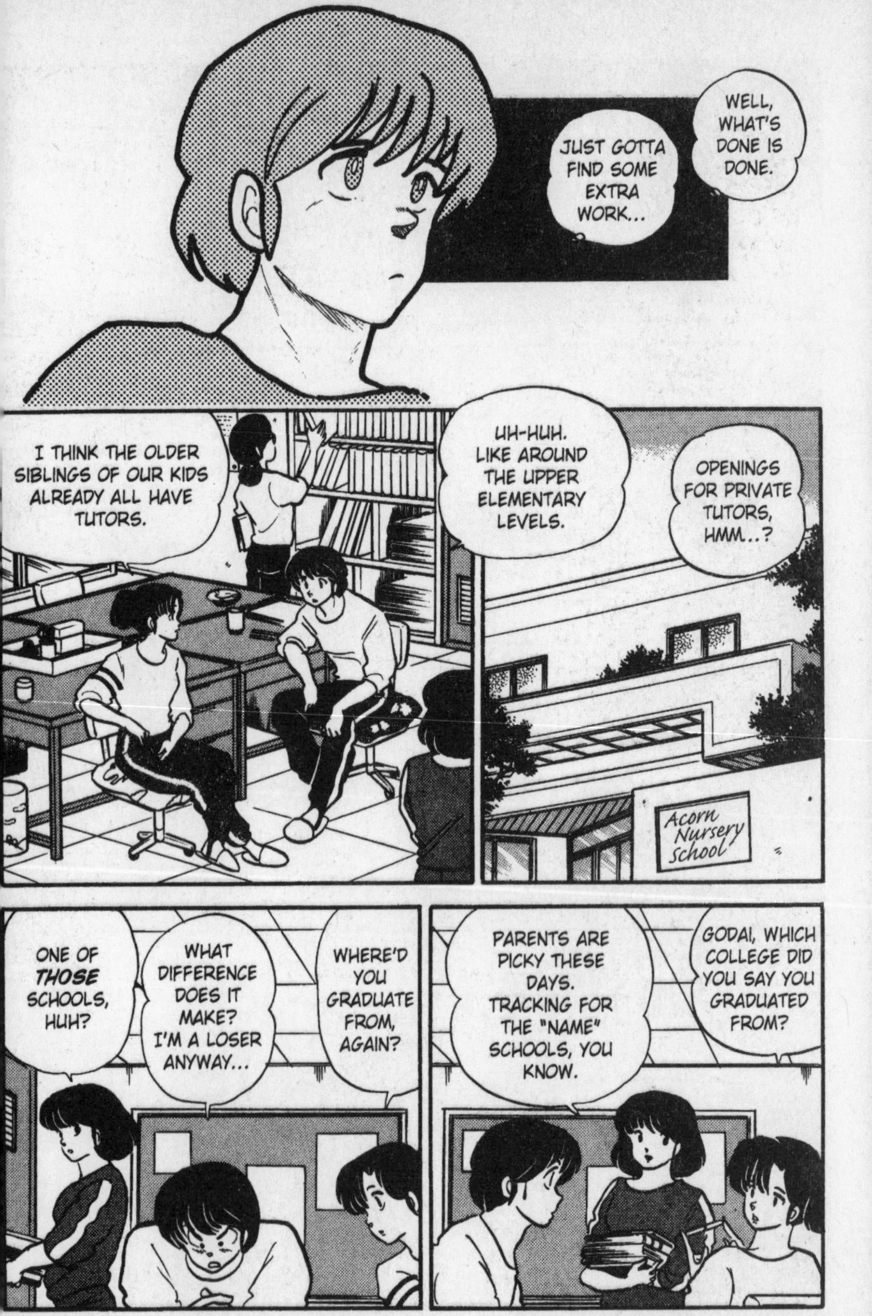
WELL, WHAT'S DONE IS DONE.
JUST GOTTA FIND SOME EXTRA WORK...
OPENINGS FOR PRIVATE TUTORS, HMM..?
Acorn Nursery School
UH-HUH. LIKE AROUND THE UPPER ELEMENTARY LEVELS.
I THINK THE OLDER SIBLINGS OF OUR KIDS ALREADY ALL HAVE TUTORS.
GODAI, WHICH COLLEGE DID YOU SAY YOU GRADUATED FROM?
PARENTS ARE PICKY THESE DAYS. TRACKING FOR THE "NAME" SCHOOLS, YOU KNOW.
WHERE'D YOU GRADUATE FROM, AGAIN?
WHAT DIFFERENCE DOES IT MAKE? I'M A LOSER ANYWAY...
ONE OF *THOSE* SCHOOLS, HUH?

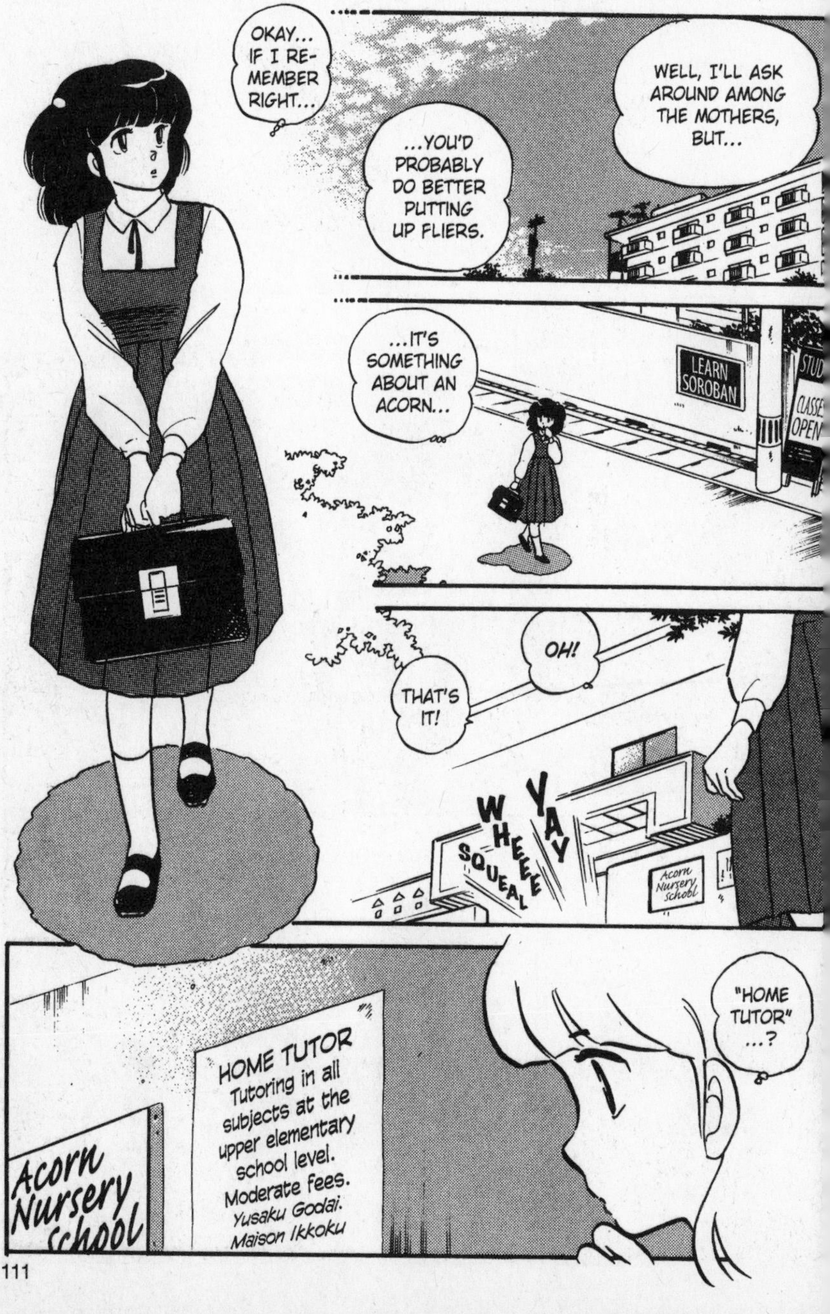
WELL, I'LL ASK AROUND AMONG THE MOTHERS, BUT...
...YOU'D PROBABLY DO BETTER PUTTING UP FLIERS.
LEARN SOROBAN
STUD
CLASSES OPEN
...IT'S SOMETHING ABOUT AN ACORN...
OH!
THAT'S IT!
YAY
WHEEEE
SQUEAL
Acorn Nursery School
OKAY... IF I RE-MEMBER RIGHT...
"HOME TUTOR" ...?
HOME TUTOR
Tutoring in all subjects at the upper elementary school level.
Moderate fees.
Yusaku Godai.
Maison Ikkoku
Acorn Nursery School

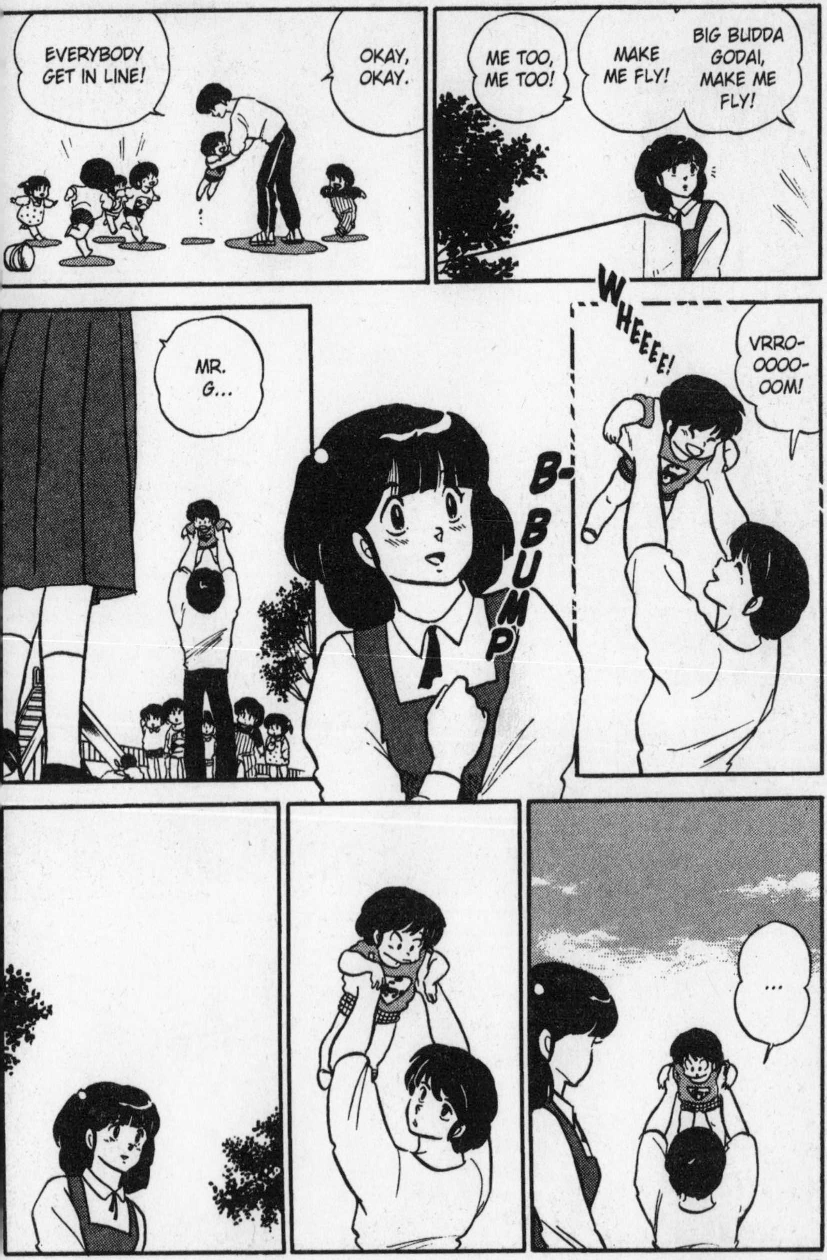
BIG BUDDA GODAI, MAKE ME FLY!
MAKE ME FLY!
ME TOO, ME TOO!
OKAY, OKAY.
EVERYBODY GET IN LINE!
WHEEEEE!
VRRO-OOOO-OOM!
B-BUMP
MR. G...
...

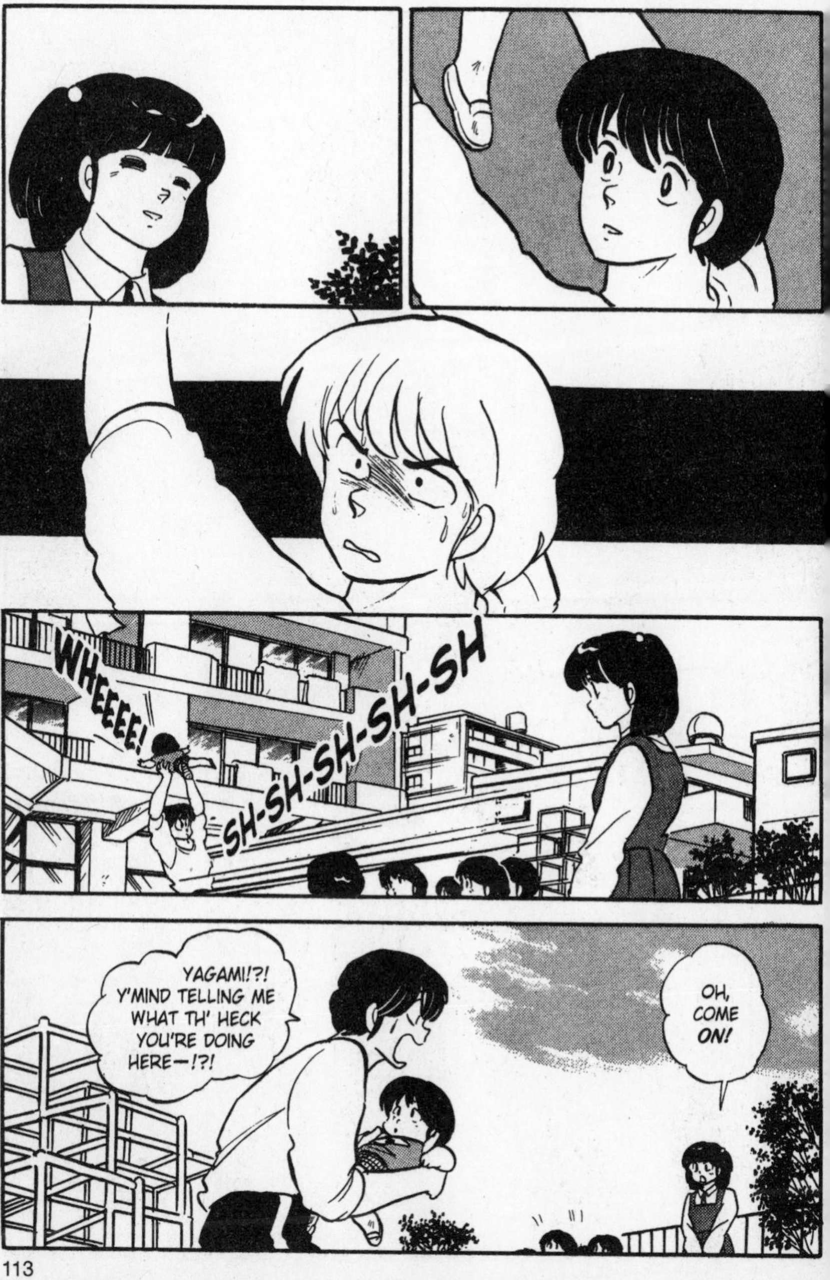
SH-SH-SH-SH-SH
WHEEEEE!
OH, COME ON!
YAGAMI!?! Y'MIND TELLING ME WHAT TH' HECK YOU'RE DOING HERE—!?!

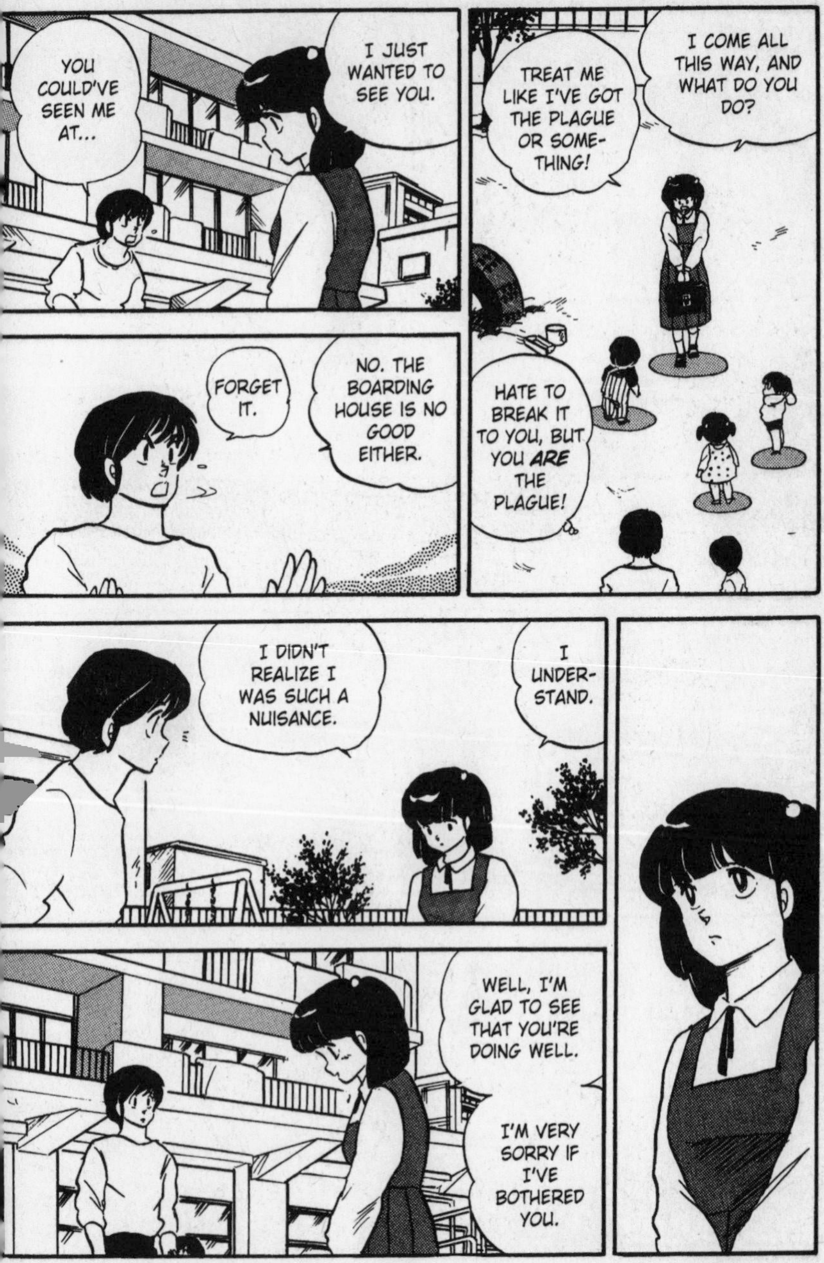
I COME ALL THIS WAY, AND WHAT DO YOU DO?
TREAT ME LIKE I'VE GOT THE PLAGUE OR SOMETHING!
HATE TO BREAK IT TO YOU, BUT YOU ARE THE PLAGUE!
I JUST WANTED TO SEE YOU.
YOU COULD'VE SEEN ME AT...
NO. THE BOARDING HOUSE IS NO GOOD EITHER.
FORGET IT.
I UNDERSTAND.
I DIDN'T REALIZE I WAS SUCH A NUISANCE.
WELL, I'M GLAD TO SEE THAT YOU'RE DOING WELL.
I'M VERY SORRY IF I'VE BOTHERED YOU.

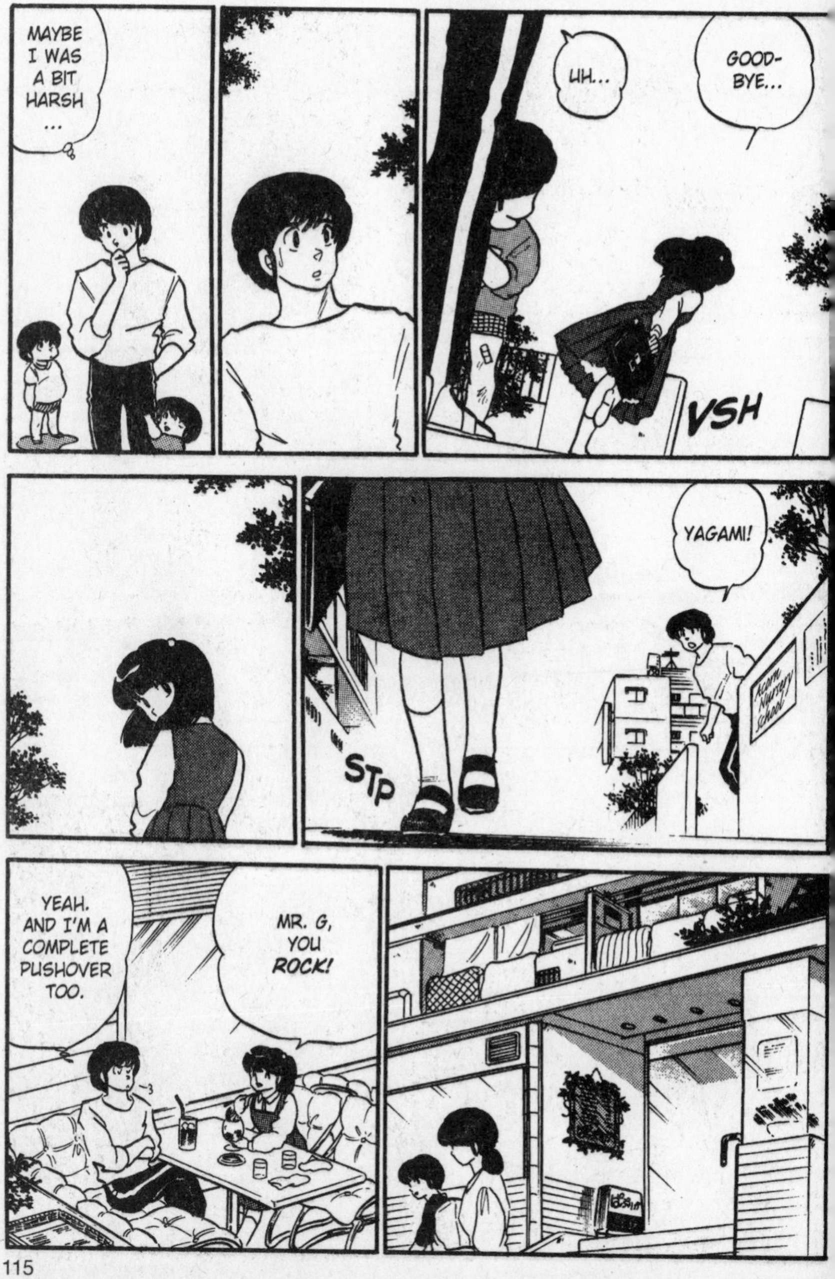
GOOD-BYE...
UH...
VSH
MAYBE I WAS A BIT HARSH ...
YAGAMI!
Acorn Nursery School
STP
MR. G, YOU ROCK!
YEAH. AND I'M A COMPLETE PUSHOVER TOO.

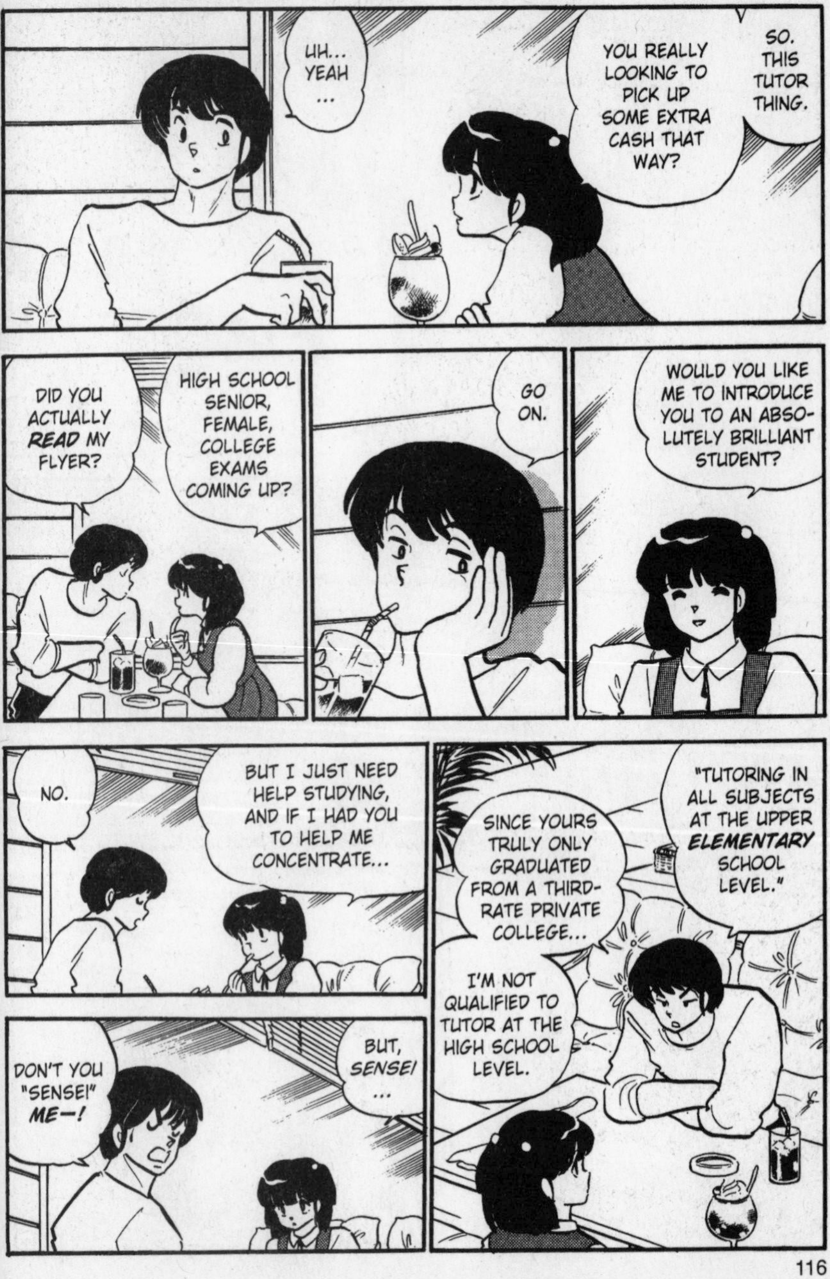
SO. THIS TUTOR THING.
YOU REALLY LOOKING TO PICK UP SOME EXTRA CASH THAT WAY?
UH... YEAH ...
WOULD YOU LIKE ME TO INTRODUCE YOU TO AN ABSO-LUTELY BRILLIANT STUDENT?
GO ON.
HIGH SCHOOL SENIOR, FEMALE, COLLEGE EXAMS COMING UP?
DID YOU ACTUALLY *READ* MY FLYER?
"TUTORING IN ALL SUBJECTS AT THE UPPER *ELEMENTARY* SCHOOL LEVEL."
SINCE YOURS TRULY ONLY GRADUATED FROM A THIRD-RATE PRIVATE COLLEGE...
I'M NOT QUALIFIED TO TUTOR AT THE HIGH SCHOOL LEVEL.
BUT I JUST NEED HELP STUDYING, AND IF I HAD YOU TO HELP ME CONCENTRATE...
NO.
BUT, *SENSEI* ...
DON'T YOU "SENSEI!" *ME—!*

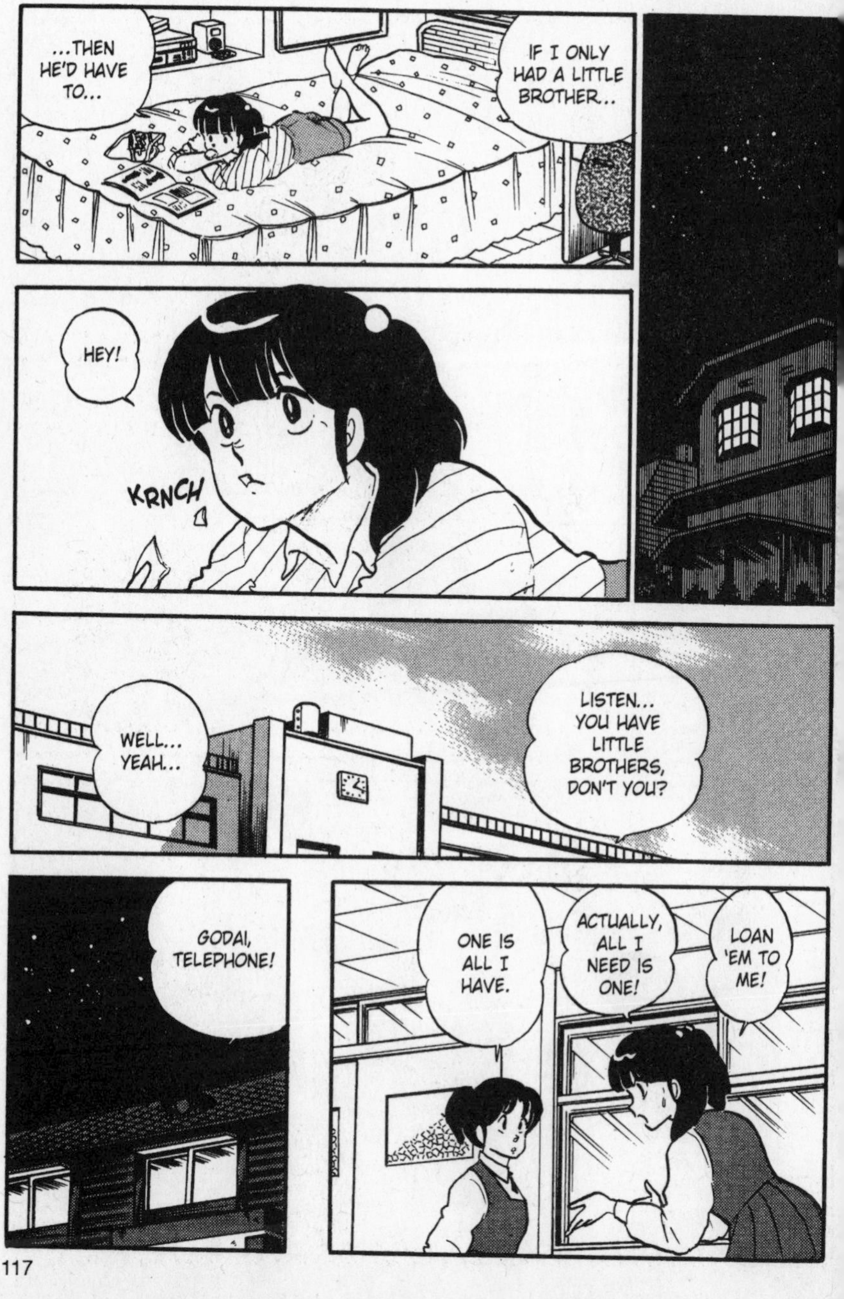
IF I ONLY HAD A LITTLE BROTHER...
...THEN HE'D HAVE TO...
HEY!
KRNCH
LISTEN... YOU HAVE LITTLE BROTHERS, DON'T YOU?
WELL... YEAH...
LOAN 'EM TO ME!
ACTUALLY, ALL I NEED IS ONE!
ONE IS ALL I HAVE.
GODAI, TELEPHONE!

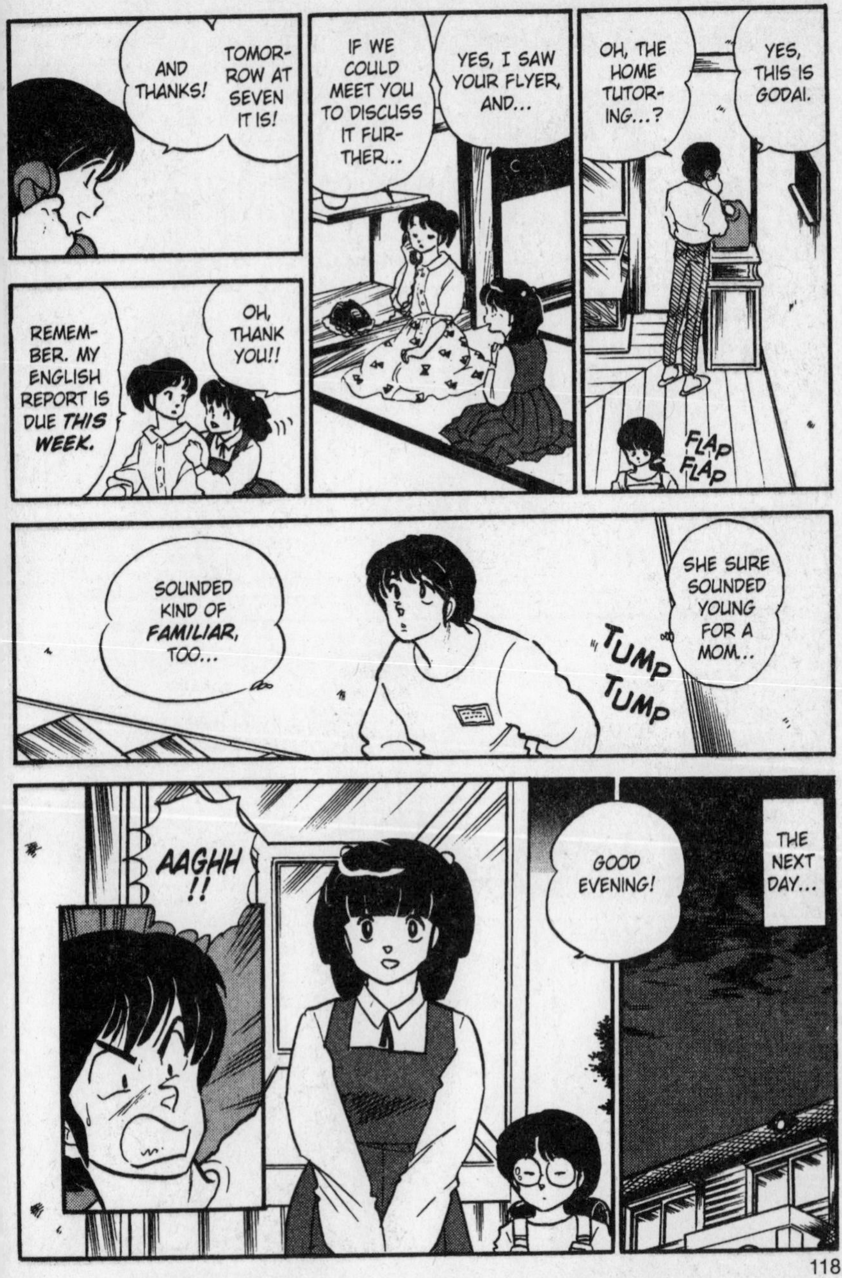
YES, THIS IS GODAI.
OH, THE HOME TUTOR-ING...?
FLAP FLAP
YES, I SAW YOUR FLYER, AND...
IF WE COULD MEET YOU TO DISCUSS IT FUR-THER...
TOMOR-ROW AT SEVEN IT IS!
AND THANKS!
OH, THANK YOU!!
REMEM-BER. MY ENGLISH REPORT IS DUE THIS WEEK.
SHE SURE SOUNDED YOUNG FOR A MOM..
TUMP TUMP
SOUNDED KIND OF FAMILIAR, TOO...
THE NEXT DAY...
GOOD EVENING!
AAGHH!!

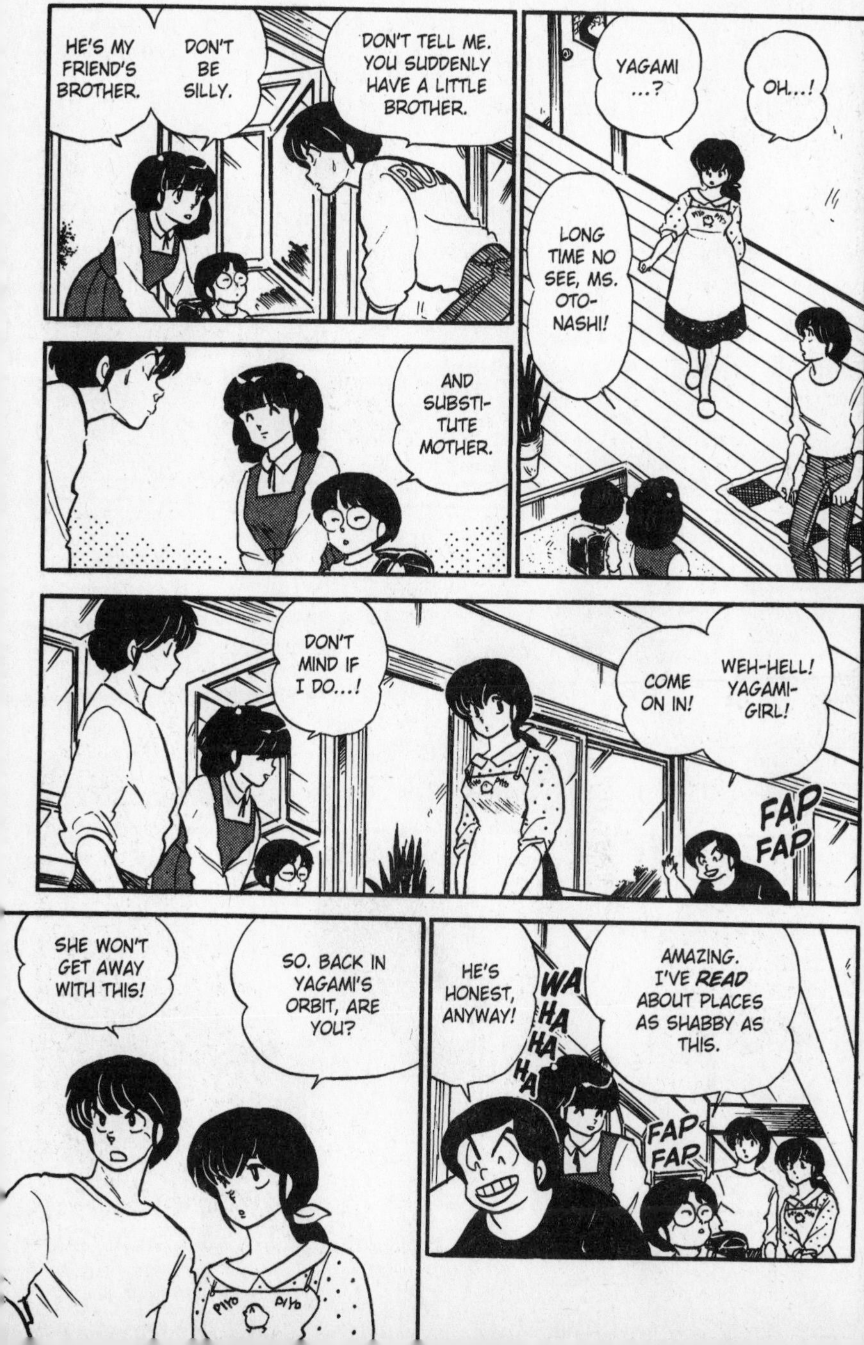
OH...!
YAGAMI ...?
LONG TIME NO SEE, MS. OTO-NASHI!
DON'T TELL ME. YOU SUDDENLY HAVE A LITTLE BROTHER.
DON'T BE SILLY.
HE'S MY FRIEND'S BROTHER.
AND SUBSTI-TUTE MOTHER.
WEH-HELL! YAGAMI-GIRL!
COME ON IN!
FAP FAP
DON'T MIND IF I DO...!
AMAZING. I'VE *READ* ABOUT PLACES AS SHABBY AS THIS.
WA HA HA HA
HE'S HONEST, ANYWAY!
FAP FAP
SO. BACK IN YAGAMI'S ORBIT, ARE YOU?
SHE WON'T GET AWAY WITH THIS!

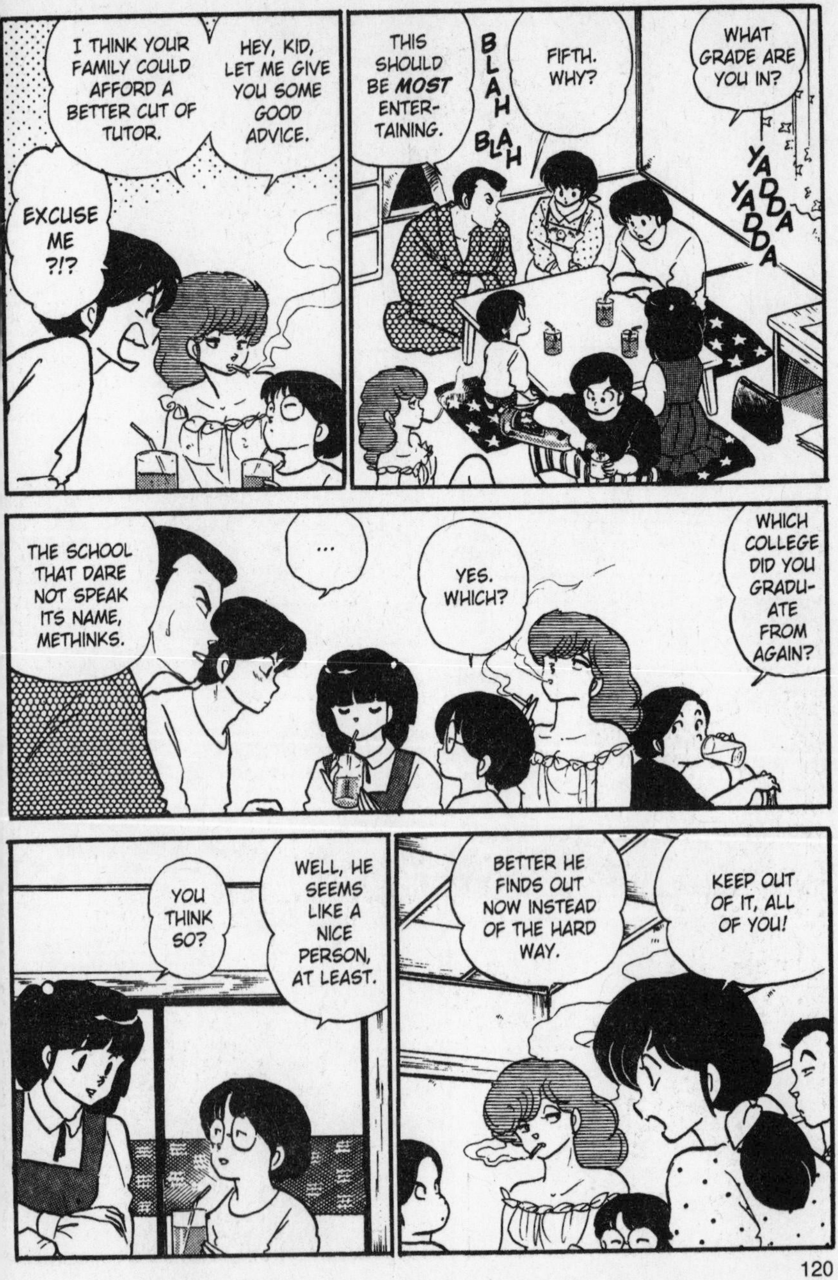
WHAT GRADE ARE YOU IN?
YADDA YADDA
FIFTH. WHY?
BLAH BLAH
THIS SHOULD BE *MOST* ENTERTAINING.
HEY, KID, LET ME GIVE YOU SOME GOOD ADVICE.
I THINK YOUR FAMILY COULD AFFORD A BETTER CUT OF TUTOR.
EXCUSE ME ?!?
WHICH COLLEGE DID YOU GRADUATE FROM AGAIN?
YES. WHICH?
...
THE SCHOOL THAT DARE NOT SPEAK ITS NAME, METHINKS.
KEEP OUT OF IT, ALL OF YOU!
BETTER HE FINDS OUT NOW INSTEAD OF THE HARD WAY.
WELL, HE SEEMS LIKE A NICE PERSON, AT LEAST.
YOU THINK SO?

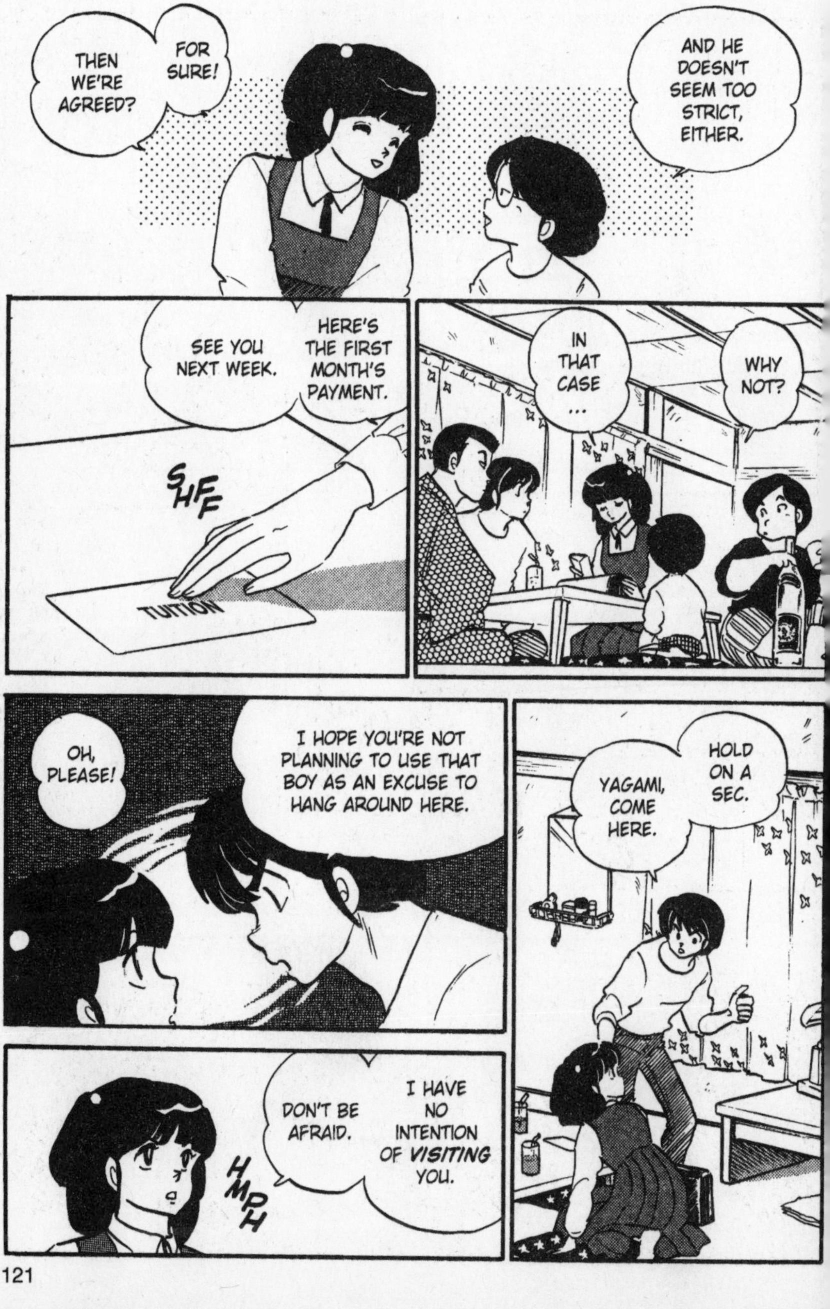
AND HE DOESN'T SEEM TOO STRICT, EITHER.
FOR SURE!
THEN WE'RE AGREED?
WHY NOT?
IN THAT CASE ...
HERE'S THE FIRST MONTH'S PAYMENT.
SEE YOU NEXT WEEK.
SHFF
TUITION
HOLD ON A SEC.
YAGAMI, COME HERE.
I HOPE YOU'RE NOT PLANNING TO USE THAT BOY AS AN EXCUSE TO HANG AROUND HERE.
OH, PLEASE!
I HAVE NO INTENTION OF *VISITING* YOU.
DON'T BE AFRAID.
HMPH

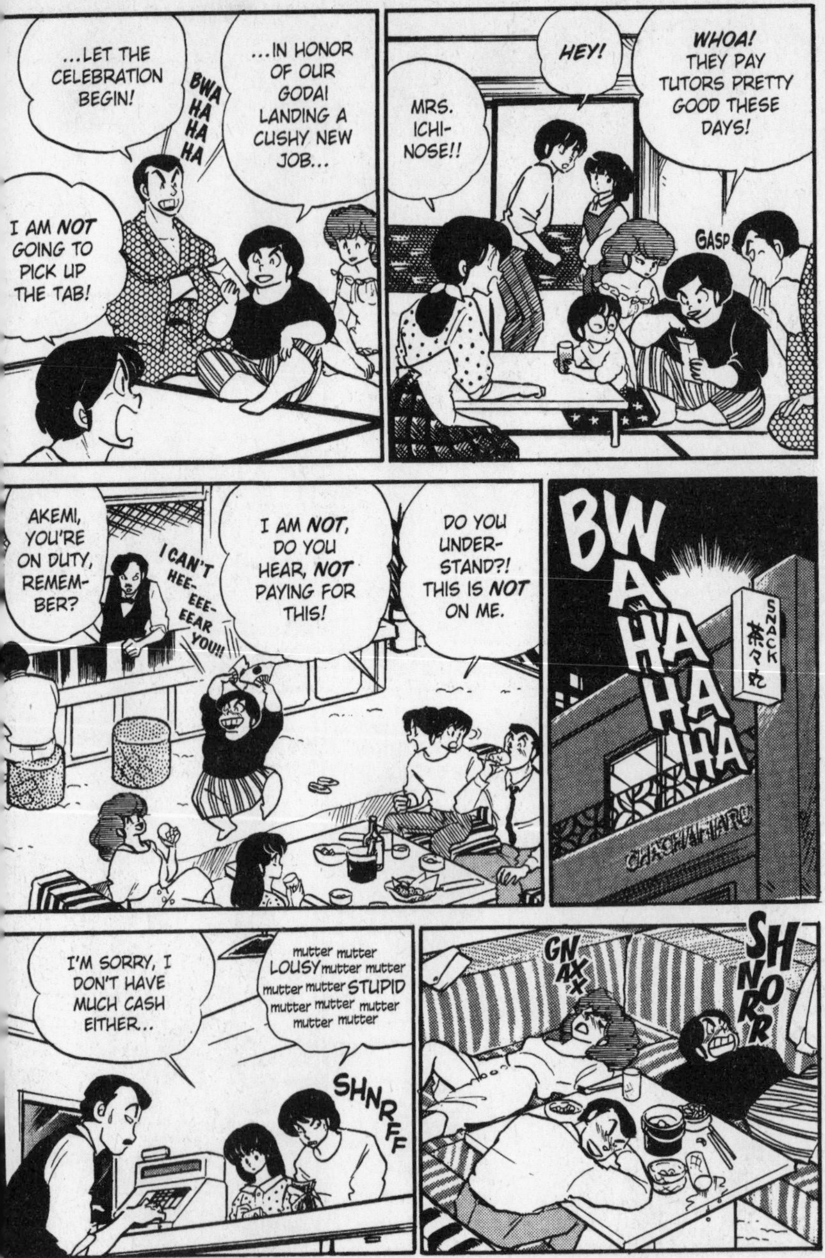
WHOA! THEY PAY TUTORS PRETTY GOOD THESE DAYS!
GASP
HEY!
MRS. ICHI-NOSE!!
...IN HONOR OF OUR GODAI LANDING A CUSHY NEW JOB...
BWA HA HA HA
...LET THE CELEBRATION BEGIN!
I AM NOT GOING TO PICK UP THE TAB!
BWAHAHAHAHA
SNACK
茶々丸
CHACHAMARU
DO YOU UNDERSTAND?! THIS IS NOT ON ME.
I AM NOT, DO YOU HEAR, NOT PAYING FOR THIS!
I CAN'T HEE-EEE-EEAR YOU!!
AKEMI, YOU'RE ON DUTY, REMEMBER?
SHNORR
GNAXX
mutter mutter LOUSY mutter mutter mutter mutter STUPID mutter mutter mutter mutter mutter
I'M SORRY, I DON'T HAVE MUCH CASH EITHER...
SHNRFF

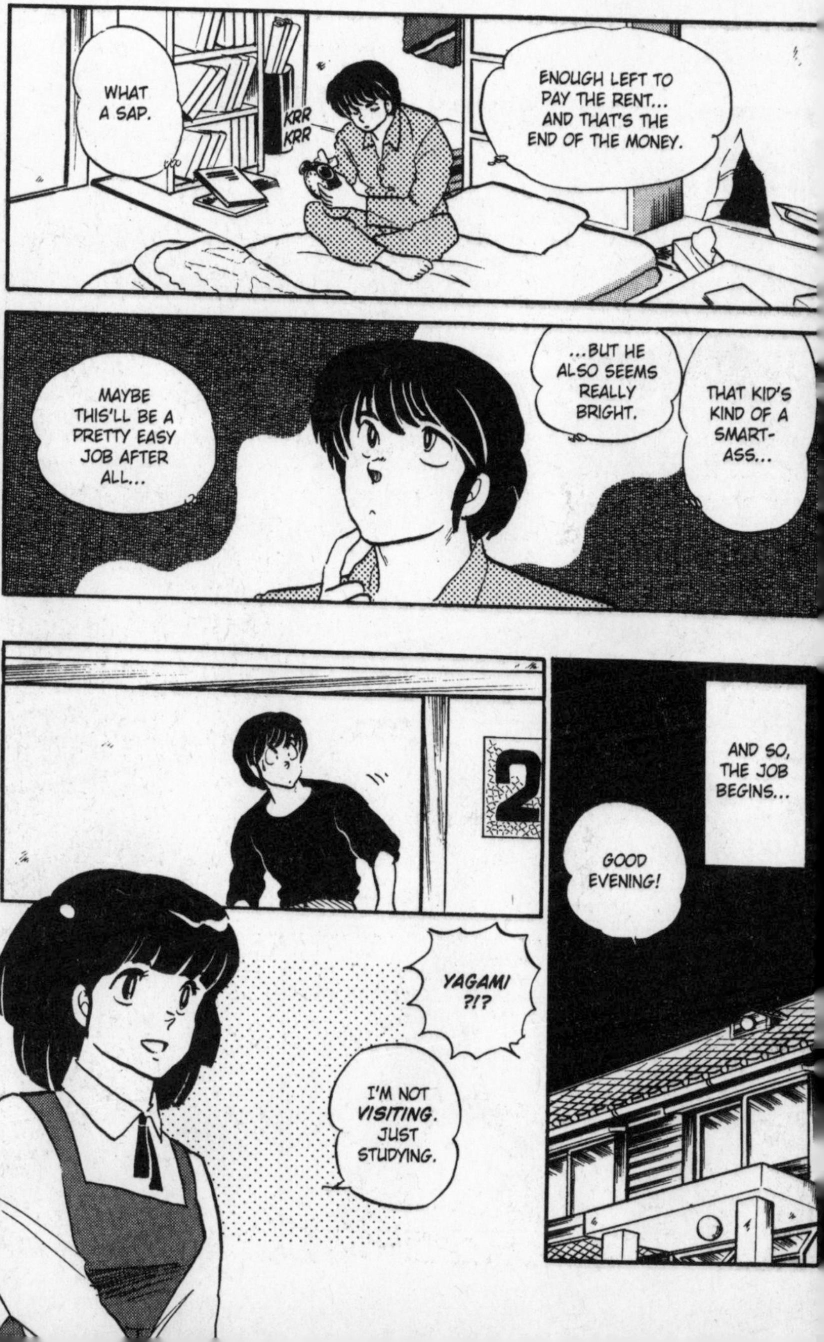
ENOUGH LEFT TO PAY THE RENT... AND THAT'S THE END OF THE MONEY.
KRR KRR
WHAT A SAP.
THAT KID'S KIND OF A SMART-ASS...
...BUT HE ALSO SEEMS REALLY BRIGHT.
MAYBE THIS'LL BE A PRETTY EASY JOB AFTER ALL...
AND SO, THE JOB BEGINS...
GOOD EVENING!
YAGAMI ?!?
I'M NOT *VISITING*. JUST STUDYING.

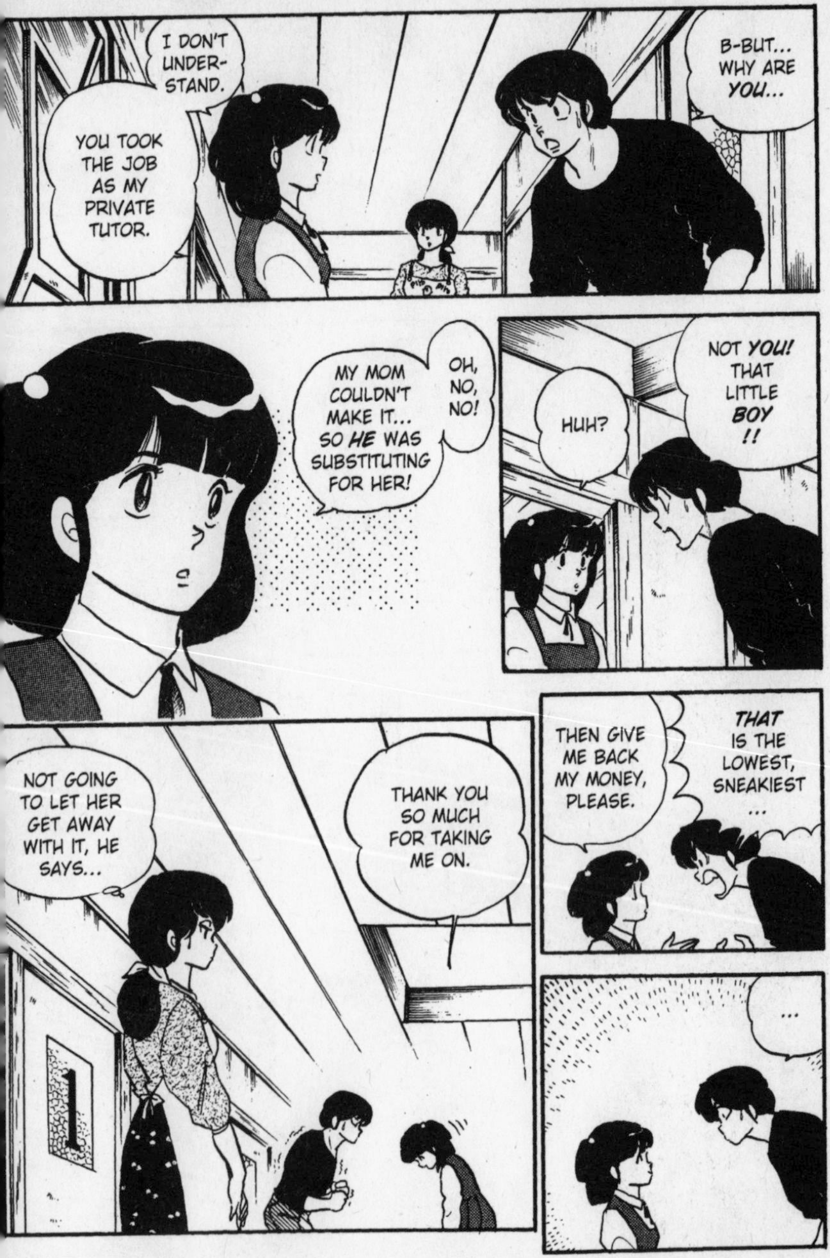
B-BUT... WHY ARE YOU...
I DON'T UNDER-STAND.
YOU TOOK THE JOB AS MY PRIVATE TUTOR.
NOT YOU! THAT LITTLE BOY !!
HUH?
OH, NO, NO!
MY MOM COULDN'T MAKE IT... SO HE WAS SUBSTITUTING FOR HER!
THAT IS THE LOWEST, SNEAKIEST ...
THEN GIVE ME BACK MY MONEY, PLEASE.
...
THANK YOU SO MUCH FOR TAKING ME ON.
NOT GOING TO LET HER GET AWAY WITH IT, HE SAYS...

PART SEVEN

HOMEWORK

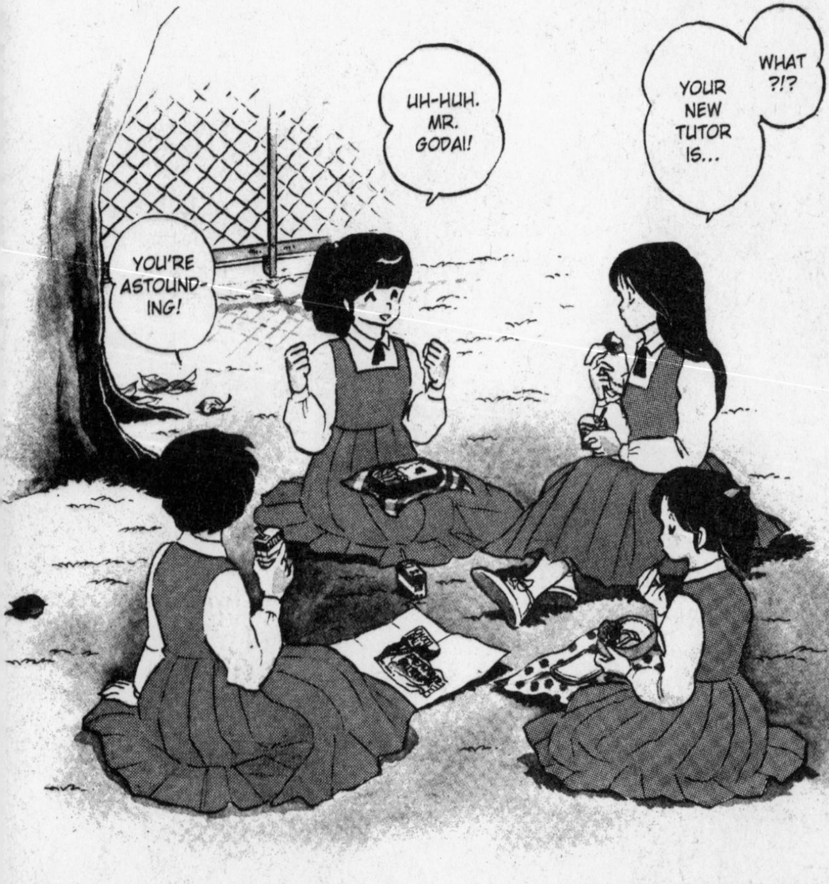
WHAT ?!?
YOUR NEW TUTOR IS...
UH-HUH. MR. GODAI!
YOU'RE ASTOUND-ING!

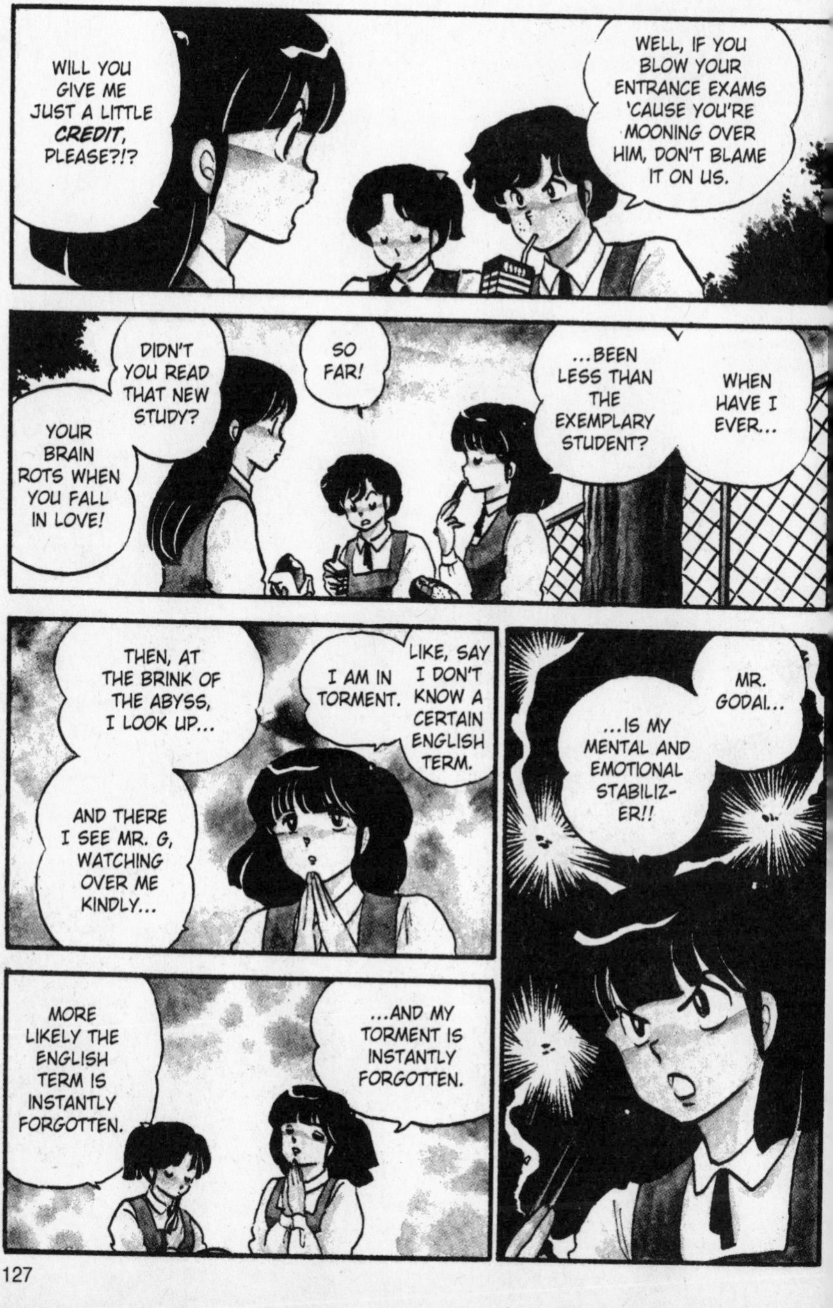
WELL, IF YOU BLOW YOUR ENTRANCE EXAMS 'CAUSE YOU'RE MOONING OVER HIM, DON'T BLAME IT ON US.
WILL YOU GIVE ME JUST A LITTLE *CREDIT*, PLEASE?!?
WHEN HAVE I EVER...
...BEEN LESS THAN THE EXEMPLARY STUDENT?
SO FAR!
DIDN'T YOU READ THAT NEW STUDY?
YOUR BRAIN ROTS WHEN YOU FALL IN LOVE!
MR. GODAI...
...IS MY MENTAL AND EMOTIONAL STABILIZ-ER!!
LIKE, SAY I DON'T KNOW A CERTAIN ENGLISH TERM.
I AM IN TORMENT.
THEN, AT THE BRINK OF THE ABYSS, I LOOK UP...
AND THERE I SEE MR. G, WATCHING OVER ME KINDLY...
...AND MY TORMENT IS INSTANTLY FORGOTTEN.
MORE LIKELY THE ENGLISH TERM IS INSTANTLY FORGOTTEN.

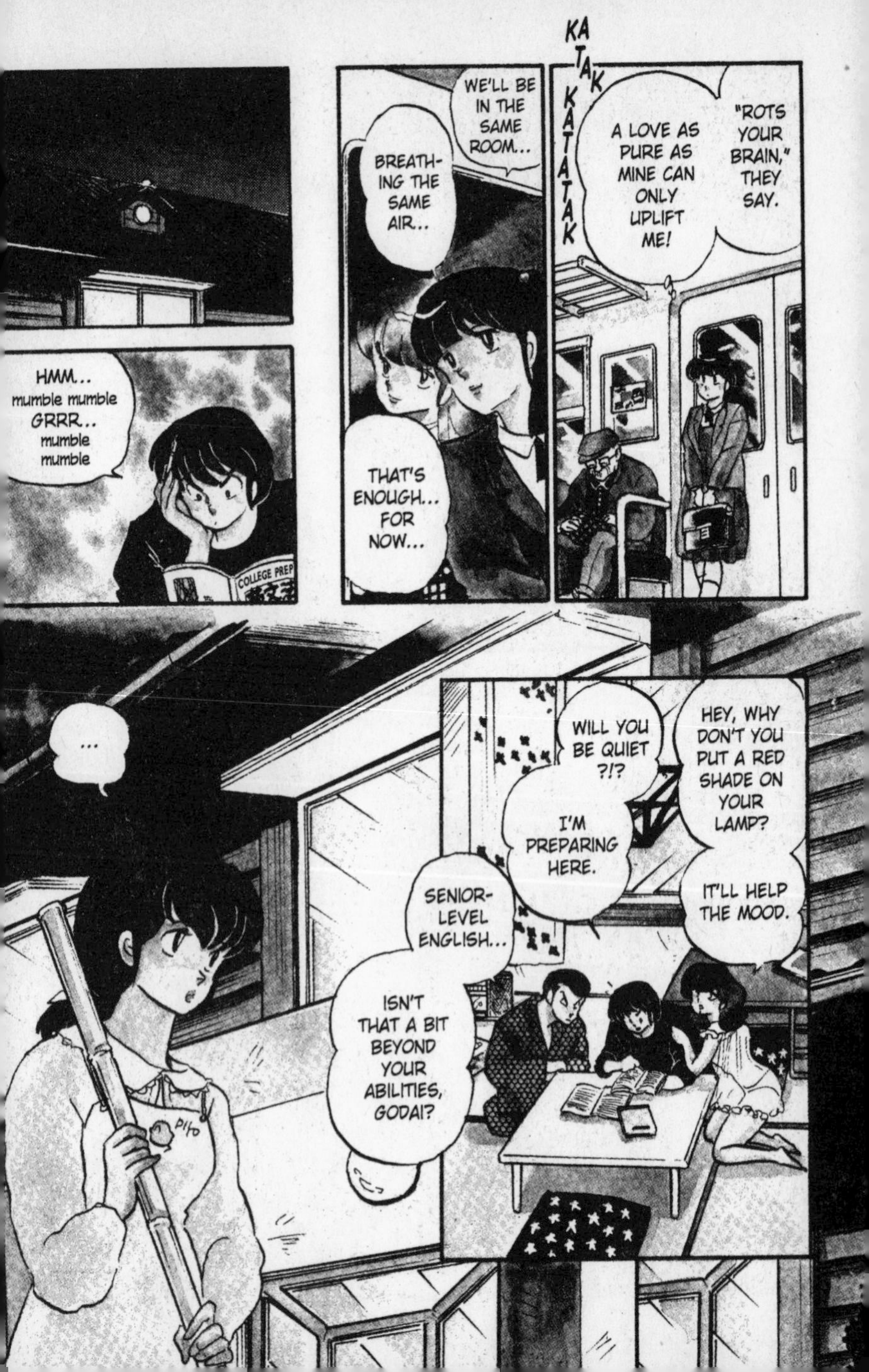
KATAK
KATATATAK
"ROTS YOUR BRAIN," THEY SAY.
A LOVE AS PURE AS MINE CAN ONLY UPLIFT ME!
WE'LL BE IN THE SAME ROOM...
BREATHING THE SAME AIR...
THAT'S ENOUGH... FOR NOW...
HMM... mumble mumble GRRR... mumble mumble
COLLEGE PREP
HEY, WHY DON'T YOU PUT A RED SHADE ON YOUR LAMP?
IT'LL HELP THE MOOD.
WILL YOU BE QUIET ?!?
I'M PREPARING HERE.
SENIOR-LEVEL ENGLISH...
ISN'T THAT A BIT BEYOND YOUR ABILITIES, GODAI?
...
piko

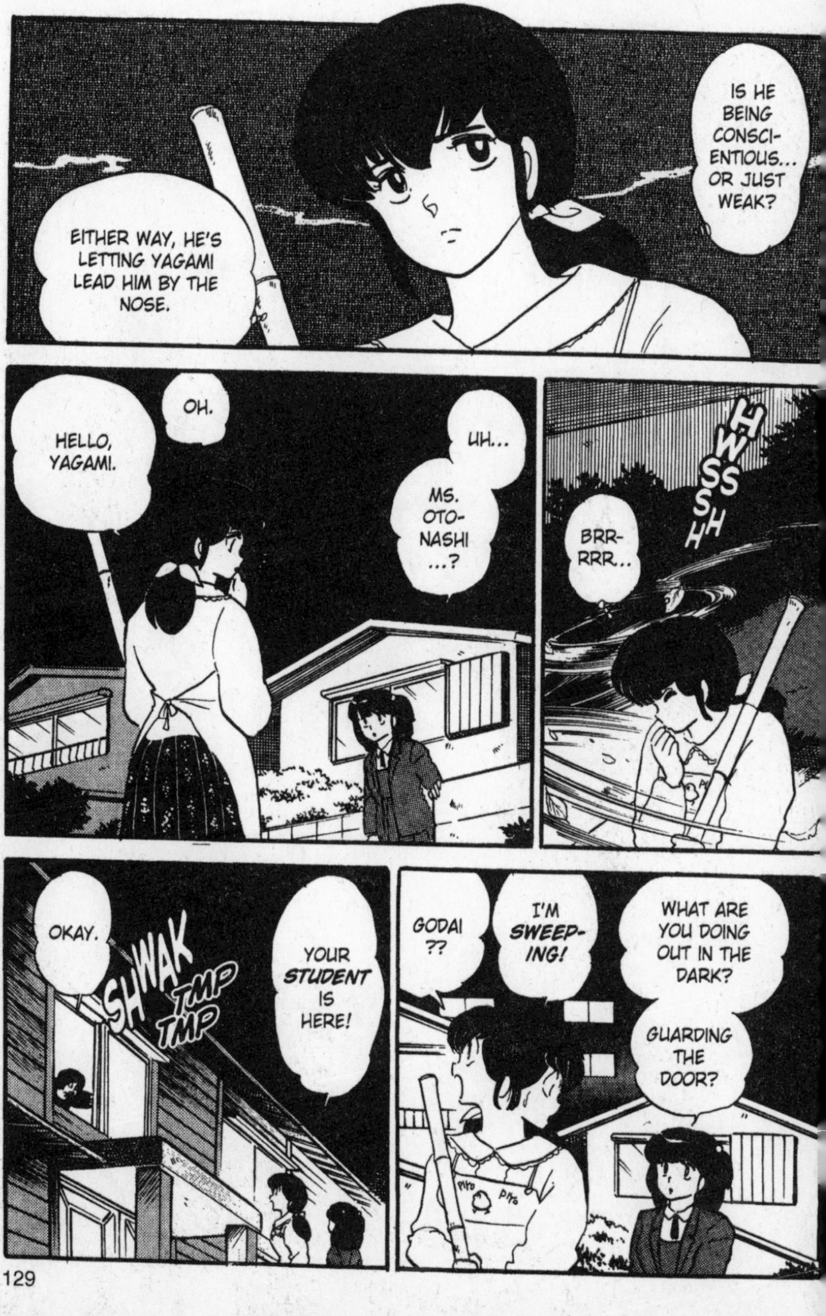
IS HE BEING CONSCI-ENTIOUS... OR JUST WEAK?
EITHER WAY, HE'S LETTING YAGAMI LEAD HIM BY THE NOSE.
HWSSSH
BRR-RRR...
UH...
MS. OTO-NASHI ...?
OH.
HELLO, YAGAMI.
WHAT ARE YOU DOING OUT IN THE DARK?
GUARDING THE DOOR?
I'M *SWEEP-ING!*
GODAI ??
YOUR *STUDENT* IS HERE!
OKAY.
SHWAK
TMP TMP

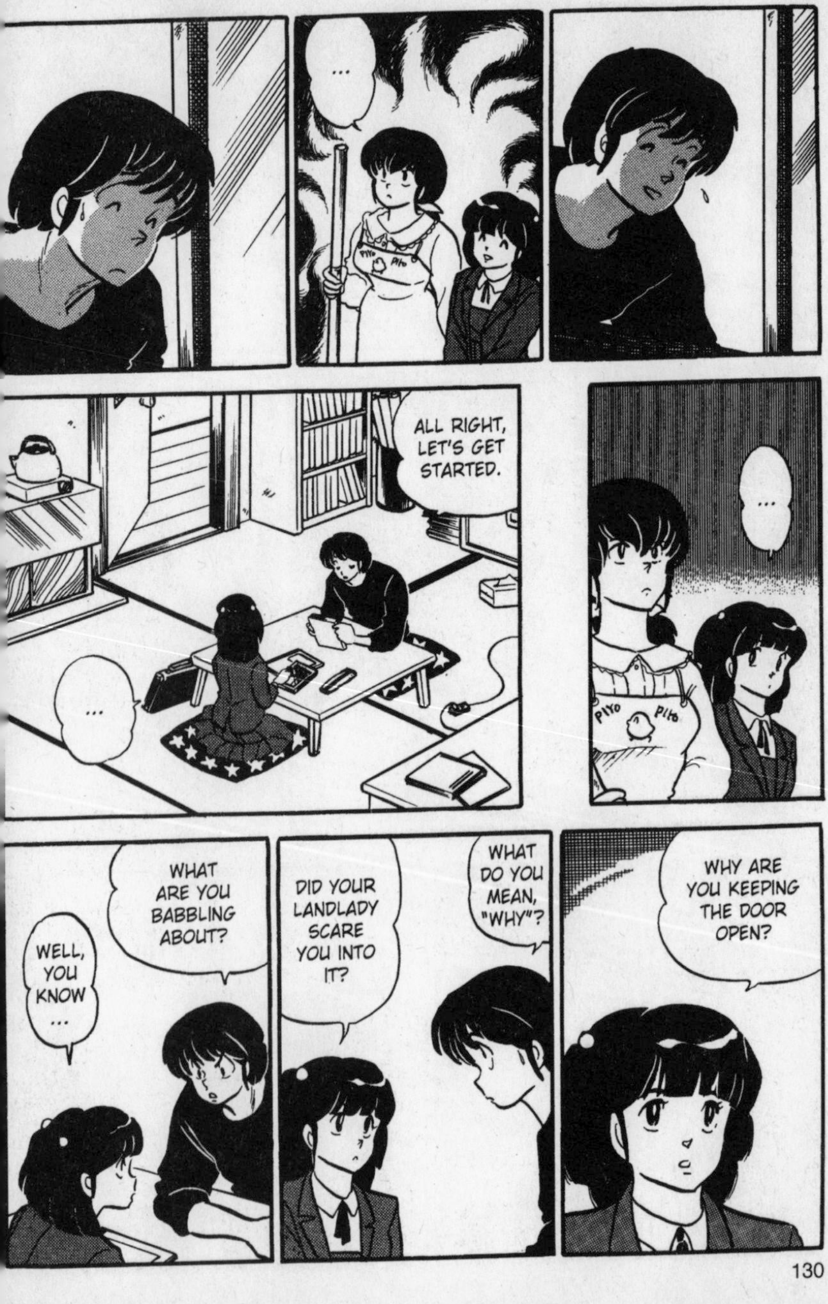
...
ALL RIGHT, LET'S GET STARTED.
...
...
WHY ARE YOU KEEPING THE DOOR OPEN?
WHAT DO YOU MEAN, "WHY"?
DID YOUR LANDLADY SCARE YOU INTO IT?
WHAT ARE YOU BABBLING ABOUT?
WELL, YOU KNOW ...

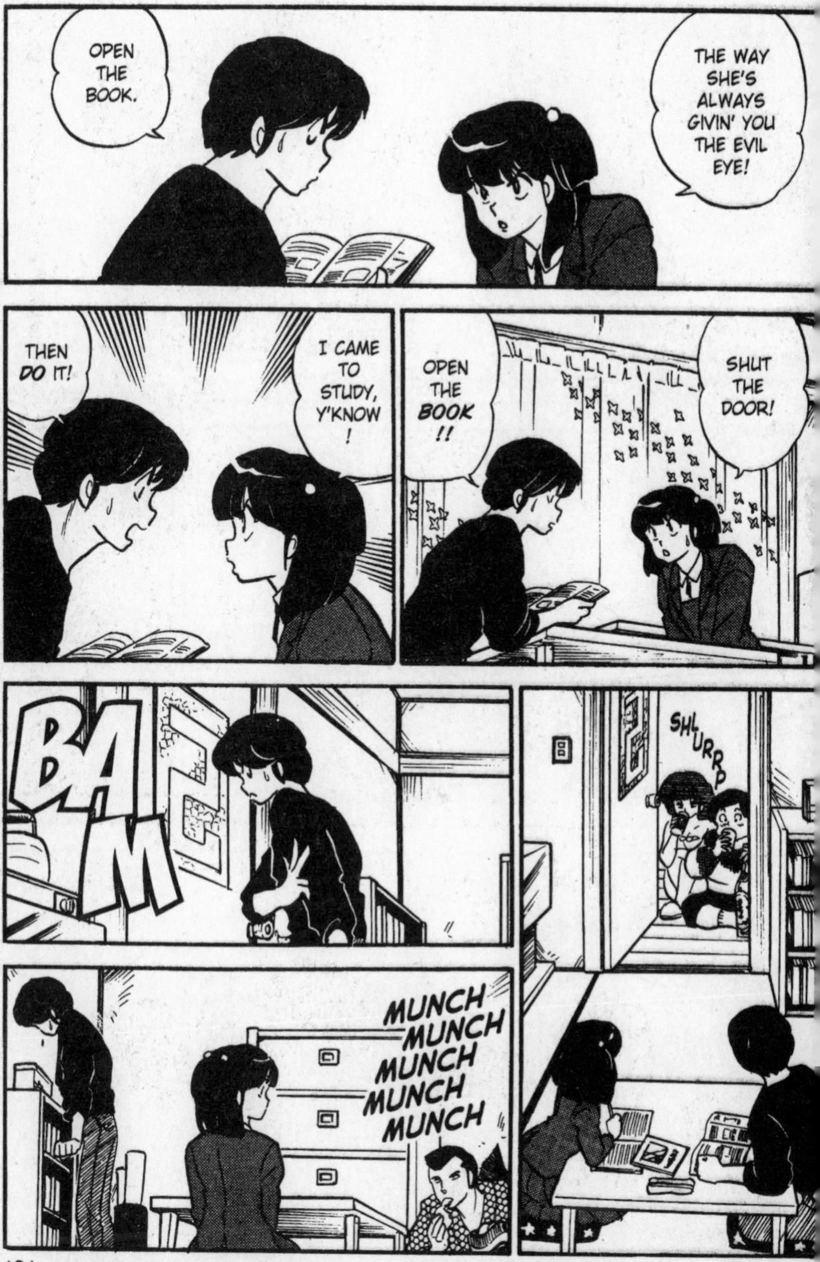
THE WAY SHE'S ALWAYS GIVIN' YOU THE EVIL EYE!
OPEN THE BOOK.
SHUT THE DOOR!
OPEN THE *BOOK* !!
I CAME TO STUDY, Y'KNOW!
THEN *DO* IT!
SHLURRP
BAM
MUNCH MUNCH MUNCH MUNCH MUNCH

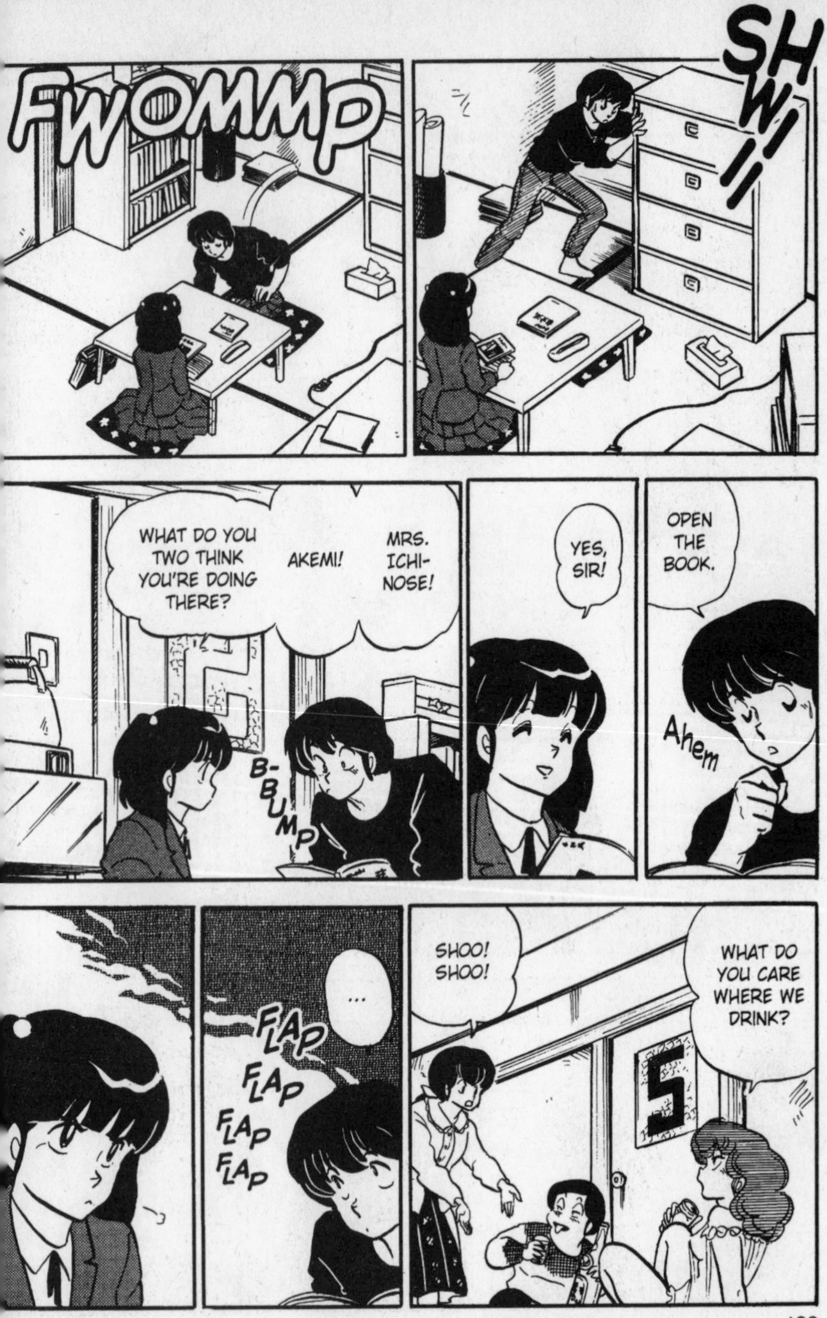
SHWIII
FWOMMP
OPEN THE BOOK.
Ahem
YES, SIR!
MRS. ICHI-NOSE!
AKEMI!
WHAT DO YOU TWO THINK YOU'RE DOING THERE?
B-BUMP
WHAT DO YOU CARE WHERE WE DRINK?
SHOO! SHOO!
...
FLAP FLAP FLAP FLAP

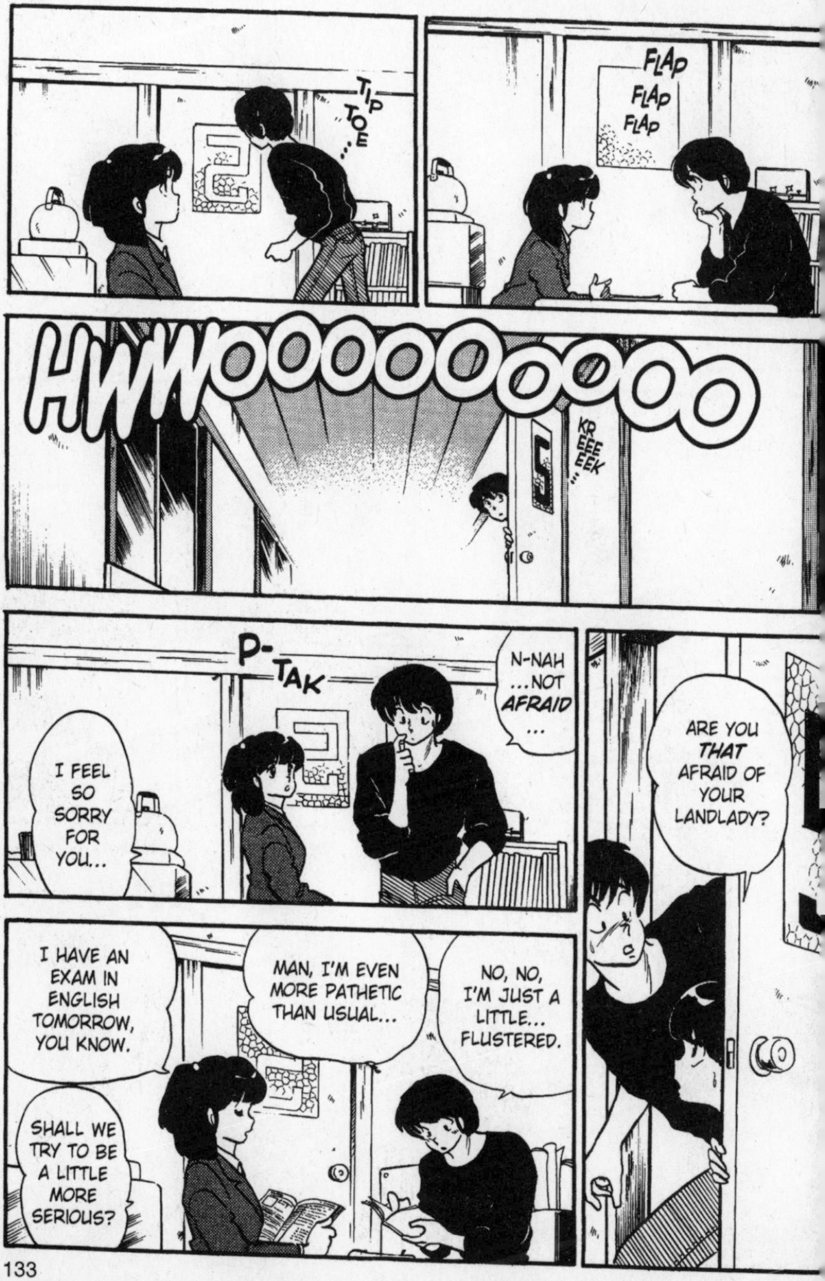
FLAP
FLAP
FLAP
TIP TOE...
HWWOOOOOOOOOO
KREEEEEEK...
ARE YOU *THAT* AFRAID OF YOUR LANDLADY?
N-NAH ...NOT *AFRAID* ...
P-TAK
I FEEL SO SORRY FOR YOU...
NO, NO, I'M JUST A LITTLE... FLUSTERED.
MAN, I'M EVEN MORE PATHETIC THAN USUAL...
I HAVE AN EXAM IN ENGLISH TOMORROW, YOU KNOW.
SHALL WE TRY TO BE A LITTLE MORE SERIOUS?

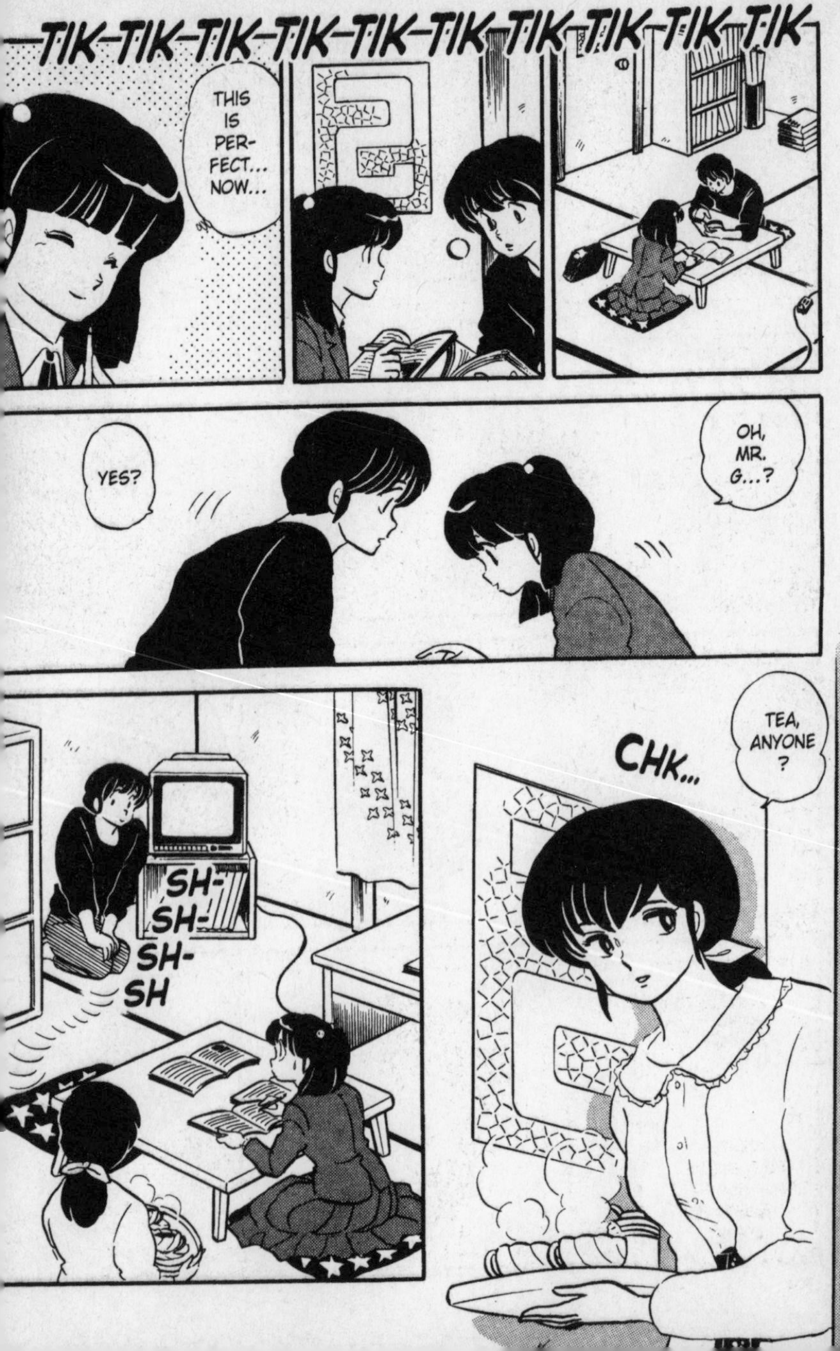
TIK-TIK-TIK-TIK-TIK-TIK-TIK-TIK-TIK-TIK
THIS IS PER-FECT... NOW...
OH, MR. G...?
YES?
CHK...
TEA, ANYONE?
SH-SH-SH-SH

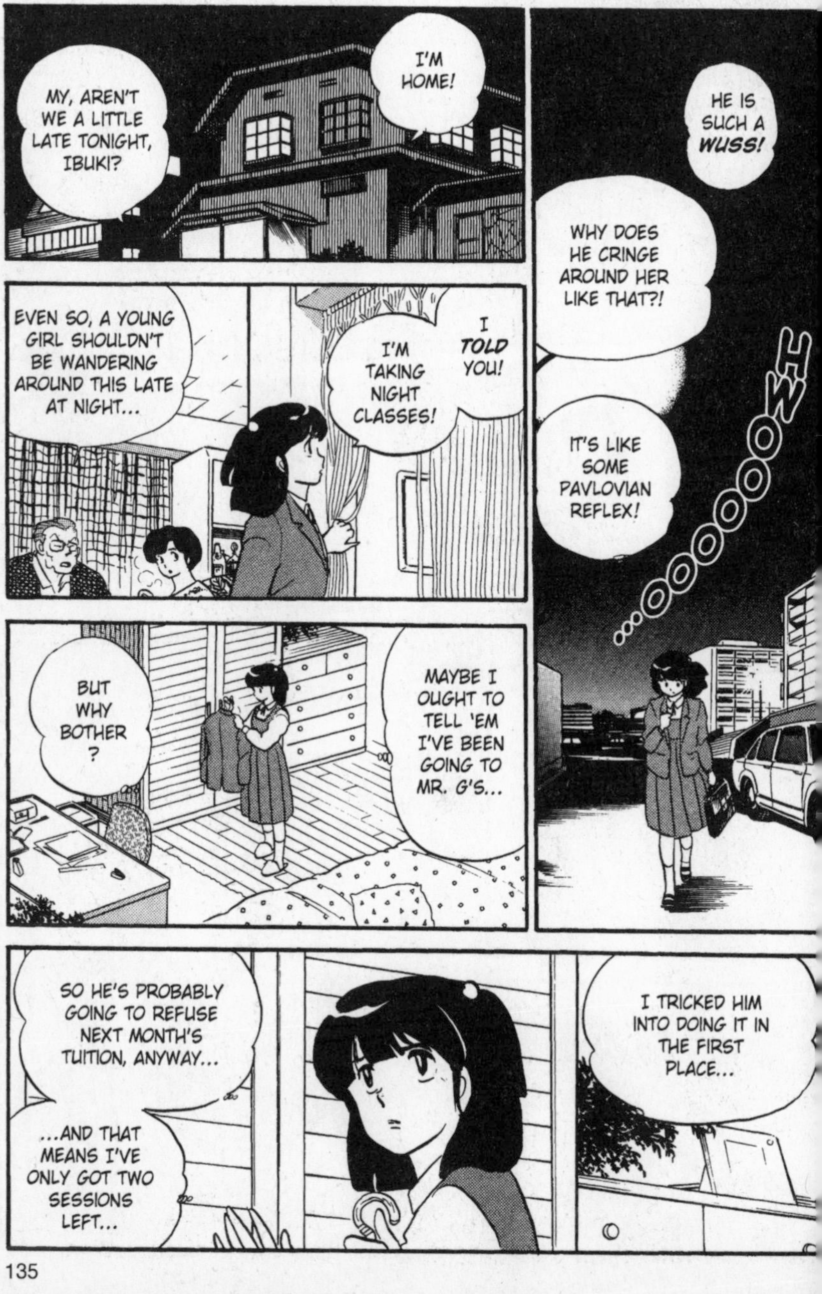
HE IS SUCH A *WUSS!*
WHY DOES HE CRINGE AROUND HER LIKE THAT?!
IT'S LIKE SOME PAVLOVIAN REFLEX!
...OOOOOOOWH
I'M HOME!
MY, AREN'T WE A LITTLE LATE TONIGHT, IBUKI?
I *TOLD* YOU!
I'M TAKING NIGHT CLASSES!
EVEN SO, A YOUNG GIRL SHOULDN'T BE WANDERING AROUND THIS LATE AT NIGHT...
MAYBE I OUGHT TO TELL 'EM I'VE BEEN GOING TO MR. G'S...
BUT WHY BOTHER ?
I TRICKED HIM INTO DOING IT IN THE FIRST PLACE...
SO HE'S PROBABLY GOING TO REFUSE NEXT MONTH'S TUITION, ANYWAY...
...AND THAT MEANS I'VE ONLY GOT TWO SESSIONS LEFT...

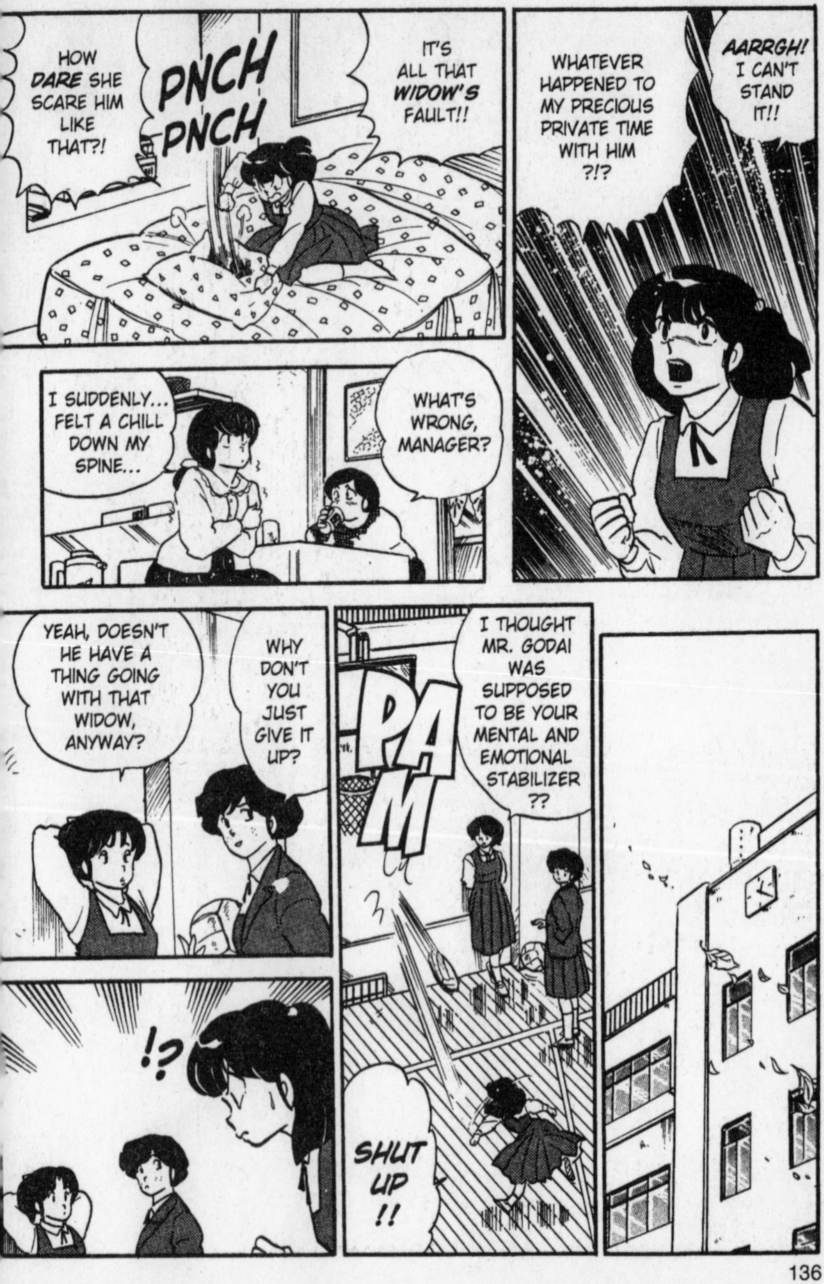
AARRGH! I CAN'T STAND IT!!
WHATEVER HAPPENED TO MY PRECIOUS PRIVATE TIME WITH HIM ?!?
IT'S ALL THAT WIDOW'S FAULT!!
PNCH PNCH
HOW DARE SHE SCARE HIM LIKE THAT?!
WHAT'S WRONG, MANAGER?
I SUDDENLY... FELT A CHILL DOWN MY SPINE...
I THOUGHT MR. GODAI WAS SUPPOSED TO BE YOUR MENTAL AND EMOTIONAL STABILIZER ??
PAM
SHUT UP !!
WHY DON'T YOU JUST GIVE IT UP?
YEAH, DOESN'T HE HAVE A THING GOING WITH THAT WIDOW, ANYWAY?
!?

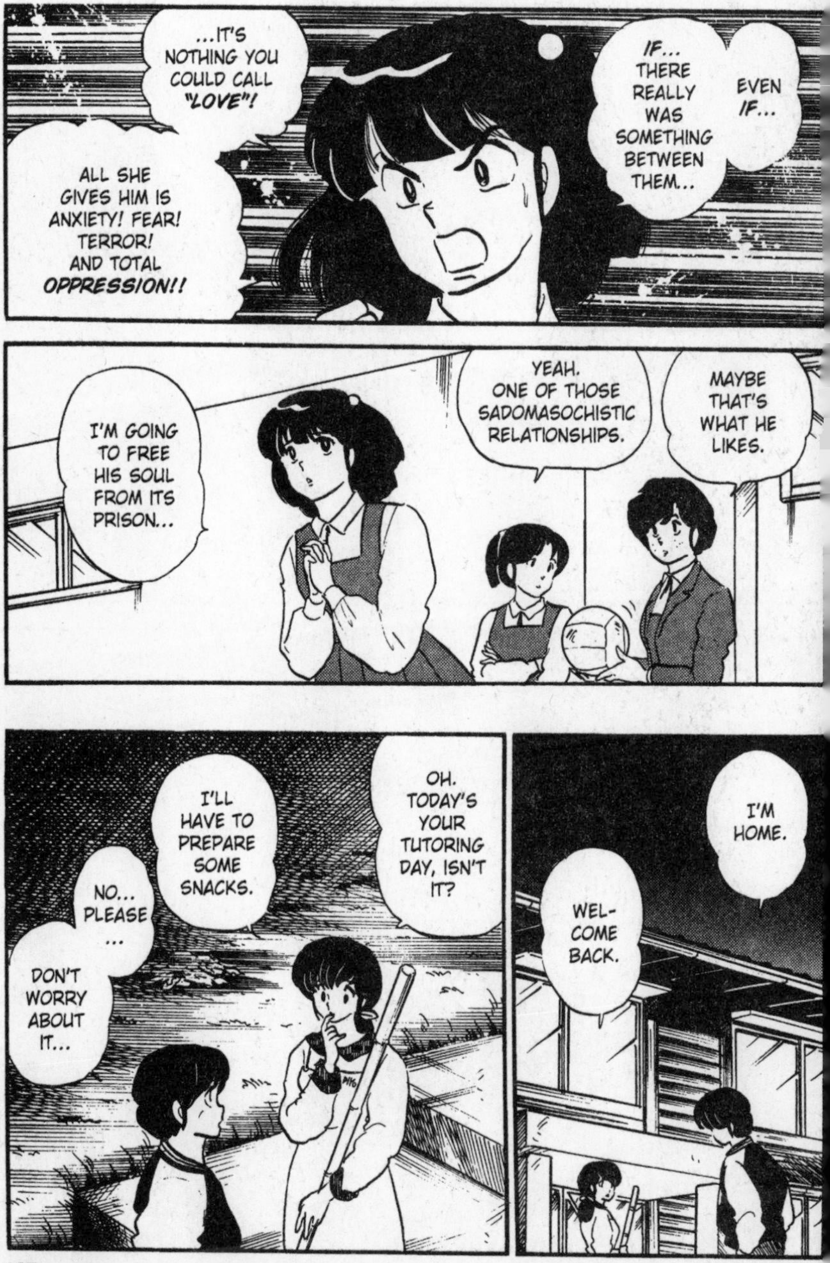
EVEN IF...
IF... THERE REALLY WAS SOMETHING BETWEEN THEM...
...IT'S NOTHING YOU COULD CALL "LOVE"!
ALL SHE GIVES HIM IS ANXIETY! FEAR! TERROR! AND TOTAL OPPRESSION!!
MAYBE THAT'S WHAT HE LIKES.
YEAH. ONE OF THOSE SADOMASOCHISTIC RELATIONSHIPS.
I'M GOING TO FREE HIS SOUL FROM ITS PRISON...
I'M HOME.
WEL-COME BACK.
OH. TODAY'S YOUR TUTORING DAY, ISN'T IT?
I'LL HAVE TO PREPARE SOME SNACKS.
NO... PLEASE ...
DON'T WORRY ABOUT IT...

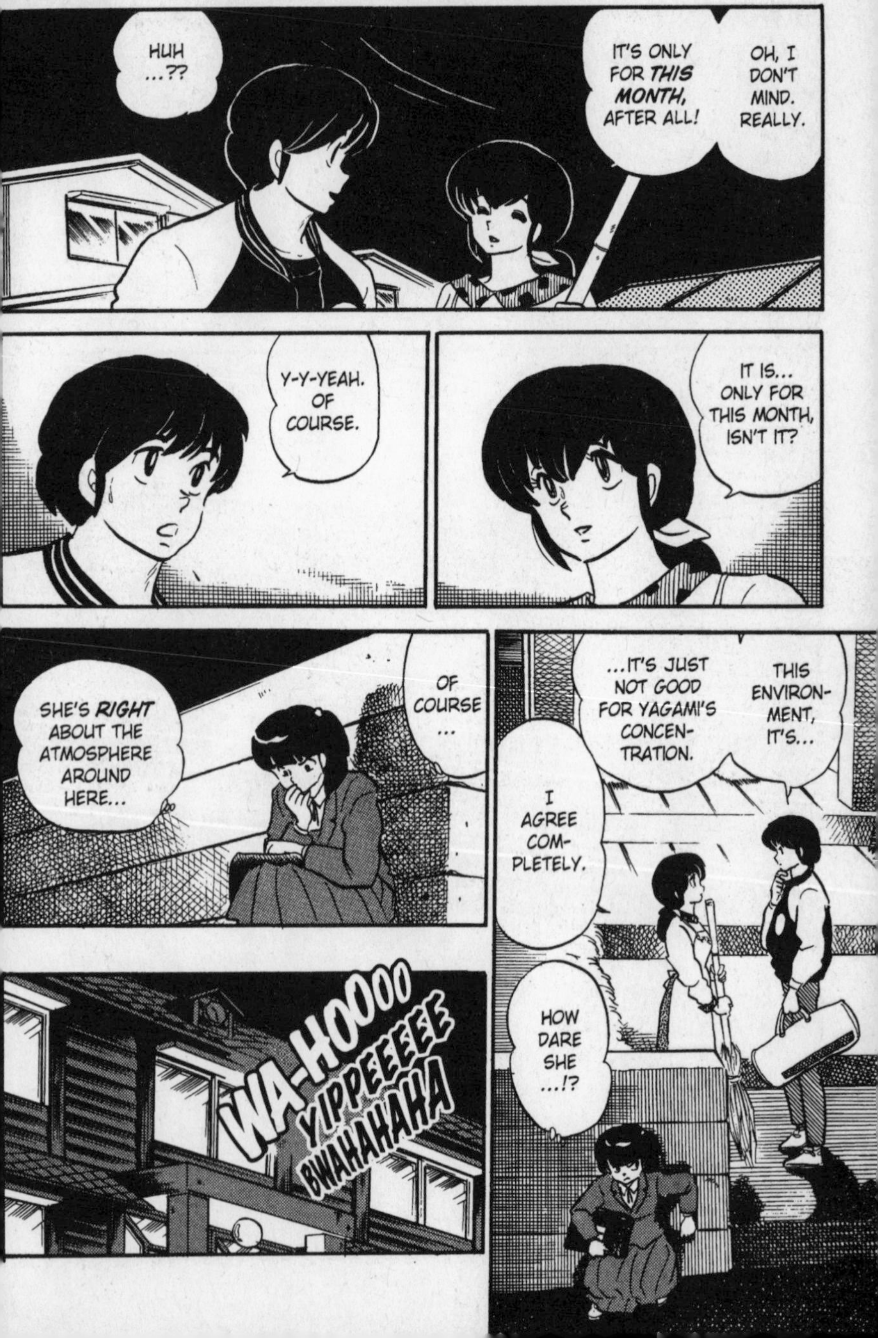
OH, I DON'T MIND. REALLY.
IT'S ONLY FOR *THIS MONTH,* AFTER ALL!
HUH ...??
IT IS... ONLY FOR THIS MONTH, ISN'T IT?
Y-Y-YEAH. OF COURSE.
CURSE
THIS ENVIRON-MENT, IT'S...
...IT'S JUST NOT GOOD FOR YAGAMI'S CONCEN-TRATION.
I AGREE COM-PLETELY.
HOW DARE SHE ...!?
OF COURSE ...
SHE'S *RIGHT* ABOUT THE ATMOSPHERE AROUND HERE...
WA-HOOOO
YIPPEEEEE
BWAHAHAHA

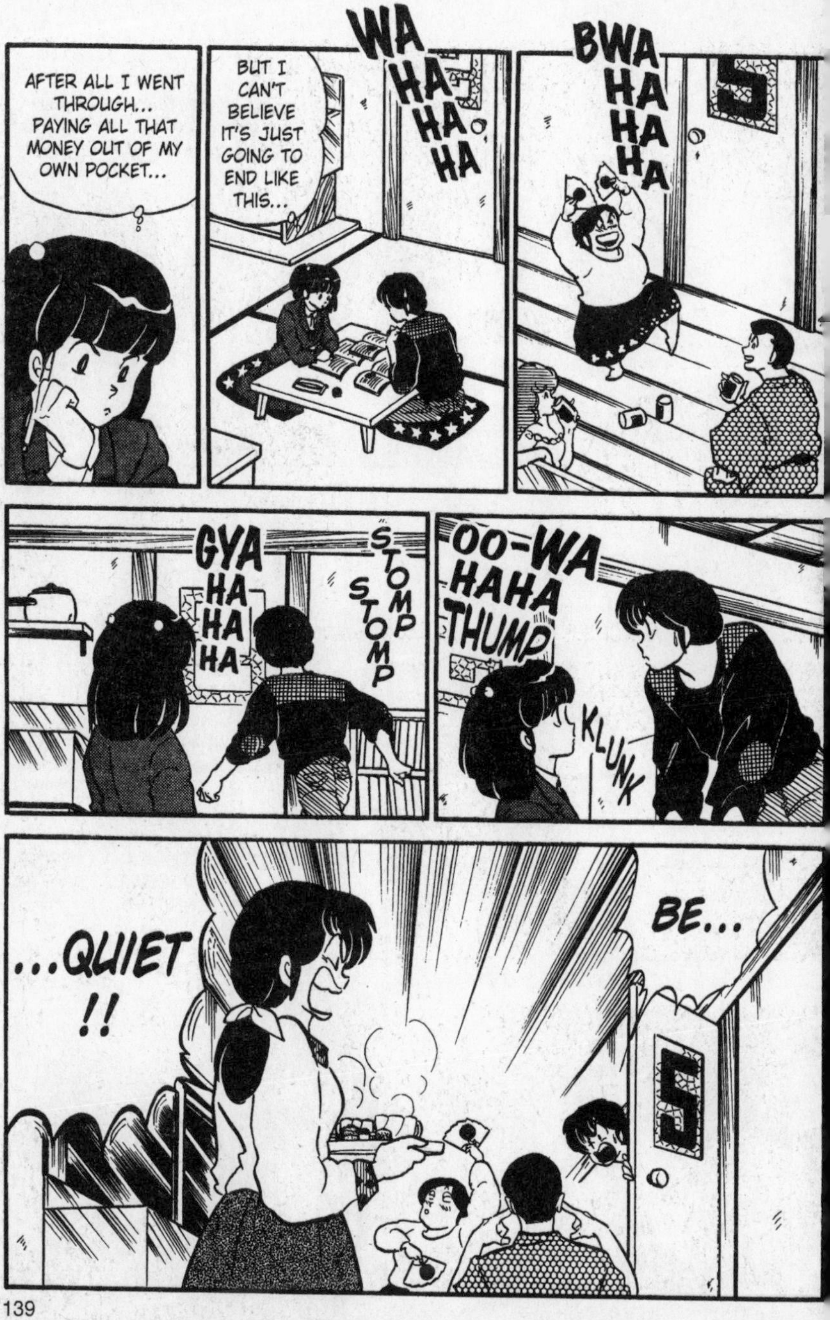
BWA HA HA HA HA
WA HA HA HA HA
BUT I CAN'T BELIEVE IT'S JUST GOING TO END LIKE THIS...
AFTER ALL I WENT THROUGH... PAYING ALL THAT MONEY OUT OF MY OWN POCKET...
OO-WA HAHA
THUMP
KLUNK
STOMP STOMP
GYA HA HA HA HA
BE...
...QUIET !!

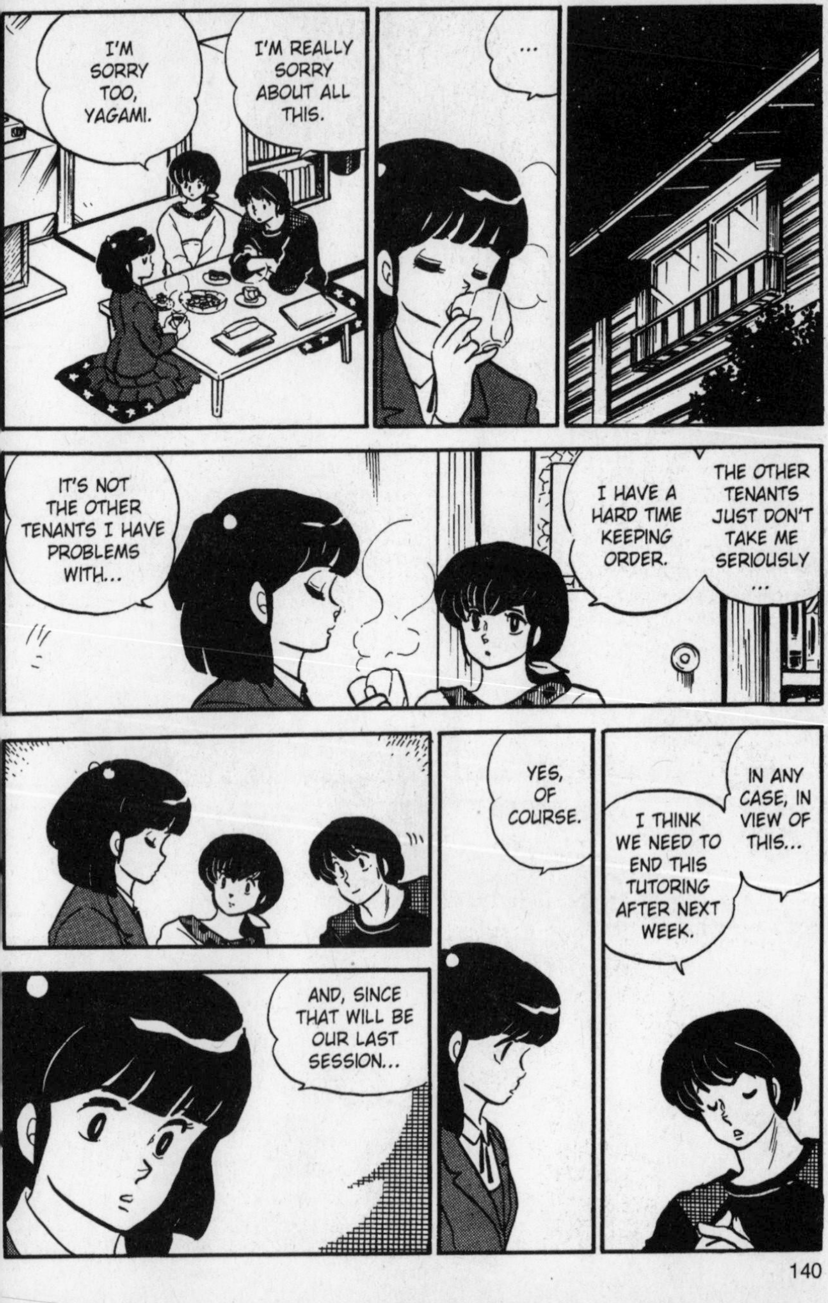
...
I'M REALLY SORRY ABOUT ALL THIS.
I'M SORRY TOO, YAGAMI.
THE OTHER TENANTS JUST DON'T TAKE ME SERIOUSLY ...
I HAVE A HARD TIME KEEPING ORDER.
IT'S NOT THE OTHER TENANTS I HAVE PROBLEMS WITH...
IN ANY CASE, IN VIEW OF THIS...
I THINK WE NEED TO END THIS TUTORING AFTER NEXT WEEK.
YES, OF COURSE.
AND, SINCE THAT WILL BE OUR LAST SESSION...

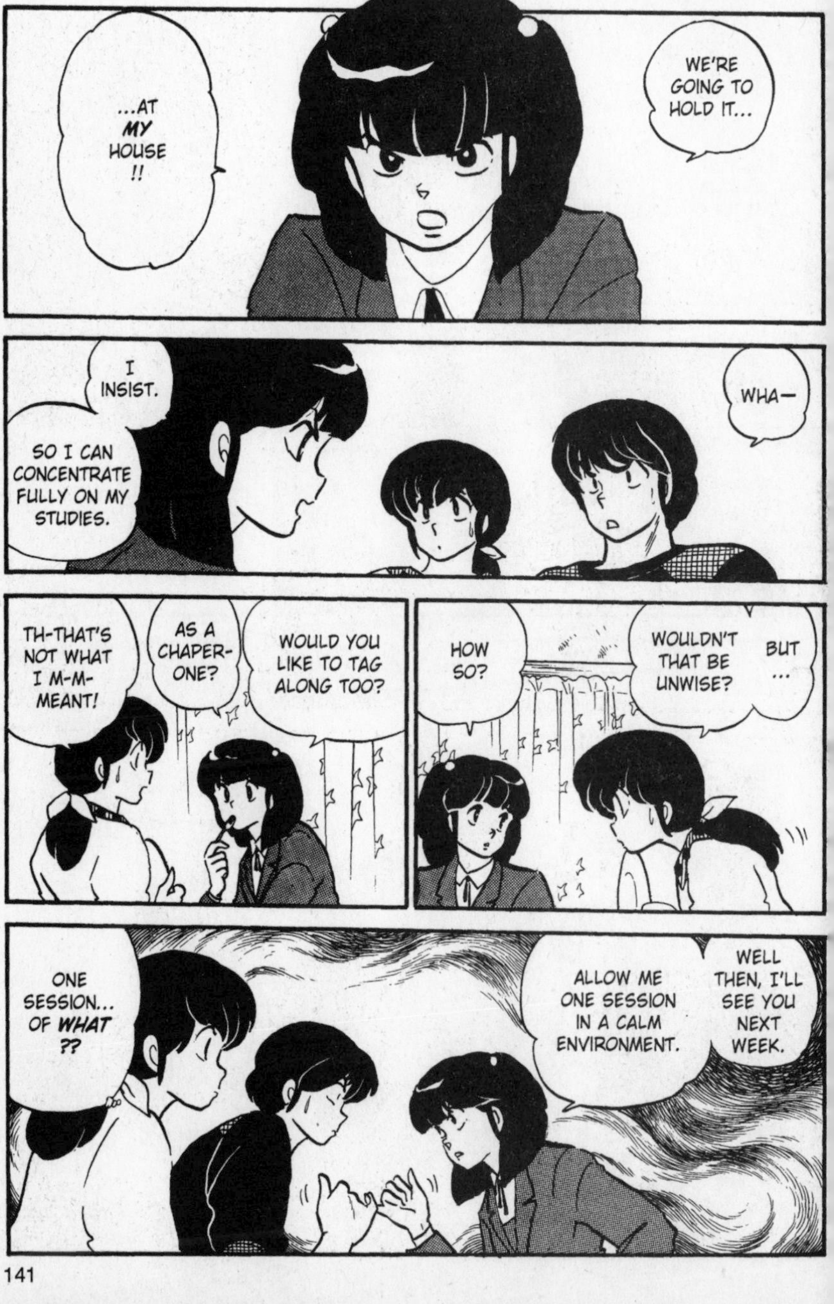
WE'RE GOING TO HOLD IT...
...AT **MY** HOUSE !!
WHA—
I INSIST.
SO I CAN CONCENTRATE FULLY ON MY STUDIES.
BUT ...
WOULDN'T THAT BE UNWISE?
HOW SO?
WOULD YOU LIKE TO TAG ALONG TOO?
AS A CHAPER-ONE?
TH-THAT'S NOT WHAT I M-M-MEANT!
WELL THEN, I'LL SEE YOU NEXT WEEK.
ALLOW ME ONE SESSION IN A CALM ENVIRONMENT.
ONE SESSION... OF **WHAT** ??

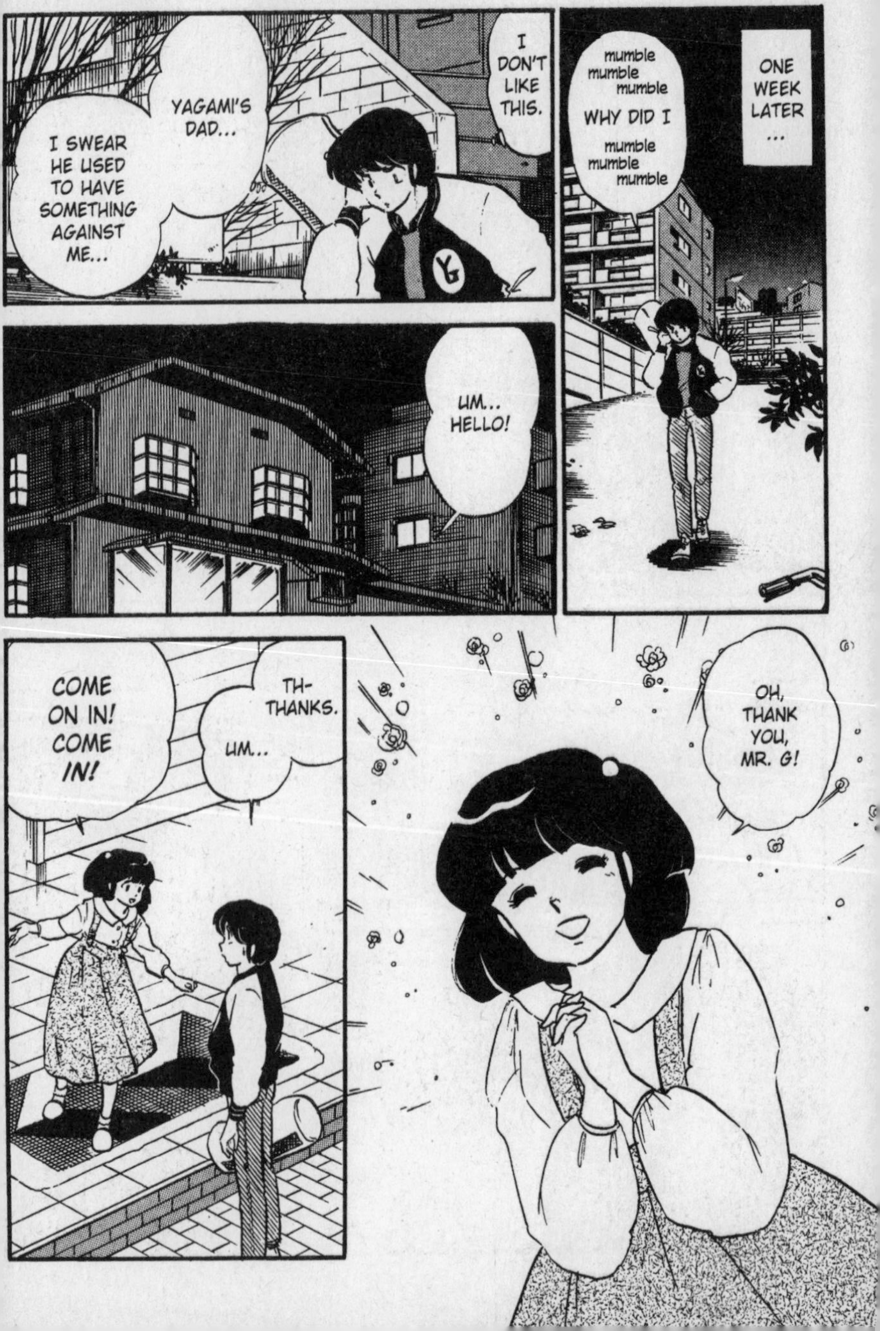
ONE WEEK LATER...
mumble mumble mumble
WHY DID I
mumble mumble mumble
I DON'T LIKE THIS.
YAGAMI'S DAD...
I SWEAR HE USED TO HAVE SOMETHING AGAINST ME...
UM... HELLO!
OH, THANK YOU, MR. G!
TH- THANKS.
UM...
COME ON IN! COME IN!

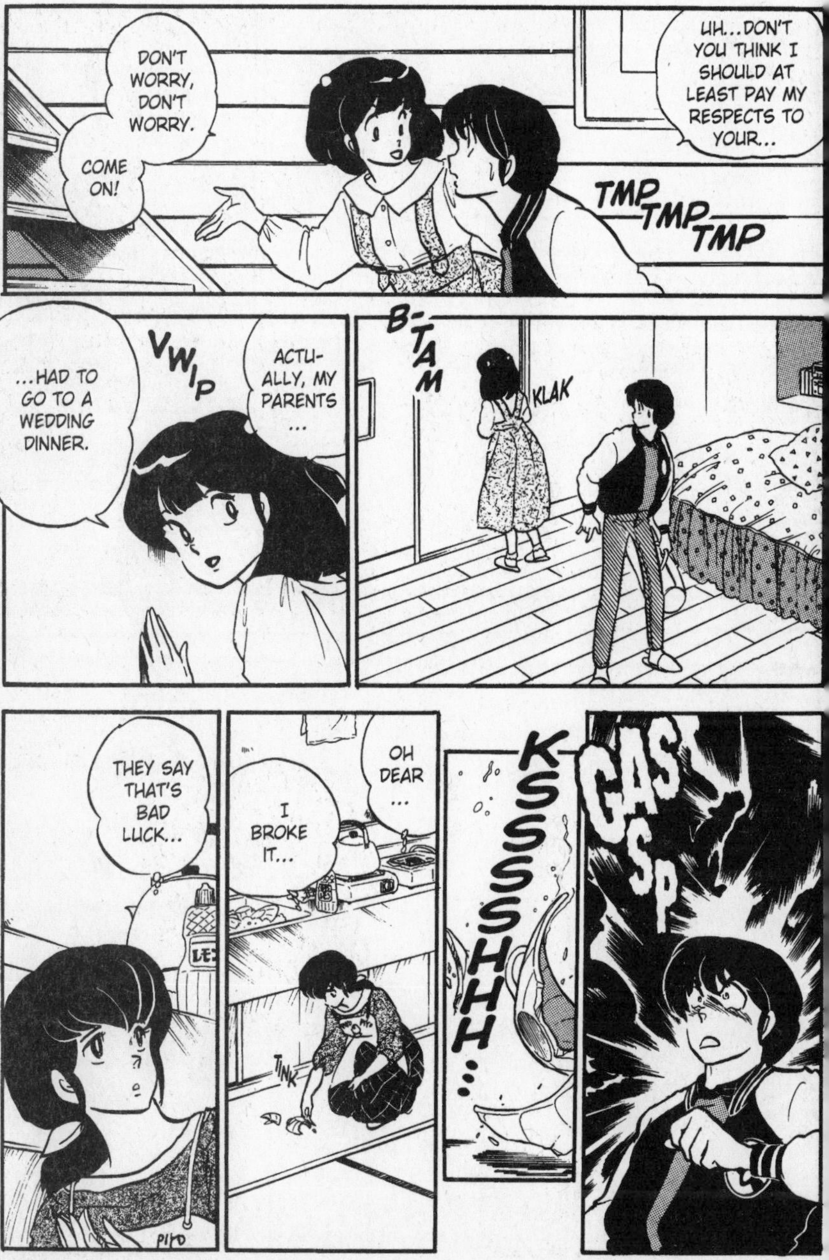
UH...DON'T YOU THINK I SHOULD AT LEAST PAY MY RESPECTS TO YOUR...
TMP TMP TMP
DON'T WORRY, DON'T WORRY.
COME ON!
B-TAM
KLAK
ACTU-ALLY, MY PARENTS ...
VWIP
...HAD TO GO TO A WEDDING DINNER.
GASSP
KSSSSSHHH...
OH DEAR ...
I BROKE IT...
TINK
THEY SAY THAT'S BAD LUCK...
PITO

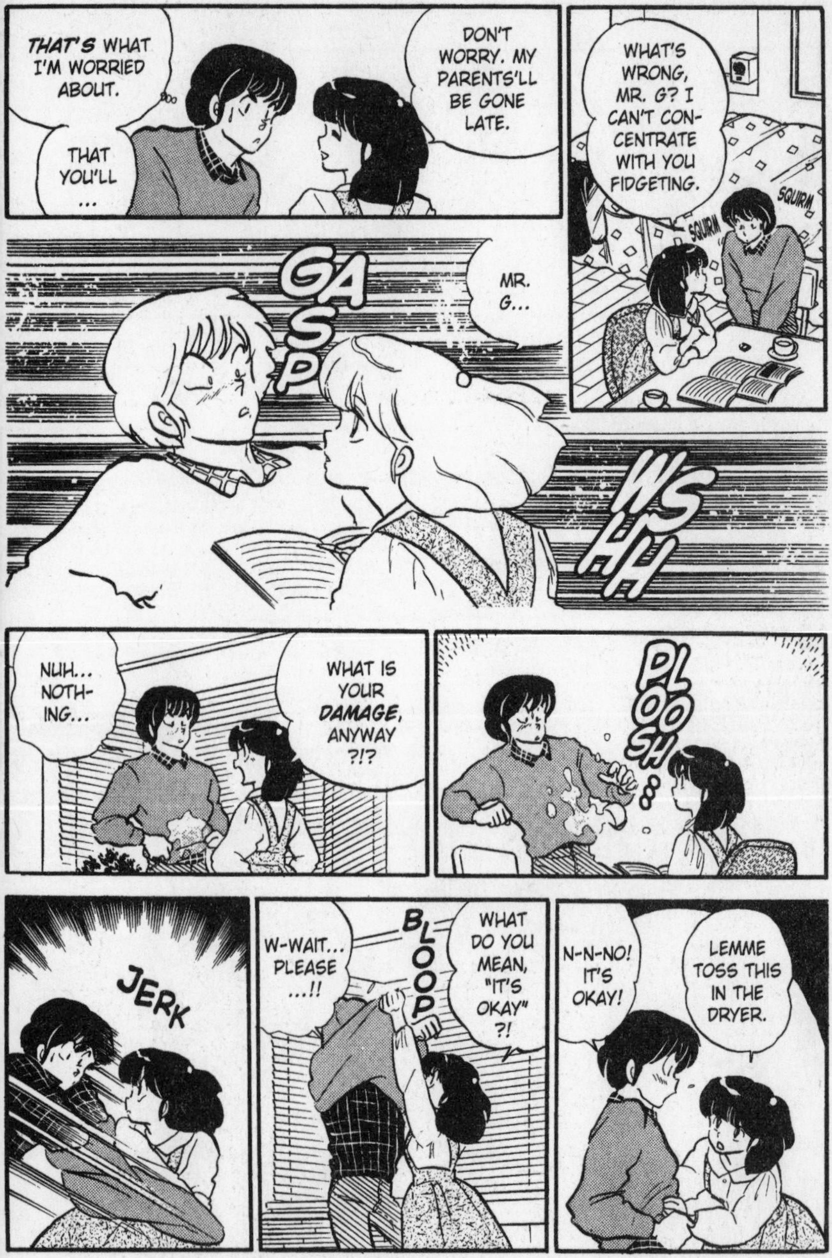
WHAT'S WRONG, MR. G? I CAN'T CONCENTRATE WITH YOU FIDGETING.
SQUIRM
SQUIRM
DON'T WORRY. MY PARENTS'LL BE GONE LATE.
THAT'S WHAT I'M WORRIED ABOUT.
THAT YOU'LL ...
MR. G...
GASP
WSHH
PLOOSH
WHAT IS YOUR DAMAGE, ANYWAY ?!?
NUH... NOTHING...
LEMME TOSS THIS IN THE DRYER.
N-N-NO! IT'S OKAY!
WHAT DO YOU MEAN, "IT'S OKAY" ?!
BLOOP
W-WAIT... PLEASE ...!!
JERK

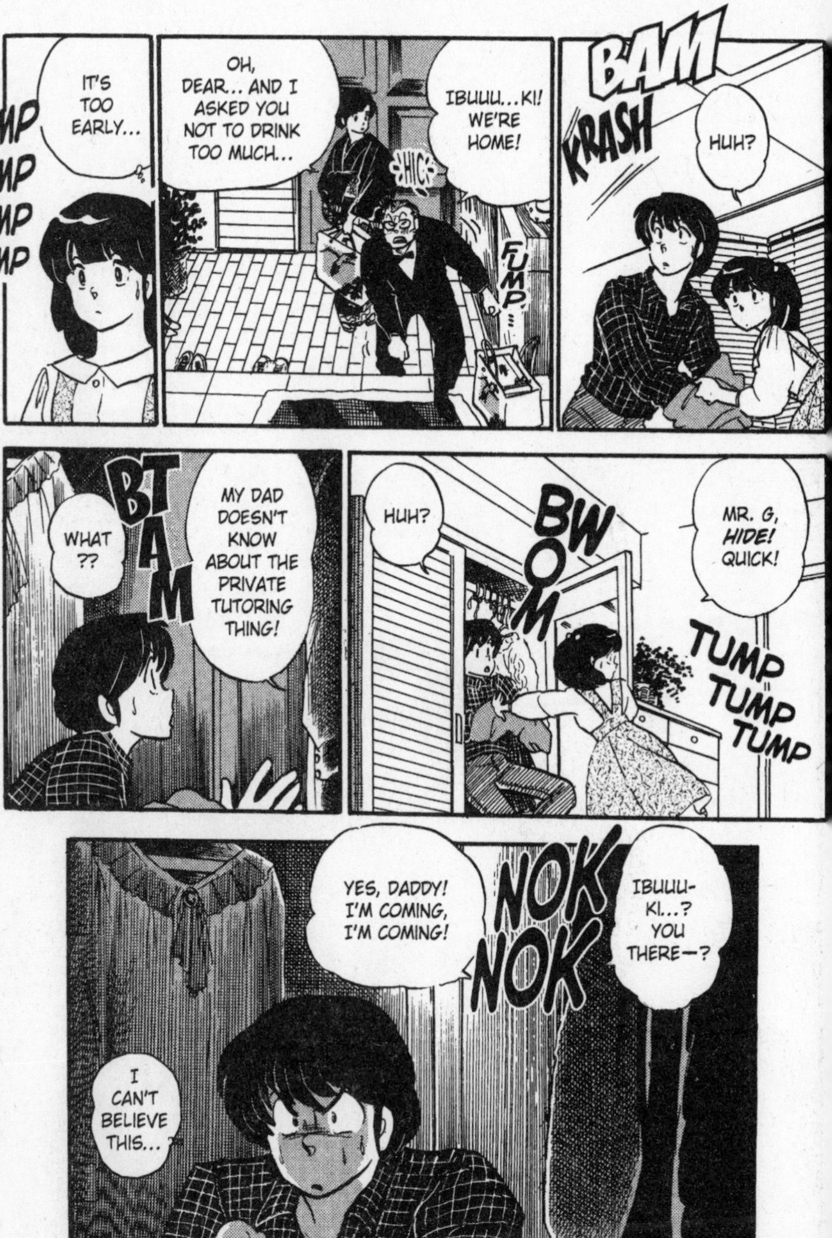
BAM
KRASH
HUH?
IBUUU...KI! WE'RE HOME!
HIC
OH, DEAR... AND I ASKED YOU NOT TO DRINK TOO MUCH...
FUMP
IT'S TOO EARLY...
TMP TMP TMP TMP
MR. G, HIDE! QUICK!
BWOM
HUH?
TUMP TUMP TUMP
MY DAD DOESN'T KNOW ABOUT THE PRIVATE TUTORING THING!
BTAM
WHAT ??
IBUUU-KI...? YOU THERE—?
NOK NOK
YES, DADDY! I'M COMING, I'M COMING!
I CAN'T BELIEVE THIS...

PART EIGHT
IF THE SHOE FITS

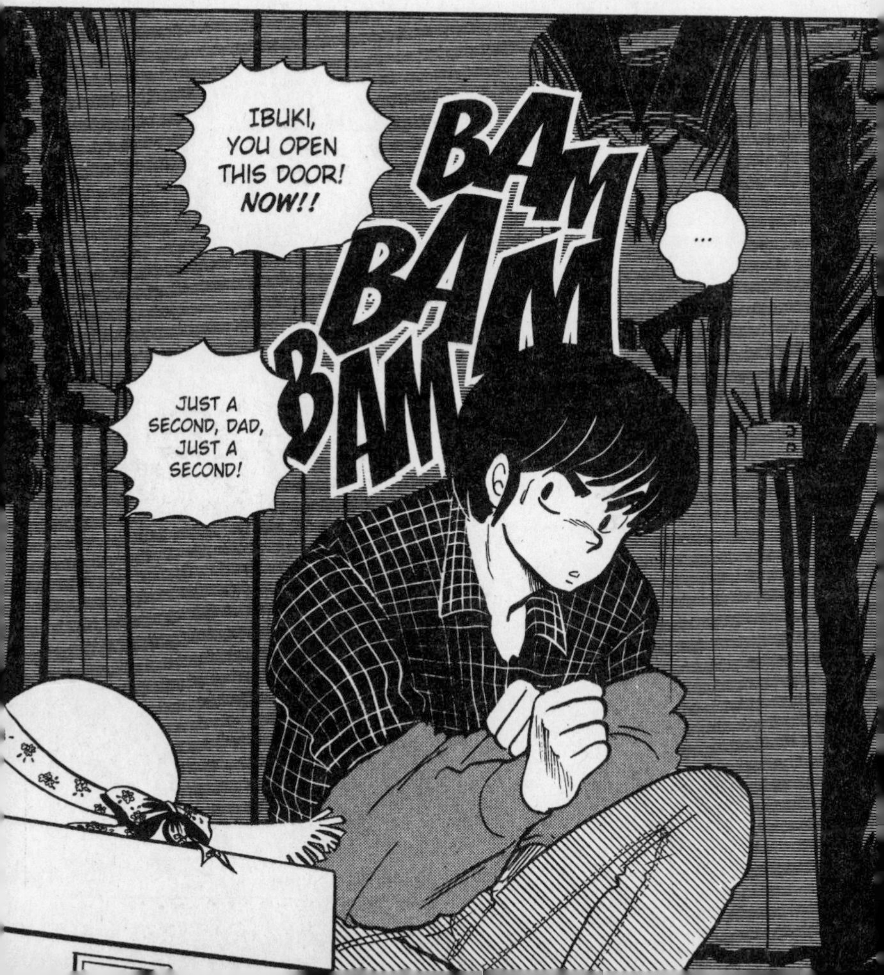
IBUKI, YOU OPEN THIS DOOR! *NOW!!*
BAM BAM BAM
...
JUST A SECOND, DAD, JUST A SECOND!

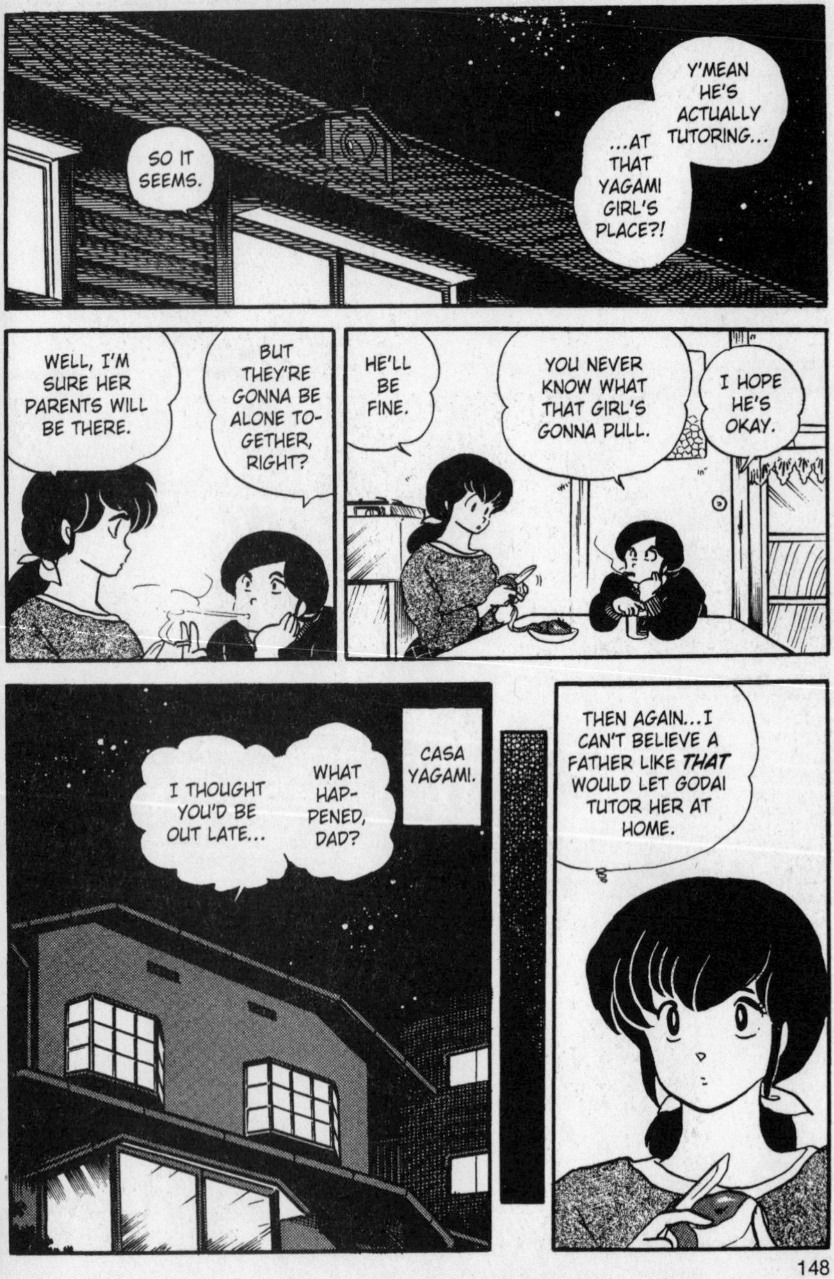
Y'MEAN HE'S ACTUALLY TUTORING...
...AT THAT YAGAMI GIRL'S PLACE?!
SO IT SEEMS.
I HOPE HE'S OKAY.
YOU NEVER KNOW WHAT THAT GIRL'S GONNA PULL.
HE'LL BE FINE.
BUT THEY'RE GONNA BE ALONE TO-GETHER, RIGHT?
WELL, I'M SURE HER PARENTS WILL BE THERE.
THEN AGAIN...I CAN'T BELIEVE A FATHER LIKE *THAT* WOULD LET GODAI TUTOR HER AT HOME.
CASA YAGAMI.
WHAT HAP-PENED, DAD?
I THOUGHT YOU'D BE OUT LATE...

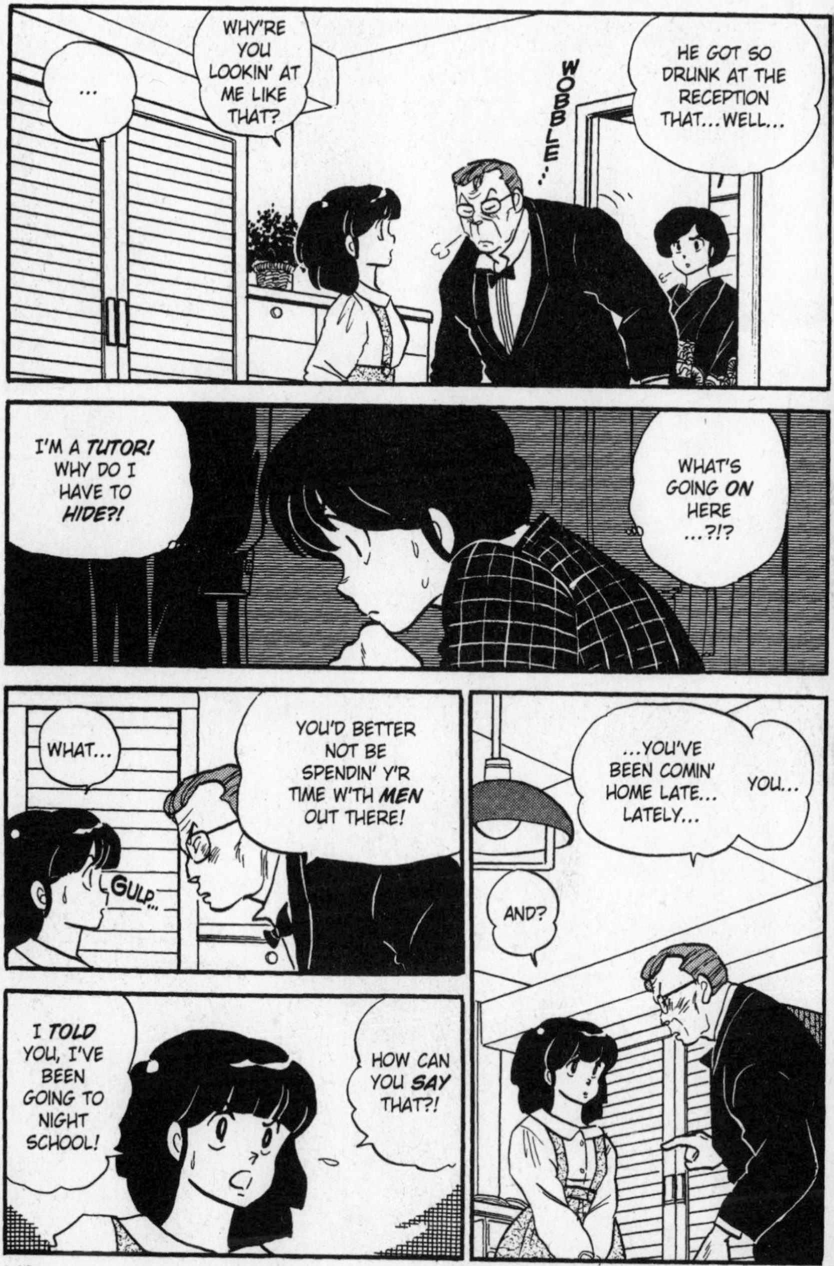
HE GOT SO DRUNK AT THE RECEPTION THAT...WELL...
WOBBLE...
WHY'RE YOU LOOKIN' AT ME LIKE THAT?
...
WHAT'S GOING ON HERE ...?!?
I'M A TUTOR! WHY DO I HAVE TO HIDE?!
YOU...
...YOU'VE BEEN COMIN' HOME LATE... LATELY...
AND?
YOU'D BETTER NOT BE SPENDIN' Y'R TIME W'TH MEN OUT THERE!
WHAT...
GULP...
HOW CAN YOU SAY THAT?!
I TOLD YOU, I'VE BEEN GOING TO NIGHT SCHOOL!

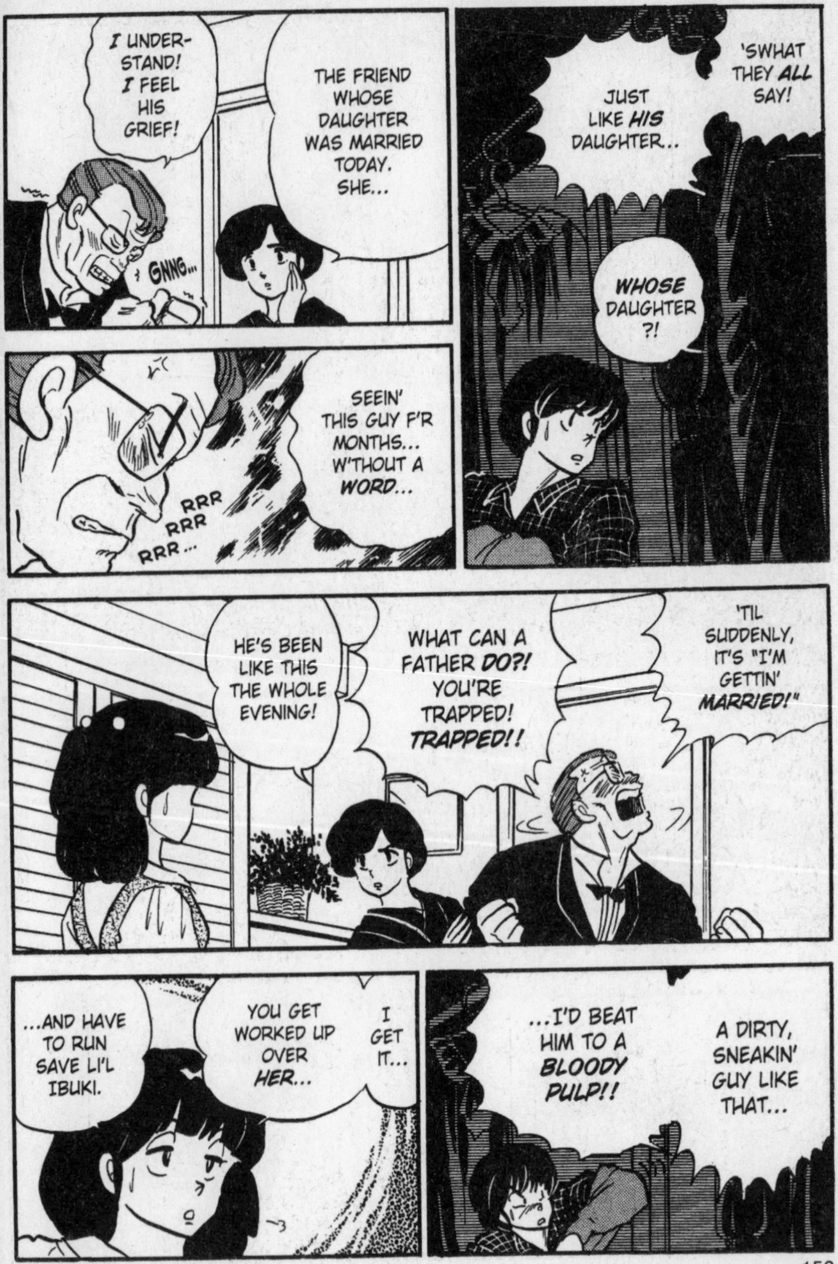
'SWHAT THEY ALL SAY!
JUST LIKE HIS DAUGHTER...
WHOSE DAUGHTER ?!
THE FRIEND WHOSE DAUGHTER WAS MARRIED TODAY. SHE...
I UNDERSTAND! I FEEL HIS GRIEF!
GNNG...
SEEIN' THIS GUY F'R MONTHS... W'THOUT A WORD...
RRR RRR RRR...
'TIL SUDDENLY, IT'S "I'M GETTIN' MARRIED!"
WHAT CAN A FATHER DO?! YOU'RE TRAPPED! TRAPPED!!
HE'S BEEN LIKE THIS THE WHOLE EVENING!
A DIRTY, SNEAKIN' GUY LIKE THAT...
...I'D BEAT HIM TO A BLOODY PULP!!
I GET IT...
YOU GET WORKED UP OVER HER...
...AND HAVE TO RUN SAVE LI'L IBUKI.

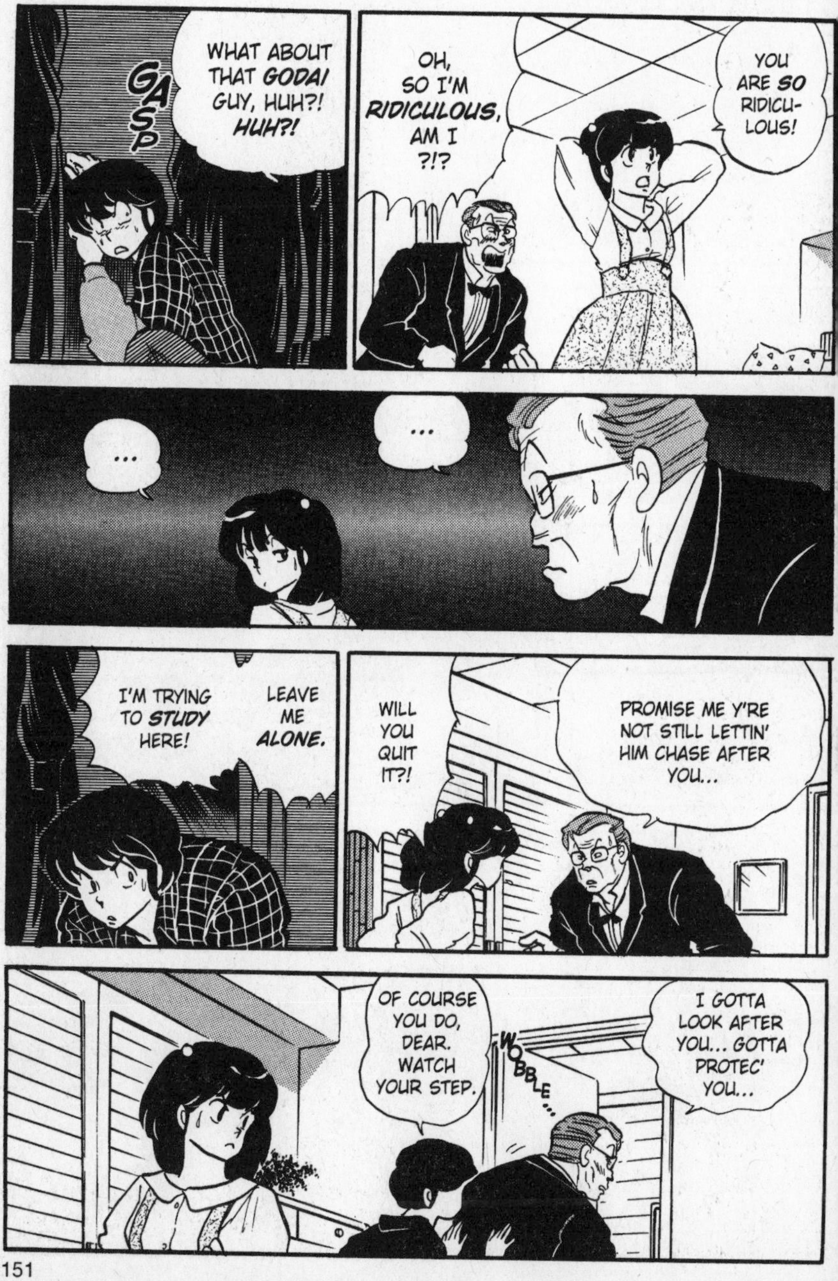
YOU ARE SO RIDICULOUS!
OH, SO I'M RIDICULOUS, AM I ?!?
WHAT ABOUT THAT GODAI GUY, HUH?! HUH?!
GASP
...
...
PROMISE ME Y'RE NOT STILL LETTIN' HIM CHASE AFTER YOU...
WILL YOU QUIT IT?!
LEAVE ME ALONE.
I'M TRYING TO STUDY HERE!
I GOTTA LOOK AFTER YOU... GOTTA PROTEC' YOU...
WOBBLE...
OF COURSE YOU DO, DEAR. WATCH YOUR STEP.

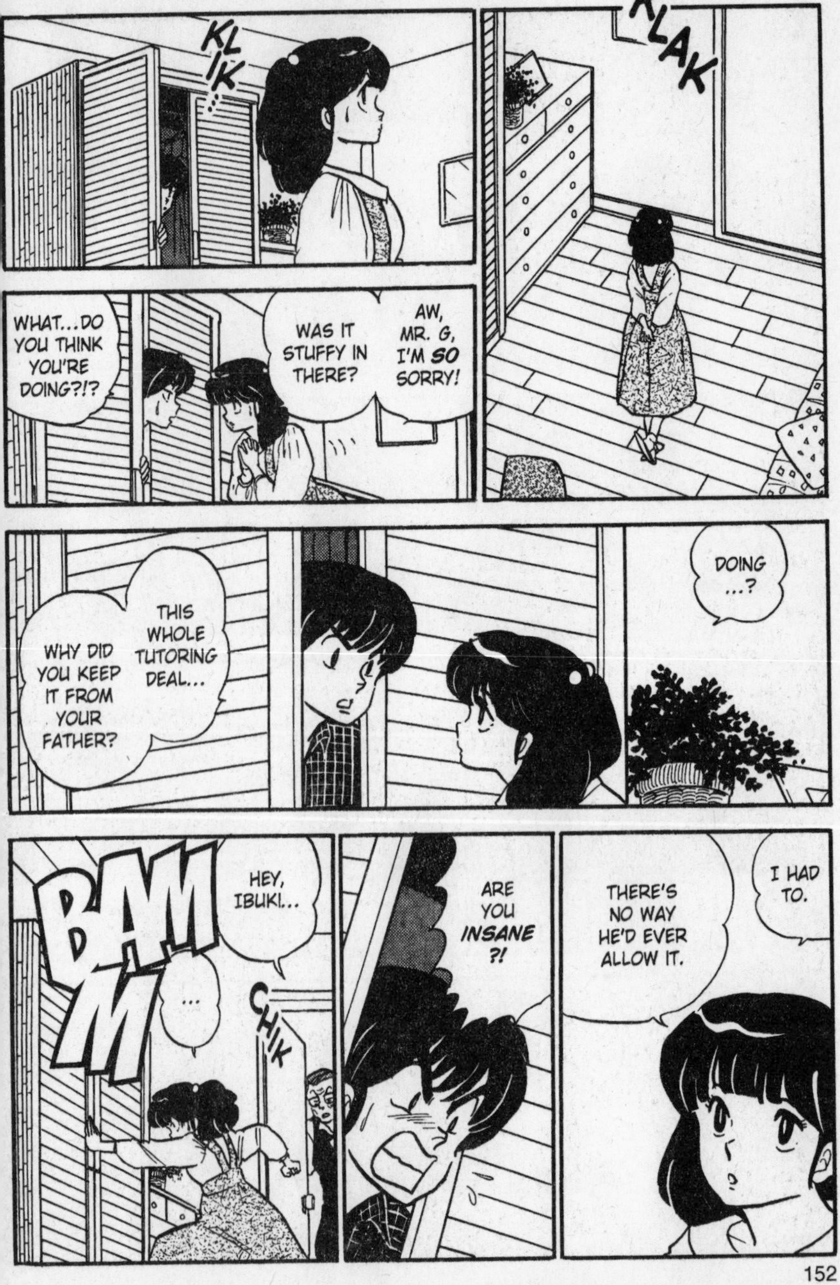
KLAK
KLIK...
AW, MR. G, I'M *SO* SORRY!
WAS IT STUFFY IN THERE?
WHAT...DO YOU THINK YOU'RE DOING?!?
DOING ...?
THIS WHOLE TUTORING DEAL...
WHY DID YOU KEEP IT FROM YOUR FATHER?
I HAD TO.
THERE'S NO WAY HE'D EVER ALLOW IT.
ARE YOU *INSANE* ?!
HEY, IBUKI...
BAM
...
CHIK

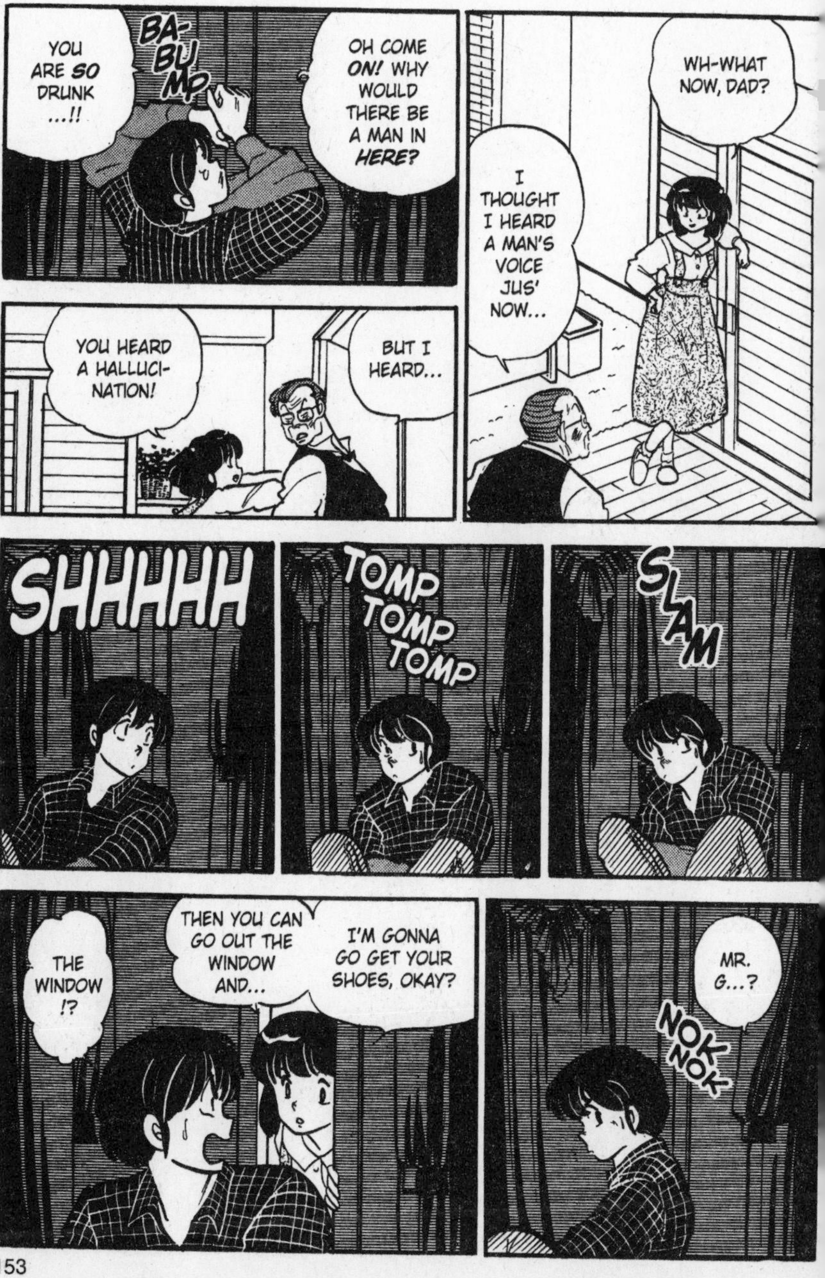
WH-WHAT NOW, DAD?
I THOUGHT I HEARD A MAN'S VOICE JUS' NOW...
OH COME ON! WHY WOULD THERE BE A MAN IN HERE?
BA-BU-MP
YOU ARE SO DRUNK ...!!
BUT I HEARD...
YOU HEARD A HALLUCI-NATION!
SLAM
TOMP TOMP TOMP
SHHHHH
MR. G...?
NOK NOK
I'M GONNA GO GET YOUR SHOES, OKAY?
THEN YOU CAN GO OUT THE WINDOW AND...
THE WINDOW !?

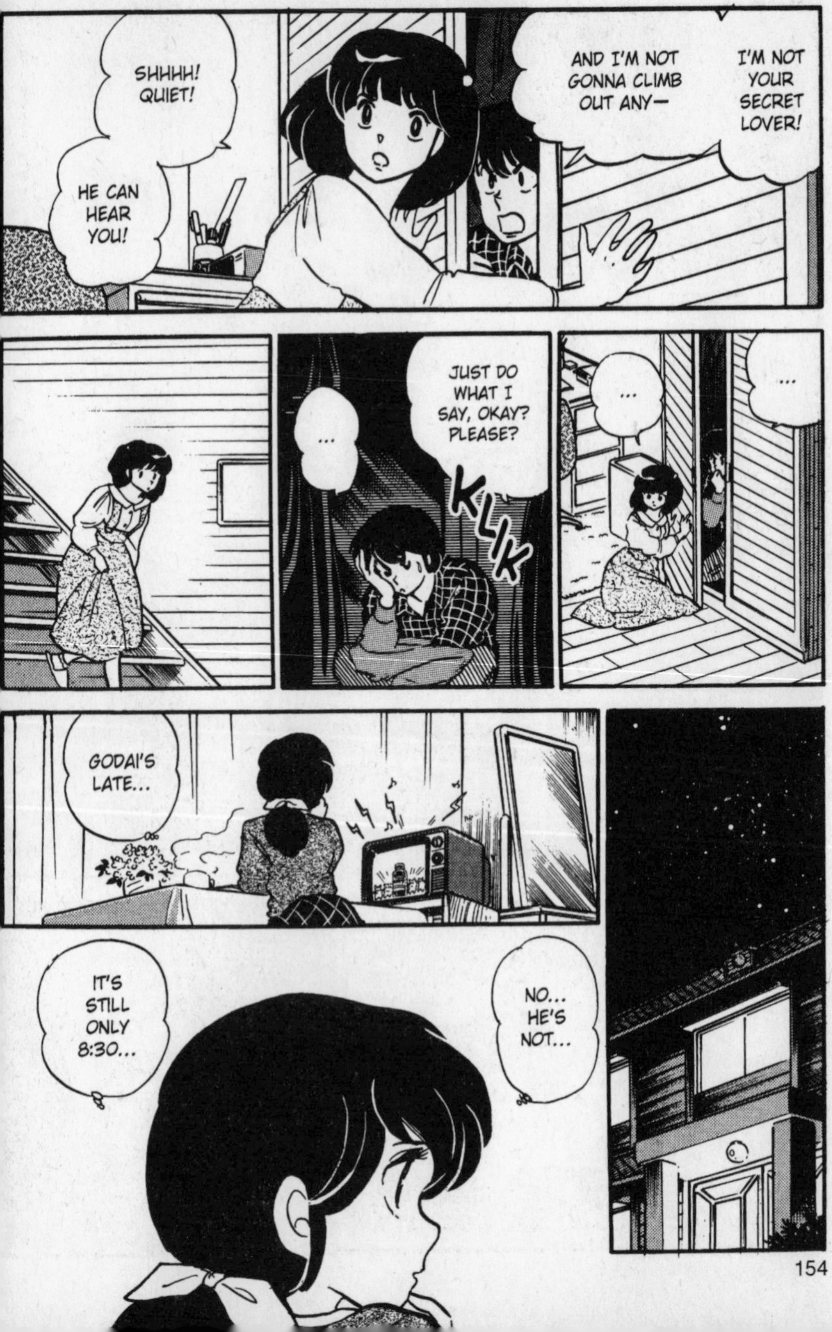
I'M NOT YOUR SECRET LOVER!
AND I'M NOT GONNA CLIMB OUT ANY—
SHHHH! QUIET!
HE CAN HEAR YOU!
...
...
JUST DO WHAT I SAY, OKAY? PLEASE?
...
KLIK
GODAI'S LATE...
NO... HE'S NOT...
IT'S STILL ONLY 8:30...

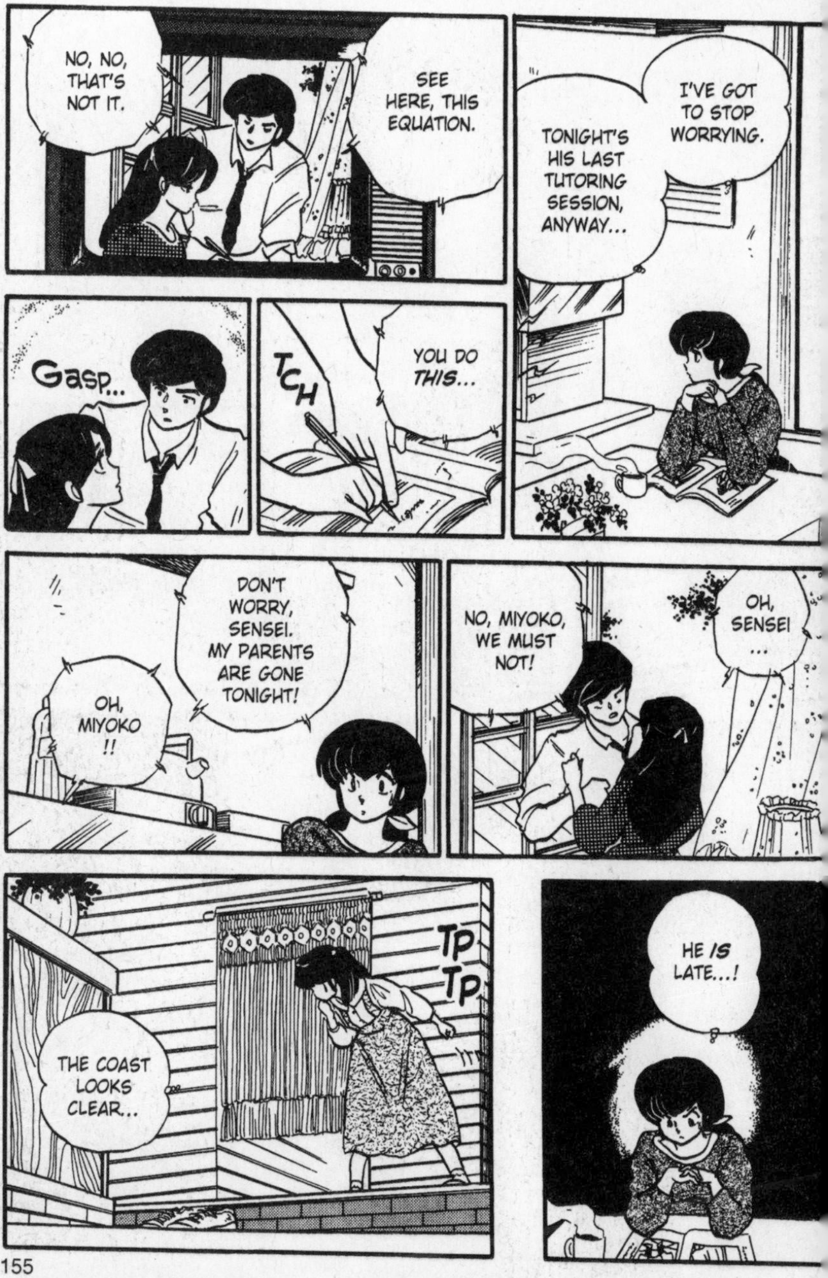

I'VE GOT TO STOP WORRYING.
TONIGHT'S HIS LAST TUTORING SESSION, ANYWAY...
SEE HERE, THIS EQUATION.
NO, NO, THAT'S NOT IT.
YOU DO *THIS*...
TCH
Gasp...
OH, SENSEI ...
NO, MIYOKO, WE MUST NOT!
DON'T WORRY, SENSEI. MY PARENTS ARE GONE TONIGHT!
OH, MIYOKO !!
HE *IS* LATE...!
TP TP
THE COAST LOOKS CLEAR...

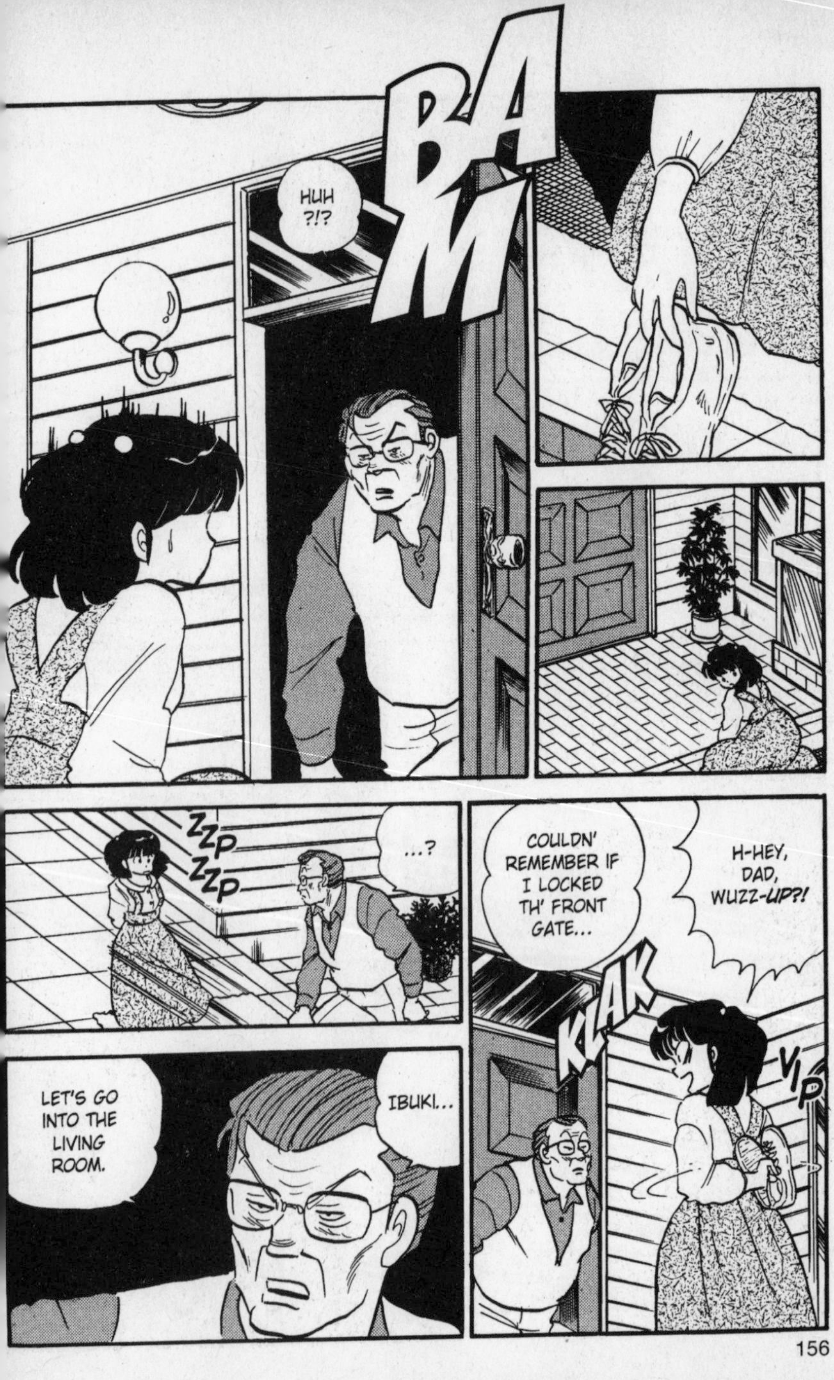
BAM
HUH ?!?
H-HEY, DAD, WUZZ-UP?!
COULDN' REMEMBER IF I LOCKED TH' FRONT GATE...
KLAK
VIP
ZZP ZZP
...?
IBUKI...
LET'S GO INTO THE LIVING ROOM.

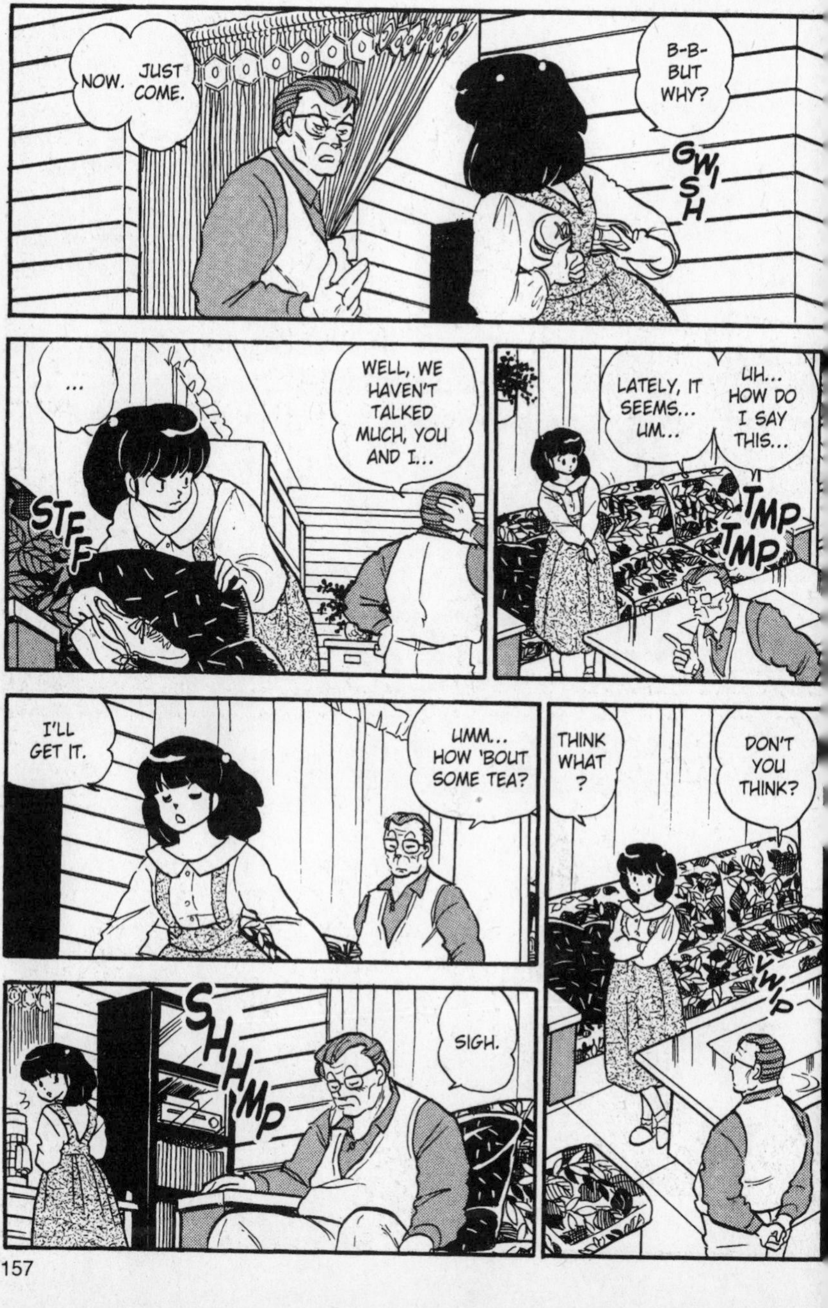
B-B-BUT WHY?
GWISH
JUST COME. NOW.
UH... HOW DO I SAY THIS...
LATELY, IT SEEMS... UM...
TMP TMP
WELL, WE HAVEN'T TALKED MUCH, YOU AND I...
...
STFF
DON'T YOU THINK?
THINK WHAT ?
VWIP
UMM... HOW 'BOUT SOME TEA?
I'LL GET IT.
SIGH.
SHHMP

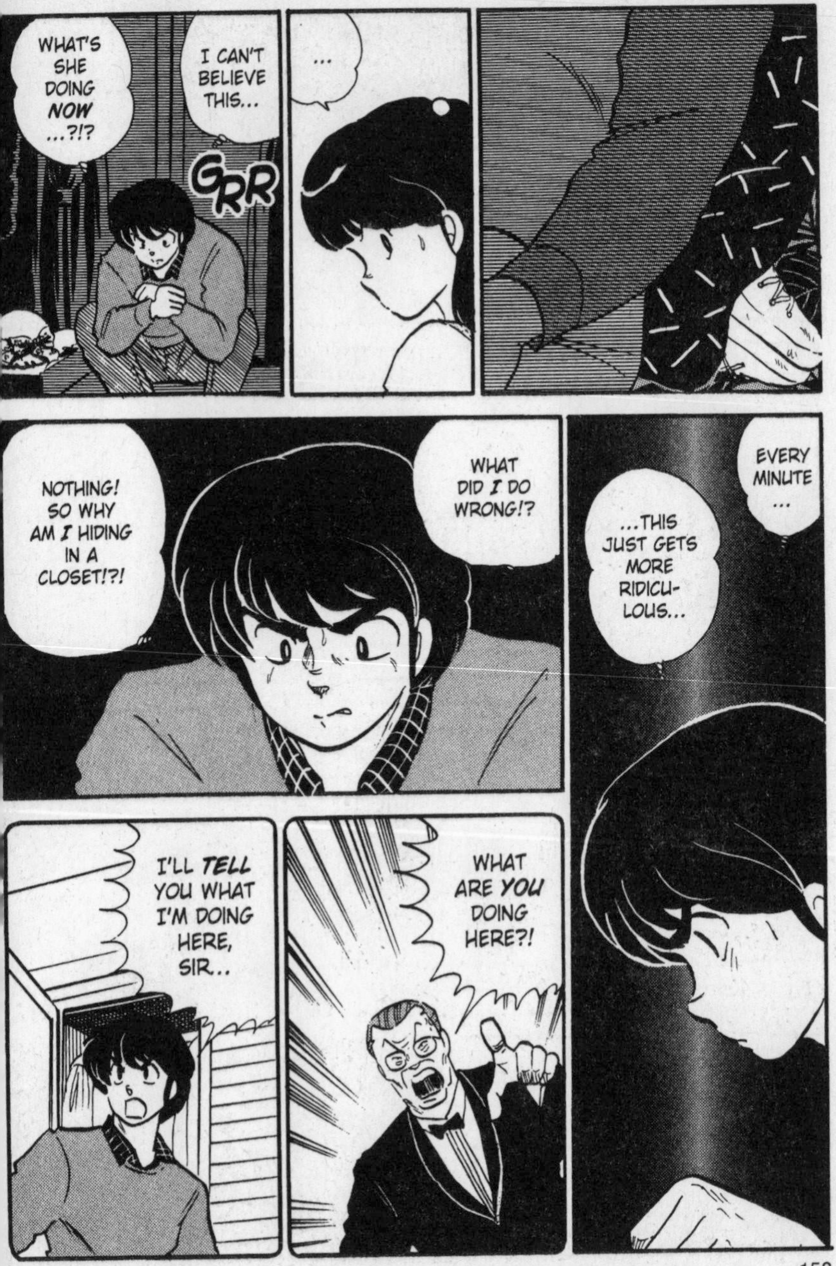
...
I CAN'T BELIEVE THIS...
WHAT'S SHE DOING NOW ...?!?
GRR
EVERY MINUTE ...
...THIS JUST GETS MORE RIDICULOUS...
WHAT DID I DO WRONG!?
NOTHING! SO WHY AM I HIDING IN A CLOSET!?!
WHAT ARE YOU DOING HERE?!
I'LL TELL YOU WHAT I'M DOING HERE, SIR...

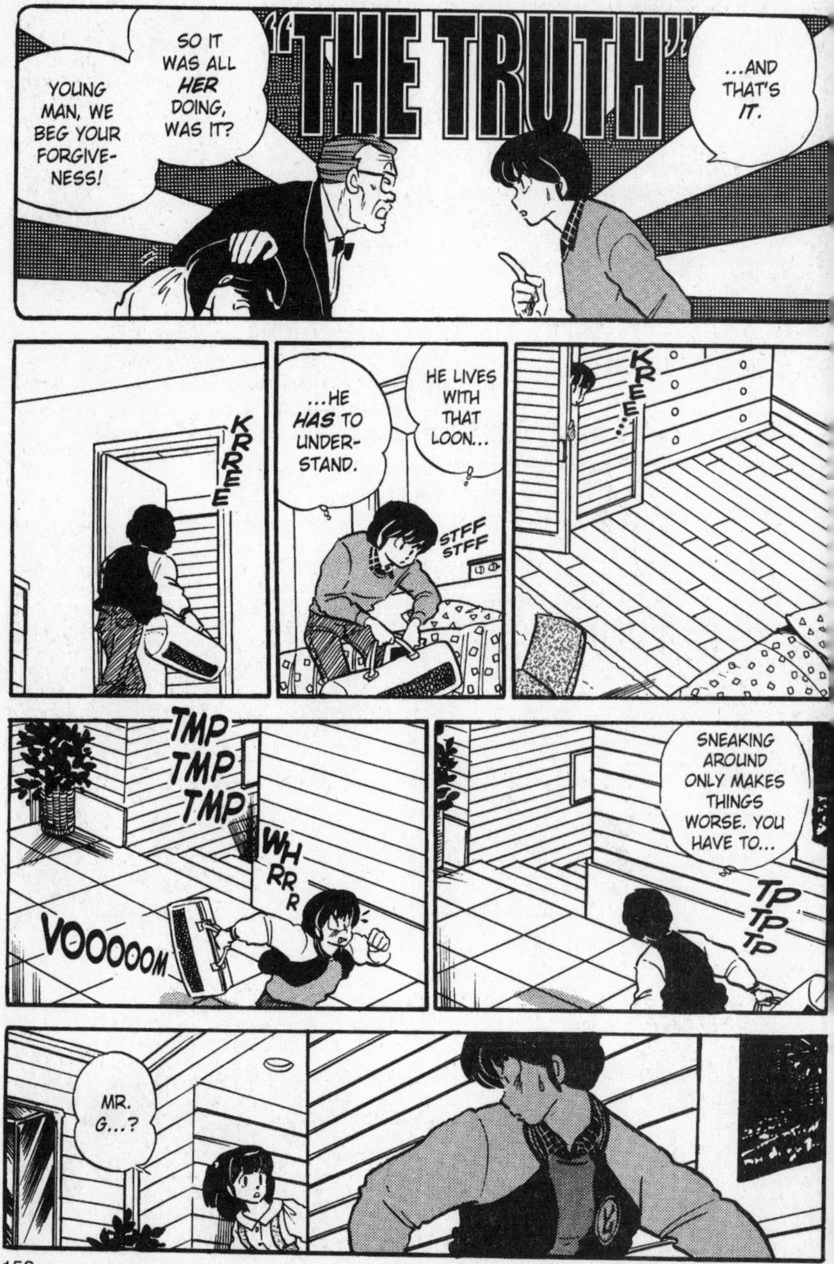

...AND THAT'S *IT.*
"THE TRUTH"
SO IT WAS ALL *HER* DOING, WAS IT?
YOUNG MAN, WE BEG YOUR FORGIVE-NESS!
KREE...
HE LIVES WITH THAT LOON...
...HE *HAS* TO UNDER-STAND.
STFF STFF
KRREE
SNEAKING AROUND ONLY MAKES THINGS WORSE. YOU HAVE TO...
TP TP TP
TMP TMP TMP
WHRRR
VOOOOOM
MR. G...?

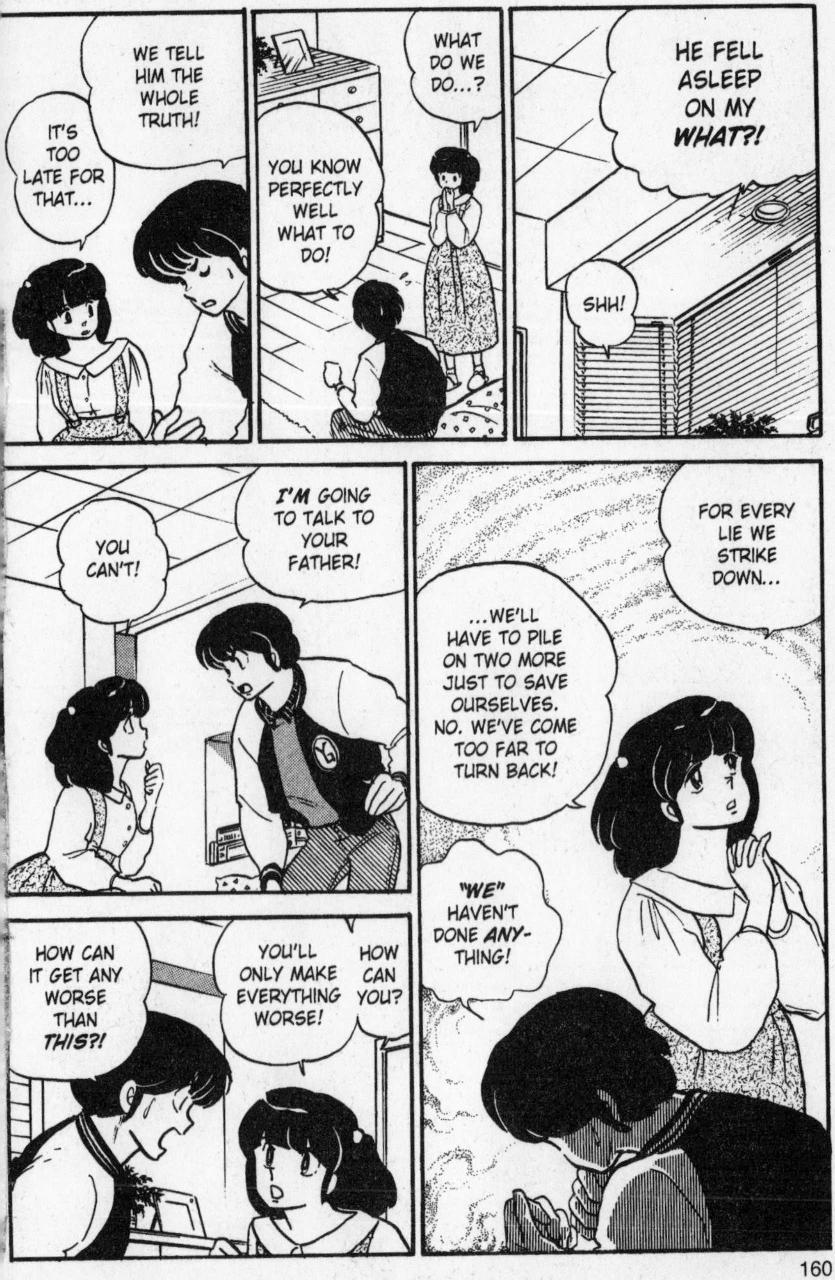
HE FELL ASLEEP ON MY WHAT?!
SHH!
WHAT DO WE DO...?
YOU KNOW PERFECTLY WELL WHAT TO DO!
WE TELL HIM THE WHOLE TRUTH!
IT'S TOO LATE FOR THAT...
FOR EVERY LIE WE STRIKE DOWN...
...WE'LL HAVE TO PILE ON TWO MORE JUST TO SAVE OURSELVES. NO. WE'VE COME TOO FAR TO TURN BACK!
"WE" HAVEN'T DONE ANY-THING!
I'M GOING TO TALK TO YOUR FATHER!
YOU CAN'T!
HOW CAN YOU?
YOU'LL ONLY MAKE EVERYTHING WORSE!
HOW CAN IT GET ANY WORSE THAN THIS?!

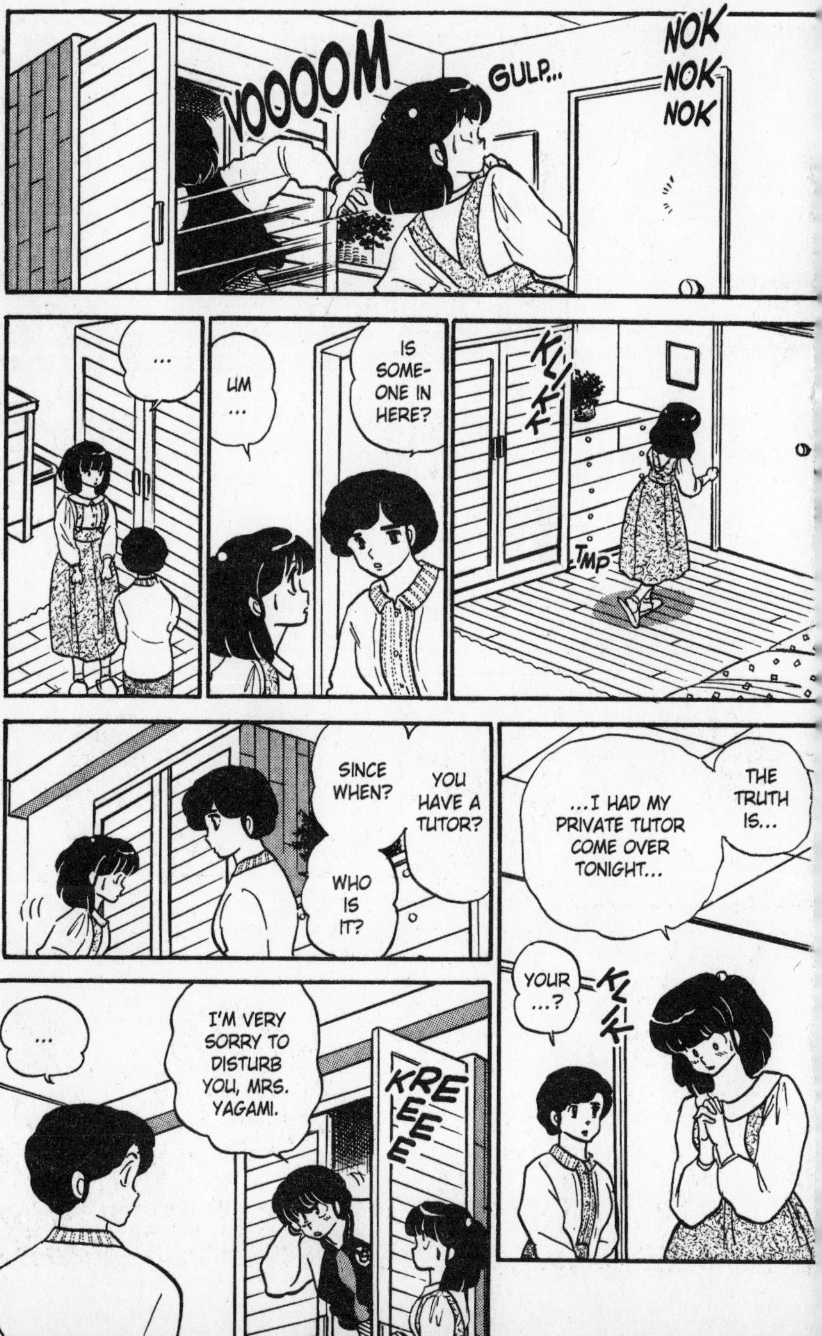
NOK NOK NOK
GULP...
VOOOOM
KLIK
TMP
IS SOMEONE IN HERE?
UM ...
...
THE TRUTH IS...
...I HAD MY PRIVATE TUTOR COME OVER TONIGHT...
YOUR ...?
KLIK
YOU HAVE A TUTOR?
SINCE WHEN?
WHO IS IT?
KREEEEE
I'M VERY SORRY TO DISTURB YOU, MRS. YAGAMI.
...

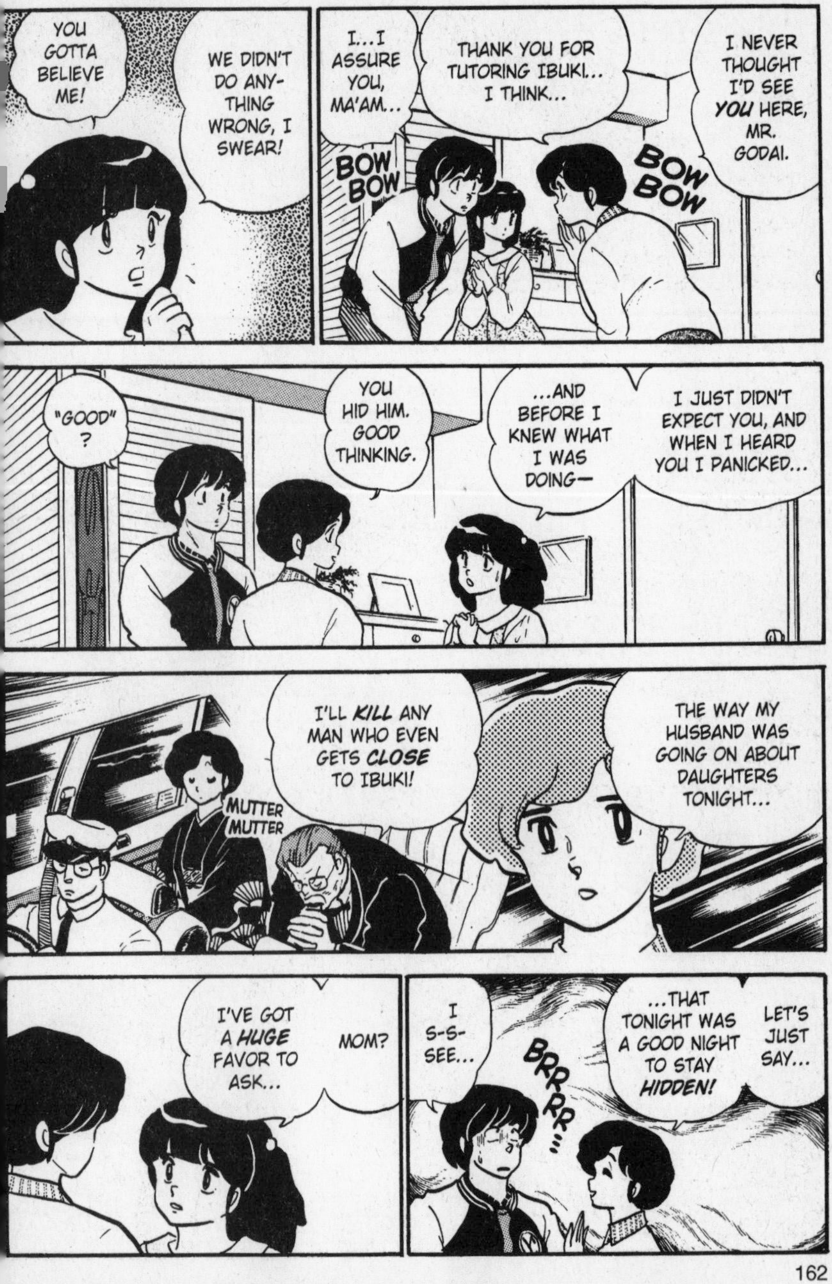
I NEVER THOUGHT I'D SEE YOU HERE, MR. GODAI.
BOW BOW
THANK YOU FOR TUTORING IBUKI... I THINK...
I...I ASSURE YOU, MA'AM...
BOW BOW
WE DIDN'T DO ANY-THING WRONG, I SWEAR!
YOU GOTTA BELIEVE ME!
I JUST DIDN'T EXPECT YOU, AND WHEN I HEARD YOU I PANICKED...
...AND BEFORE I KNEW WHAT I WAS DOING—
YOU HID HIM. GOOD THINKING.
"GOOD" ?
THE WAY MY HUSBAND WAS GOING ON ABOUT DAUGHTERS TONIGHT...
I'LL KILL ANY MAN WHO EVEN GETS CLOSE TO IBUKI!
MUTTER MUTTER
LET'S JUST SAY...
...THAT TONIGHT WAS A GOOD NIGHT TO STAY HIDDEN!
BRRRRR!!
I S-S-SEE...
MOM?
I'VE GOT A HUGE FAVOR TO ASK...

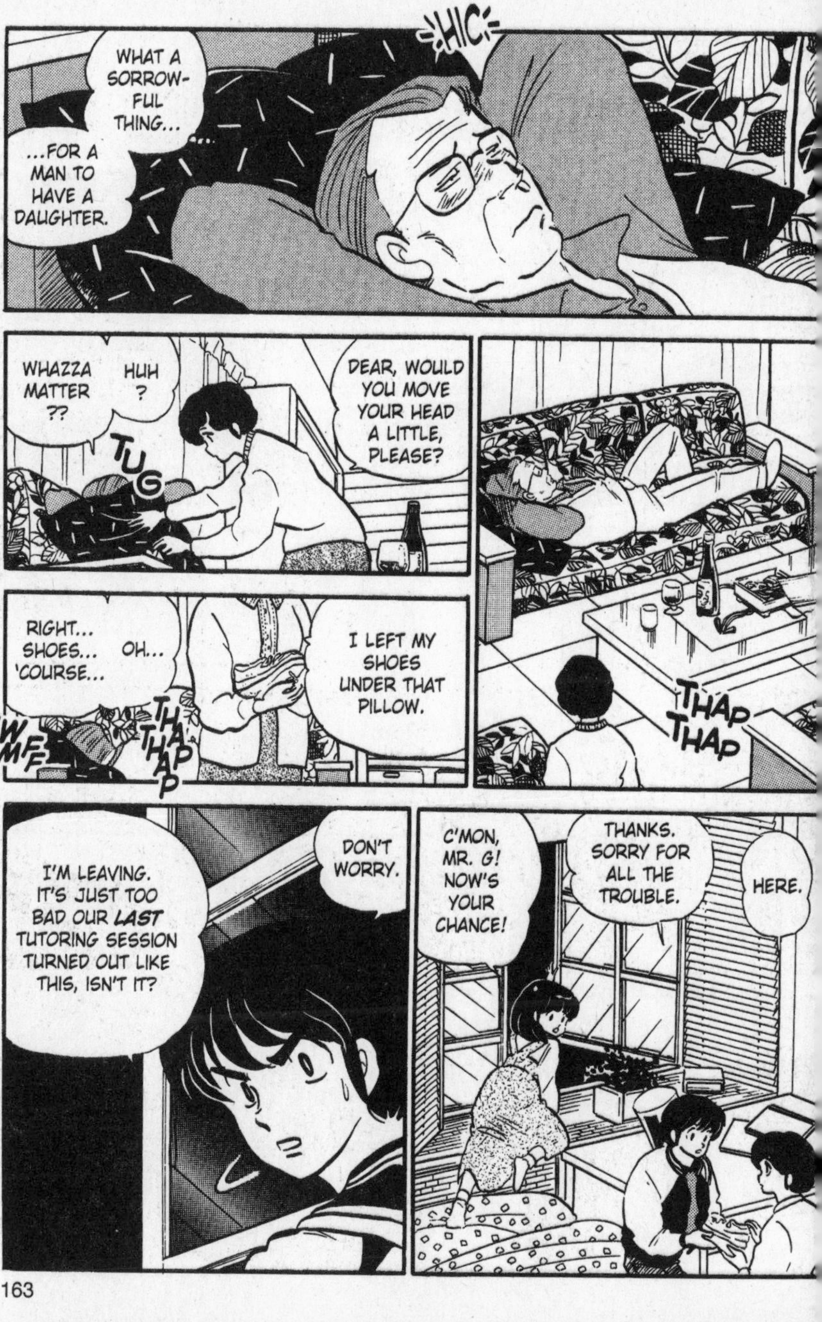
HIC
WHAT A SORROWFUL THING...
...FOR A MAN TO HAVE A DAUGHTER.
THAP THAP
DEAR, WOULD YOU MOVE YOUR HEAD A LITTLE, PLEASE?
HUH ?
WHAZZA MATTER ??
TUG
I LEFT MY SHOES UNDER THAT PILLOW.
OH...
RIGHT... SHOES... 'COURSE...
THAP THAP
GWMFF
HERE.
THANKS. SORRY FOR ALL THE TROUBLE.
C'MON, MR. G! NOW'S YOUR CHANCE!
DON'T WORRY.
I'M LEAVING. IT'S JUST TOO BAD OUR LAST TUTORING SESSION TURNED OUT LIKE THIS, ISN'T IT?

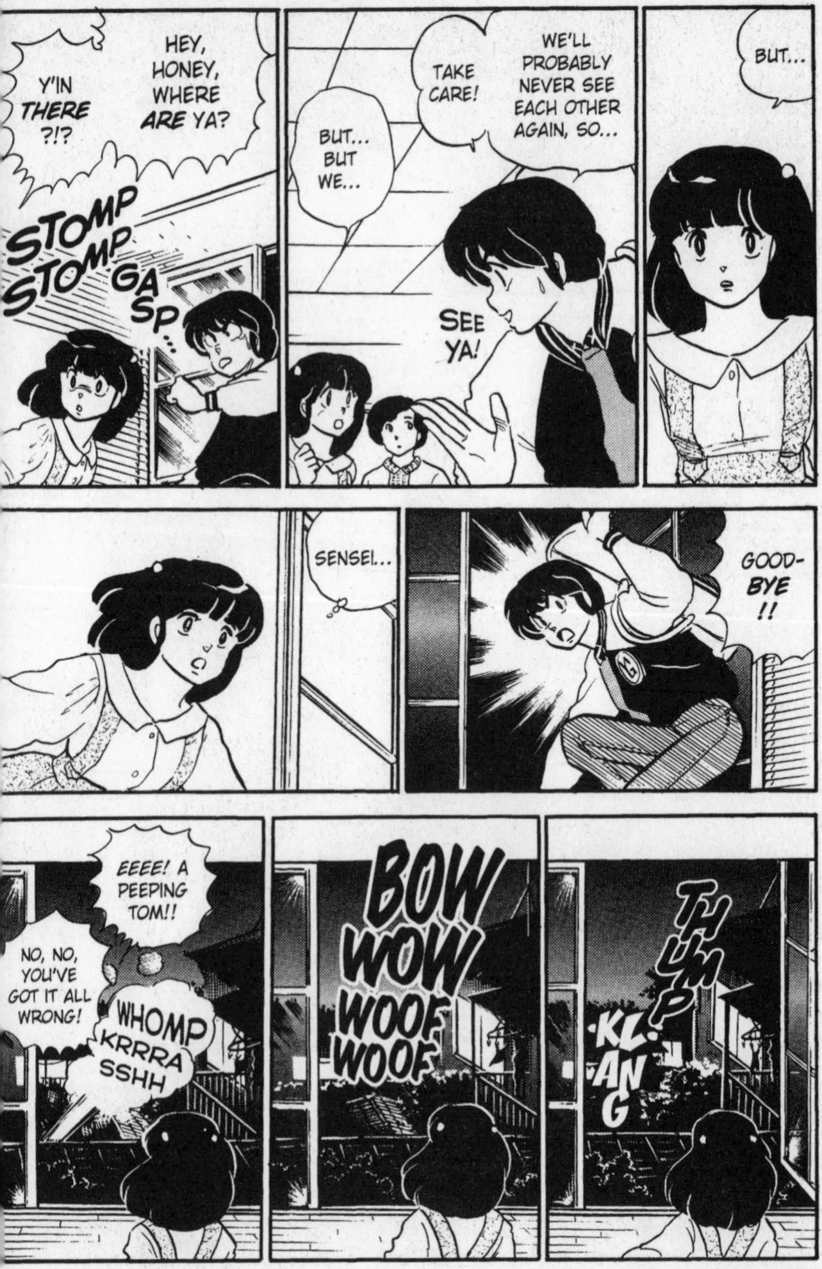
HEY, HONEY, WHERE ARE YA?
Y'IN THERE ?!?
STOMP STOMP
GASP...
SEE YA!
TAKE CARE!
WE'LL PROBABLY NEVER SEE EACH OTHER AGAIN, SO...
BUT... BUT WE...
BUT...
SENSEI...
GOOD-BYE !!
EEEE! A PEEPING TOM!!
NO, NO, YOU'VE GOT IT ALL WRONG!
WHOMP KRRRASSHH
BOW WOW WOOF WOOF
THUMP
KLANG

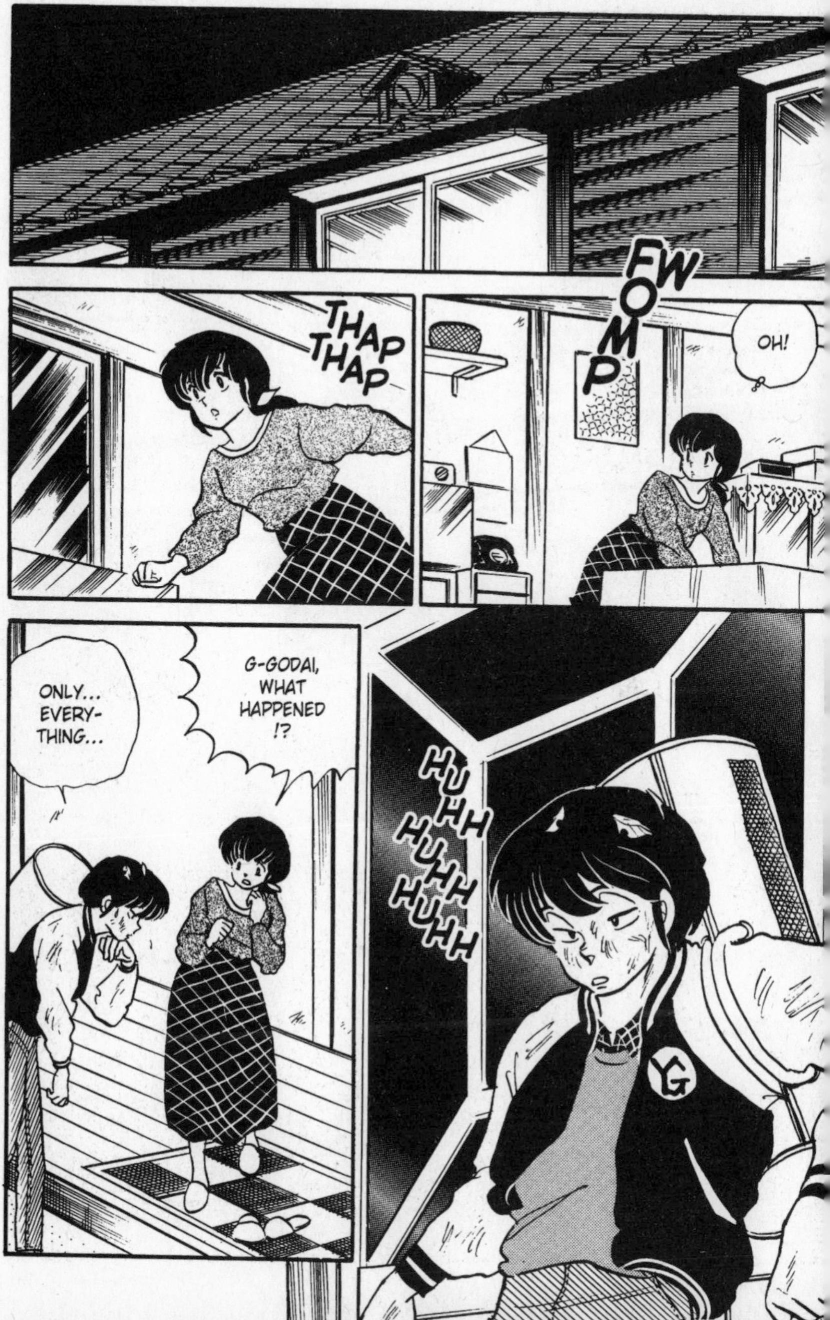
FWOMP
OH!
THAP THAP
HUHH HUHH HUHH
G-GODAI, WHAT HAPPENED !?
ONLY... EVERY-THING...

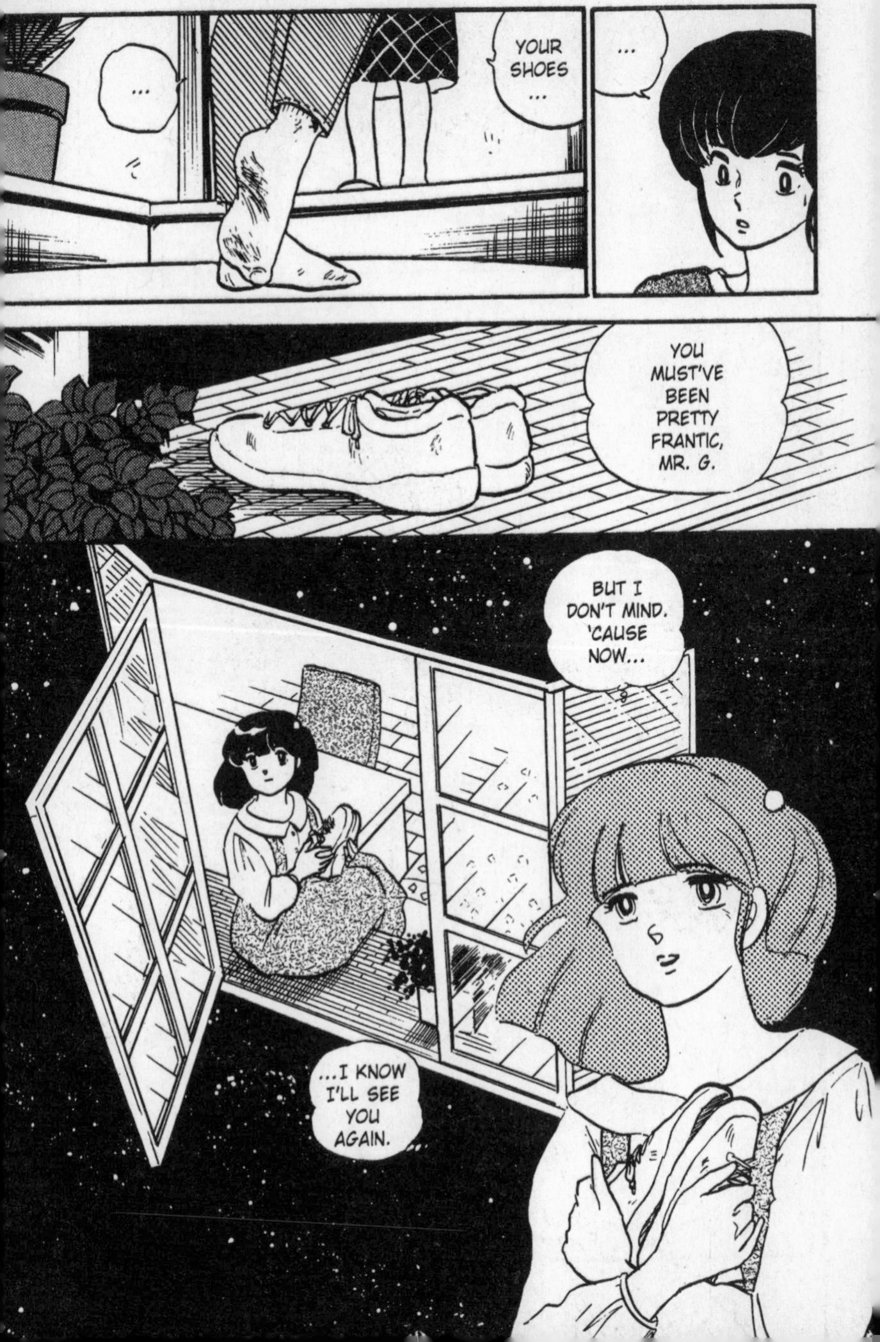
...
YOUR SHOES ...
...
YOU MUST'VE BEEN PRETTY FRANTIC, MR. G.
BUT I DON'T MIND. 'CAUSE NOW...
...I KNOW I'LL SEE YOU AGAIN.

PART NINE

DROP THE OTHER SHOE

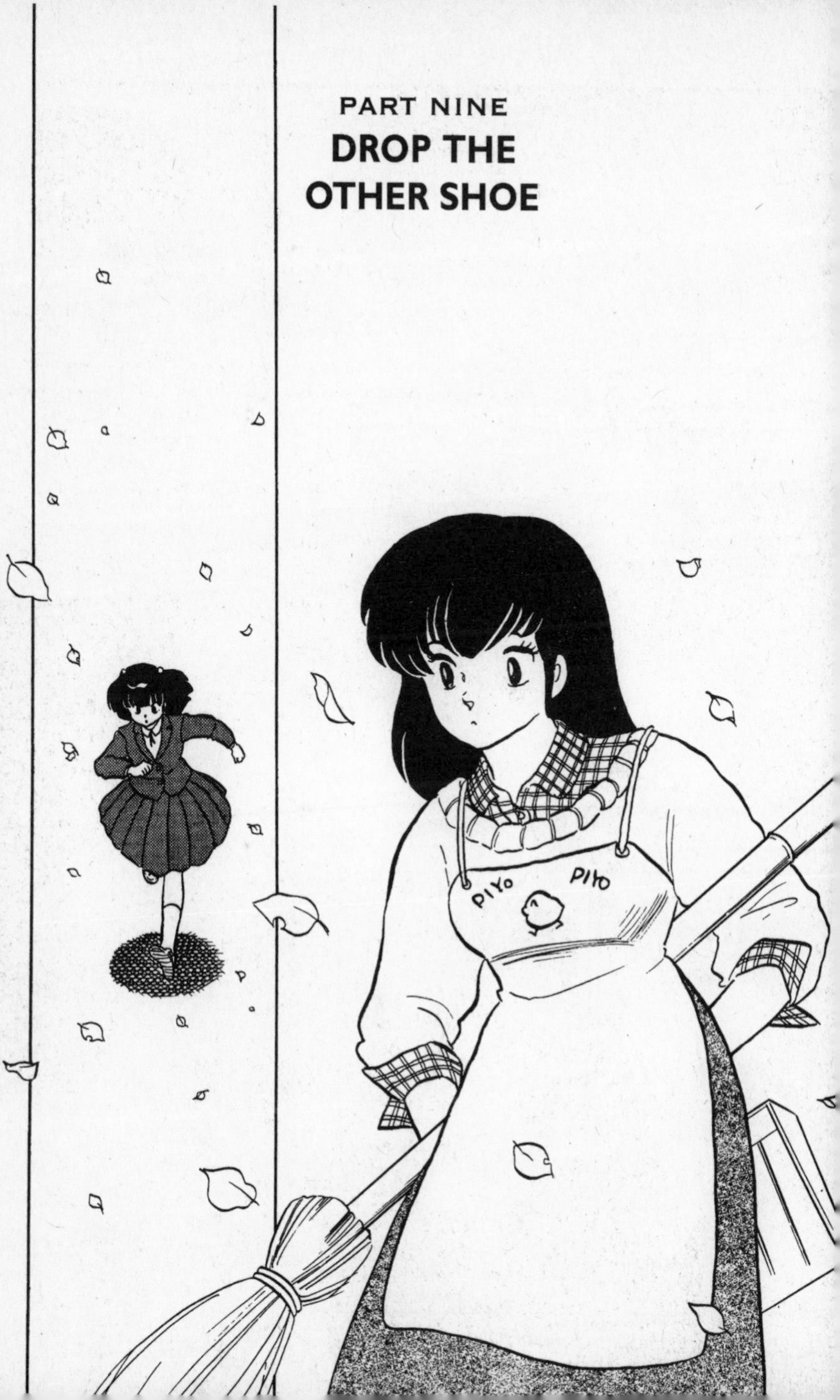
PIYO
PIYO

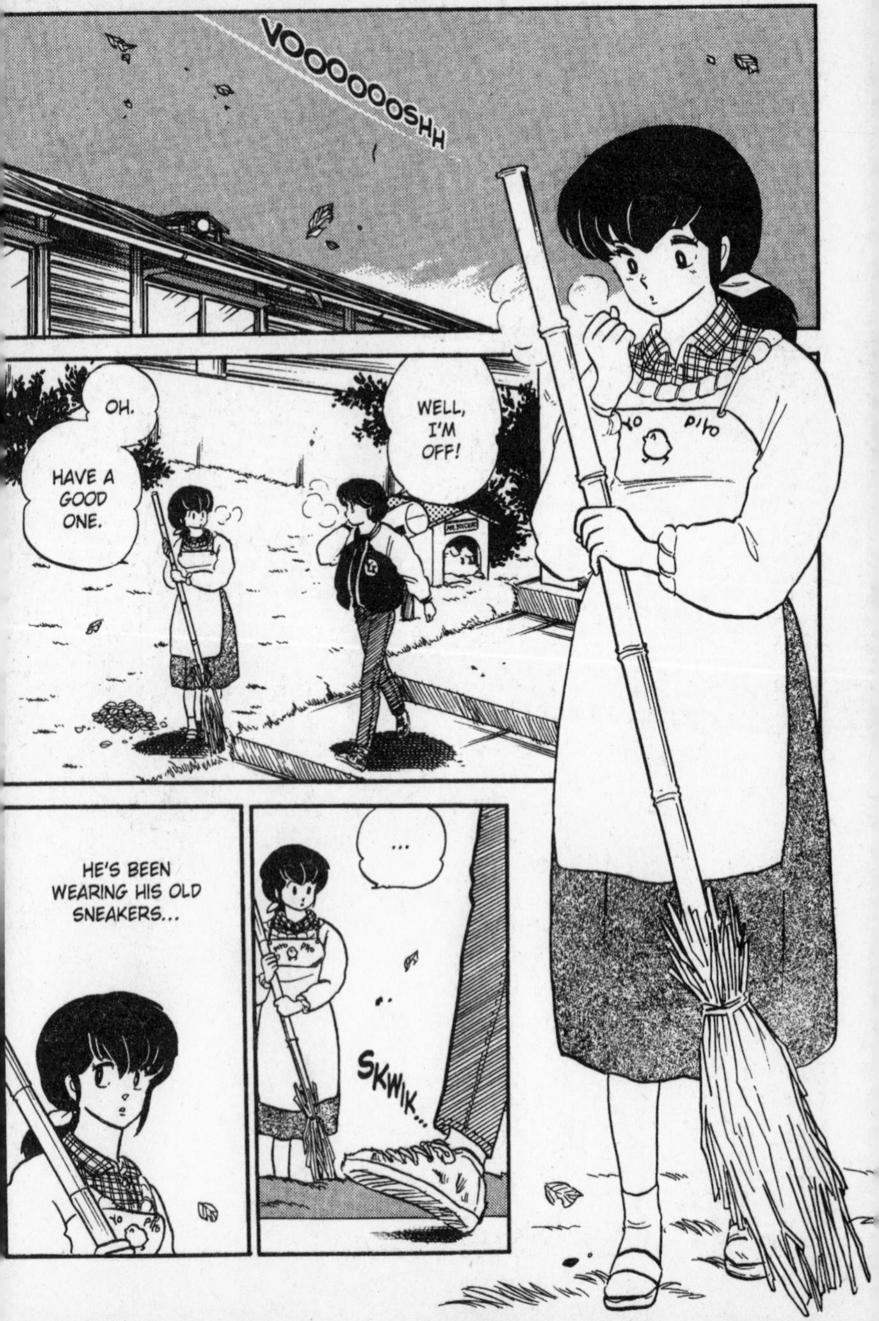
VOOOOOOOSHH
WELL, I'M OFF!
OH.
HAVE A GOOD ONE.
...
SKWIK...
HE'S BEEN WEARING HIS OLD SNEAKERS...

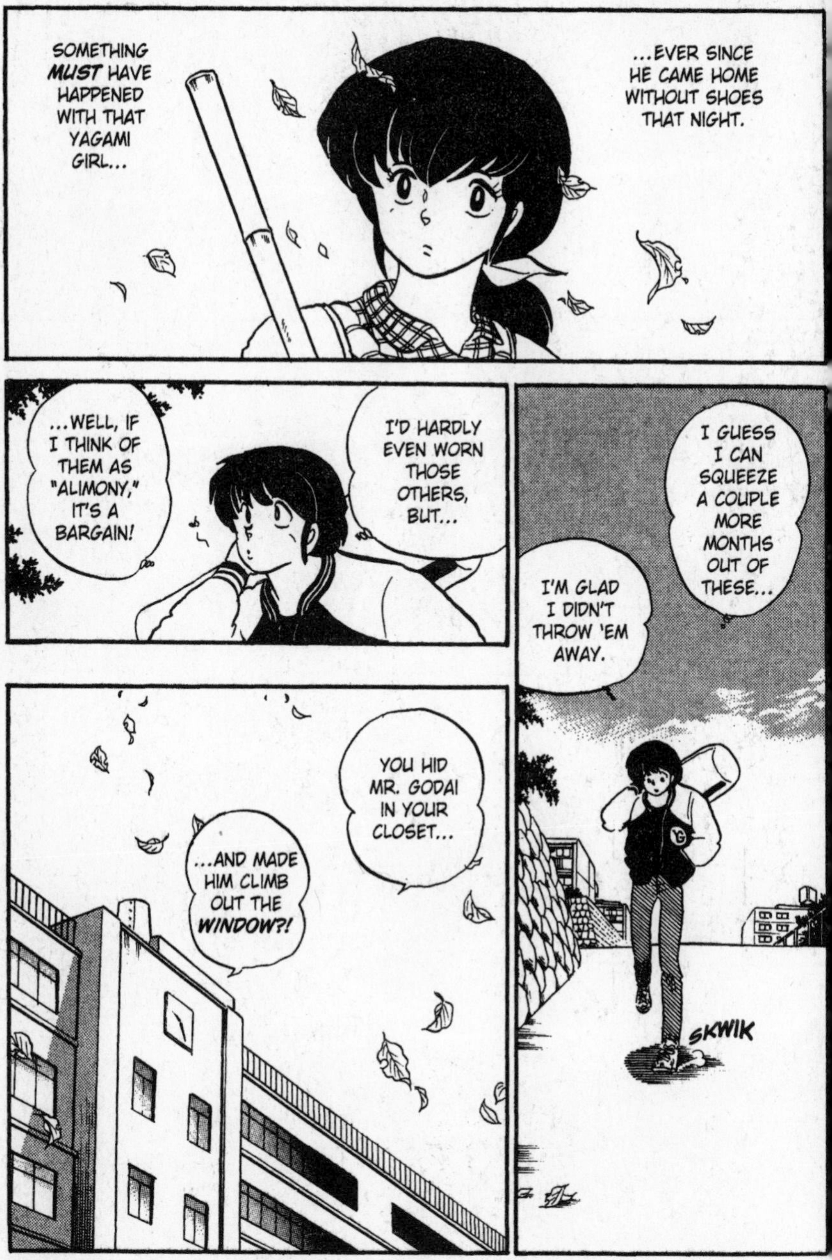
...EVER SINCE HE CAME HOME WITHOUT SHOES THAT NIGHT.
SOMETHING MUST HAVE HAPPENED WITH THAT YAGAMI GIRL...
I GUESS I CAN SQUEEZE A COUPLE MORE MONTHS OUT OF THESE...
I'M GLAD I DIDN'T THROW 'EM AWAY.
SKWIK
I'D HARDLY EVEN WORN THOSE OTHERS, BUT...
...WELL, IF I THINK OF THEM AS "ALIMONY," IT'S A BARGAIN!
YOU HID MR. GODAI IN YOUR CLOSET...
...AND MADE HIM CLIMB OUT THE WINDOW?!

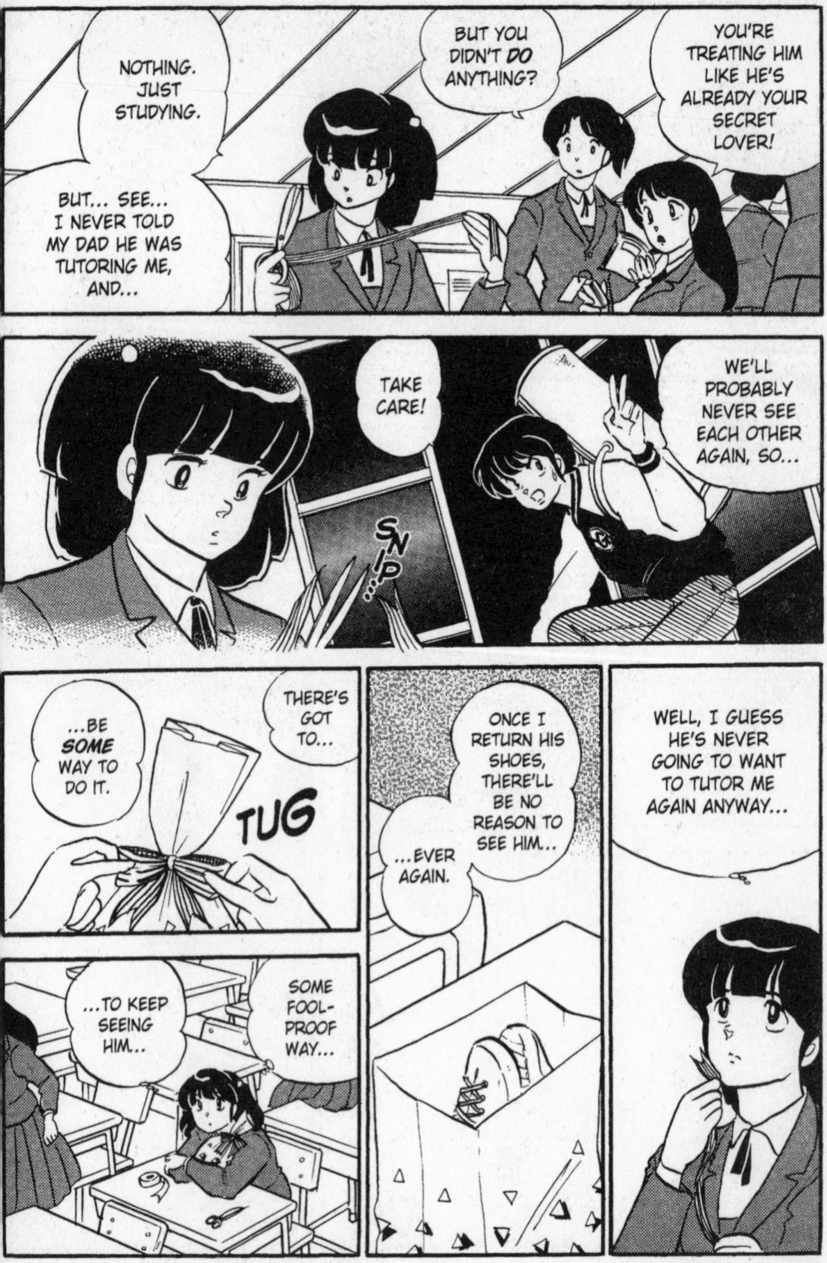
YOU'RE TREATING HIM LIKE HE'S ALREADY YOUR SECRET LOVER!
BUT YOU DIDN'T *DO* ANYTHING?
NOTHING. JUST STUDYING.
BUT... SEE... I NEVER TOLD MY DAD HE WAS TUTORING ME, AND...
WE'LL PROBABLY NEVER SEE EACH OTHER AGAIN, SO...
TAKE CARE!
SNIP...
WELL, I GUESS HE'S NEVER GOING TO WANT TO TUTOR ME AGAIN ANYWAY...
ONCE I RETURN HIS SHOES, THERE'LL BE NO REASON TO SEE HIM...
...EVER AGAIN.
THERE'S GOT TO...
TUG
...BE **SOME** WAY TO DO IT.
SOME FOOL-PROOF WAY...
...TO KEEP SEEING HIM...

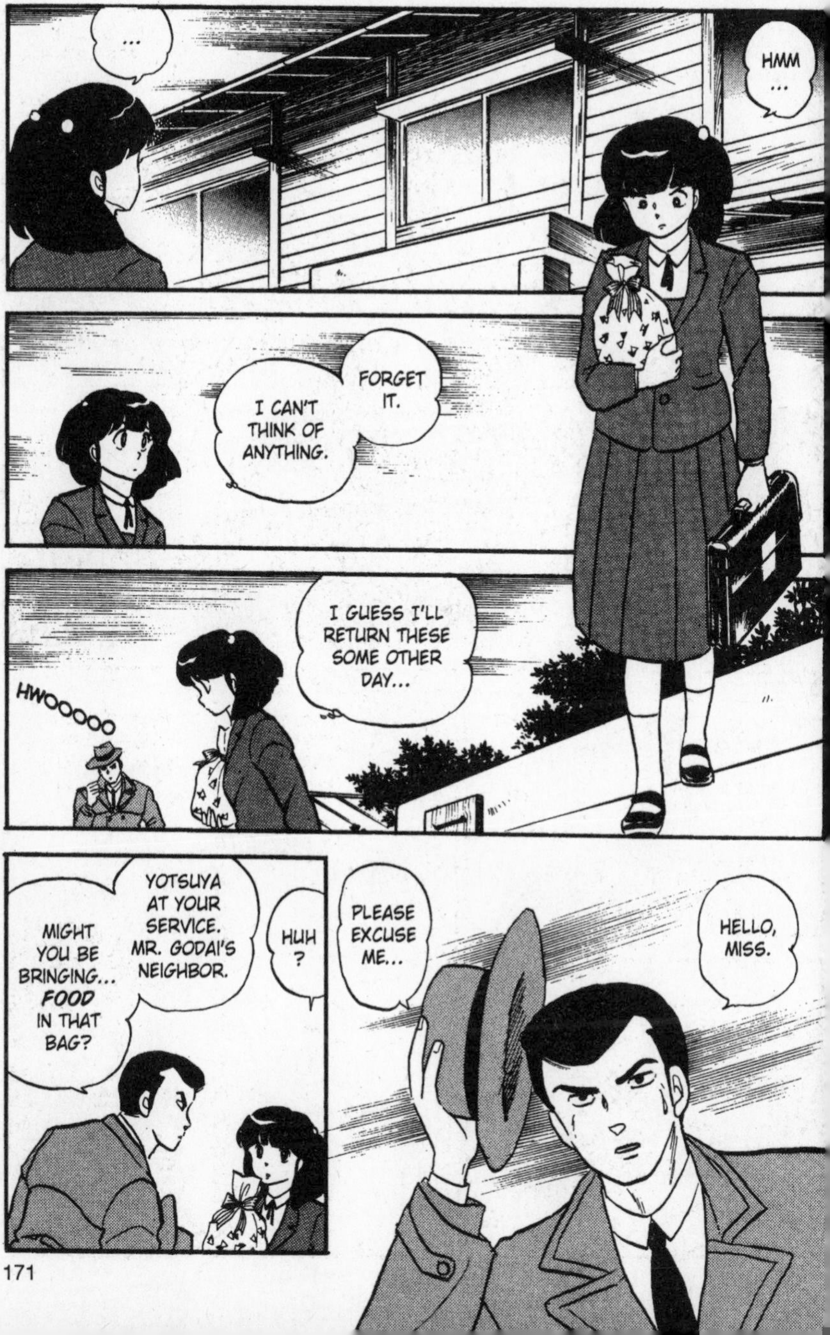
HMM ...
...
FORGET IT.
I CAN'T THINK OF ANYTHING.
I GUESS I'LL RETURN THESE SOME OTHER DAY...
HWOOOOOO
HELLO, MISS.
PLEASE EXCUSE ME...
HUH ?
YOTSUYA AT YOUR SERVICE. MR. GODAI'S NEIGHBOR.
MIGHT YOU BE BRINGING... FOOD IN THAT BAG?

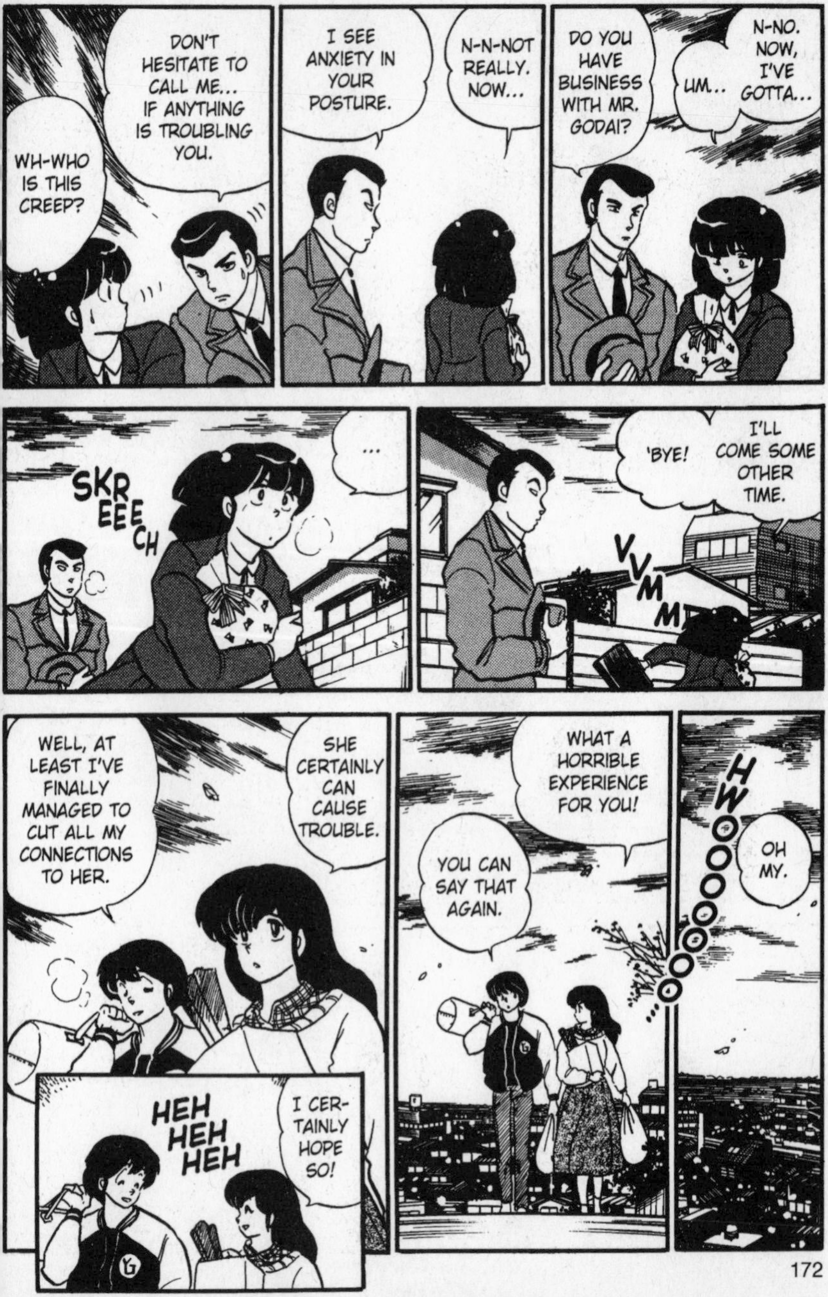
N-NO. NOW, I'VE GOTTA...
UM...
DO YOU HAVE BUSINESS WITH MR. GODAI?
N-N-NOT REALLY. NOW...
I SEE ANXIETY IN YOUR POSTURE.
DON'T HESITATE TO CALL ME... IF ANYTHING IS TROUBLING YOU.
WH-WHO IS THIS CREEP?
I'LL COME SOME OTHER TIME.
'BYE!
VVMMM
...
SKREEECH
HWOOOOOOOOO...
OH MY.
WHAT A HORRIBLE EXPERIENCE FOR YOU!
YOU CAN SAY THAT AGAIN.
SHE CERTAINLY CAN CAUSE TROUBLE.
WELL, AT LEAST I'VE FINALLY MANAGED TO CUT ALL MY CONNECTIONS TO HER.
I CER-TAINLY HOPE SO!
HEH HEH HEH

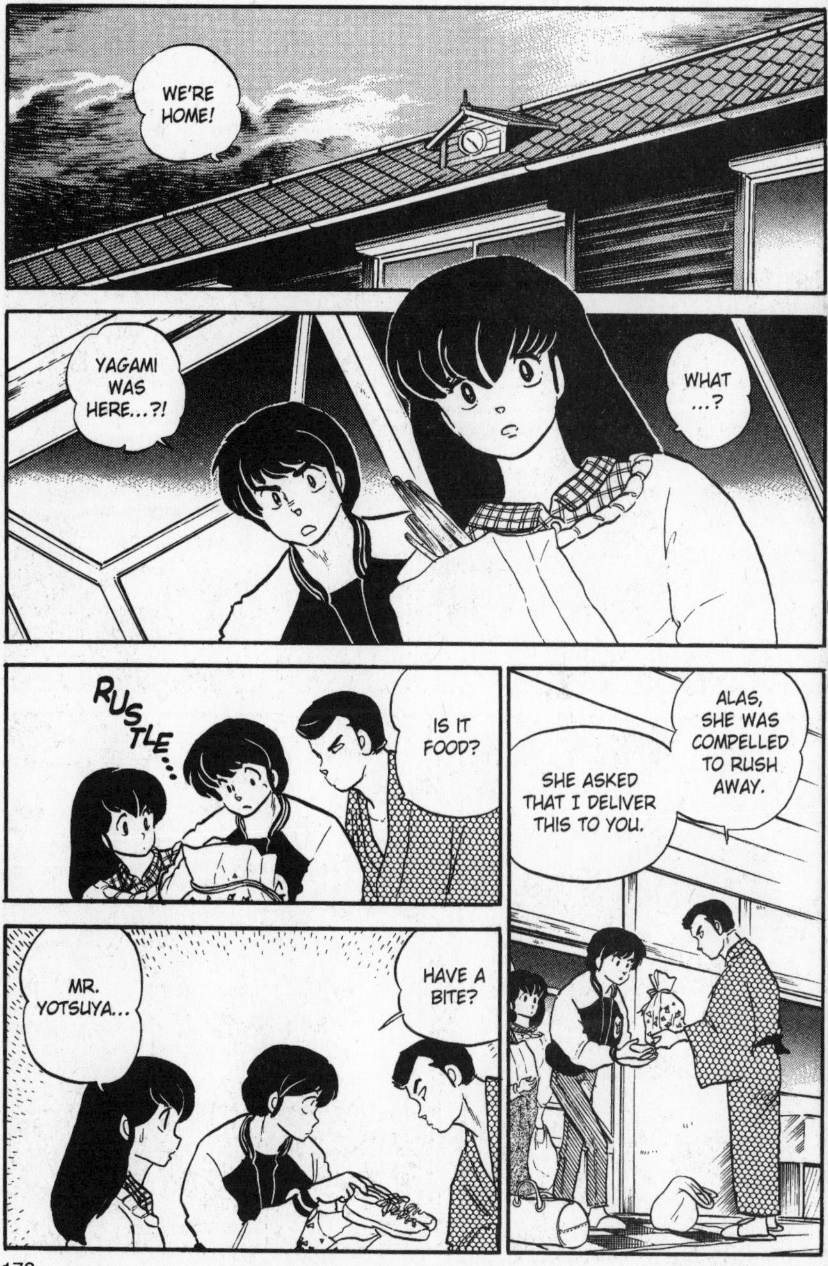

WE'RE HOME!
WHAT ...?
YAGAMI WAS HERE...?!
ALAS, SHE WAS COMPELLED TO RUSH AWAY.
SHE ASKED THAT I DELIVER THIS TO YOU.
IS IT FOOD?
RUSTLE...
HAVE A BITE?
MR. YOTSUYA...

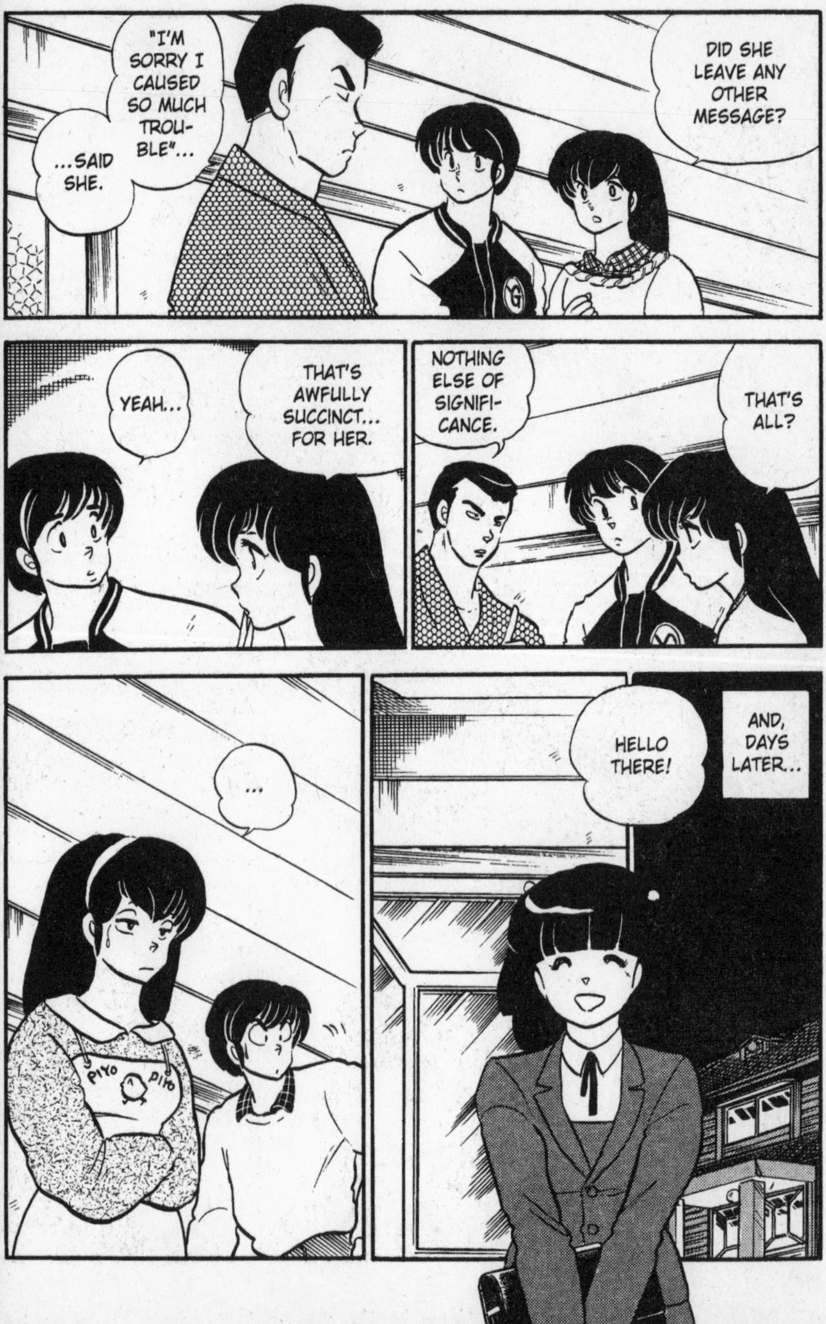
DID SHE LEAVE ANY OTHER MESSAGE?
"I'M SORRY I CAUSED SO MUCH TROUBLE"...
...SAID SHE.
THAT'S ALL?
NOTHING ELSE OF SIGNIFICANCE.
THAT'S AWFULLY SUCCINCT... FOR HER.
YEAH...
AND, DAYS LATER...
HELLO THERE!
...

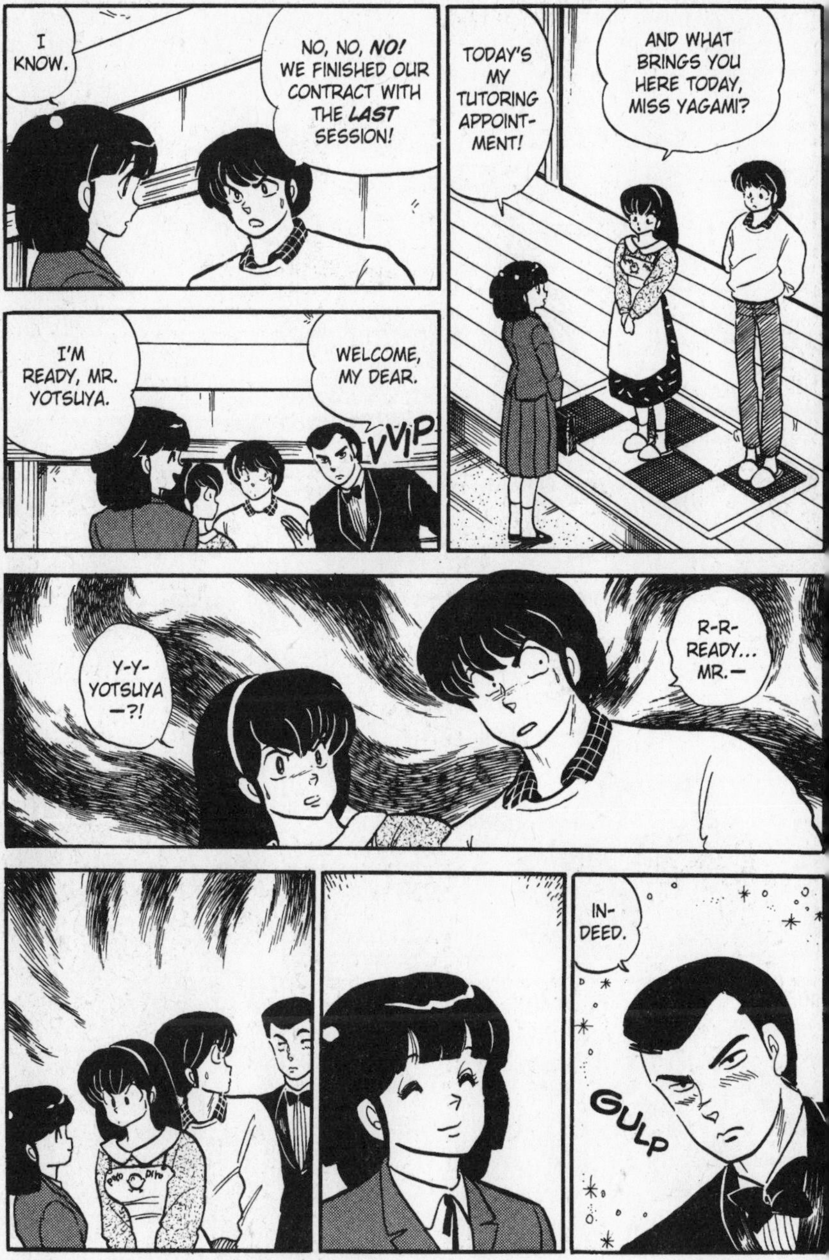
AND WHAT BRINGS YOU HERE TODAY, MISS YAGAMI?
TODAY'S MY TUTORING APPOINT-MENT!
NO, NO, NO! WE FINISHED OUR CONTRACT WITH THE LAST SESSION!
I KNOW.
WELCOME, MY DEAR.
VVIP
I'M READY, MR. YOTSUYA.
R-R-READY... MR.—
Y-Y-YOTSUYA—?!
IN-DEED.
GULP

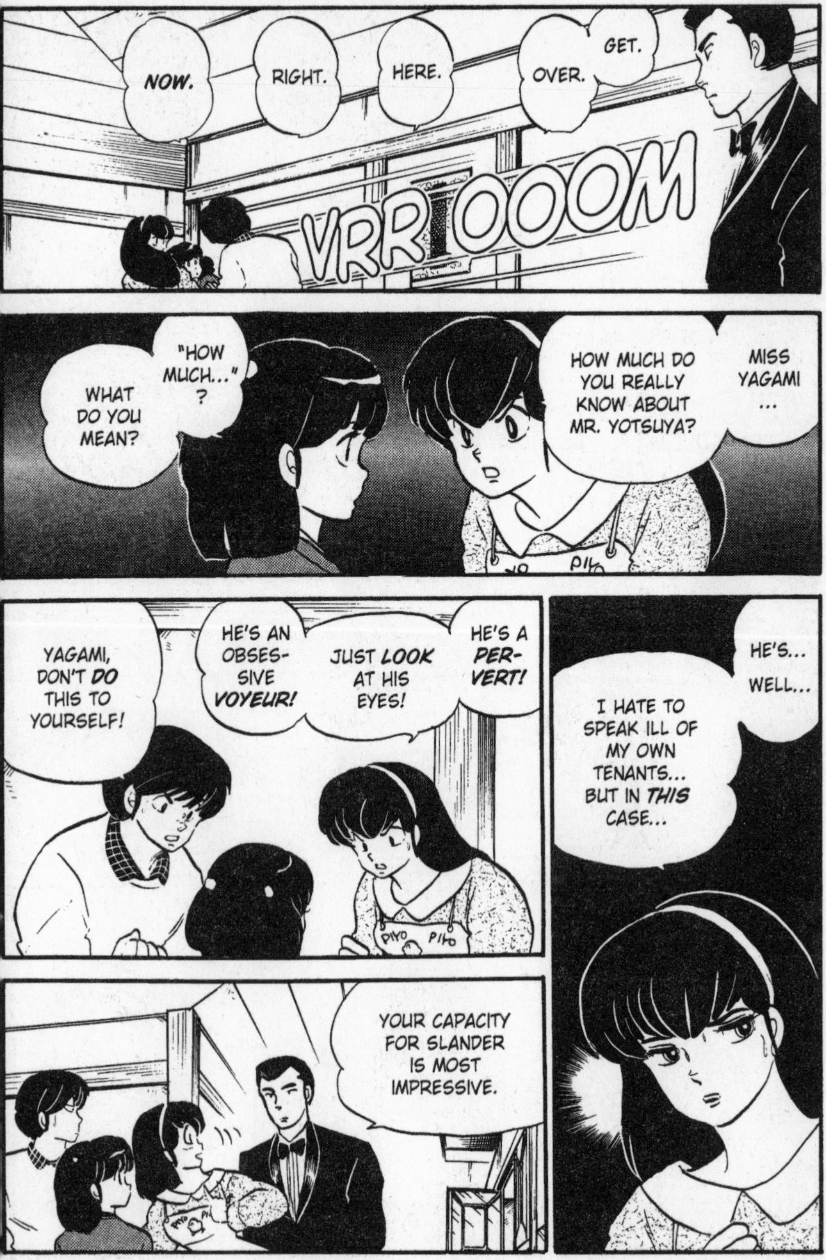
GET.
OVER.
HERE.
RIGHT.
NOW.
VRRIOOOM
MISS YAGAMI...
HOW MUCH DO YOU REALLY KNOW ABOUT MR. YOTSUYA?
"HOW MUCH..." ?
WHAT DO YOU MEAN?
HE'S... WELL...
I HATE TO SPEAK ILL OF MY OWN TENANTS... BUT IN THIS CASE...
HE'S A PERVERT!
JUST LOOK AT HIS EYES!
HE'S AN OBSESSIVE VOYEUR!
YAGAMI, DON'T DO THIS TO YOURSELF!
PIYO PIYO
YOUR CAPACITY FOR SLANDER IS MOST IMPRESSIVE.

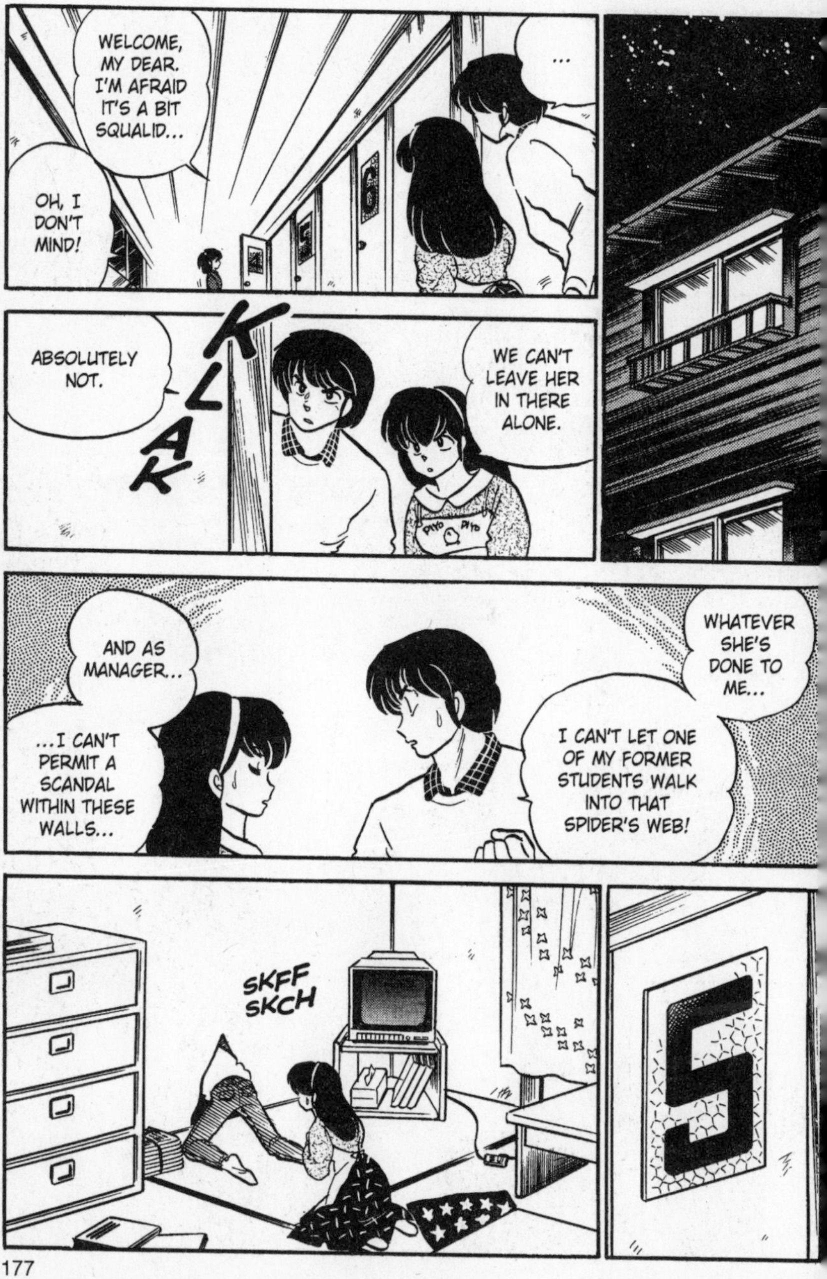
...
WELCOME, MY DEAR. I'M AFRAID IT'S A BIT SQUALID...
OH, I DON'T MIND!
WE CAN'T LEAVE HER IN THERE ALONE.
KLAK
ABSOLUTELY NOT.
WHATEVER SHE'S DONE TO ME...
I CAN'T LET ONE OF MY FORMER STUDENTS WALK INTO THAT SPIDER'S WEB!
AND AS MANAGER...
...I CAN'T PERMIT A SCANDAL WITHIN THESE WALLS...
SKFF SKCH

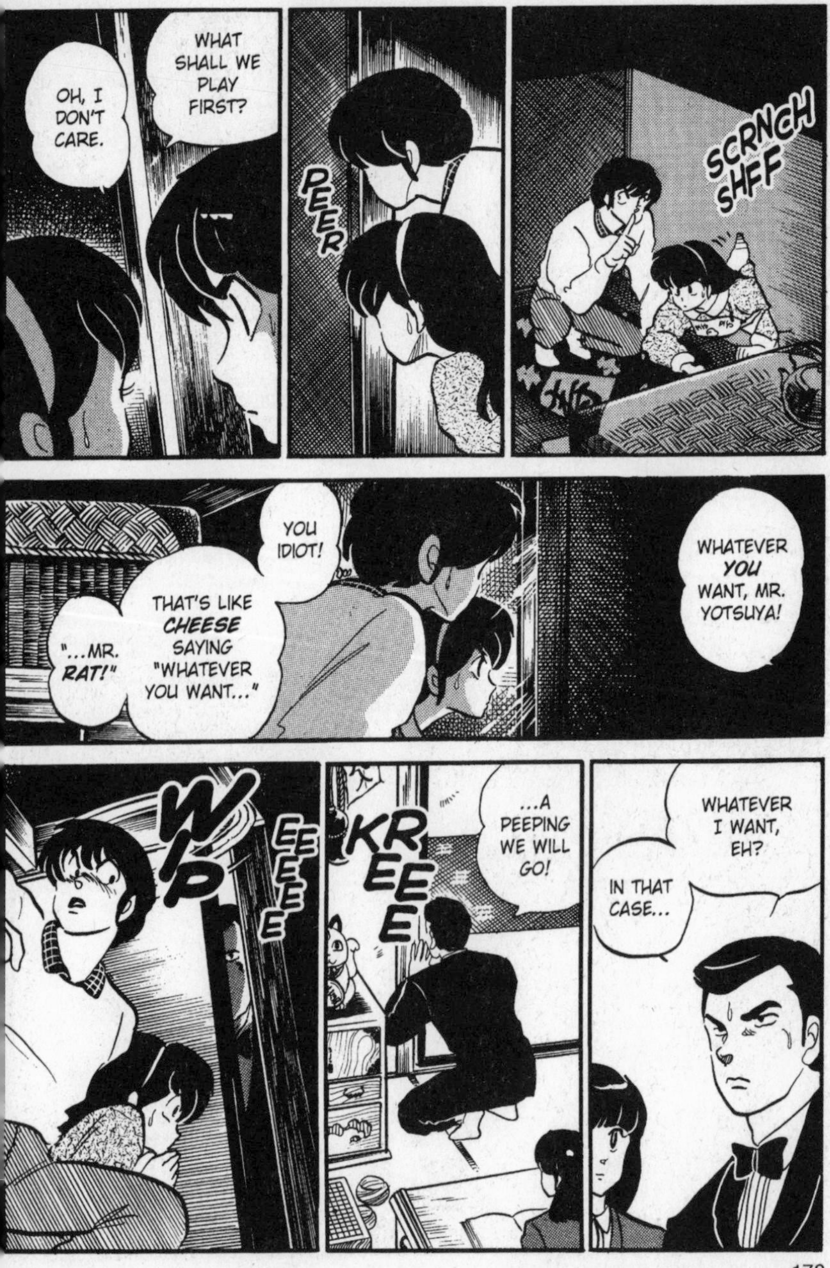
SCRNCH SHFF
PEER
WHAT SHALL WE PLAY FIRST?
OH, I DON'T CARE.
WHATEVER YOU WANT, MR. YOTSUYA!
YOU IDIOT!
THAT'S LIKE CHEESE SAYING "WHATEVER YOU WANT..."
"...MR. RAT!"
WHATEVER I WANT, EH?
IN THAT CASE...
...A PEEPING WE WILL GO!
KREEE
EEEEE
WIP

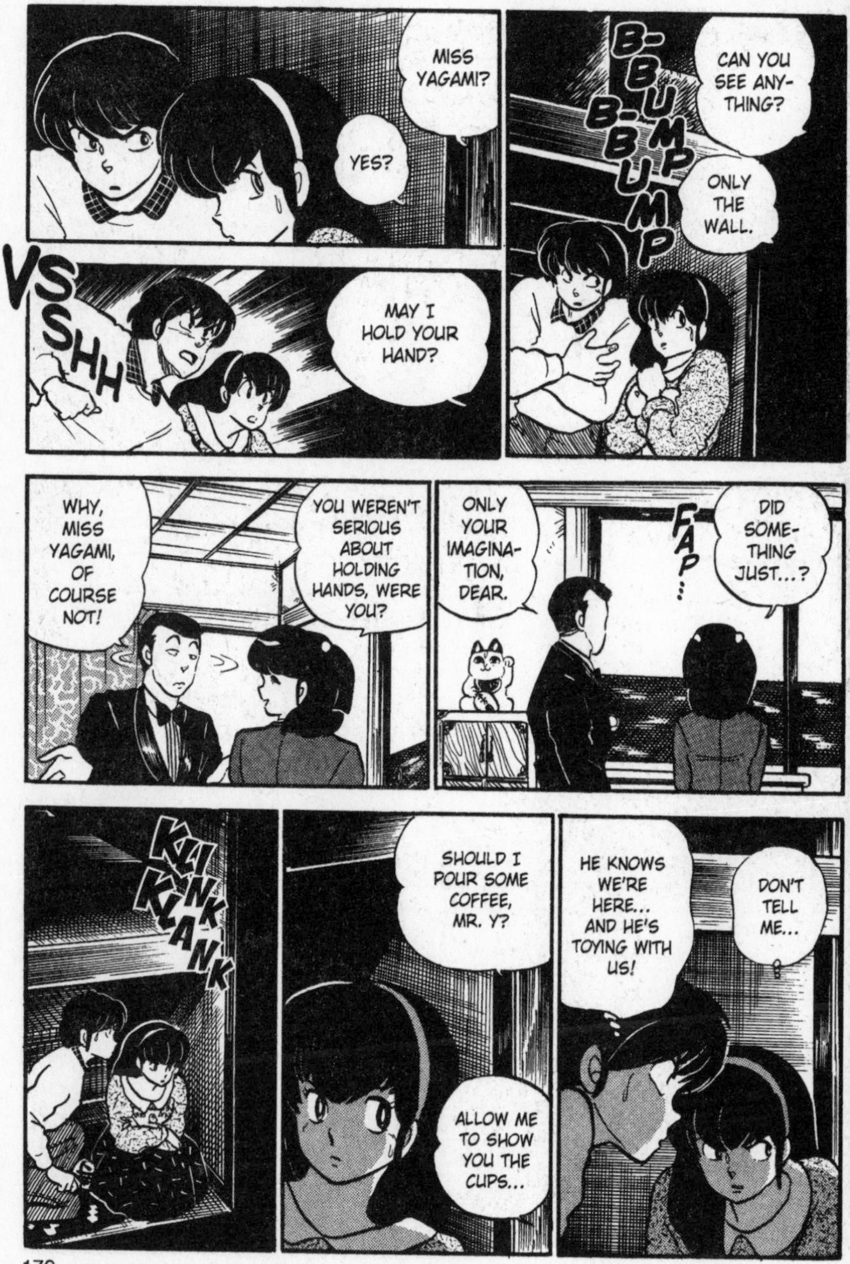
B-BUMP B-BUMP
CAN YOU SEE ANYTHING?
ONLY THE WALL.
MISS YAGAMI?
YES?
VSSHH
MAY I HOLD YOUR HAND?
FAP...
DID SOMETHING JUST...?
ONLY YOUR IMAGINATION, DEAR.
YOU WEREN'T SERIOUS ABOUT HOLDING HANDS, WERE YOU?
WHY, MISS YAGAMI, OF COURSE NOT!
DON'T TELL ME...
HE KNOWS WE'RE HERE... AND HE'S TOYING WITH US!
SHOULD I POUR SOME COFFEE, MR. Y?
ALLOW ME TO SHOW YOU THE CUPS...
KLINK KLANK

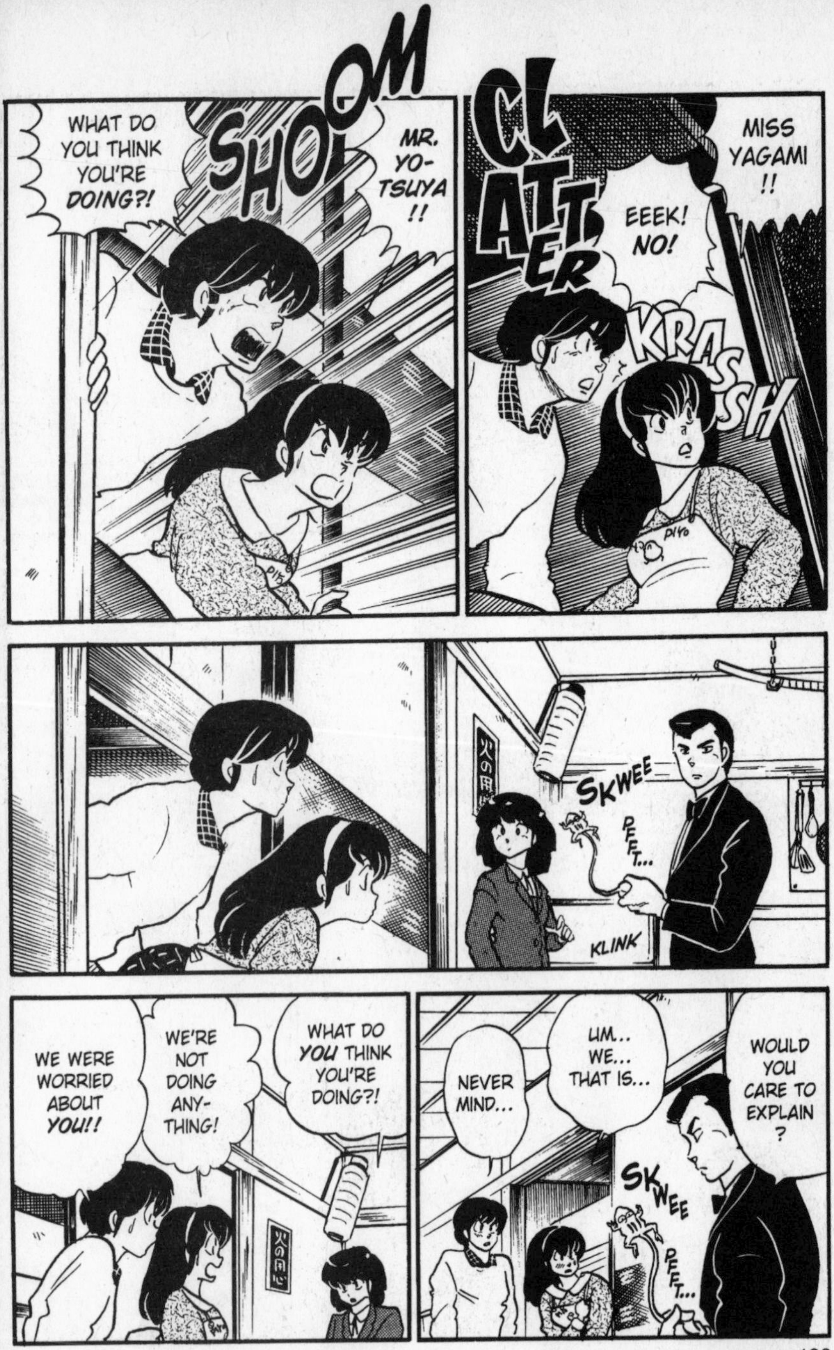
MISS YAGAMI !!
EEEK! NO!
CLATTER
KRASSH
MR. YO-TSUYA !!
SHOOOM
WHAT DO YOU THINK YOU'RE *DOING*?!
SKWEE
PFFT...
KLINK
WOULD YOU CARE TO EXPLAIN ?
UM.. WE... THAT IS...
NEVER MIND...
SKWEE
PFFT...
WHAT DO *YOU* THINK YOU'RE DOING?!
WE'RE NOT DOING ANY-THING!
WE WERE WORRIED ABOUT *YOU*!!

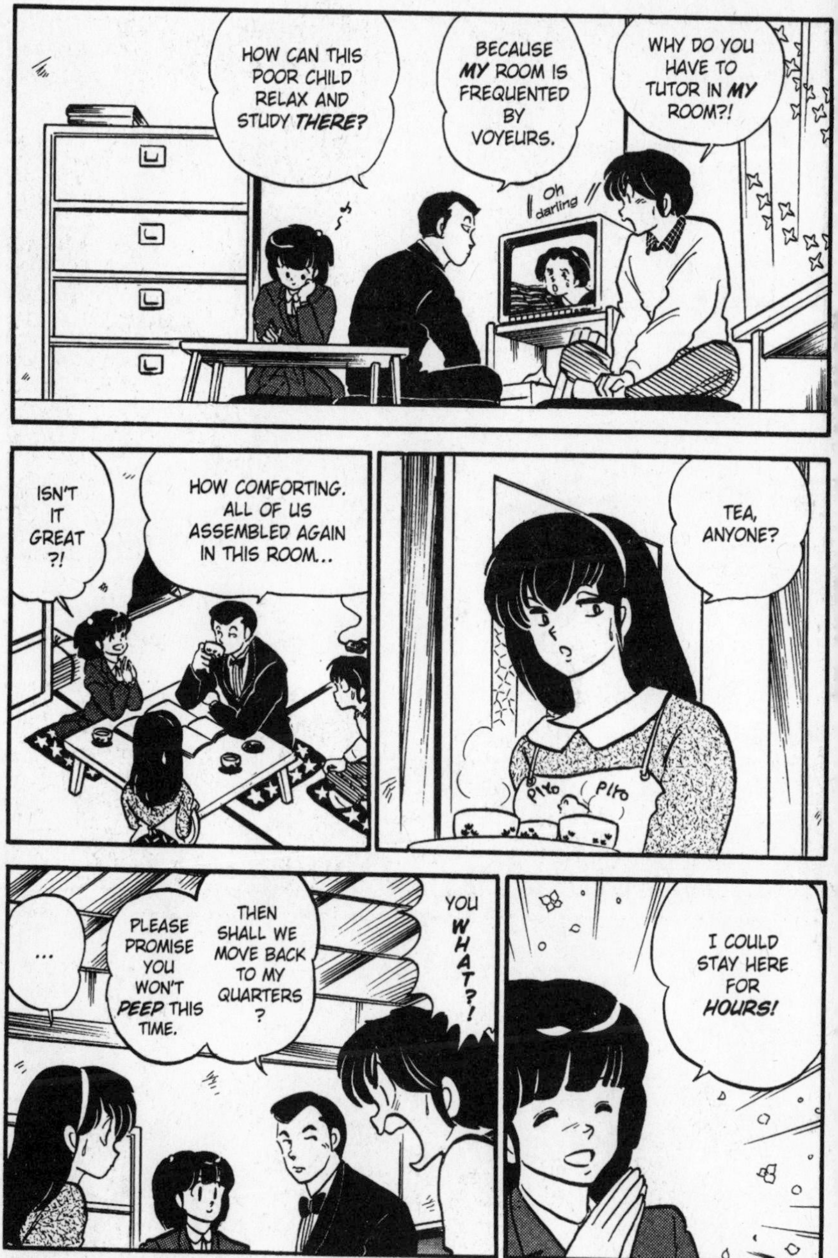
WHY DO YOU HAVE TO TUTOR IN MY ROOM?!
Oh darling
BECAUSE MY ROOM IS FREQUENTED BY VOYEURS.
HOW CAN THIS POOR CHILD RELAX AND STUDY THERE?
TEA, ANYONE?
Piyo
Piyo
HOW COMFORTING. ALL OF US ASSEMBLED AGAIN IN THIS ROOM...
ISN'T IT GREAT?!
I COULD STAY HERE FOR HOURS!
YOU WHAT?!
THEN SHALL WE MOVE BACK TO MY QUARTERS?
PLEASE PROMISE YOU WON'T PEEP THIS TIME.
...

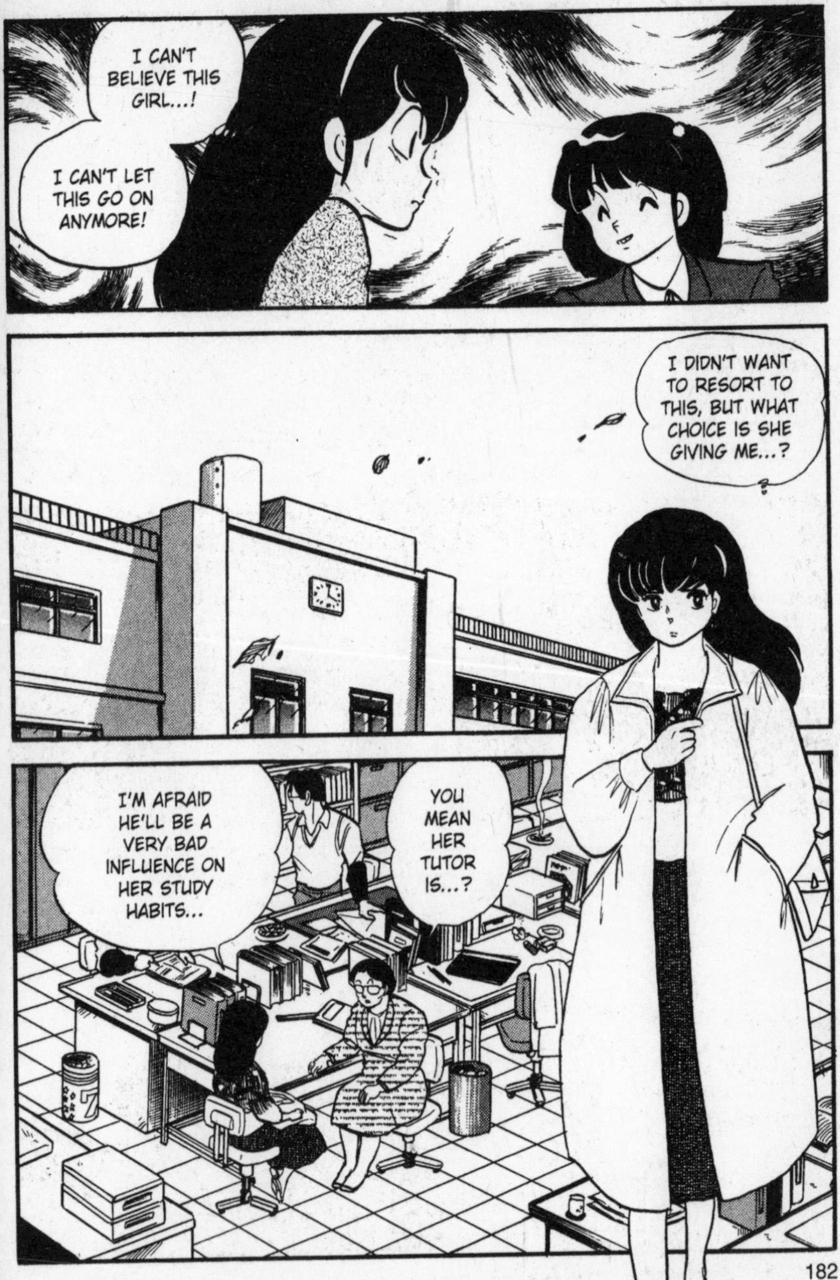
I CAN'T BELIEVE THIS GIRL...!
I CAN'T LET THIS GO ON ANYMORE!
I DIDN'T WANT TO RESORT TO THIS, BUT WHAT CHOICE IS SHE GIVING ME...?
YOU MEAN HER TUTOR IS...?
I'M AFRAID HE'LL BE A VERY BAD INFLUENCE ON HER STUDY HABITS...

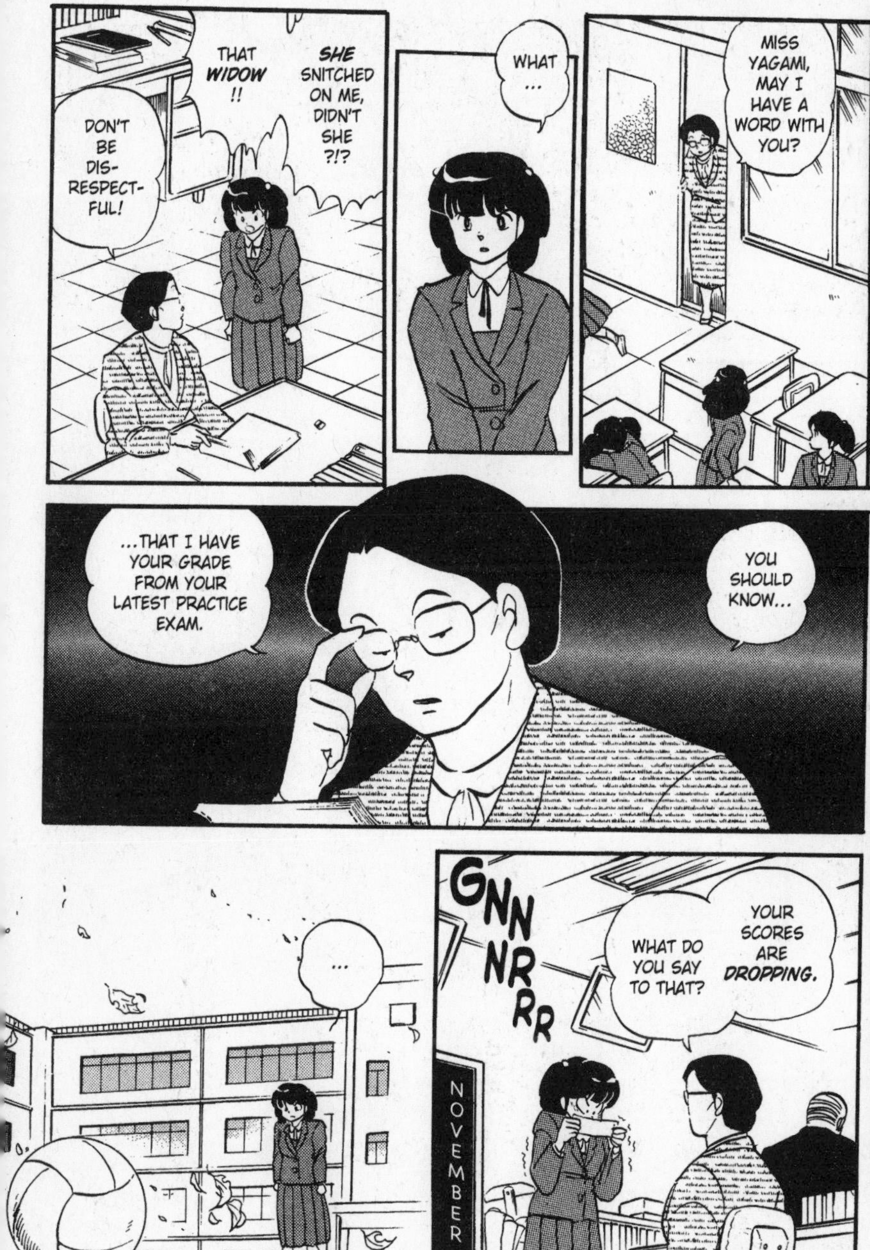
MISS YAGAMI, MAY I HAVE A WORD WITH YOU?
WHAT ...
SHE SNITCHED ON ME, DIDN'T SHE ?!?
THAT WIDOW !!
DON'T BE DIS-RESPECT-FUL!
YOU SHOULD KNOW...
...THAT I HAVE YOUR GRADE FROM YOUR LATEST PRACTICE EXAM.
YOUR SCORES ARE DROPPING.
WHAT DO YOU SAY TO THAT?
GNN NRRR
NOVEMBER
...

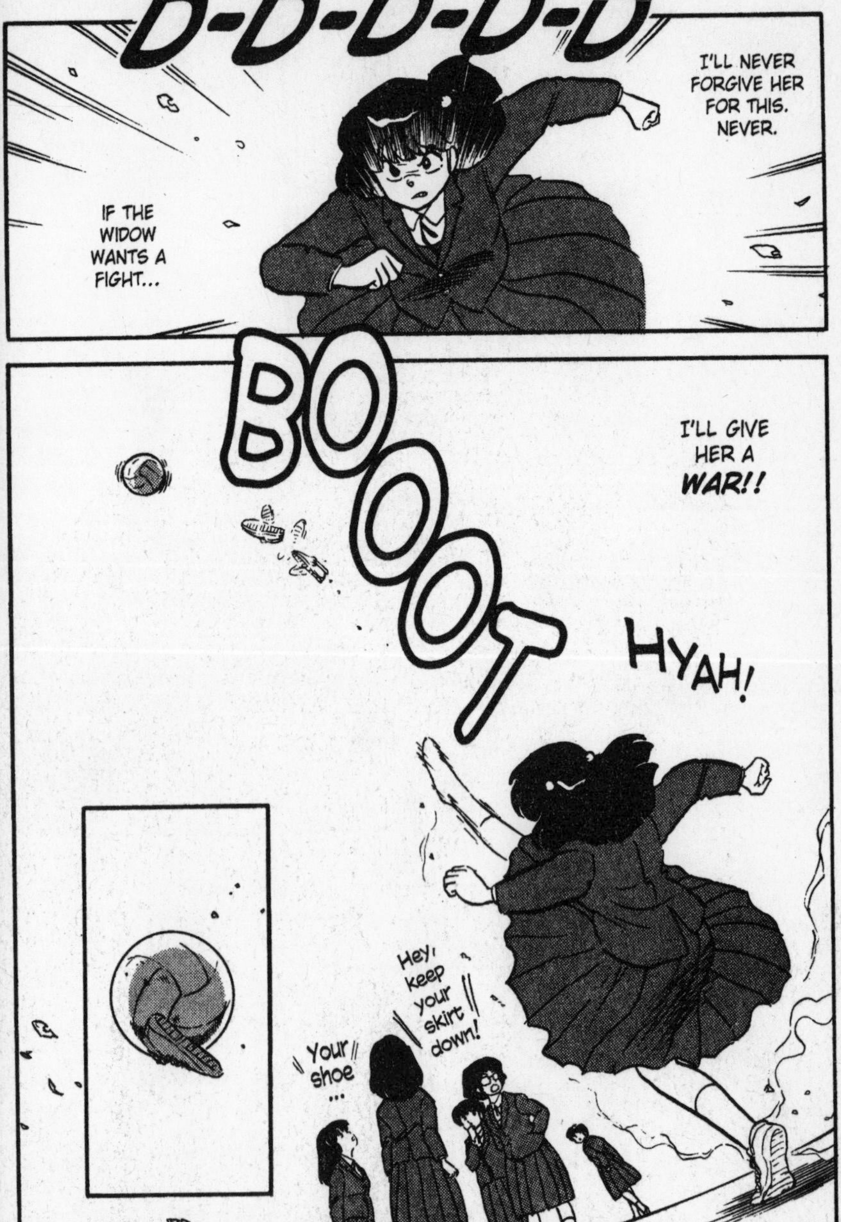
D-D-D-D-D-D
I'LL NEVER FORGIVE HER FOR THIS. NEVER.
IF THE WIDOW WANTS A FIGHT...
BOOOOT
I'LL GIVE HER A WAR!!
HYAH!
Hey, keep your skirt down!
Your shoe ...

PART TEN
VERTIGO

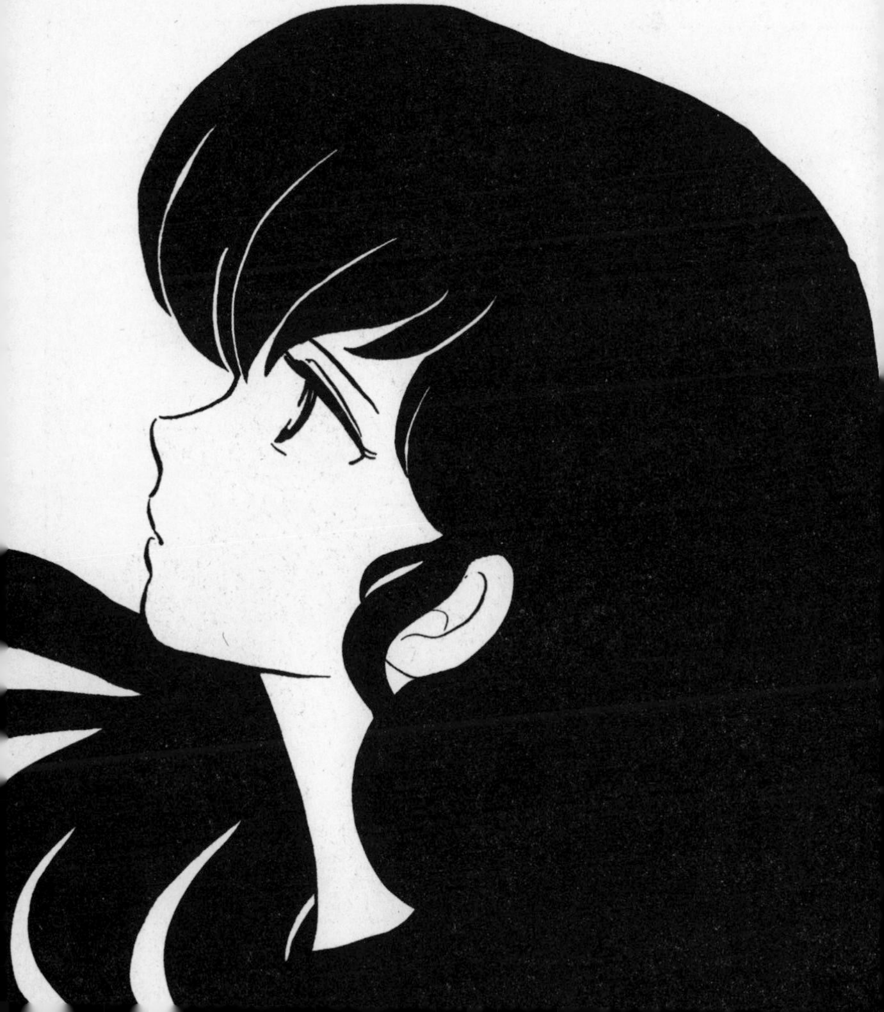

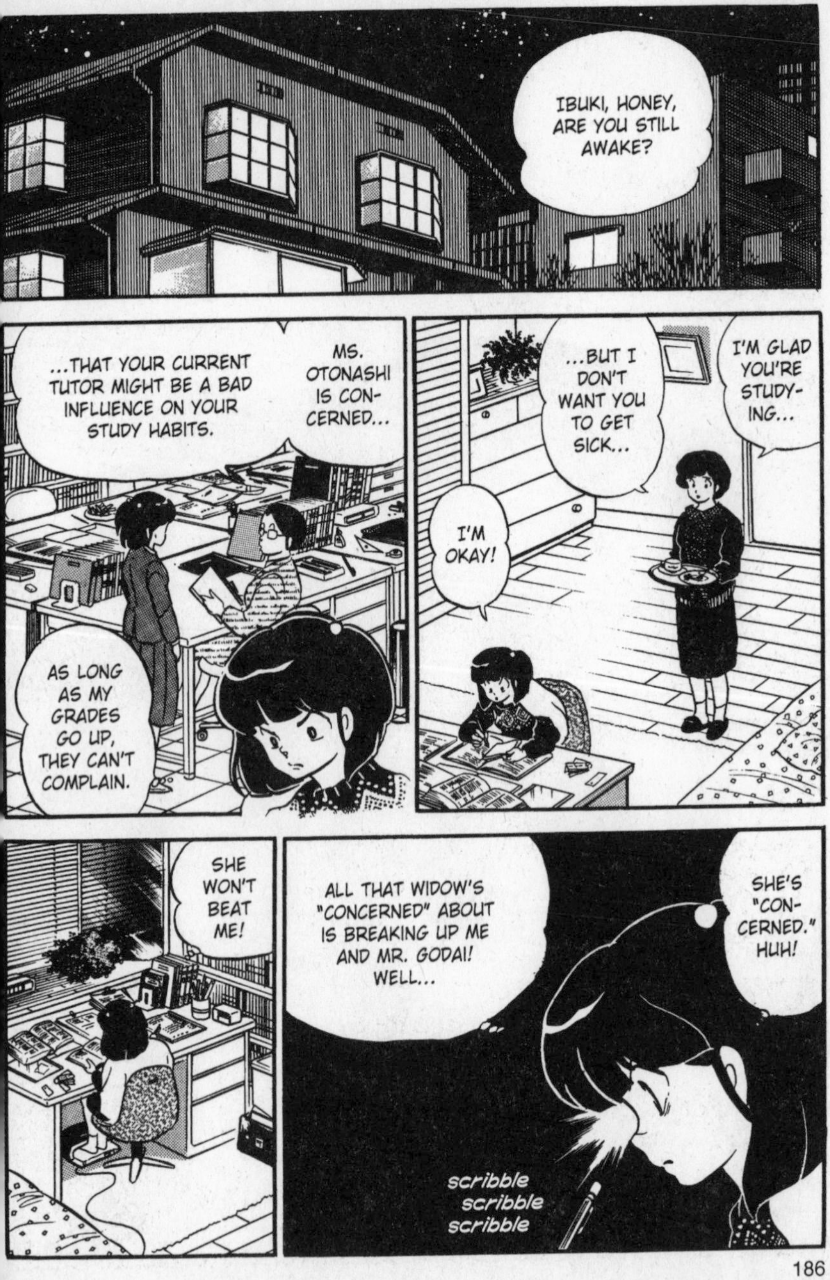
IBUKI, HONEY, ARE YOU STILL AWAKE?
I'M GLAD YOU'RE STUDY-ING...
...BUT I DON'T WANT YOU TO GET SICK...
I'M OKAY!
MS. OTONASHI IS CON-CERNED...
...THAT YOUR CURRENT TUTOR MIGHT BE A BAD INFLUENCE ON YOUR STUDY HABITS.
AS LONG AS MY GRADES GO UP, THEY CAN'T COMPLAIN.
SHE'S "CON-CERNED." HUH!
ALL THAT WIDOW'S "CONCERNED" ABOUT IS BREAKING UP ME AND MR. GODAI! WELL...
scribble scribble scribble
SHE WON'T BEAT ME!

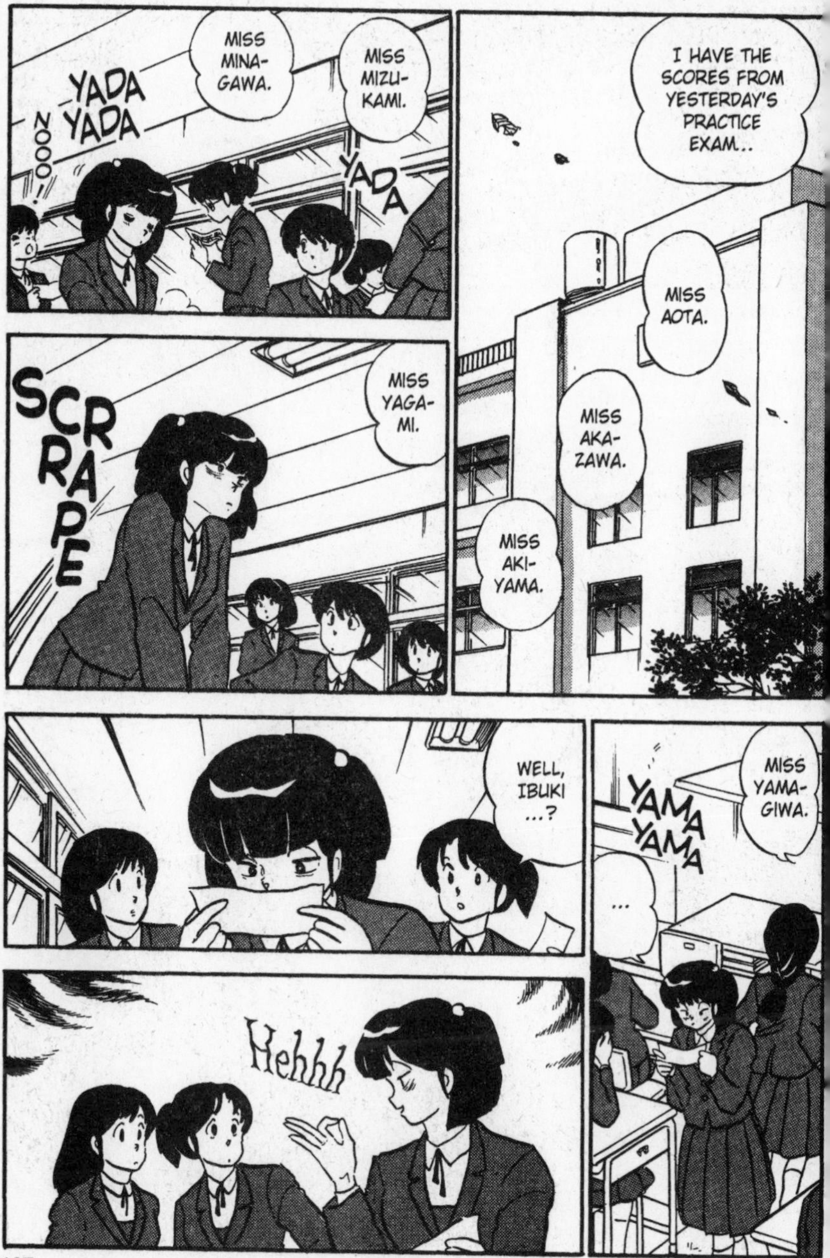
I HAVE THE SCORES FROM YESTERDAY'S PRACTICE EXAM...
MISS AOTA.
MISS AKAZAWA.
MISS AKIYAMA.
MISS MIZUKAMI.
YADA
MISS MINAGAWA.
YADA YADA
NOOO!!
MISS YAGAMI.
SCRRAPE
MISS YAMAGIWA.
YAMA YAMA
...
WELL, IBUKI ...?
Hehhh

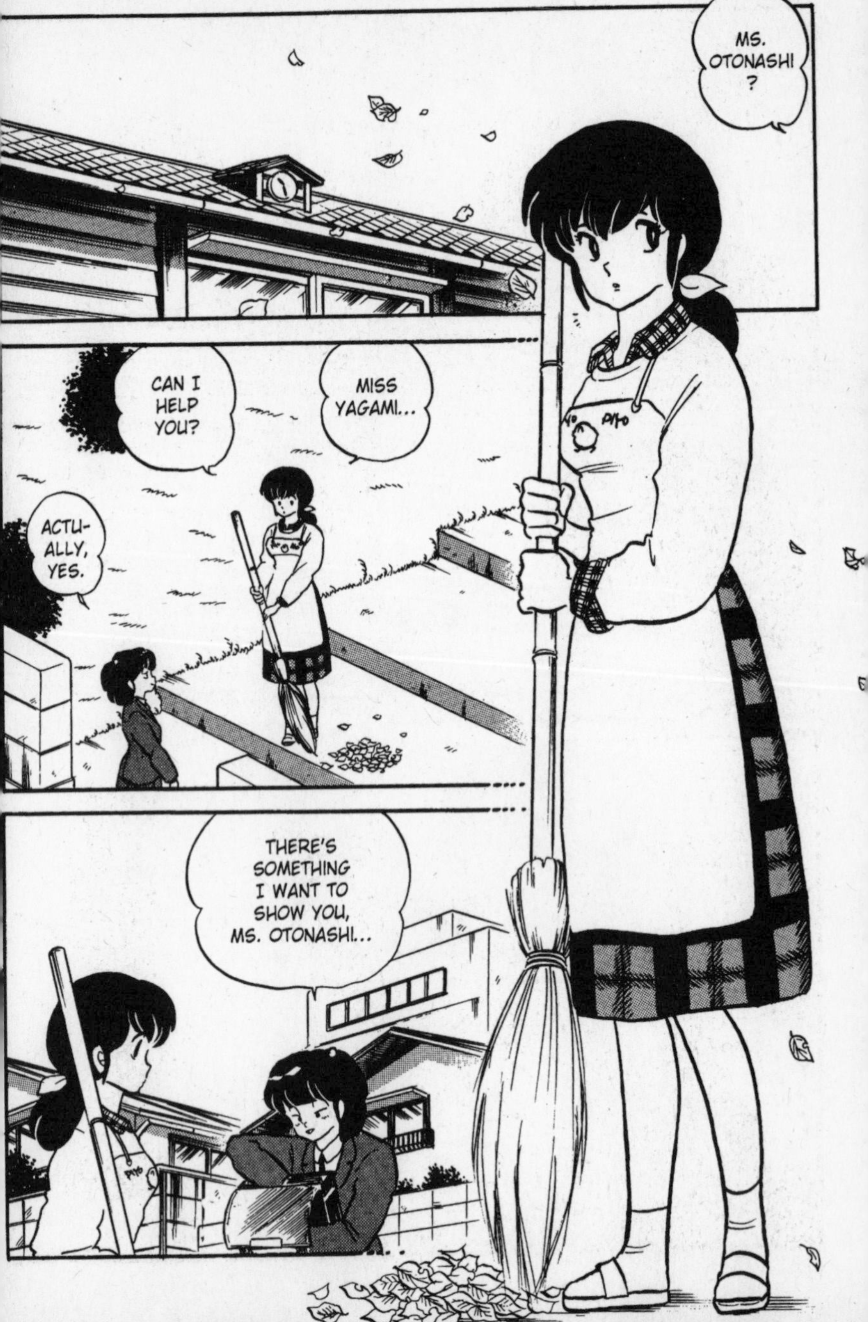
MS. OTONASHI?
MISS YAGAMI...
CAN I HELP YOU?
ACTU-ALLY, YES.
THERE'S SOMETHING I WANT TO SHOW YOU, MS. OTONASHI...

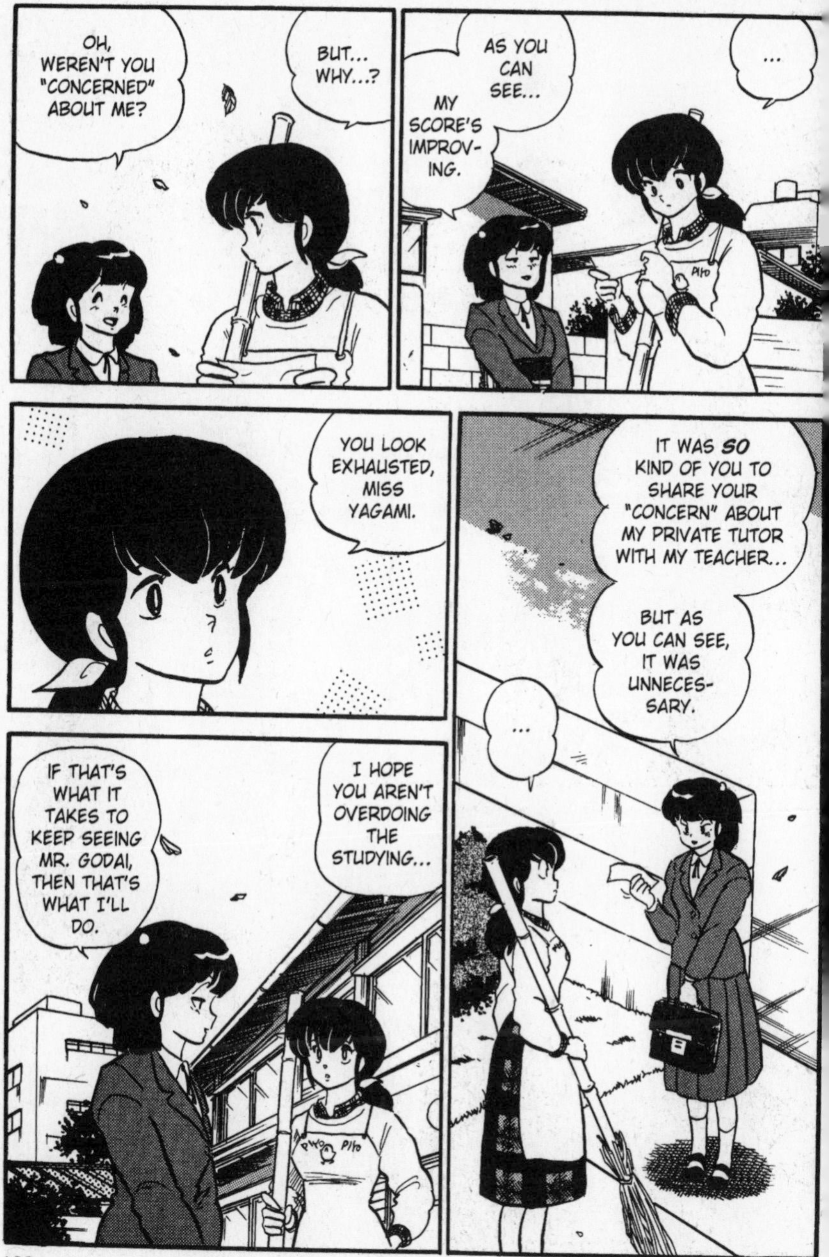
...
AS YOU CAN SEE...
MY SCORE'S IMPROV-ING.
BUT... WHY...?
OH, WEREN'T YOU "CONCERNED" ABOUT ME?
IT WAS **SO** KIND OF YOU TO SHARE YOUR "CONCERN" ABOUT MY PRIVATE TUTOR WITH MY TEACHER...
BUT AS YOU CAN SEE, IT WAS UNNECES-SARY.
...
YOU LOOK EXHAUSTED, MISS YAGAMI.
I HOPE YOU AREN'T OVERDOING THE STUDYING...
IF THAT'S WHAT IT TAKES TO KEEP SEEING MR. GODAI, THEN THAT'S WHAT I'LL DO.

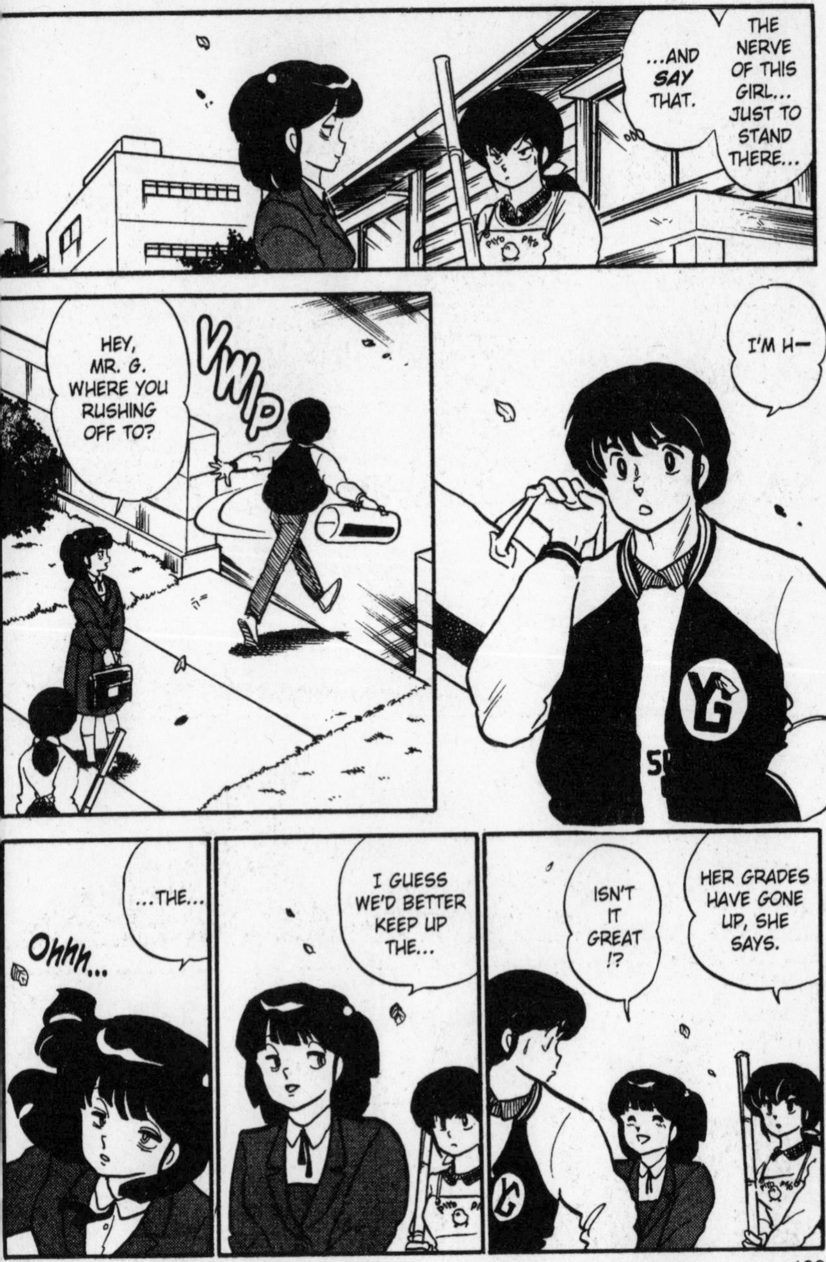
THE NERVE OF THIS GIRL... JUST TO STAND THERE...
...AND SAY THAT.
I'M H—
HEY, MR. G. WHERE YOU RUSHING OFF TO?
VWIP
HER GRADES HAVE GONE UP, SHE SAYS.
ISN'T IT GREAT!?
I GUESS WE'D BETTER KEEP UP THE...
...THE...
Ohhh...

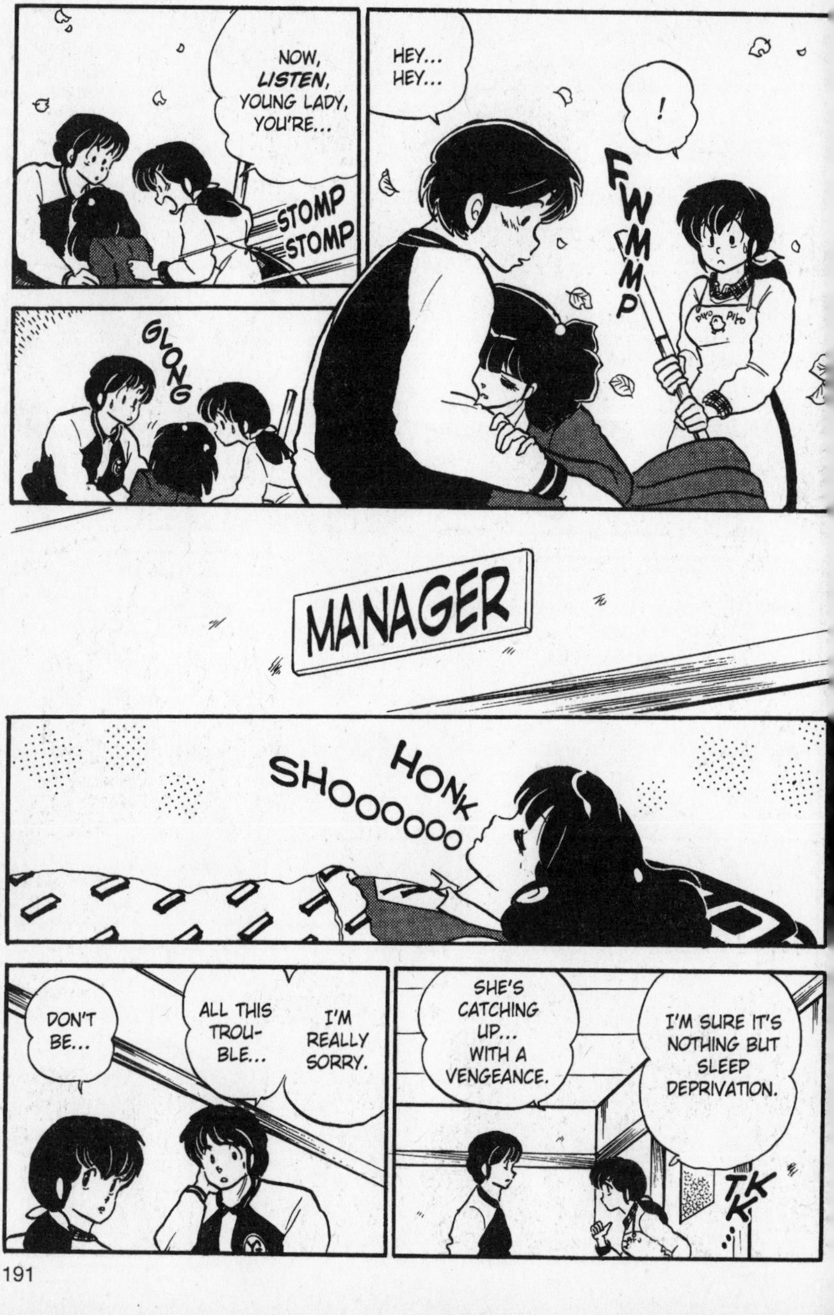
!
FWMMP
HEY... HEY...
NOW, *LISTEN*, YOUNG LADY, YOU'RE...
STOMP STOMP
GLONG
MANAGER
HONK
SHOOOOOO
I'M SURE IT'S NOTHING BUT SLEEP DEPRIVATION.
SHE'S CATCHING UP... WITH A VENGEANCE.
TKK
I'M REALLY SORRY.
ALL THIS TROUBLE...
DON'T BE...

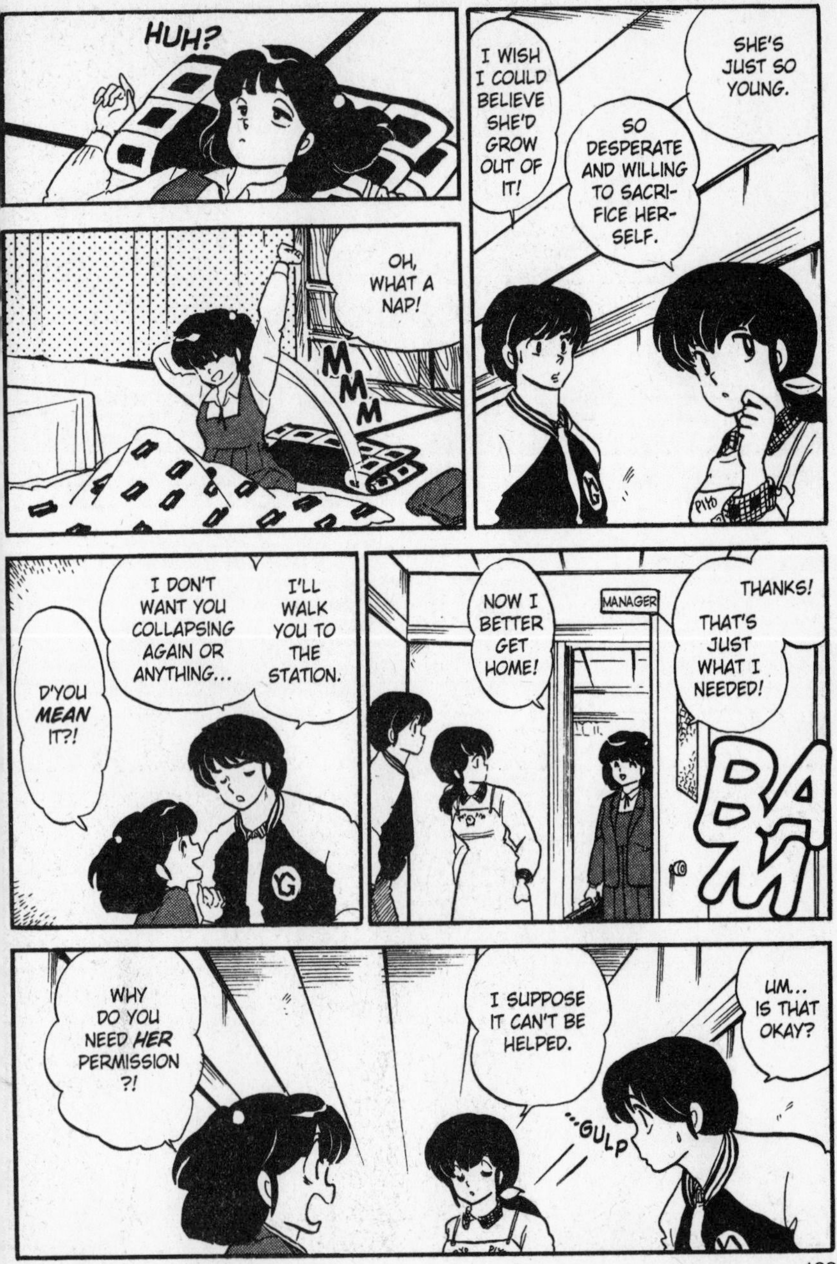
SHE'S JUST SO YOUNG.
SO DESPERATE AND WILLING TO SACRIFICE HERSELF.
I WISH I COULD BELIEVE SHE'D GROW OUT OF IT!
HUH?
OH, WHAT A NAP!
MMMM
PIYO
MANAGER
THANKS!
THAT'S JUST WHAT I NEEDED!
BAM
NOW I BETTER GET HOME!
I'LL WALK YOU TO THE STATION.
I DON'T WANT YOU COLLAPSING AGAIN OR ANYTHING...
D'YOU *MEAN* IT?!
UM... IS THAT OKAY?
I SUPPOSE IT CAN'T BE HELPED.
...GULP
WHY DO YOU NEED *HER* PERMISSION?!

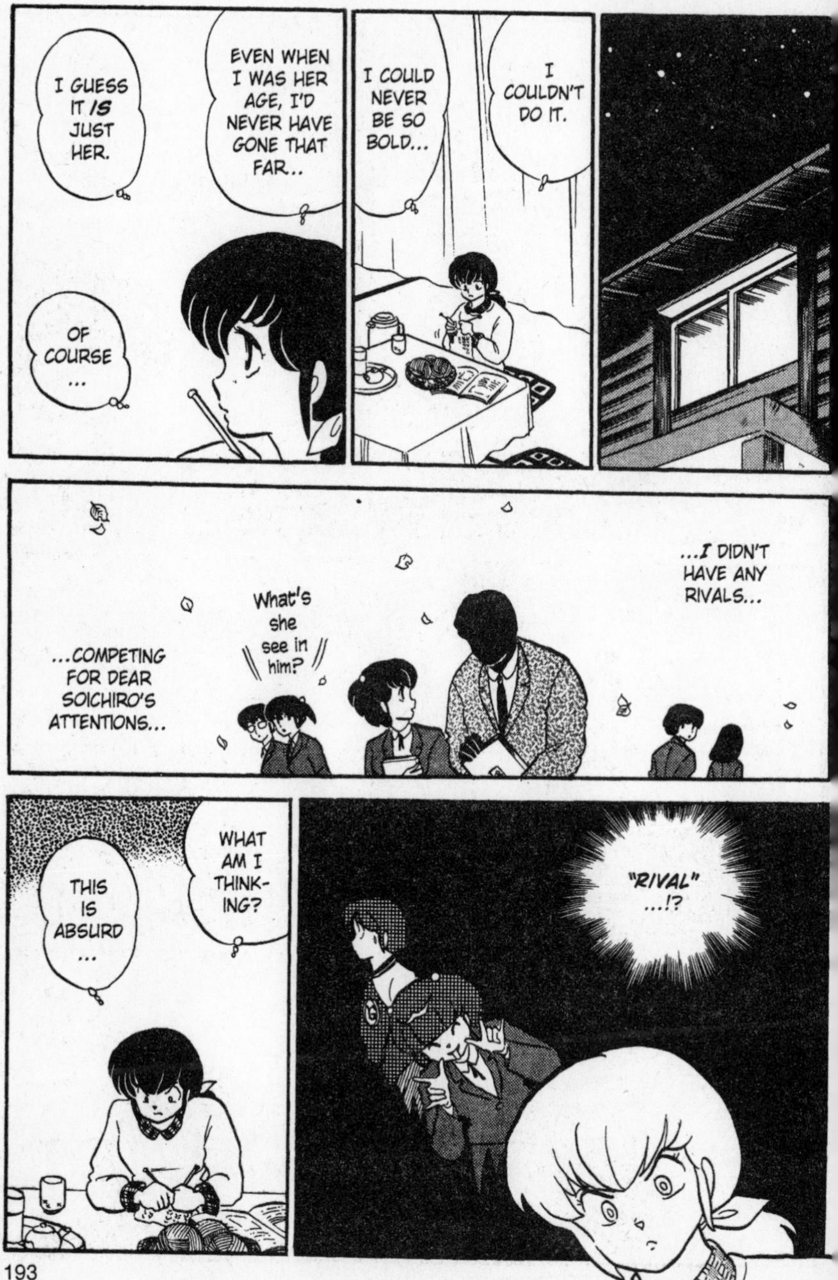
I COULDN'T DO IT.
I COULD NEVER BE SO BOLD...
EVEN WHEN I WAS HER AGE, I'D NEVER HAVE GONE THAT FAR..
I GUESS IT *IS* JUST HER.
OF COURSE ...
...*I* DIDN'T HAVE ANY RIVALS...
What's she see in him?
...COMPETING FOR DEAR SOICHIRO'S ATTENTIONS...
"RIVAL" ...!?
WHAT AM I THINKING?
THIS IS ABSURD ...

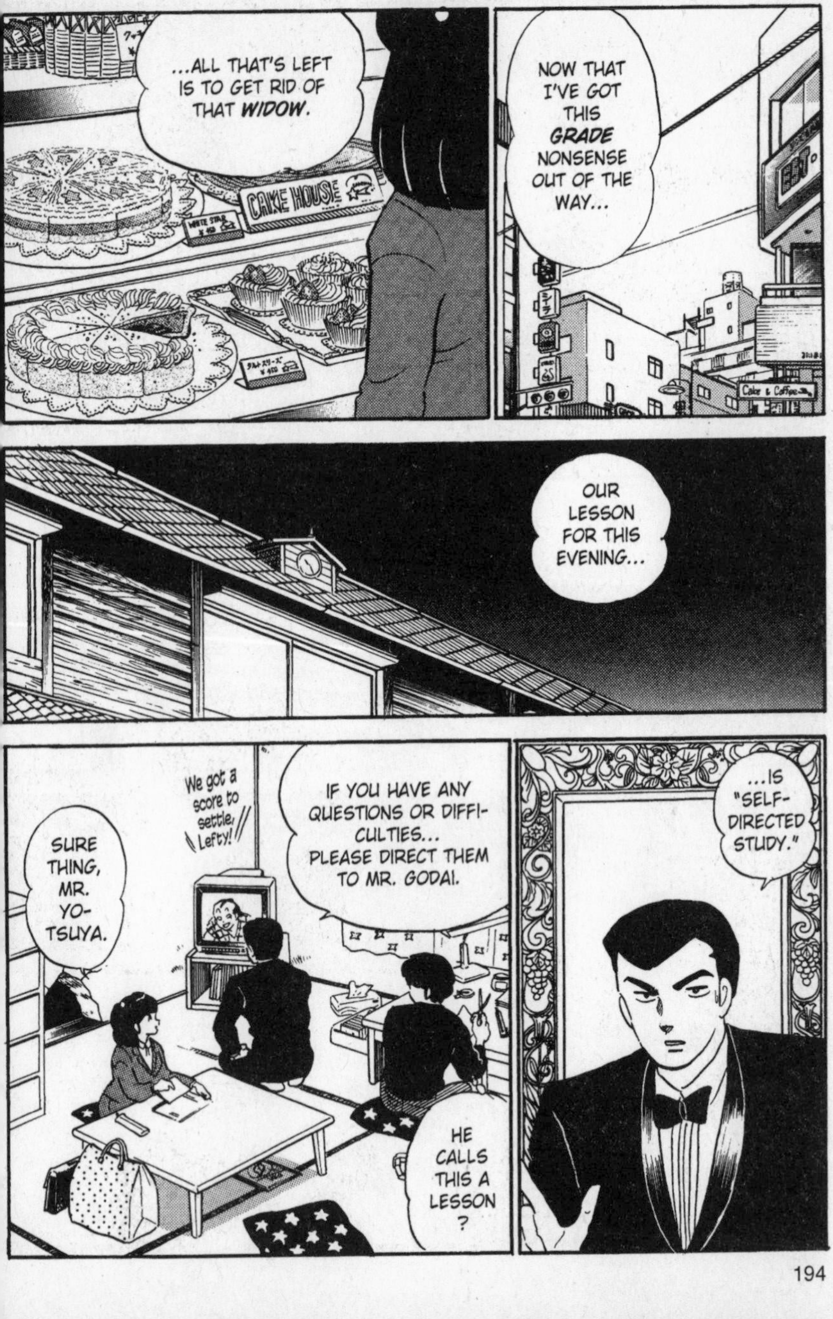
NOW THAT I'VE GOT THIS GRADE NONSENSE OUT OF THE WAY...
...ALL THAT'S LEFT IS TO GET RID OF THAT WIDOW.
CAKE HOUSE
OUR LESSON FOR THIS EVENING...
...IS "SELF-DIRECTED STUDY."
IF YOU HAVE ANY QUESTIONS OR DIFFICULTIES... PLEASE DIRECT THEM TO MR. GODAI.
We got a score to settle, Lefty!
SURE THING, MR. YOTSUYA.
HE CALLS THIS A LESSON?

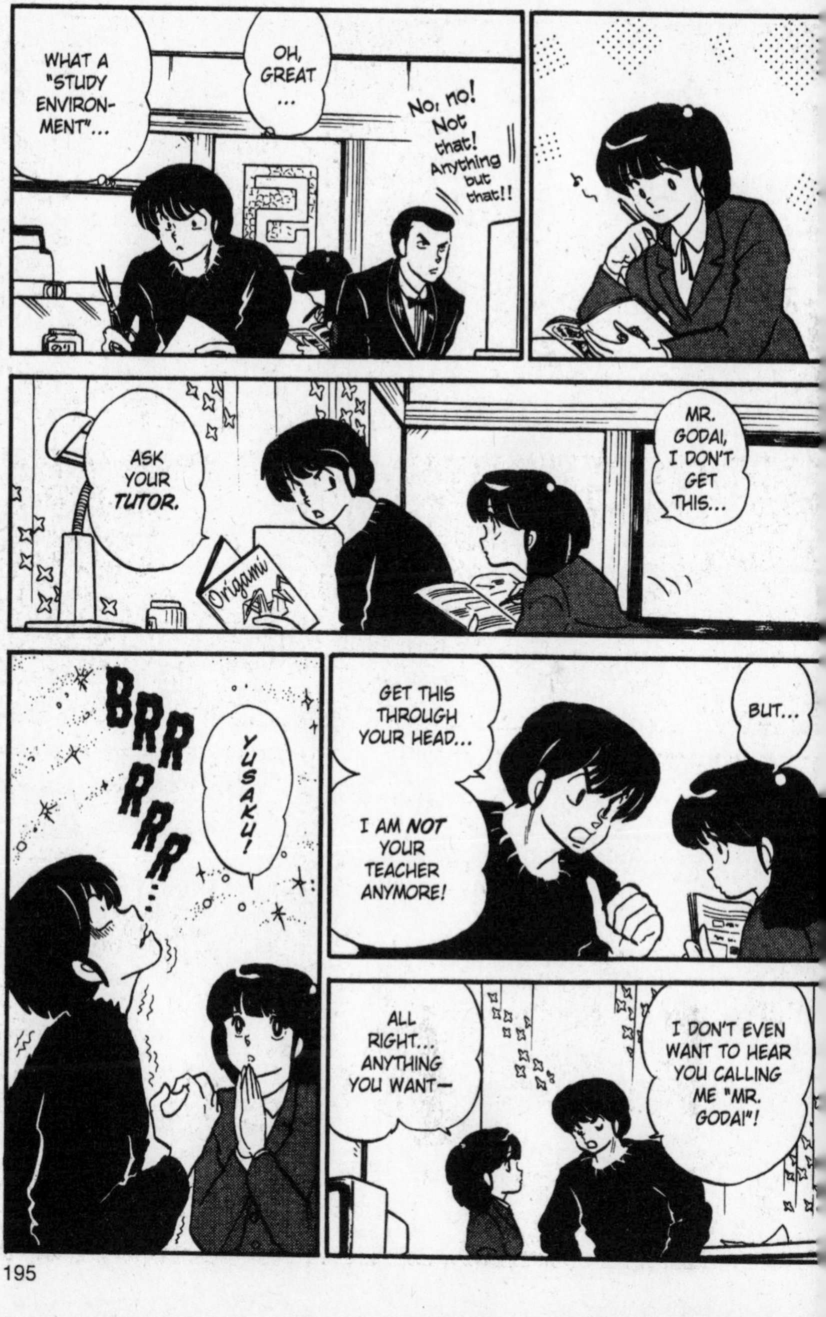
No, no! Not that! Anything but that!!
OH, GREAT ...
WHAT A "STUDY ENVIRONMENT"...
MR. GODAI, I DON'T GET THIS...
ASK YOUR *TUTOR.*
Origami
BUT...
GET THIS THROUGH YOUR HEAD...
I AM *NOT* YOUR TEACHER ANYMORE!
I DON'T EVEN WANT TO HEAR YOU CALLING ME "MR. GODAI"!
ALL RIGHT... ANYTHING YOU WANT—
YUSAKU!
BRRRRRR...

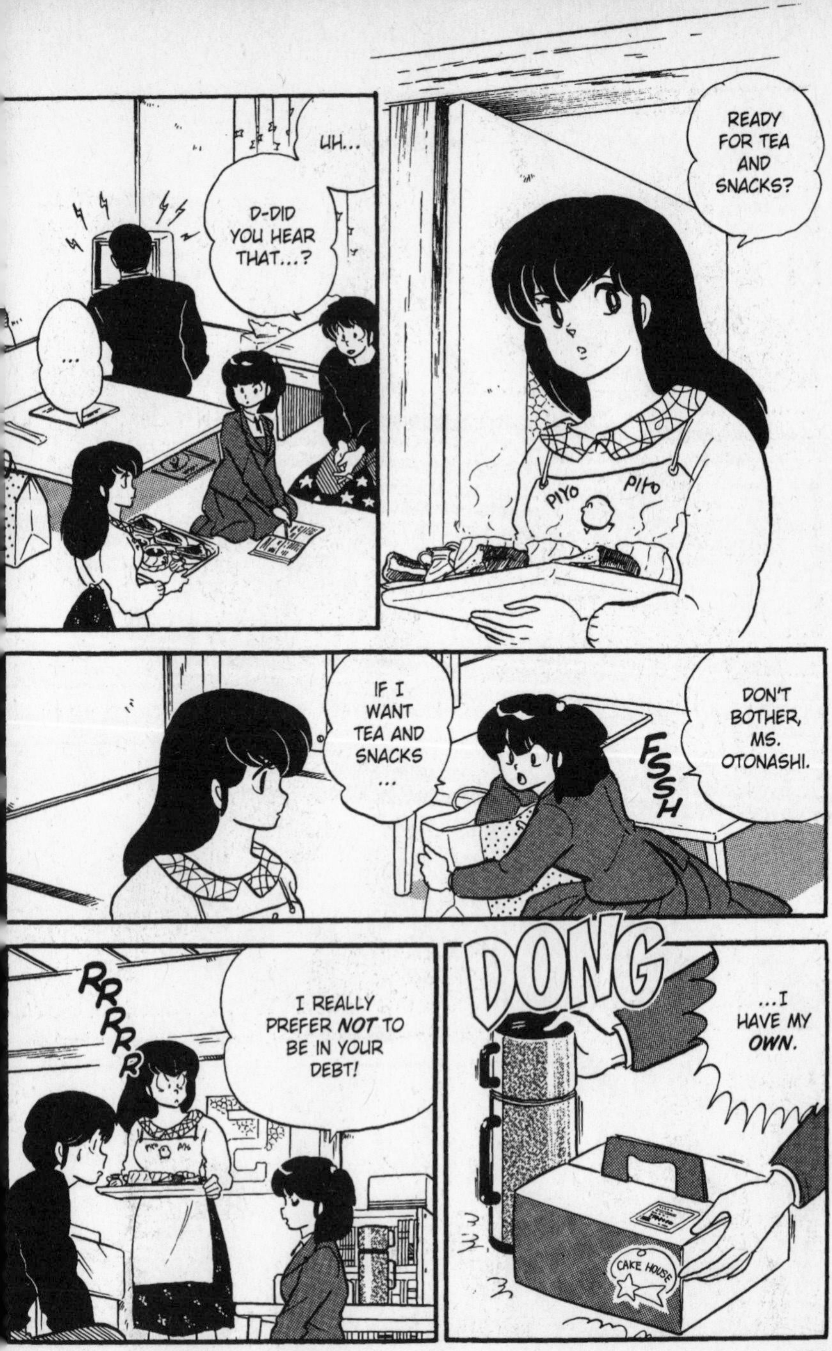
READY FOR TEA AND SNACKS?
PIYO PIYO
UH...
D-DID YOU HEAR THAT...?
...
DON'T BOTHER, MS. OTONASHI.
FSSH
IF I WANT TEA AND SNACKS ...
DONG
...I HAVE MY OWN.
CAKE HOUSE
RRRRR
I REALLY PREFER NOT TO BE IN YOUR DEBT!

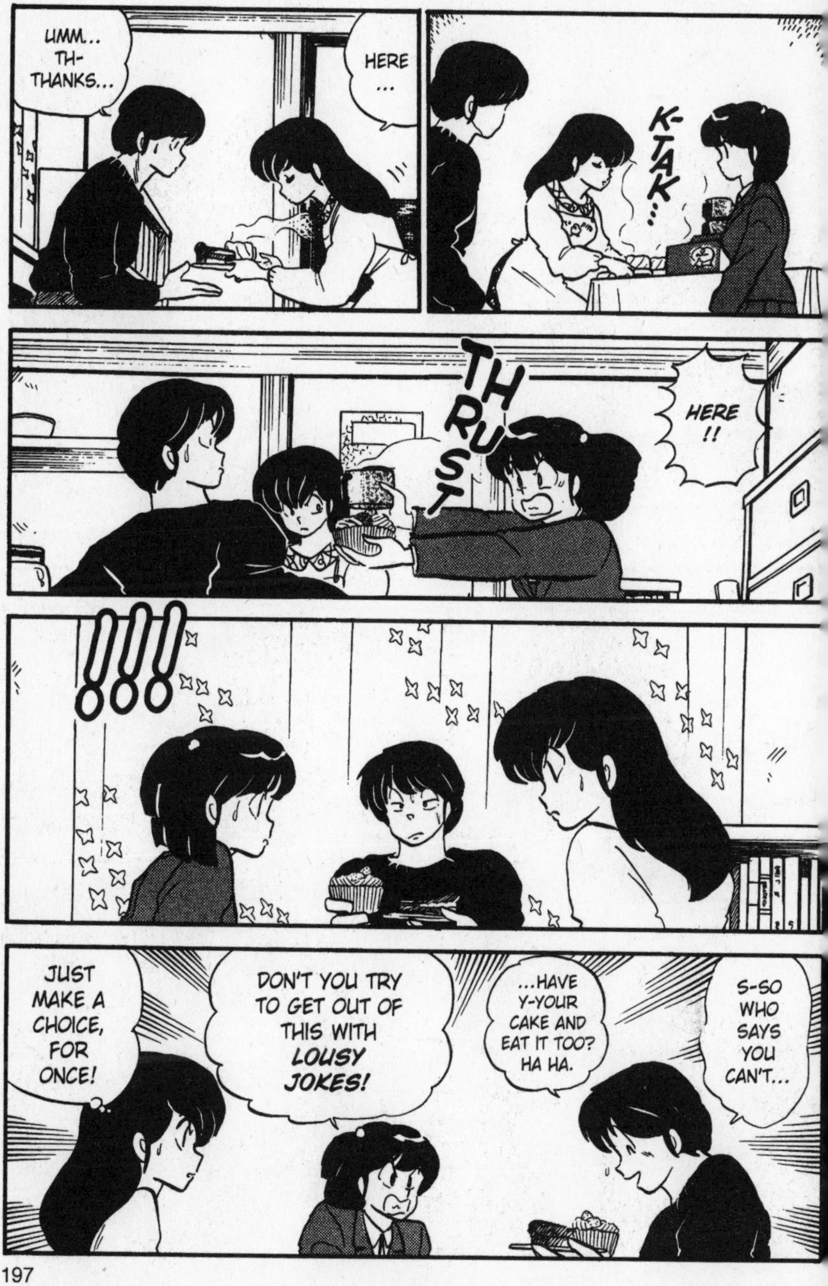
K-TAK...
HERE ...
UMM... TH-THANKS...
HERE !!
THRUST
!!!
S-SO WHO SAYS YOU CAN'T...
...HAVE Y-YOUR CAKE AND EAT IT TOO? HA HA.
DON'T YOU TRY TO GET OUT OF THIS WITH LOUSY JOKES!
JUST MAKE A CHOICE, FOR ONCE!

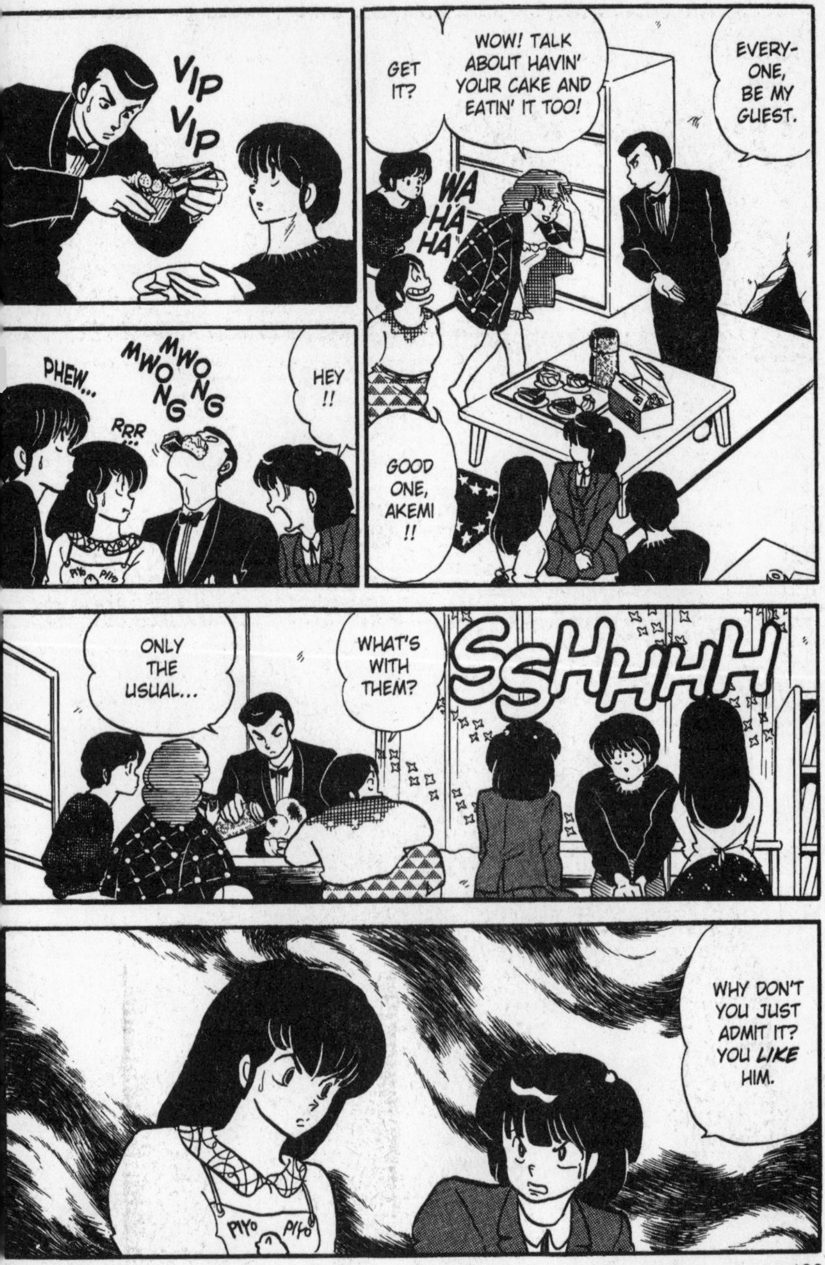
EVERY-ONE, BE MY GUEST.
WOW! TALK ABOUT HAVIN' YOUR CAKE AND EATIN' IT TOO!
GET IT?
WA HA HA
GOOD ONE, AKEMI !!
VIP VIP
HEY !!
MWONG MWONG
RRR...
PHEW...
SSHHHH
WHAT'S WITH THEM?
ONLY THE USUAL...
WHY DON'T YOU JUST ADMIT IT? YOU *LIKE* HIM.

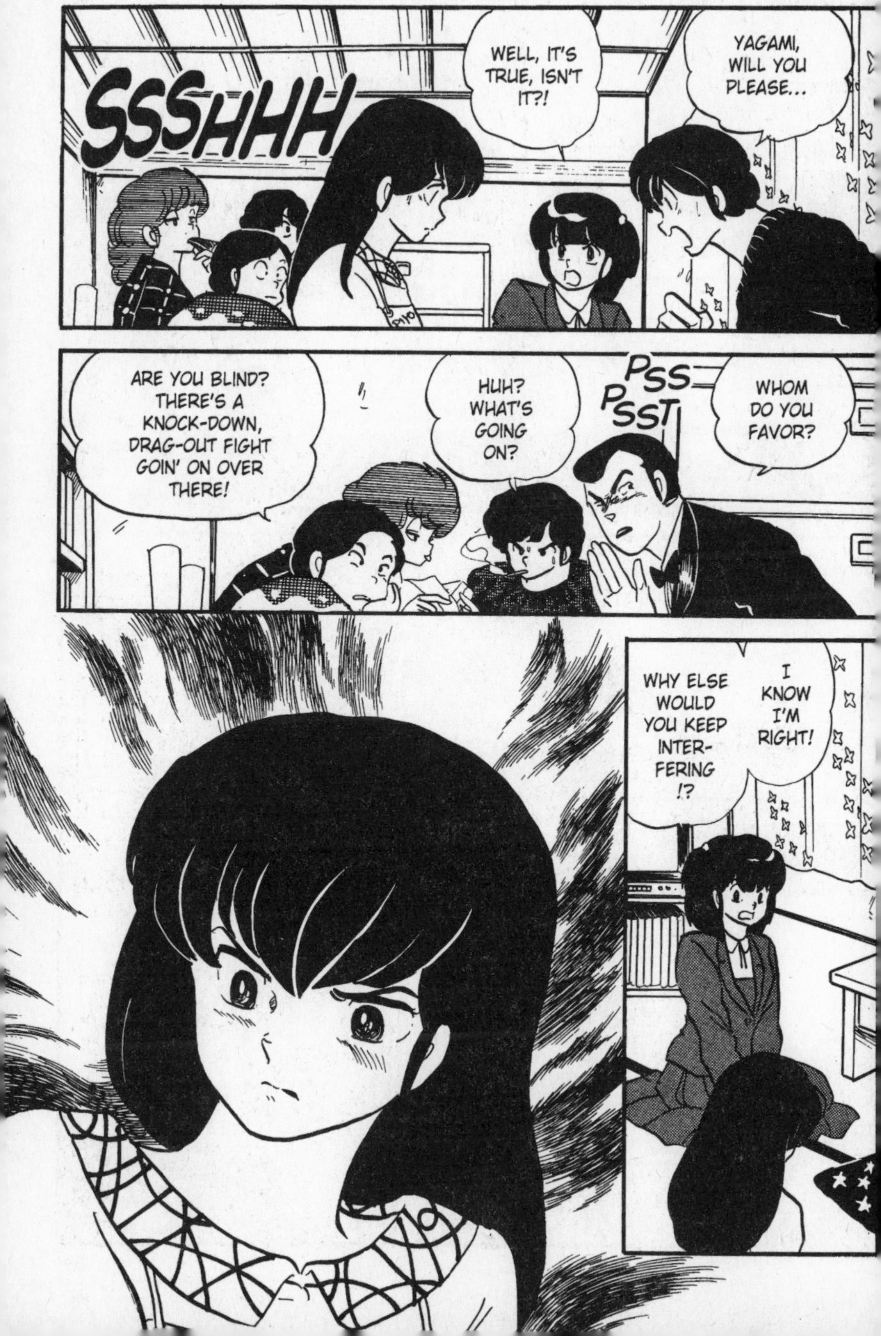
YAGAMI, WILL YOU PLEASE...
WELL, IT'S TRUE, ISN'T IT?!
SSSHHH
WHOM DO YOU FAVOR?
PSS PSST
HUH? WHAT'S GOING ON?
ARE YOU BLIND? THERE'S A KNOCK-DOWN, DRAG-OUT FIGHT GOIN' ON OVER THERE!
I KNOW I'M RIGHT!
WHY ELSE WOULD YOU KEEP INTER-FERING!?

TAP TAP
KLIK
SHE'S DOWN ...
SHAA
MR. G!
WHOA, WHOA, WHOA.
LET ME GO!! IF SHE GETS HIM ALONE NOW...
FEAR NOT.
NOTHING'LL HAPPEN. I GUARANTEE IT.
MANAGER !!
TM TM TM
SLAP...
PLEASE ...
DON'T LISTEN TO WHAT ANY OF THEM SAY...
TM

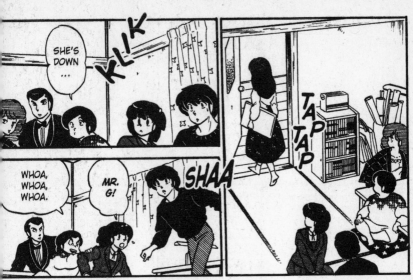

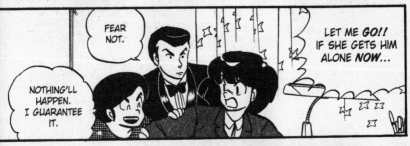

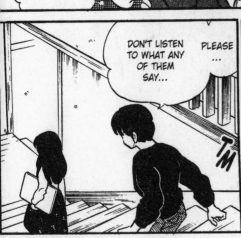

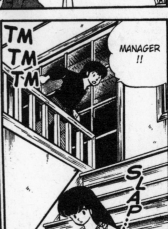

AND IN REACTION TO A TEEN-AGER.

NO, REALLY... YOU...

NO ...

I'M SORRY ...

I ACTED SO IMMATURELY.

SUDDENLY, IT REALLY MATTERED... NOT TO LET HER WIN...

MANA-GER ...?

UH...

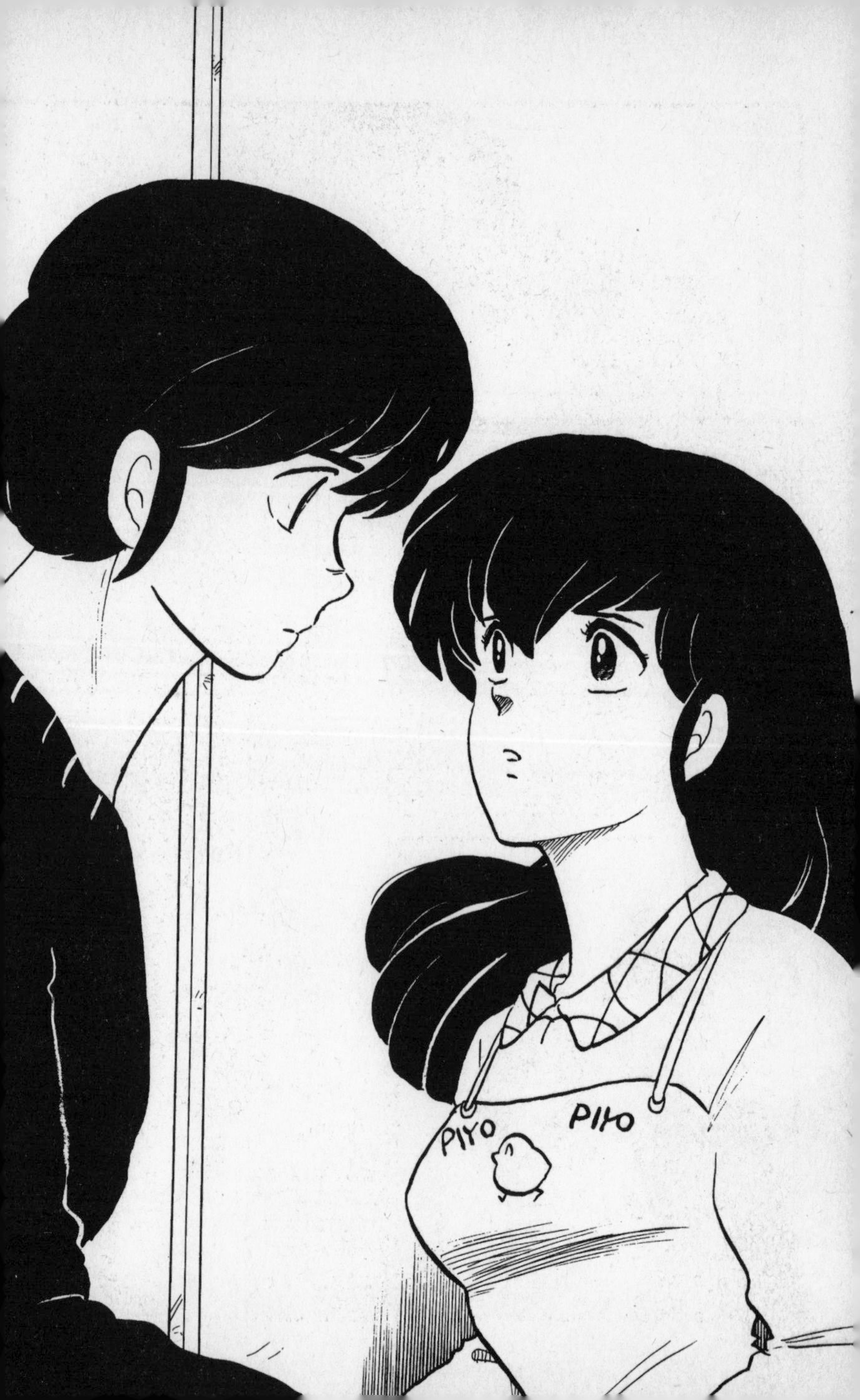
PIYO
PIYO

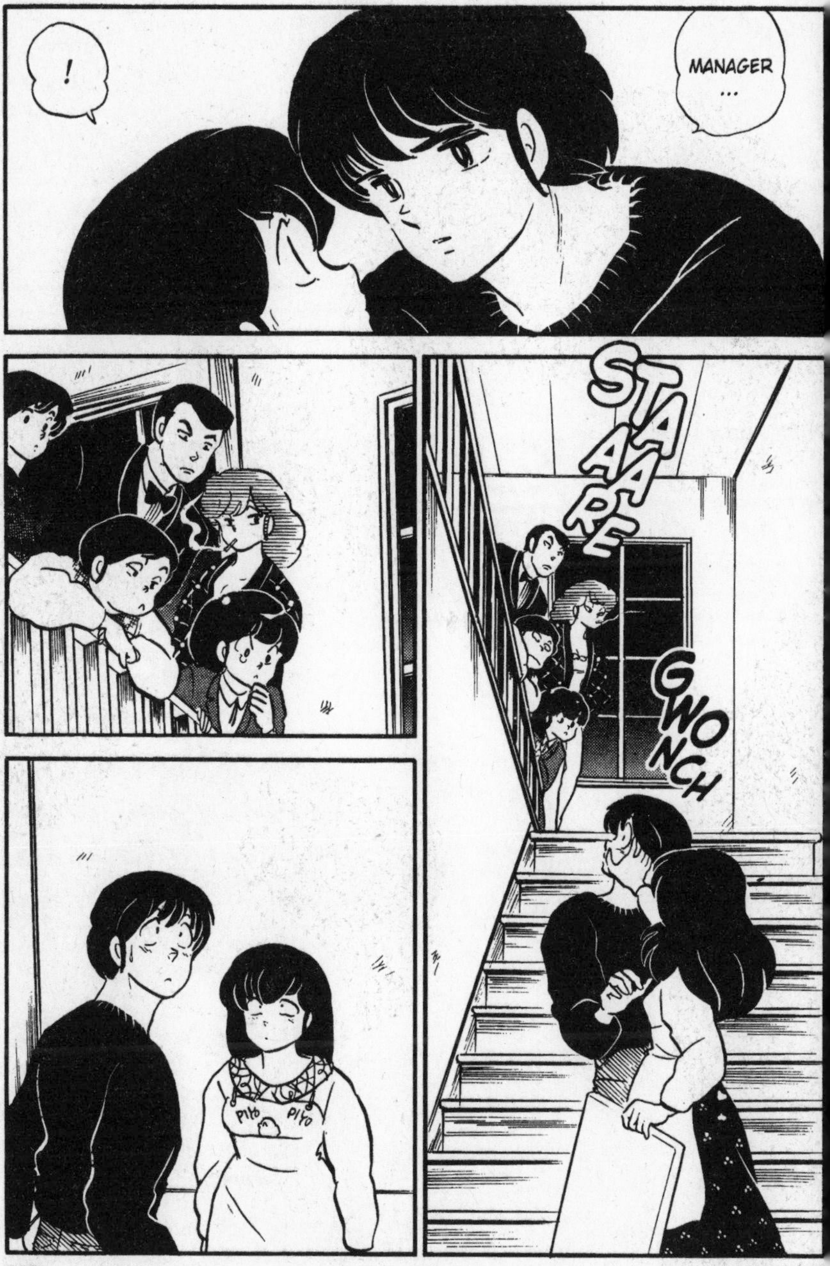
MANAGER ...
!
STAAARE
GWONCH

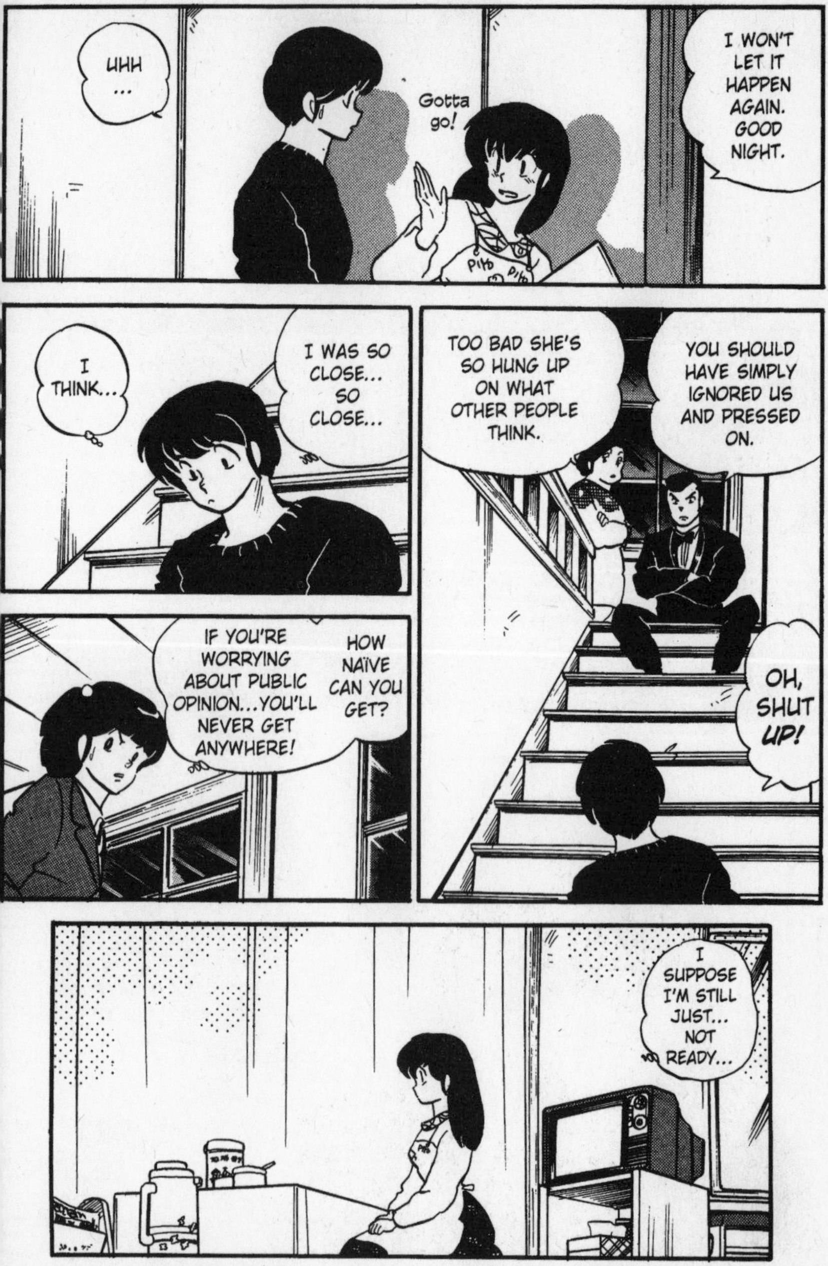
I WON'T LET IT HAPPEN AGAIN. GOOD NIGHT.
Gotta go!
UHH ...
YOU SHOULD HAVE SIMPLY IGNORED US AND PRESSED ON.
TOO BAD SHE'S SO HUNG UP ON WHAT OTHER PEOPLE THINK.
OH, SHUT UP!
I WAS SO CLOSE... SO CLOSE...
I THINK...
HOW NAÏVE CAN YOU GET?
IF YOU'RE WORRYING ABOUT PUBLIC OPINION...YOU'LL NEVER GET ANYWHERE!
I SUPPOSE I'M STILL JUST... NOT READY...

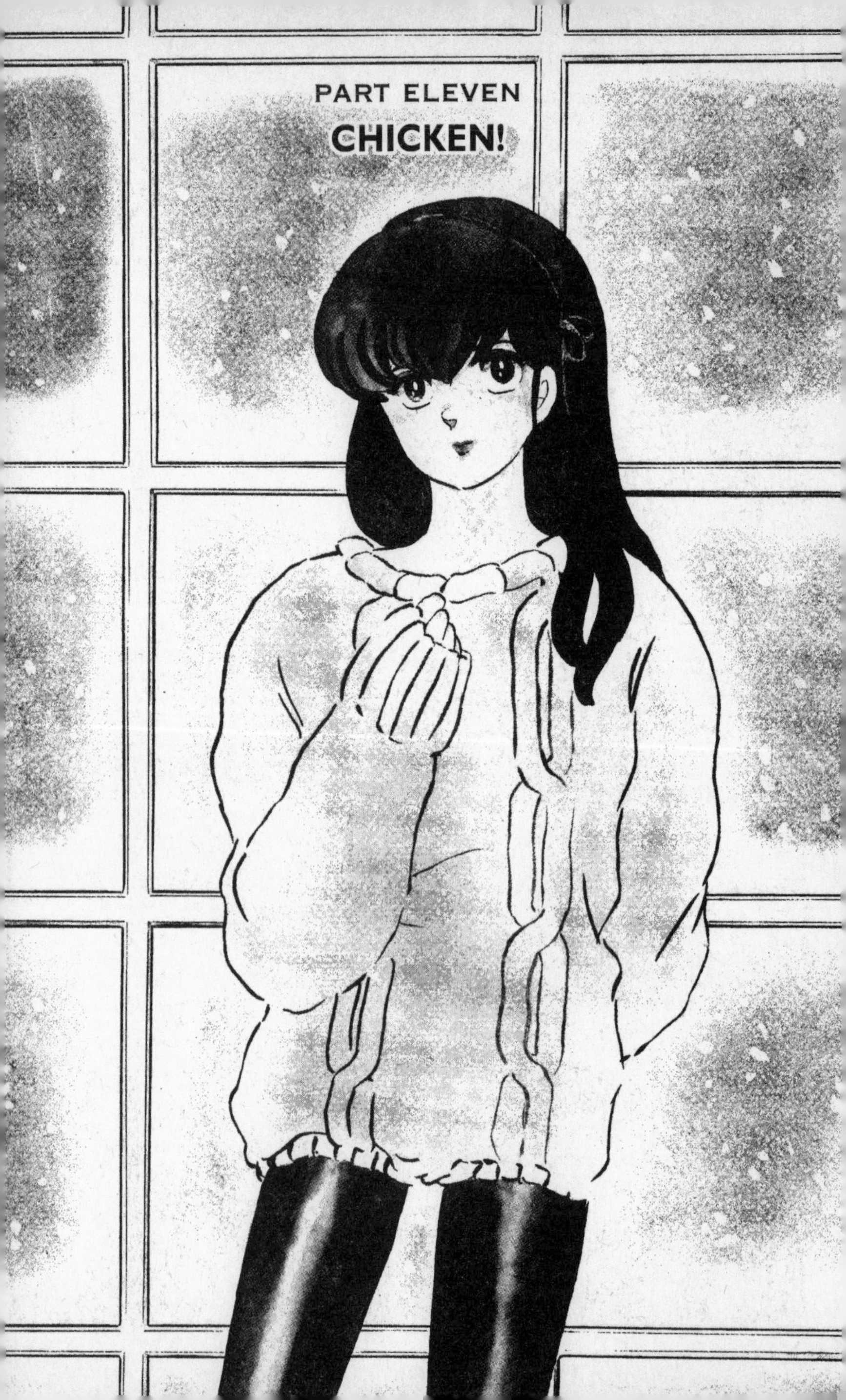
PART ELEVEN
CHICKEN!

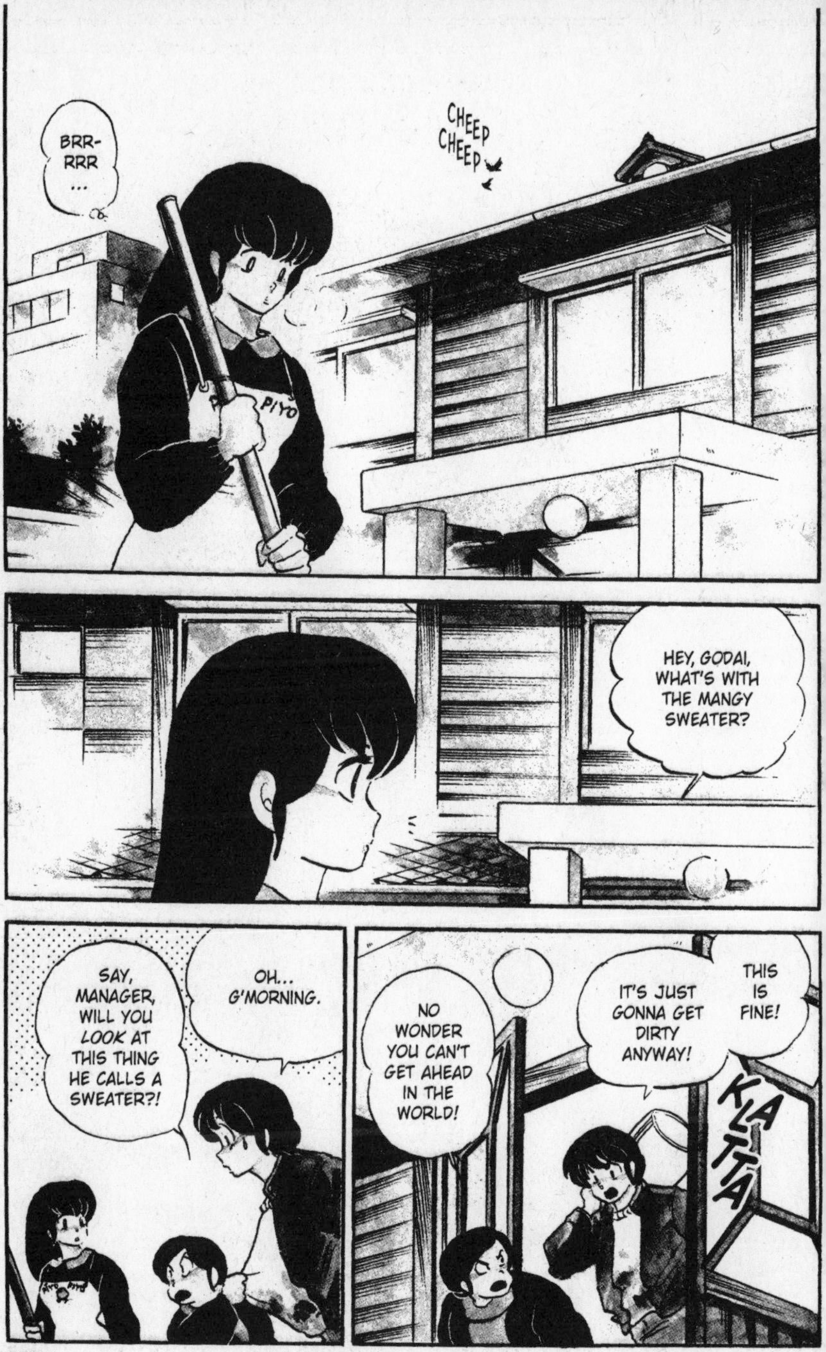
CHEEP CHEEP
BRR-RRR ...
PIYO
HEY, GODAI, WHAT'S WITH THE MANGY SWEATER?
THIS IS FINE!
IT'S JUST GONNA GET DIRTY ANYWAY!
KLATTA
NO WONDER YOU CAN'T GET AHEAD IN THE WORLD!
OH... G'MORNING.
SAY, MANAGER, WILL YOU *LOOK* AT THIS THING HE CALLS A SWEATER?!

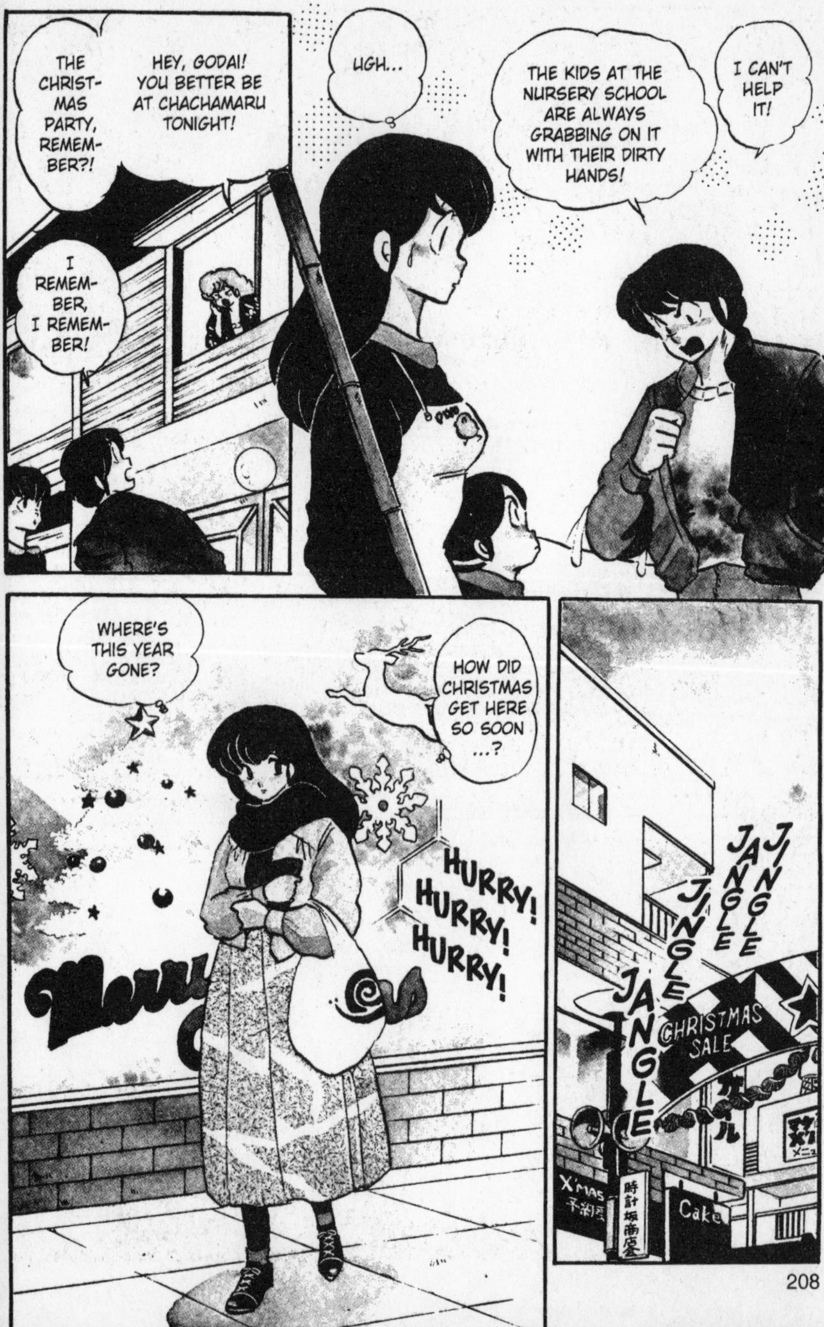
I CAN'T HELP IT!
THE KIDS AT THE NURSERY SCHOOL ARE ALWAYS GRABBING ON IT WITH THEIR DIRTY HANDS!
UGH...
HEY, GODAI! YOU BETTER BE AT CHACHAMARU TONIGHT!
THE CHRISTMAS PARTY, REMEMBER?!
I REMEMBER, I REMEMBER!
JINGLE JANGLE JINGLE JANGLE
CHRISTMAS SALE
X'MAS
Cake
HOW DID CHRISTMAS GET HERE SO SOON ...?
WHERE'S THIS YEAR GONE?
HURRY! HURRY! HURRY!

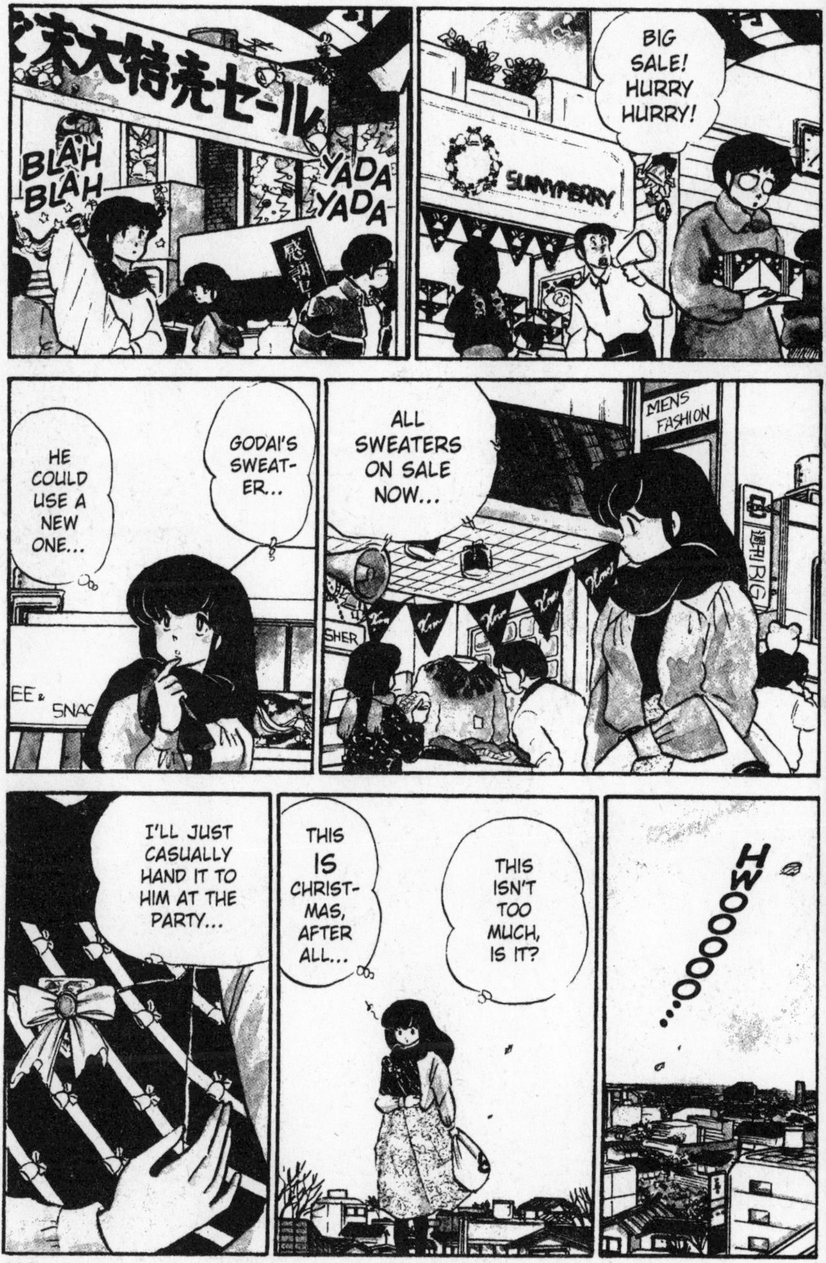
BIG SALE! HURRY HURRY!
SUNNYBERRY
末大特売セール
BLAH BLAH
YADA YADA
MENS FASHION
ALL SWEATERS ON SALE NOW...
SHER
GODAI'S SWEATER...
HE COULD USE A NEW ONE...
EE & SNAC
HWOOOOOO...
THIS ISN'T TOO MUCH, IS IT?
THIS IS CHRISTMAS, AFTER ALL...
I'LL JUST CASUALLY HAND IT TO HIM AT THE PARTY...

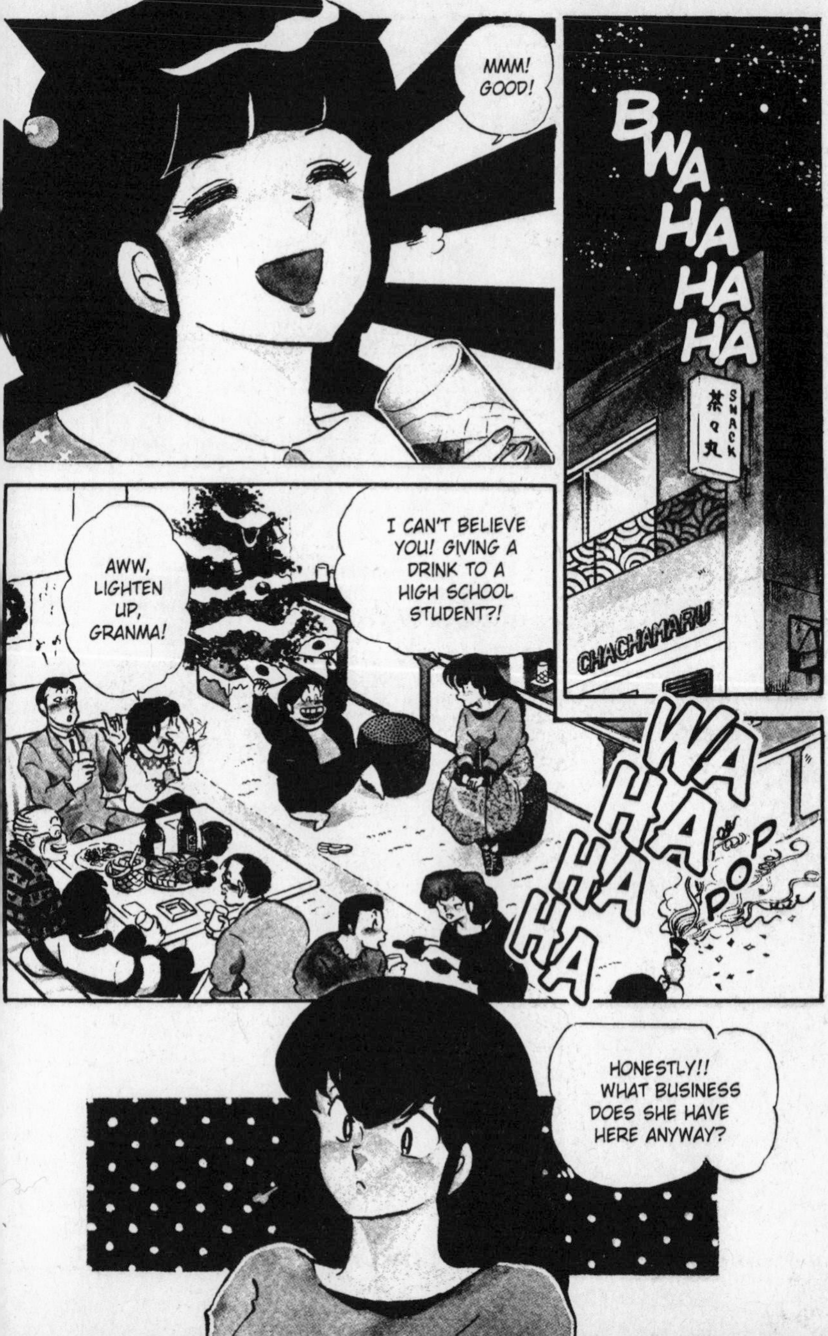
BWAHAHAHA
茶々丸
SNACK
CHACHAMARU
MMM! GOOD!
I CAN'T BELIEVE YOU! GIVING A DRINK TO A HIGH SCHOOL STUDENT?!
AWW, LIGHTEN UP, GRANMA!
WAHAHAHAHA
POP
HONESTLY!! WHAT BUSINESS DOES SHE HAVE HERE ANYWAY?

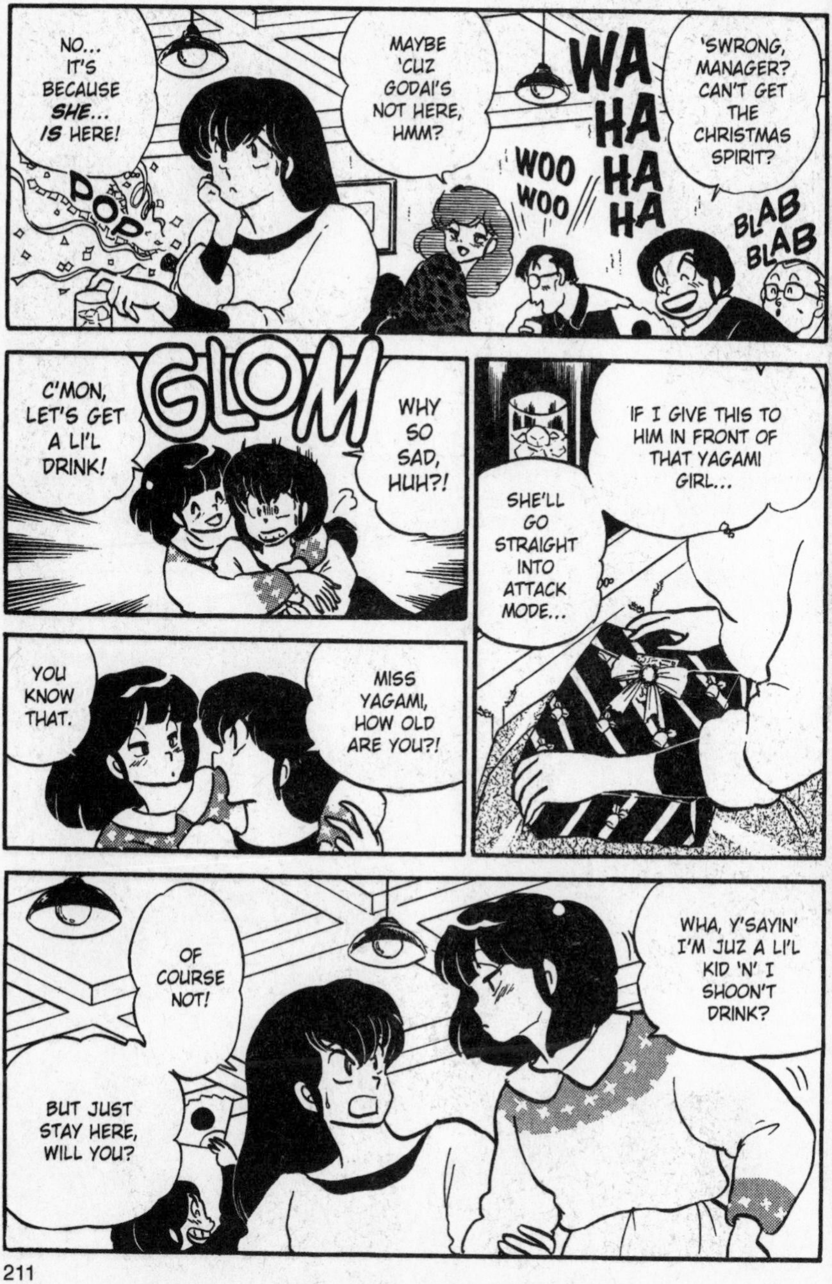
'SWRONG, MANAGER? CAN'T GET THE CHRISTMAS SPIRIT?
BLAB BLAB
WA HA HA HA
WOO WOO
MAYBE 'CUZ GODAI'S NOT HERE, HMM?
NO... IT'S BECAUSE SHE... IS HERE!
POP
IF I GIVE THIS TO HIM IN FRONT OF THAT YAGAMI GIRL...
SHE'LL GO STRAIGHT INTO ATTACK MODE...
WHY SO SAD, HUH?!
GLOM
C'MON, LET'S GET A LI'L DRINK!
MISS YAGAMI, HOW OLD ARE YOU?!
YOU KNOW THAT.
WHA, Y'SAYIN' I'M JUZ A LI'L KID 'N' I SHOON'T DRINK?
OF COURSE NOT!
BUT JUST STAY HERE, WILL YOU?

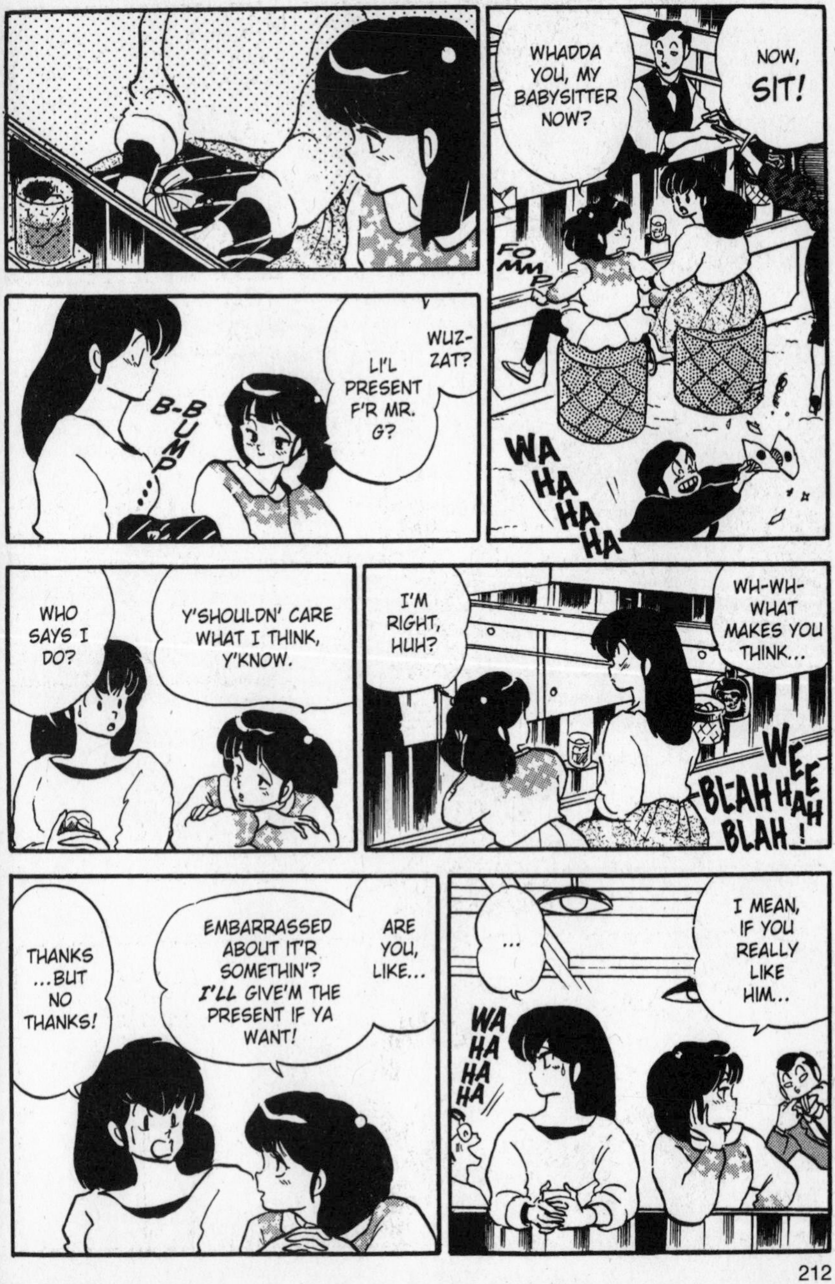
NOW, SIT!
WHADDA YOU, MY BABYSITTER NOW?
FOMMP
WAHAHAHAHA
WUZ-ZAT?
LI'L PRESENT F'R MR. G?
B-BUMP...
WH-WH-WHAT MAKES YOU THINK...
I'M RIGHT, HUH?
WEEHAHAH!
BLAH BLAH BLAH
Y'SHOULDN' CARE WHAT I THINK, Y'KNOW.
WHO SAYS I DO?
I MEAN, IF YOU REALLY LIKE HIM...
...
WAHAHAHAHA
ARE YOU, LIKE...
EMBARRASSED ABOUT IT'R SOMETHIN'? *I'LL* GIVE'M THE PRESENT IF YA WANT!
THANKS ...BUT NO THANKS!

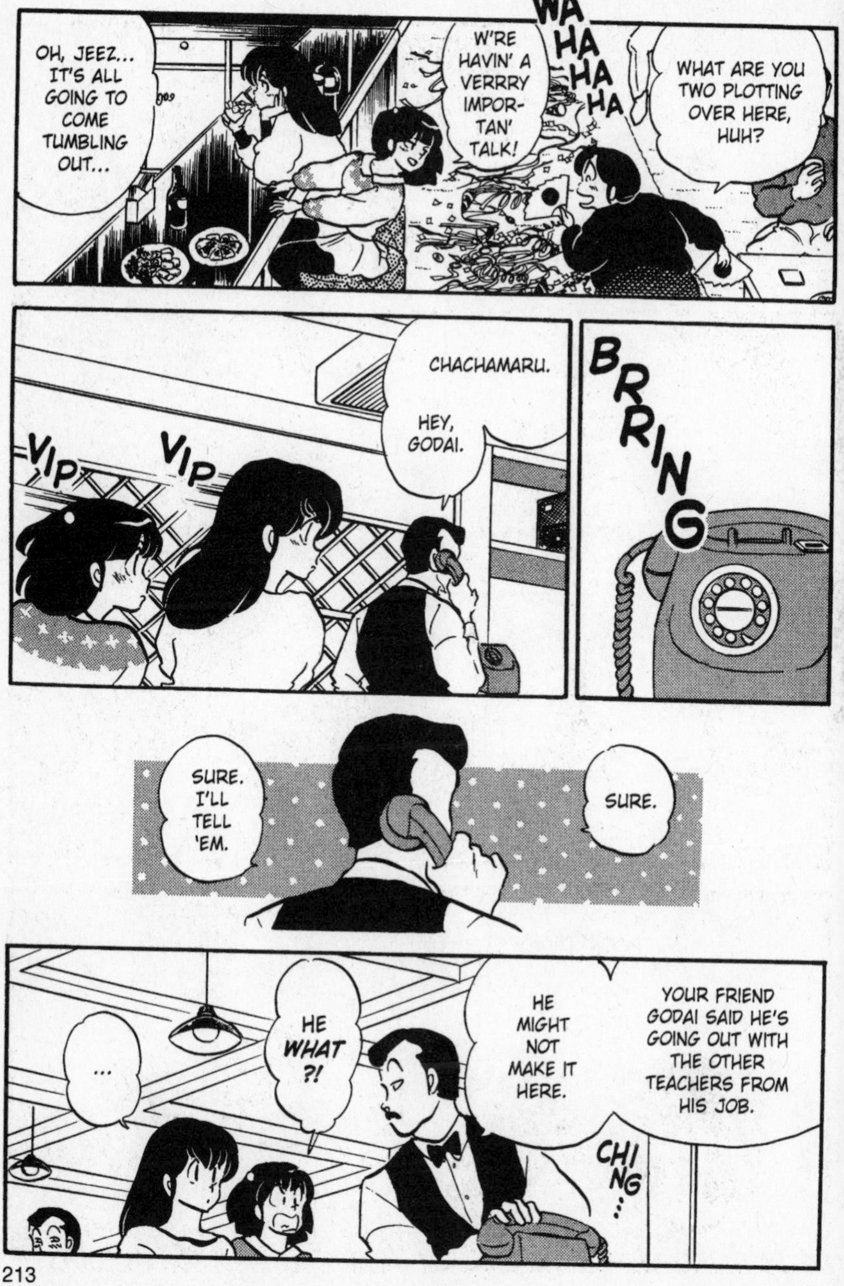
WHAT ARE YOU TWO PLOTTING OVER HERE, HUH?
WA HA HA HA
W'RE HAVIN' A VERRRY IMPOR-TAN' TALK!
OH, JEEZ... IT'S ALL GOING TO COME TUMBLING OUT...
BRRRING
CHACHAMARU.
HEY, GODAI.
VIP VIP
SURE.
SURE. I'LL TELL 'EM.
YOUR FRIEND GODAI SAID HE'S GOING OUT WITH THE OTHER TEACHERS FROM HIS JOB.
HE MIGHT NOT MAKE IT HERE.
CHING...
HE *WHAT* ?!
...

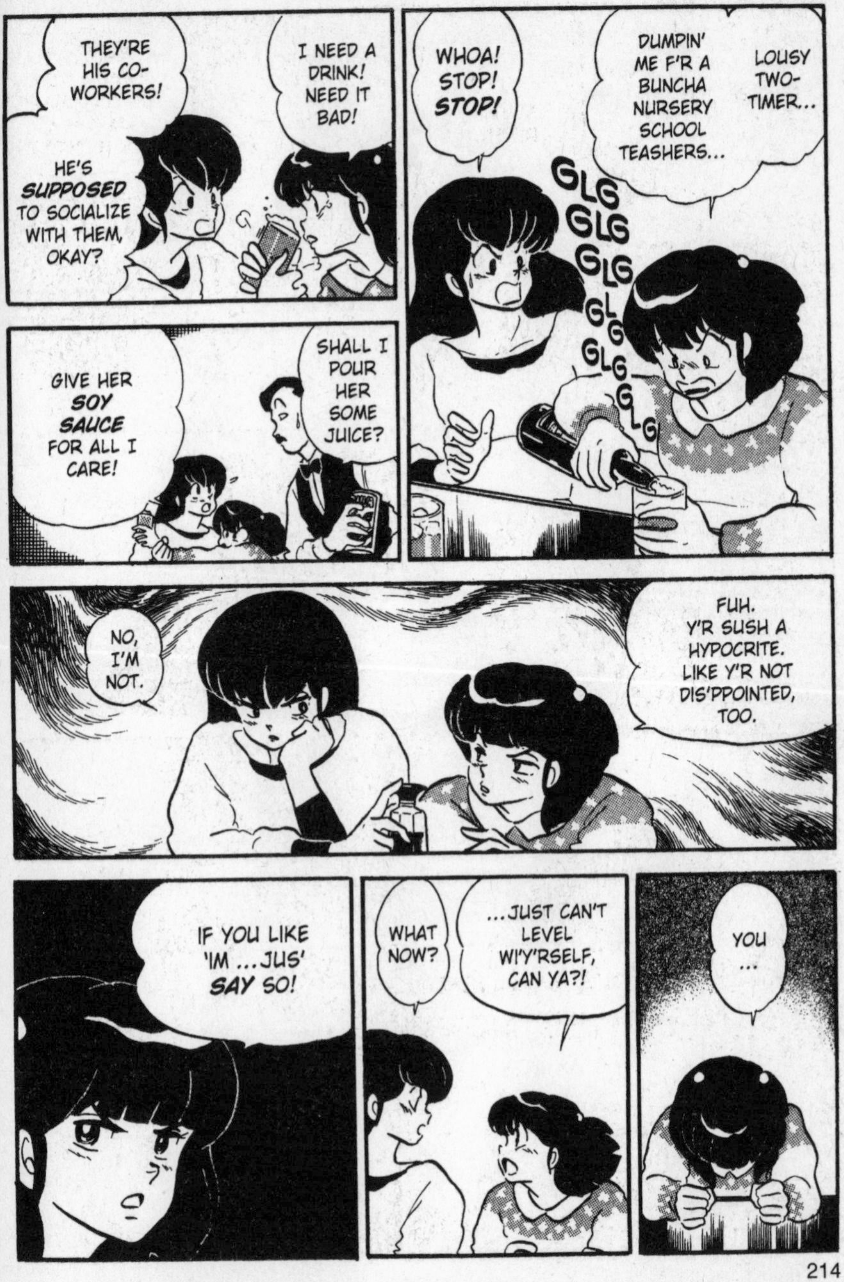
LOUSY TWO-TIMER...
DUMPIN' ME F'R A BUNCHA NURSERY SCHOOL TEASHERS...
WHOA! STOP! **STOP!**
GLG GLG GLG GLG GLG
I NEED A DRINK! NEED IT BAD!
THEY'RE HIS CO-WORKERS!
HE'S **SUPPOSED** TO SOCIALIZE WITH THEM, OKAY?
SHALL I POUR HER SOME JUICE?
GIVE HER **SOY SAUCE** FOR ALL I CARE!
FUH. Y'R SUSH A HYPOCRITE. LIKE Y'R NOT DIS'PPOINTED, TOO.
NO, I'M NOT.
YOU ...
...JUST CAN'T LEVEL WI'Y'RSELF, CAN YA?!
WHAT NOW?
IF YOU LIKE 'IM ...JUS' **SAY** SO!

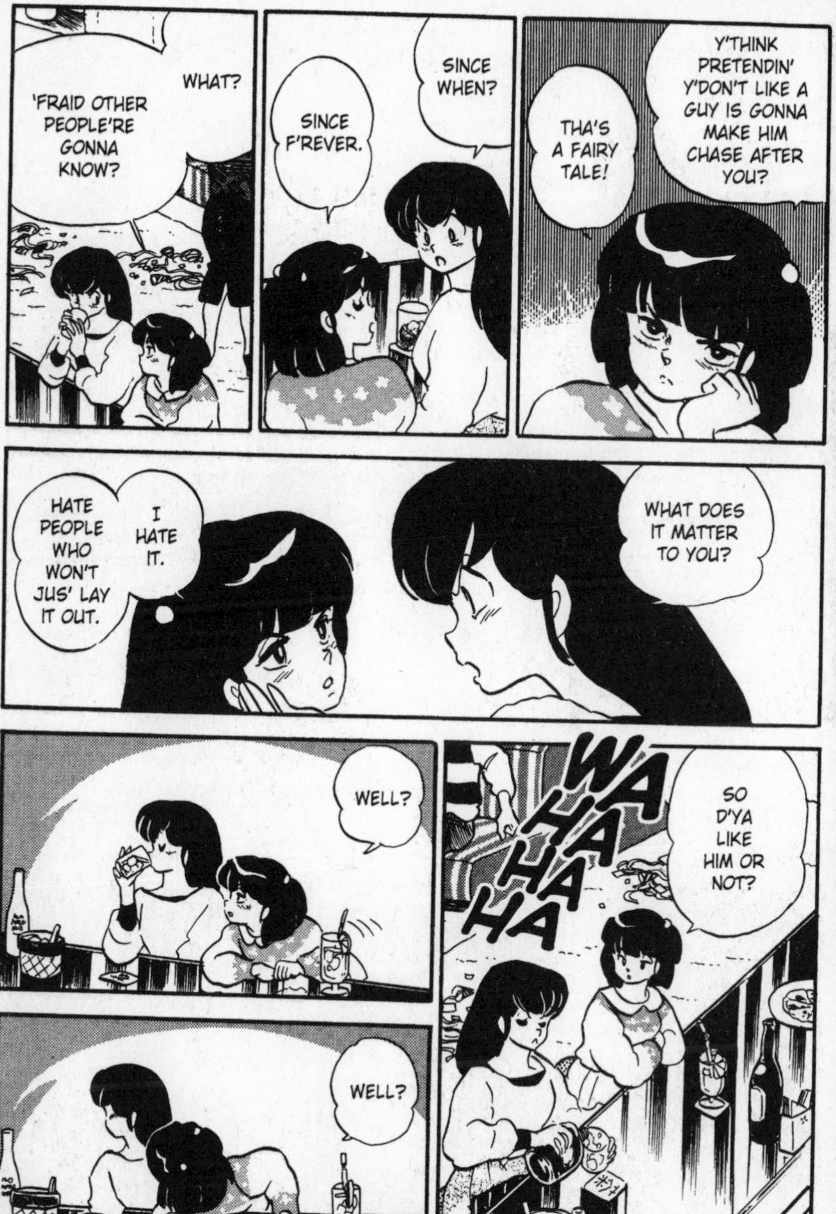

Y'THINK PRETENDIN' Y'DON'T LIKE A GUY IS GONNA MAKE HIM CHASE AFTER YOU?
THA'S A FAIRY TALE!
SINCE WHEN?
SINCE F'REVER.
WHAT?
'FRAID OTHER PEOPLE'RE GONNA KNOW?
WHAT DOES IT MATTER TO YOU?
I HATE IT.
HATE PEOPLE WHO WON'T JUS' LAY IT OUT.
WAHAHAHAHA
SO D'YA LIKE HIM OR NOT?
WELL?
WELL?

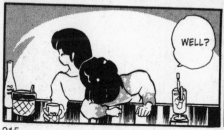

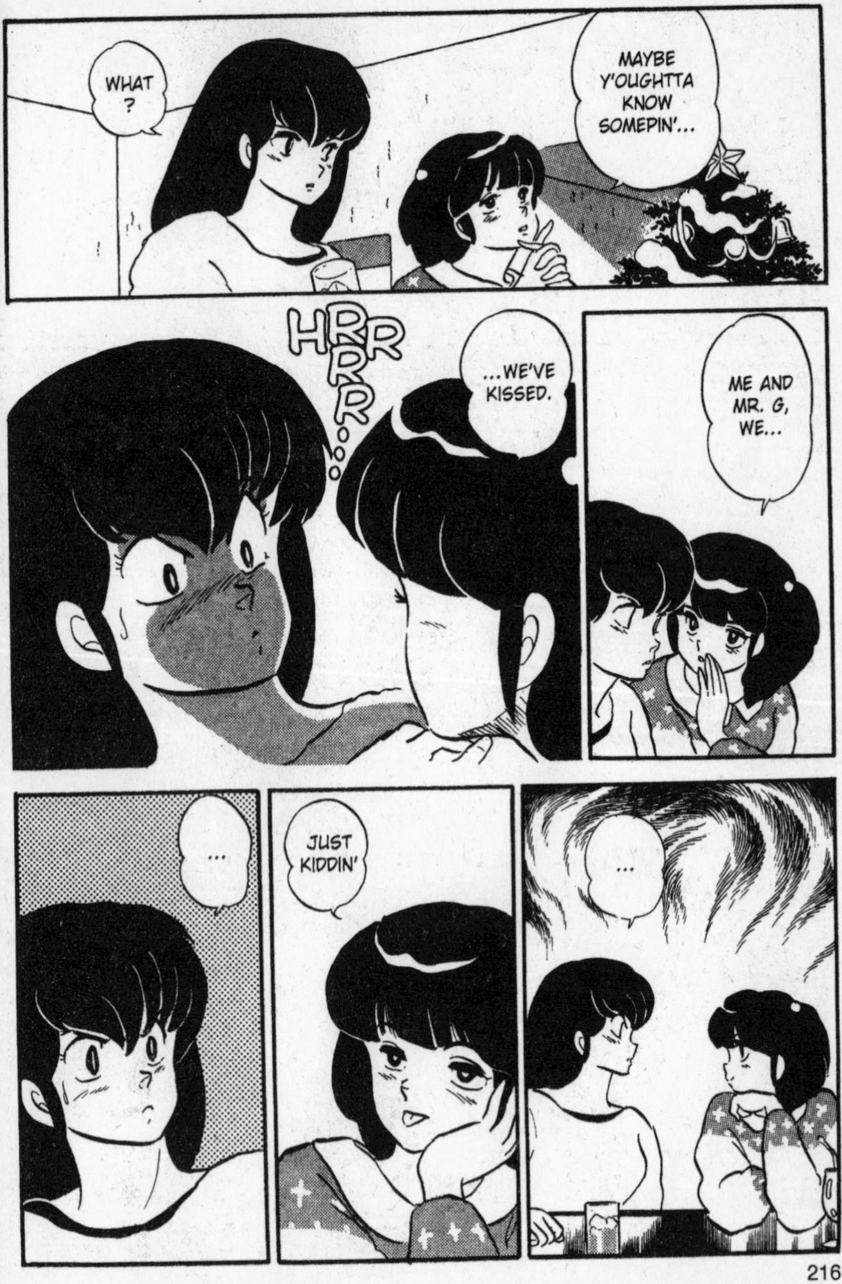
MAYBE Y'OUGHTTA KNOW SOMEPIN'...
WHAT ?
ME AND MR. G, WE...
...WE'VE KISSED.
HRRRR
...
JUST KIDDIN'
...

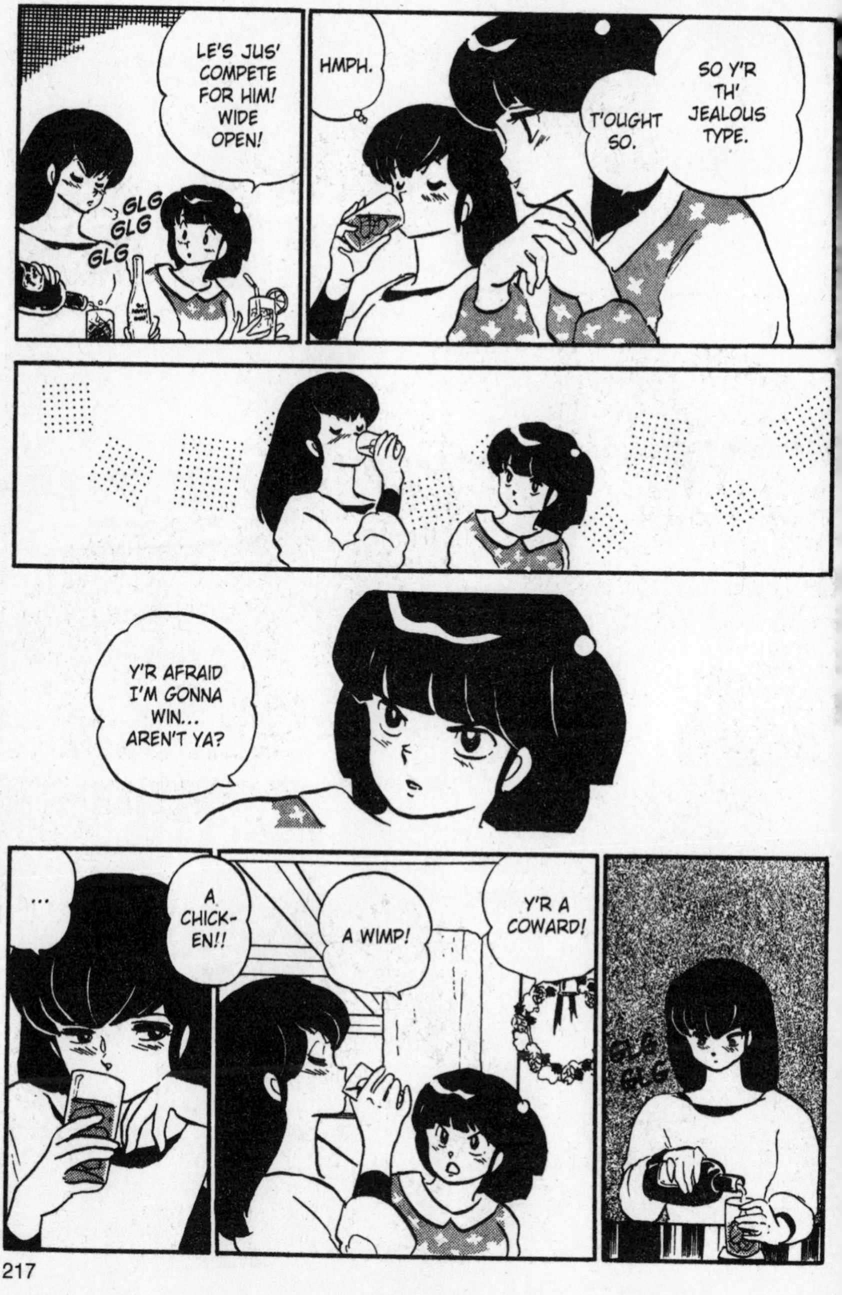
SO Y'R TH' JEALOUS TYPE.
T'OUGHT SO.
HMPH.
LE'S JUS' COMPETE FOR HIM! WIDE OPEN!
GLG GLG GLG
Y'R AFRAID I'M GONNA WIN... AREN'T YA?
GLG GLG
Y'R A COWARD!
A WIMP!
A CHICK-EN!!
...

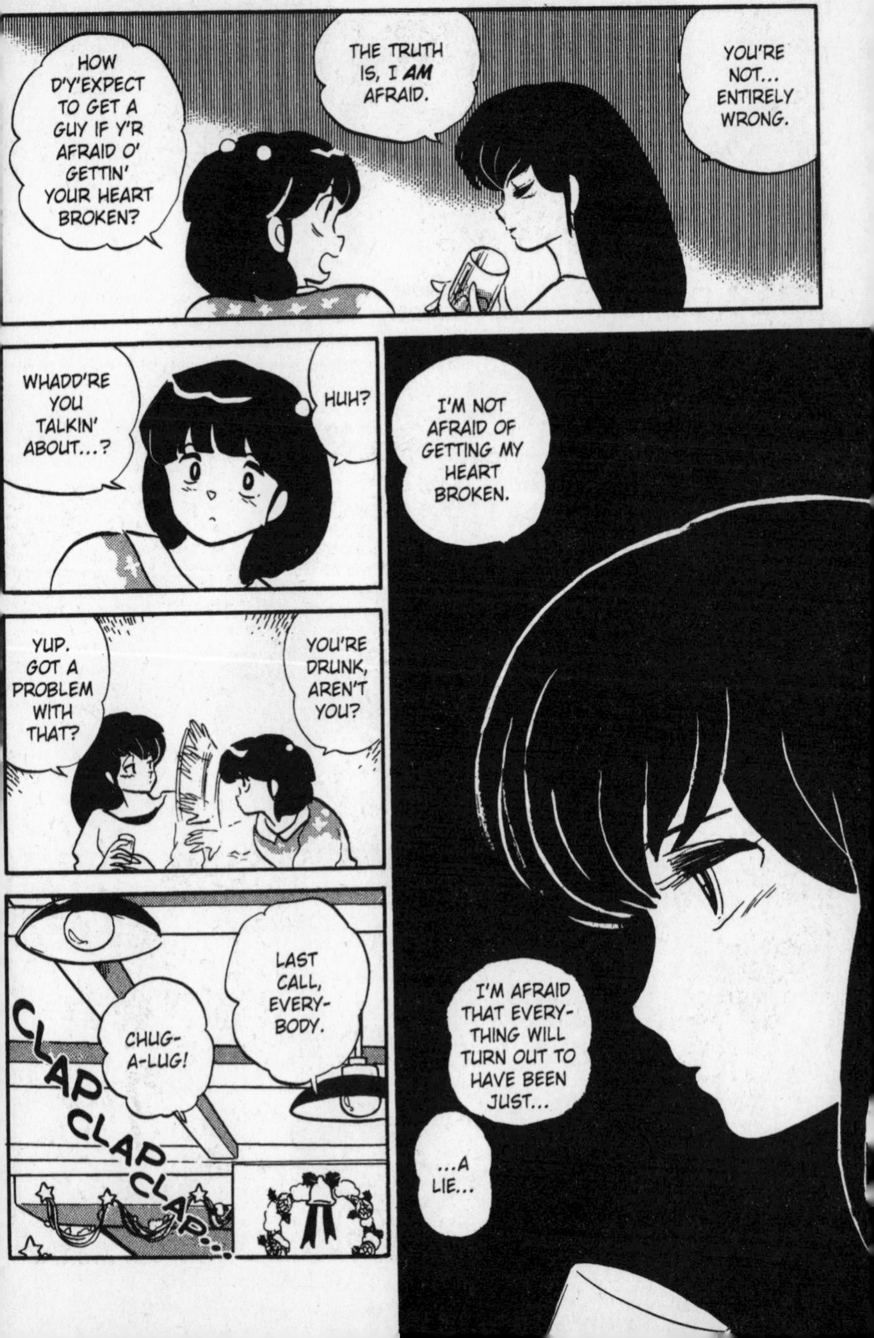
YOU'RE NOT... ENTIRELY WRONG.
THE TRUTH IS, I **AM** AFRAID.
HOW D'Y'EXPECT TO GET A GUY IF Y'R AFRAID O' GETTIN' YOUR HEART BROKEN?
I'M NOT AFRAID OF GETTING MY HEART BROKEN.
I'M AFRAID THAT EVERY-THING WILL TURN OUT TO HAVE BEEN JUST...
...A LIE...
HUH?
WHADD'RE YOU TALKIN' ABOUT...?
YOU'RE DRUNK, AREN'T YOU?
YUP. GOT A PROBLEM WITH THAT?
LAST CALL, EVERY-BODY.
CHUG-A-LUG!
CLAP CLAP CLAP CLAP CLAP...

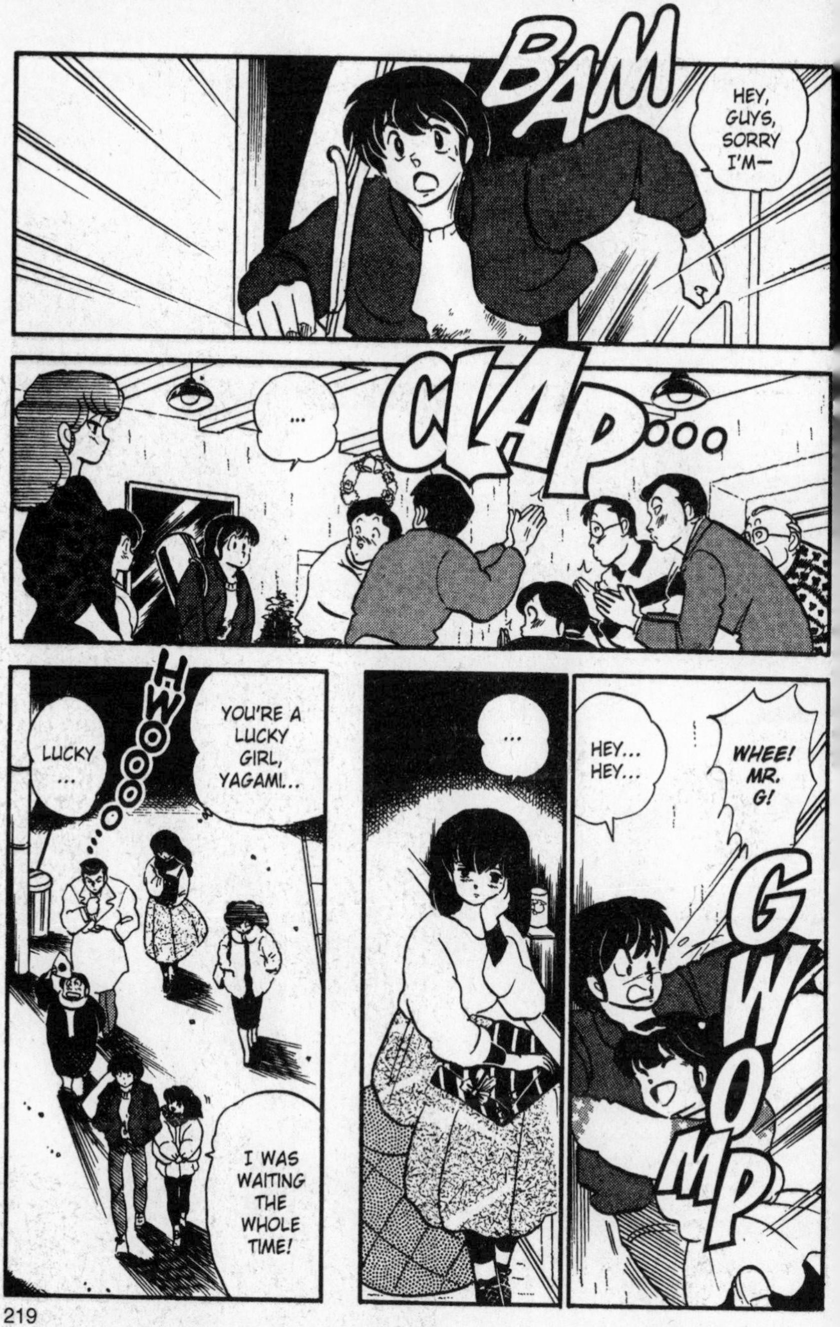
BAM
HEY, GUYS, SORRY I'M—
CLAPooo
...
WHEE! MR. G!
HEY... HEY...
GWOMP
...
YOU'RE A LUCKY GIRL, YAGAMI...
LUCKY ...
HWOOOOO
I WAS WAITING THE WHOLE TIME!

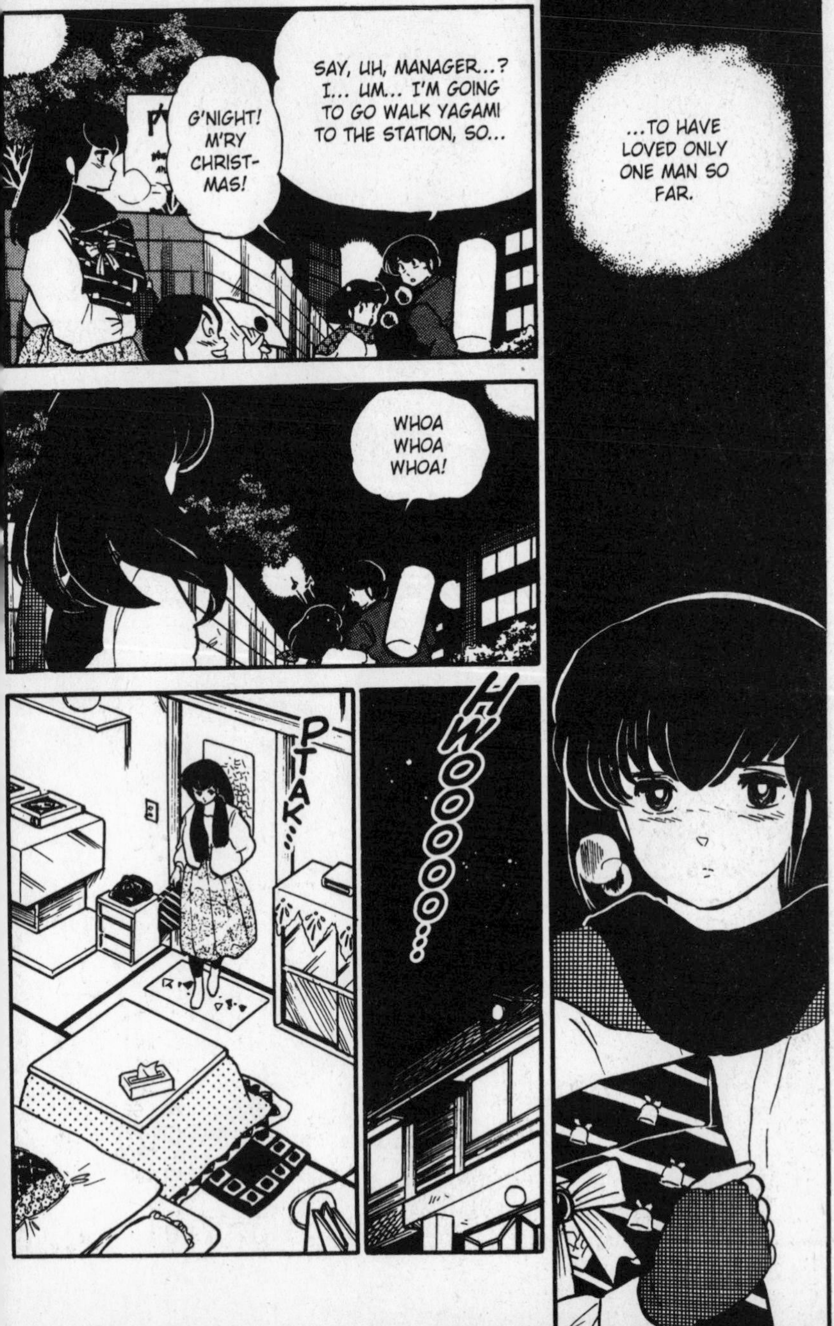
...TO HAVE LOVED ONLY ONE MAN SO FAR.
SAY, UH, MANAGER...? I... UM... I'M GOING TO GO WALK YAGAMI TO THE STATION, SO...
G'NIGHT! M'RY CHRIST-MAS!
WHOA WHOA WHOA!
HWOOOOOOOO...
PTAK...

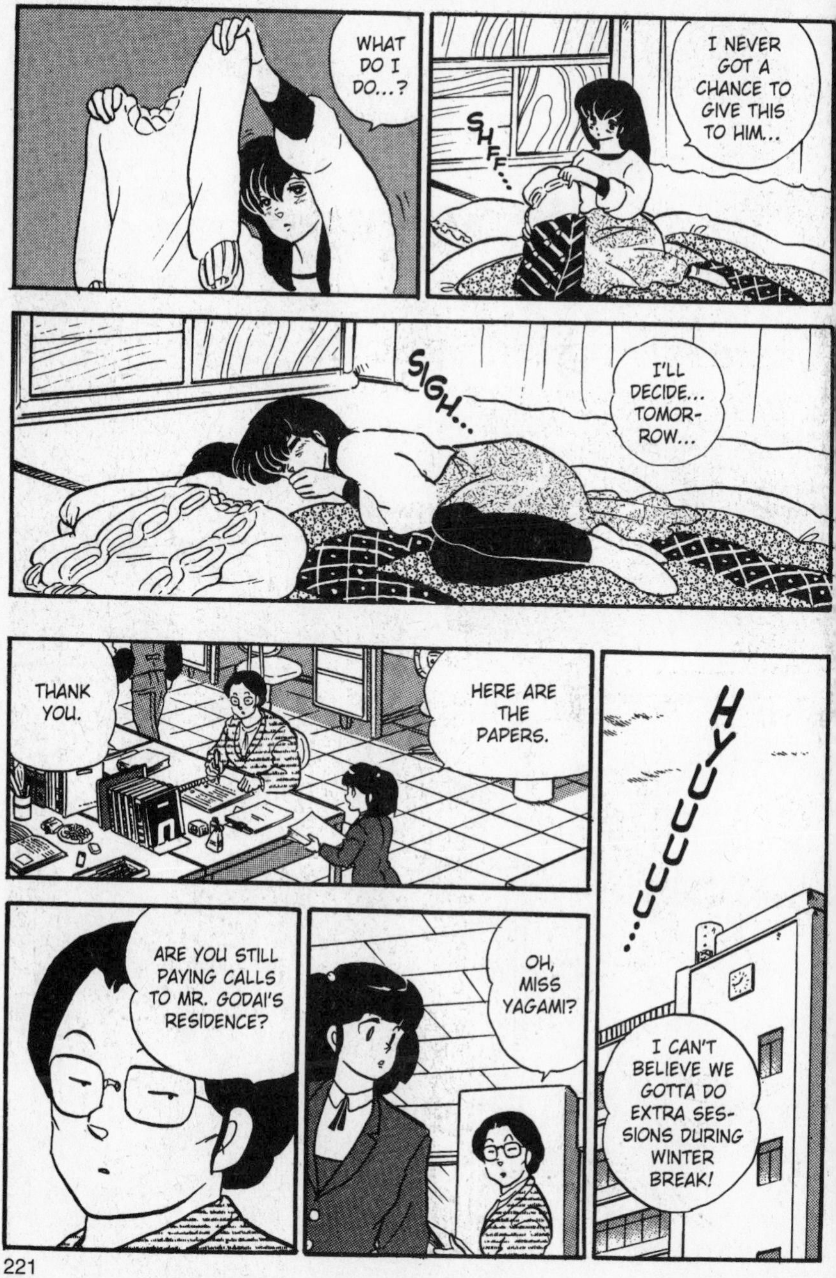
I NEVER GOT A CHANCE TO GIVE THIS TO HIM...
SHFF...
WHAT DO I DO...?
I'LL DECIDE... TOMORROW...
SIGH...
HYUUUUUU...
I CAN'T BELIEVE WE GOTTA DO EXTRA SESSIONS DURING WINTER BREAK!
HERE ARE THE PAPERS.
THANK YOU.
OH, MISS YAGAMI?
ARE YOU STILL PAYING CALLS TO MR. GODAI'S RESIDENCE?

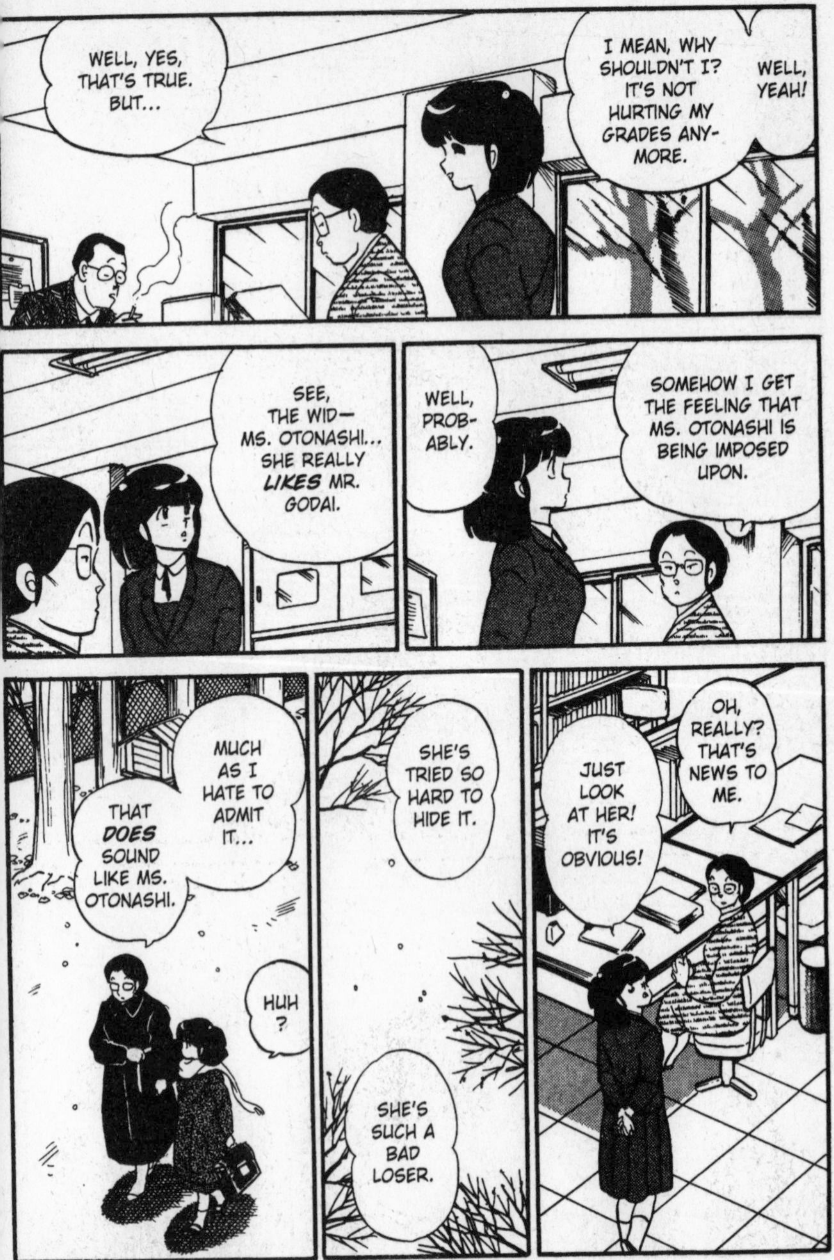
WELL, YEAH!
I MEAN, WHY SHOULDN'T I? IT'S NOT HURTING MY GRADES ANY-MORE.
WELL, YES, THAT'S TRUE. BUT...
SOMEHOW I GET THE FEELING THAT MS. OTONASHI IS BEING IMPOSED UPON.
WELL, PROB-ABLY.
SEE, THE WID— MS. OTONASHI... SHE REALLY ***LIKES*** MR. GODAI.
OH, REALLY? THAT'S NEWS TO ME.
JUST LOOK AT HER! IT'S OBVIOUS!
SHE'S TRIED SO HARD TO HIDE IT.
SHE'S SUCH A BAD LOSER.
MUCH AS I HATE TO ADMIT IT...
THAT ***DOES*** SOUND LIKE MS. OTONASHI.
HUH?

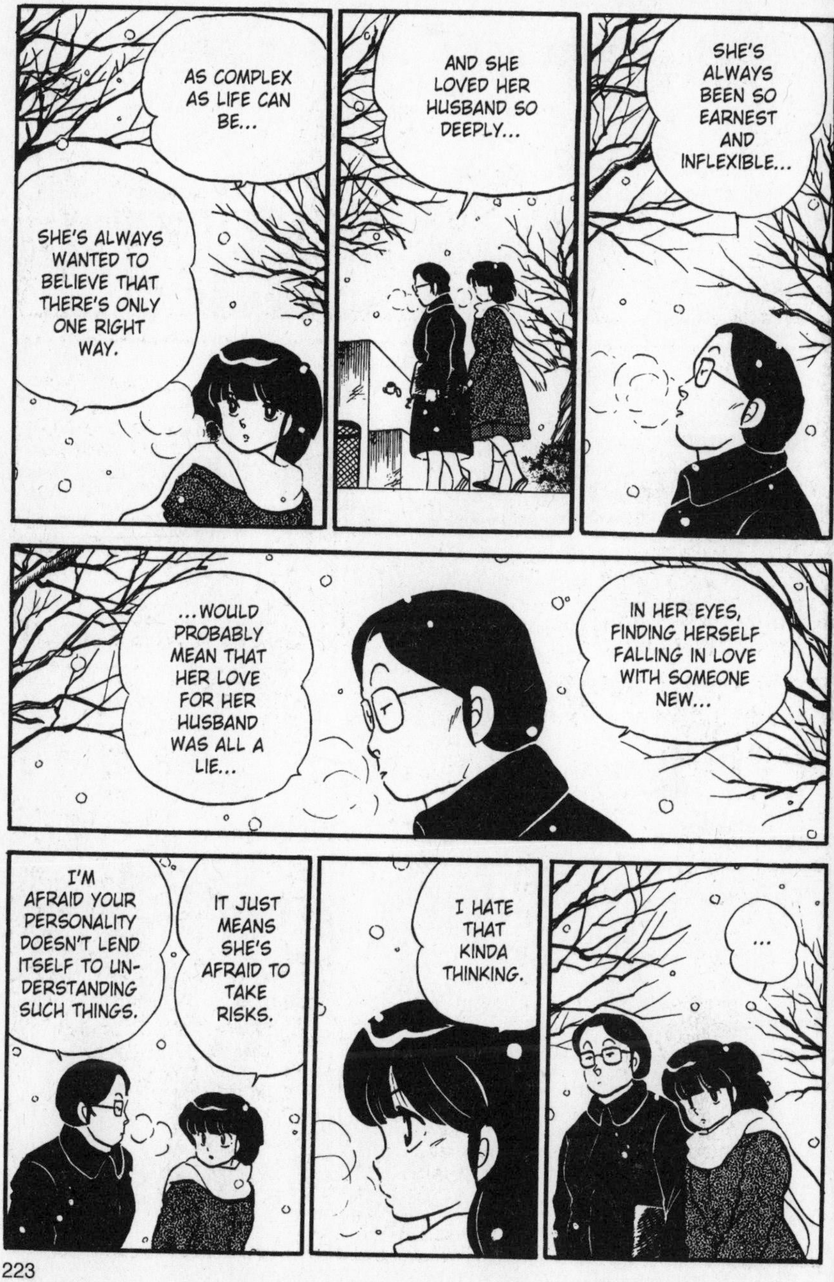
SHE'S ALWAYS BEEN SO EARNEST AND INFLEXIBLE...
AND SHE LOVED HER HUSBAND SO DEEPLY...
AS COMPLEX AS LIFE CAN BE...
SHE'S ALWAYS WANTED TO BELIEVE THAT THERE'S ONLY ONE RIGHT WAY.
IN HER EYES, FINDING HERSELF FALLING IN LOVE WITH SOMEONE NEW...
...WOULD PROBABLY MEAN THAT HER LOVE FOR HER HUSBAND WAS ALL A LIE...
...
I HATE THAT KINDA THINKING.
IT JUST MEANS SHE'S AFRAID TO TAKE RISKS.
I'M AFRAID YOUR PERSONALITY DOESN'T LEND ITSELF TO UN-DERSTANDING SUCH THINGS.

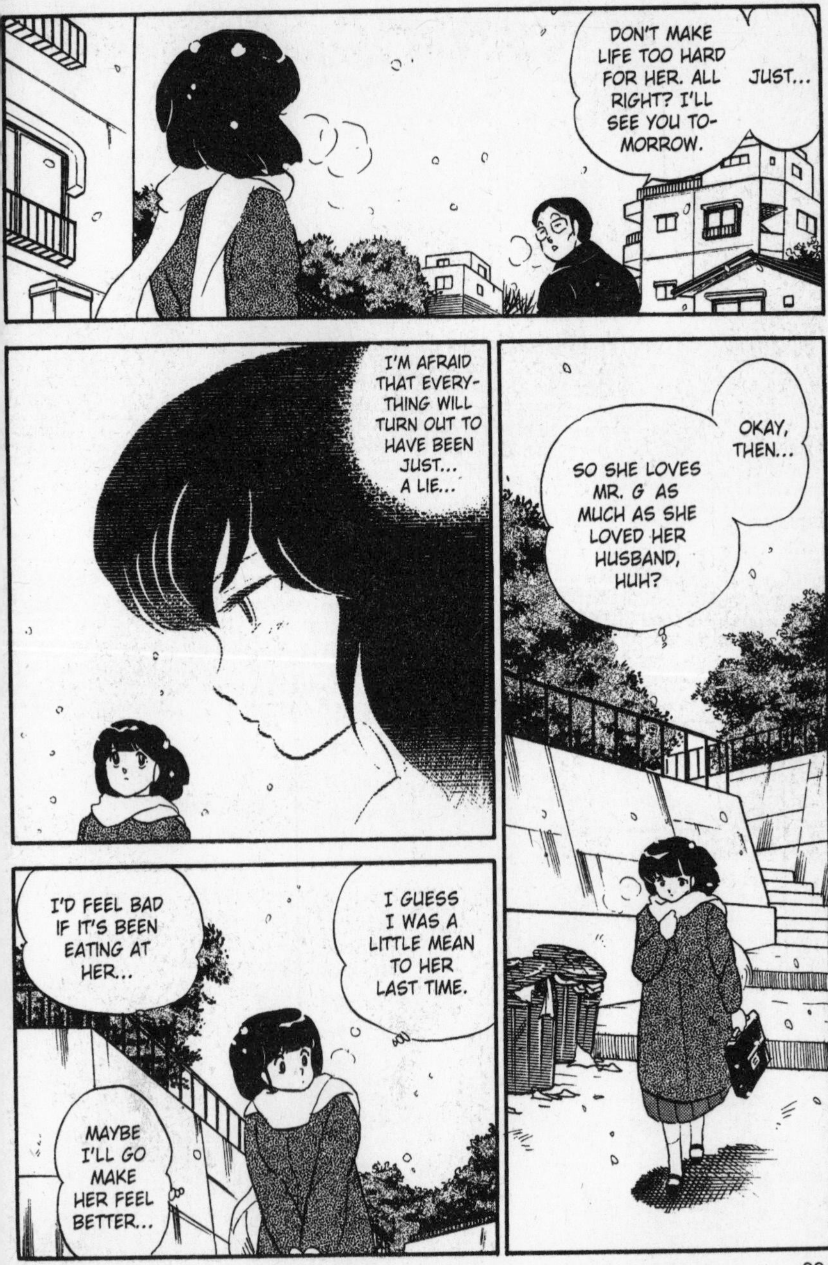
JUST...
DON'T MAKE LIFE TOO HARD FOR HER. ALL RIGHT? I'LL SEE YOU TO-MORROW.
OKAY, THEN...
SO SHE LOVES MR. G AS MUCH AS SHE LOVED HER HUSBAND, HUH?
I'M AFRAID THAT EVERY-THING WILL TURN OUT TO HAVE BEEN JUST... A LIE...
I GUESS I WAS A LITTLE MEAN TO HER LAST TIME.
I'D FEEL BAD IF IT'S BEEN EATING AT HER...
MAYBE I'LL GO MAKE HER FEEL BETTER...

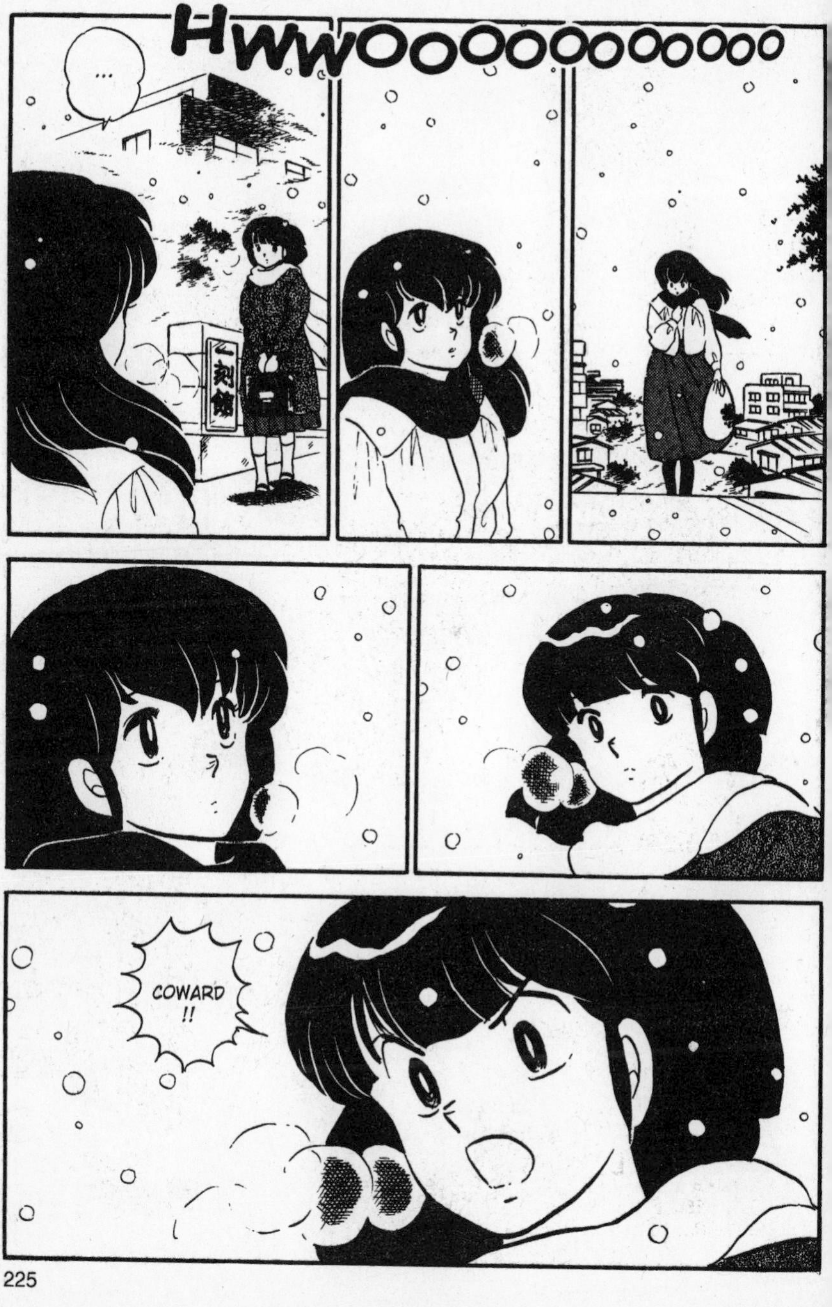
HWWOOOOOOOOOOO
...
COWARD !!

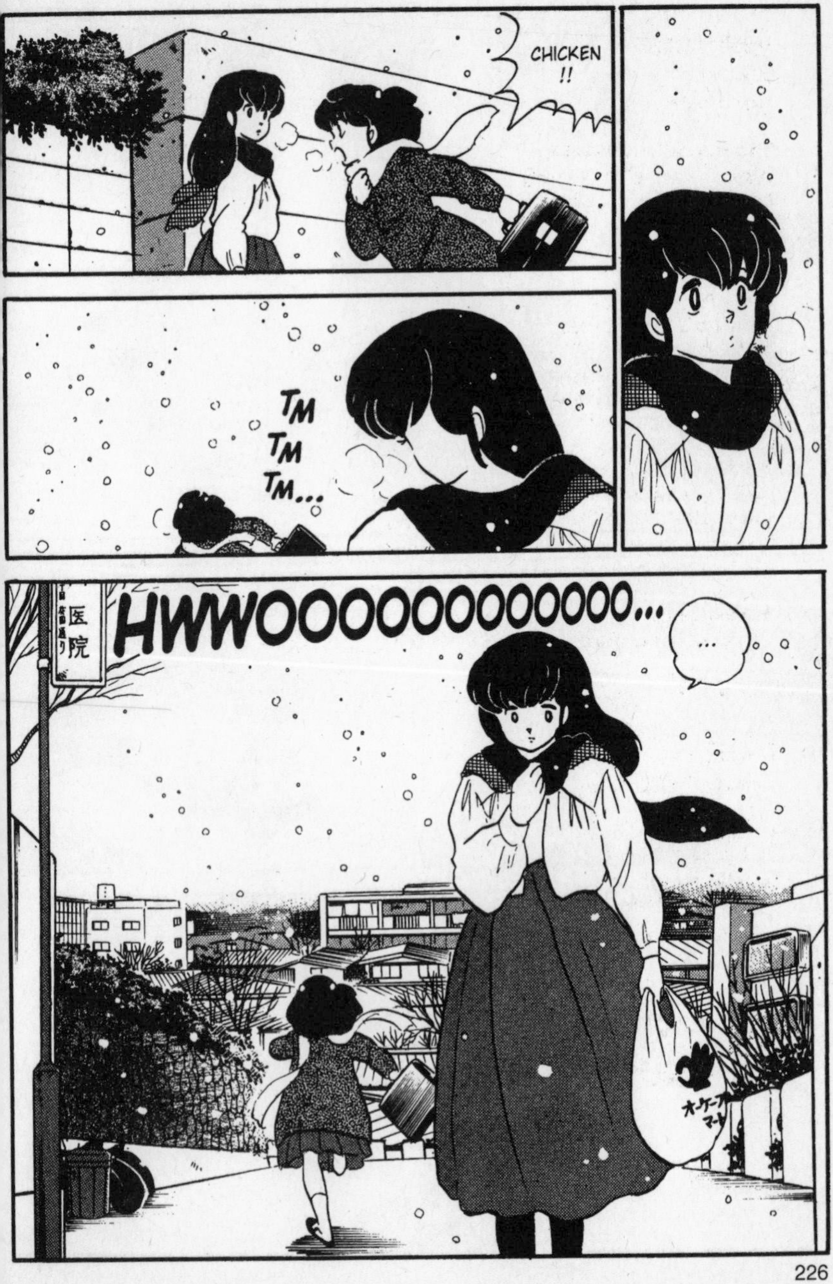
CHICKEN !!
TM TM TM...
HWWOOOOOOOOOOOOO...
...
医院

MAISON IKKOKU

VOLUME 11

Story and Art by Rumiko Takahashi

Translation/Gerard Jones & Mari Morimoto
Touch-Up Art & Lettering/Susan Daigle-Leach
Design/Nozomi Akashi
Editor — 1st Edition/Trish Ledoux
Editor — Editor's Choice Edition/Kit Fox

Managing Editor/Annette Roman
Director of Production/Noboru Watanabe
Vice President of Publishing/Alvin Lu
Sr. Director of Acquisitions/Rika Inouye
Vice President of Sales & Marketing/Liza Coppola
Publisher/Hyoe Narita

Printed in Canada

Published by VIZ, LLC
P.O. Box 77010
San Francisco, CA 94107

Editor's Choice Edition
10 9 8 7 6 5 4 3 2 1
First printing, May 2005
First English edition published 1998

www.viz.com

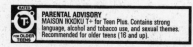

ABOUT THE ARTIST

Rumiko Takahashi, born in 1957 in Niigata, Japan, is the acclaimed creator and artist of *Maison Ikkoku, InuYasha, Ranma 1/2* and *Lum * Urusei Yatsura*.

She lived in a small student apartment in Nakano, Japan, which was the basis for the *Maison Ikkoku* series, while she attended the prestigious Nihon Joseidai (Japan Women's University). At the same time, Takahashi also began studying comics at Gekiga Sonjuku, a famous school for manga artists run by Kazuo Koike, author of *Crying Freeman* and *Lone Wolf and Cub*. In 1978, Takahashi won a prize in Shogakukan's annual New Comic Artist Contest and her boy-meets-alien comedy *Lum * Urusei Yatsura* began appearing in the weekly manga magazine *Shonen Sunday*.

Takahashi's success and critical acclaim continues to grow, with popular titles including *Ranma 1/2* and *InuYasha*. Many of her graphic novel series have also been animated, and are widely available in several languages.

EDITOR'S RECOMMENDATIONS

More manga!
More manga!

Fans of

maison ikkoku

should also read:

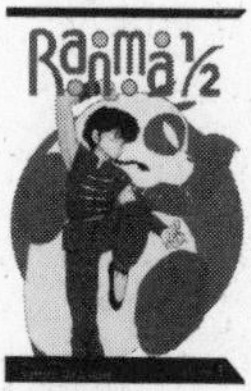
Ranma 1/2

©1988 Rumiko Takahashi/Shogakukan, Inc.

RANMA 1/2
Rumiko Takahashi's gender-bending comedy series is the tale of a father and son who fall into cursed springs in China, and their lives are transformed, literally. When they get wet, the father turns into a panda and the son, Ranma, turns into a girl. Comic situations ensue as they try and keep their friends and family, especially Ranma's fiancée and her family, from finding out their secret.

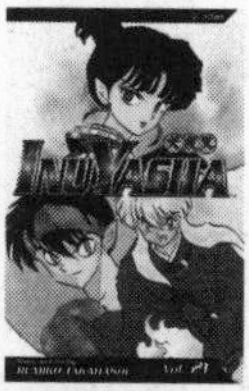

© 1997 Rumiko Takahashi/Shogakukan, Inc.

INUYASHA
Takahashi returned to her fantasy roots with this exciting manga that combines elements of historical action, exciting horror, touching romance, and ridiculously physical comedy. Modern schoolgirl Kagome is pulled into Japan's mystical past and must join forces with a scabrous half-demon named Inu-Yasha. This series has also spawned an immensely popular TV series as well!

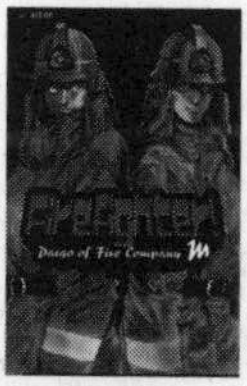
Daigo of Fire Company M

© 1996 Masahito Soda/Shogakukan, Inc.

FIREFIGHTER!: Daigo of Fire Company M
Tired of magical girls and romantic misunderstandings? Would you sooner take a long walk off a short pier than slog through another tale of a prebubescent-boy-coming-into-his-own-thanks-to-his-father's-giant-robot? Than look no further than *FIREFIGHTER!*, an immensely readable and entertaining manga about a cocky young man who, despite the feelings of his superior officers (and the public at large), has been earmarked for fire-fighting greatness. Daigo takes "going over the top" to new, heretofore unheard of levels.

COMPLETE OUR SURVEY AND LET US KNOW WHAT YOU THINK!

☐ Please do NOT send me information about VIZ products, news and events, special offers, or other information.

☐ Please do NOT send me information from VIZ's trusted business partners.

Name: _____

Address: _____

City: _____ **State:** _____ **Zip:** _____

E-mail: _____

☐ Male ☐ Female **Date of Birth** (mm/dd/yyyy): ___/___/_____ (Under 13? Parental consent required)

What race/ethnicity do you consider yourself? (please check one)

☐ Asian/Pacific Islander   ☐ Black/African American   ☐ Hispanic/Latino

☐ Native American/Alaskan Native   ☐ White/Caucasian   ☐ Other: _____

What VIZ product did you purchase? (check all that apply and indicate title purchased)

☐ DVD/VHS _____

☐ Graphic Novel _____

☐ Magazines _____

☐ Merchandise _____

Reason for purchase: (check all that apply)

☐ Special offer   ☐ Favorite title   ☐ Gift

☐ Recommendation   ☐ Other _____

Where did you make your purchase? (please check one)

☐ Comic store   ☐ Bookstore   ☐ Mass/Grocery Store

☐ Newsstand   ☐ Video/Video Game Store ☐ Other: _____

☐ Online (site: _____)

What other VIZ properties have you purchased/own? _____

_____

How many anime and/or manga titles have you purchased in the last year? How many were VIZ titles? (please check one from each column)

ANIME	MANGA	VIZ
☐ None	☐ None	☐ None
☐ 1-4	☐ 1-4	☐ 1-4
☐ 5-10	☐ 5-10	☐ 5-10
☐ 11+	☐ 11+	☐ 11+

I find the pricing of VIZ products to be: (please check one)

☐ Cheap ☐ Reasonable ☐ Expensive

What genre of manga and anime would you like to see from VIZ? (please check two)

☐ Adventure ☐ Comic Strip ☐ Science Fiction ☐ Fighting
☐ Horror ☐ Romance ☐ Fantasy ☐ Sports

What do you think of VIZ's new look?

☐ Love It ☐ It's OK ☐ Hate It ☐ Didn't Notice ☐ No Opinion

Which do you prefer? (please check one)

☐ Reading right-to-left

☐ Reading left-to-right

Which do you prefer? (please check one)

☐ Sound effects in English

☐ Sound effects in Japanese with English captions

☐ Sound effects in Japanese only with a glossary at the back

THANK YOU! Please send the completed form to:

NJW Research
42 Catharine St.
Poughkeepsie, NY 12601

All information provided will be used for internal purposes only. We promise not to sell or otherwise divulge your information.